60

FARRAR
STRAUS
GIROUX

Once Upon a Country

A PALESTINIAN LIFE

Sari Nusseibeh

with Anthony David

Farrar, Straus and Giroux
New York

Farrar, Straus and Giroux
19 Union Square West, New York 10003

        Library of Congress Cataloging-in-Publication Data
Nusseibeh, Sari.
    Once upon a country : a Palestinian life / Sari Nusseibeh with
Anthony David.
        p.   cm.
    Includes bibliographical references.
    ISBN-13: 978-0-374-29950-7 (hardcover : alk. paper)
    ISBN-10: 0-374-29950-1 (hardcover : alk. paper)
    1. Nusseibeh, Sari.   2. Palestinian Arabs—Biography.   3. Arab-
Israeli conflict.   I. David, Anthony, Ph.D.   II. Title.

DS119.7.N825 2007
956.94'42054092—dc22
[B]   2006013272

To my father

Contents

Once Upon a Country

A Fairy Tale

ALMOST FORTY YEARS ago the Israeli army conquered Jerusalem, a city my family had lived in since the days of Omar the Great, and soon afterward I fell in love with Lucy. Everyone agreed at the time, including the two of us, that it was an odd match. We were both students at Oxford, which at least on the surface was where our similarities ended. Lucy was the daughter of John Austin, one of England's mightiest modern philosophers, and I was the nineteen-year-old son of a man who had spent the last twenty years serving a Jordanian-administered Palestine, an entity recently wiped off the map in six brief days. Lucy was expected to marry into the British intelligentsia and to pursue a dazzling academic career of her own. By contrast, I no longer had a country, and the old ruling class my father represented had been plunged into a crisis from which it would never recover. The children of the privileged and educated, including all five of my siblings, began heading for the exits.

Had I intended to stay in exile, the love that Lucy and I shared perhaps would have raised fewer eyebrows. But I wanted to return, and I wanted her to go with me. But how do you ask the daughter of a famous

Oxford don to follow you to the war-scarred, embattled, poor, and occupied city of Jerusalem? How do you break the news that your fate will be tied to one of the most volatile corners on the planet, with two major wars in its recent history and the Arab leaders worldwide calling for another? It seemed too preposterous even to try, so I wrote a fairy tale instead.

It was second nature for me to use myth to get across something so important. At the time I was, as I remain, under the thrall of Lewis Carroll's *Alice's Adventures in Wonderland*, for in it I saw how a children's yarn could say more than a dozen philosophical treatises.

Fairy tales are also in my blood, and how could it be otherwise, with my having been raised surrounded by such a timeless and magical landscape? When my ancestors arrived in Jerusalem from Arabia thirteen centuries ago, the city's history was already so hallowed by time—and of course by the ancient Jewish prophets who once roamed its streets—that it left the newcomers from the desert in awe. That awe was so strong that as a child 1,300 years later, I couldn't walk to the corner market without feeling it all the way to my fingertips. Sometimes, when I watched my uncle's camels graze among ruins of Suq al-Khawajat, or Goldsmith's Souk, which had belonged to the Nusseibehs from time immemorial, the sensation of being a character in an ancient story swept through me—as it did when I watched a different uncle, the doorkeeper of the Church of the Holy Sepulcher, take a foot-long skeleton key and, as in the story that my Christian friends told me of St. Peter and the Pearly Gates, unlock a door thick enough to withstand a battering ram. In a city whose lanes were too narrow and crooked for a tank, this massive oak door still gave off a sense of impenetrability.

After snatching the city away from the Byzantine Empire in the seventh century, Omar the Great made our family's ancestor High Judge of Jerusalem, and from that point on my family has served the Holy City as judges, teachers, Sufi sages, politicians, and as doorkeepers to the Church of the Holy Sepulcher.

With all this in my background, my fairy tale's first line was as truthful as it was unsubtle: "Oh how I *wish* I could go to the Holy Land."

The rest of the story is about an angel on a flying donkey who takes an English girl named Louise on a ride to Jerusalem. The model for my story was Mohammed's Night Journey to Jerusalem, my favorite childhood fable. One evening the Prophet mounted a winged steed named al-Burak, Arabic for "lightning," and took a magical trip that over time would inspire the tales of flying carpets. Apart from the revelation of the Koran, in the only miracle ever associated with the Muslim prophet, Mohammed flew on al-Burak's back over the endless dunes and rock deserts of Arabia to a land described in the Koran as holy and blessed.

The destination of the Night Journey was the site of Solomon's ancient temple in Jerusalem and the place, according to Jewish tradition, of Abraham's sacrifice. To be more precise, he and his steed landed on the rock where some say Adam was created, and where he first set foot on earth after his expulsion from Paradise. (They'll also tell you that if you look closely enough, you'll see his footprints.) It is from that rock that the Prophet then ascended to heaven to receive instructions for the Abrahamic message of Islam, or *faith* in the one God.

In the yarn I wrote for Lucy, after an angel wearing a turban and riding the magical donkey whisks Louise away to Jerusalem, she meets a variety of characters, including Mr. Seems, who is never what he seems to be. Another figure she encounters stands guard at the Church of the Holy Sepulcher. Since the time of the Crusades, this knight of the Holy Sepulcher has been asleep at the same spot, as rigid as the tin man in *The Wizard of Oz*, and just as teary eyed, because a thousand years ago he vowed not to budge until there was peace in the Holy Land.

While at Oxford, I never finished the tale. I got Louise as far as Jerusalem, but I couldn't figure out what to do with her once she arrived. Would she help awaken the Crusader knight outside the Holy Sepulcher? Would she help bring peace to the Holy Land? I was stumped.

Anyway, Lucy didn't need a fairy tale to fall in love with Jerusalem: before I wrote the story she had already spent time in the Holy Land, while on tour with an Oxford choir, and had begun to identify with the landscape, history, language, and people with as much avidity as a native.

And so for more than thirty-five years my tale sat in a drawer, untitled and unfinished, and the knight remained very much asleep. More pressing matters—academic work, family life, and three decades of war and upheaval—got in the way. It was only last year, as I was preparing for my upcoming fellowship at the Radcliffe Institute at Harvard, that I picked up the tale again. I asked my twelve-year-old daughter, Nuzha, bedridden with the flu at the time, for her opinion on its merits. An avid and critical reader of stories and an aspiring writer herself, she gave me the thumbs-up, and I packed the tale along with the rest of my things to take to America. So as the institute's distinguished mathematicians, historians, and biologists pursued their academic and scientific endeavors, I worked on my fairy tale.

The aim, of course, was no longer to persuade Lucy to run off with me to Jerusalem. Now other motives had surfaced. Lucy and I now had our own children, who had to make their own decision as to whether to stay in a land far more mired in tragedy and seething with resentment than it was after the Six-Day War. Could I so easily say to my children, as I said to Lucy back then, that a life in Palestine would be an adventure? Even if I tried, they would never respond as Louise does in the tale. ("It would be *so* exciting . . . Just *think*," she pleaded, with her palms pressed together as if in prayer.) The only way to convince them about the possibility of a future in Palestine was to make a good case that our conflict with Israel could be solved. Somehow I had to wake up the sleeping knight in front of the Holy Sepulcher.

Weeks of toil resulted in some new characters and a couple of mystical Sufi riddles. But I still didn't know how to awaken the sleeping knight. No wonder, for after decades of effort, the magical formula for solving the Israeli-Palestinian conflict seemed more elusive than ever. The Goldsmith's Souk, my favorite haunt as a child, had been taken over by a sect of messianic Israeli settlers, who had turned the ruins into a flourishing colony—but also a strategic dagger thrust into the center of the Muslim Quarter. More seriously, the country had been ruined by armed conflict. Suicide bombers had invaded Israeli cities, and the Israeli army had responded by reoccupying the West Bank. The Oslo Agreement was in shambles, and whatever was left of Arafat's rule in the Occupied Territories was being challenged by Islamic extremism. Meanwhile, the Israelis were using terrorism as a pretext for erecting the "Security Fence," a twenty-foot-high concrete wall that began to weave its way through the West Bank like some malevolent snake. Each time I returned to Jerusalem for important meetings at Al-Quds University, where I work, I had to be shadowed by my two bodyguards, ubiquitous, like characters in Kafka's *The Castle*. Far from peaceful New England, my bodyguards reminded me just how asleep my fictional knight remained.

The solution to the riddle came to me on a plane returning to Boston after Chairman Arafat's funeral.

A few days earlier, I had been at the Skidmore College lodge preparing for a lecture I was to deliver the following day when an urgent message came from Jerusalem. Chairman Arafat, enfeebled and holed up in his destroyed compound encircled by Israeli tanks, had succumbed to a mysterious illness. Chairman Arafat hadn't been a well man for some years. The last time I met with him, before leaving for my sabbatical, he had looked gaunt and frail. When he fell ill this last time, he was flown to Paris, where a few days later he died. The Old Man, as he was known, was gone. That evening I cut short my stay in beautiful Saratoga Springs and took an overnight flight to Jerusalem.

Predictably, Arafat's death unleashed a variety of crackpot theories. There were some who accused the Shin Bet, Israel's shadowy security service, of having poisoned him; others alleged that AIDS had done him in; still others pointed the finger at rival Palestinian factions, or at the PLO itself. Some Israelis, thinking that divine justice had finally been meted out, let out a chorus of hallelujahs. "The wicked witch of the east is dead," said a prominent Brooklyn-born rabbi. Whatever the cause, everyone agreed that Arafat's death had reshuffled the deck.

In an ancient world such as ours, the truth inevitably gets embellished with a thick layer of legend. Depending on your point of view, Arafat was a freedom fighter, a terrorist, or both. (As if to complicate things for those who needed to see him as either one or the other, when he showed up at the United Nations for his first speech to the world body, his holster was empty and he spoke about "guns" *and* "olive branches.") Above all, he was a symbol of the scattered, defeated, humiliated Palestinian people. Through rousing slogans and by means both foul and fair, he had forged a nation out of people without leadership and divided by clan, geography, religion, and class, many of whom were refugees living in squalor and despair. He had rekindled their national identity and provided them with hope. This no one can take from him.

Upon my arrival at Ben Gurion Airport the following morning, my two bodyguards picked me up and we drove directly to Ramallah. Arafat's body was to arrive by helicopter from Cairo three hours later.

Rather than take the normal Jerusalem-Ramallah route, which we figured would be crammed with people, we drove into Ramallah from the west. The Israeli army, expecting foreign dignitaries and the odd Israeli well-wisher, allowed us to pass the roadblocks without undue delay, and within an hour we arrived at the head office of HASHD, the Arabic name for the People's Campaign for Peace and Democracy.

At the office, a motley team of young leaders, nearly all of them veterans of Israeli prisons, made black flags and banners with the message THE PEOPLE'S CAMPAIGN MOURNS THE DEATH OF ARAFAT. The plan was to use the occasion of the funeral to distribute fifty thousand leaflets calling for nonviolence and a two-state solution with Israel.

From there we continued on to the Muqata, Arafat's rubble-strewn compound at the edge of town. My colleagues had made special arrangements for me to enter through the VIP gate. When we arrived, the large iron gate was shut. Palestinian security guards pushed back a crowd of hundreds of people screaming to get in. My bodyguards managed to clear a path. "The president of Al-Quds University has arrived!" they called out to the guards. Suddenly, in what seemed like a military operation, a narrow slit in the gate opened, and out streamed a column of Palestinian security guards, who swept me off my feet and hauled me in, slamming the gate behind them. The banging and screams of the crowd reverberated in my ears. I pulled my blue worry beads from my pocket and started rubbing them.

Once inside the compound, I made my way upstairs to the PLO offices. Gathered there were public figures, some top PLO people, Prime Minister Abu Ala, and a number of leaders from Gaza whom I hadn't seen in years thanks to Israeli closures. The mood was grim.

Everyone was waiting for the helicopter carrying Arafat's body, along with Arafat's widow, Suha Arafat, Abu Mazen, Abed Rabbo (the cofounder, with the Israeli Yossi Belin, of the Geneva Agreement), and my longtime ally and friend Jibril Rajoub. The plan was for the dignitaries on the ground to join those in the helicopter in conducting a dignified ceremony.

The best-laid plans of mice and men! By the time the helicopter appeared on the horizon, hundreds of people had already stormed the gate and scaled the walls. Crowds were everywhere. A group of Moonies from Maryland even mingled peacefully in the horde.

In the meantime, I left the whispering dignitaries and went downstairs into the crowded compound. The entire area, the size of four soccer fields, was teeming with people. Young activists clambered atop heaps of rubble and twisted rebar to get a better view. The mood was strangely expectant, even jubilant. The solemn recital of the Koran was drowned out by the cheering and chanting of the crowd. Among those assembled, I saw colleagues and friends from ten years past, and activists with whom I had worked in the first intifada, and earlier. One was Mohammed Dahlan, the so-called "strongman" of Gaza, who headed up much of Arafat's security apparatus.

A few minutes later, a column of dignitaries led by Abu Ala emerged from the building and walked toward the helicopter landing site. Mounted security guards trotted through the crowds, trying to carve a path between the helicopter landing site and the main hall where the official burial ceremony was supposed to take place. But as soon as the guards managed to push back the crowds, the space they'd cleared filled in again, more tightly packed than before.

The helicopter finally appeared; it hovered over the crowd, unable to land. People now rushed forward, clambering on top of one another, trying to get close to the landing helicopter. Emotions began to spin out of control, and the incoherent screams turned into chants, like at a sporting match: "With our blood, with our souls, we are yours!" Lovingly they called Arafat "Abu Ammar," or "Father of Ammar." People didn't seem to believe that their leader was dead. Maybe they expected him to pull off another of his daredevil stunts, like the time he crash-landed in the Sahara and walked away with barely a scratch. Perhaps they thought the Old Man could trick death itself.

The people pushed harder and the chants grew louder, as did the din of crackling gunfire from rifles discharged skyward, and the shouted quotes from the Koran. One man, a member of the Central Committee of Fatah, Arafat's faction of the PLO, fainted in front of me, having been deprived of air by the pressing crowd. Others fell to the ground, hit by falling bullets.

The helicopter eventually managed to land. From a distance, I watched as people snatched Arafat's coffin out of the cargo section. Carried by the outstretched hands of hundreds of mourners, it was pushed for a few feet in one direction only to be pulled back in another by people wanting to lay hands on it, like worshippers seeking a magic-working relic.

I was now squeezed against a wall, and adding to my general sense of discomfort were the spent bullet casings and the pieces of masonry, dislodged by the weight of onlookers, raining down around me from the balconies above. Fearing the entire building would crumble, and having seen enough, I decided not to stick around for the funeral. I had done my duty and paid my respects.

Slipping quietly out, I had my bodyguards drive me to the home of some friends in Ramallah, and watched the rest on television.

During the flight back to Boston my mind shifted between Arafat's legacy and the future of Palestine on the one hand, and the book I was reading, Amos Oz's masterpiece *A Tale of Love and Darkness*, on the other. It was then that I thought of a way to conclude my fairy tale.

What now? I asked myself somewhere over the Mediterranean. For forty years Arafat had juggled various factions and interests and ideologies. Now that he was gone there was a sense of dread among many of the Palestinian leaders I had spoken to in Ramallah. With the father gone, would the children be at one another's throats? Would Hamas and the other Islamic extremists take over? Would our nation come apart at the seams? I felt certain that the Palestinian nation wouldn't degenerate into armed pandemonium, like post-Saddam Iraq. Arafat was not your run-of-the-mill Arab despot; he never took on the role of godlike Pharaoh. He may have brought together a shattered nation, but he hadn't created it.

It would be more accurate to say that the nation created Arafat than to say that Arafat created the nation. In particular, since the first intifada, in matters involving peace and national independence, Arafat and the PLO leadership had always lagged behind the people. Over the decades the Palestinian people had developed a will to live in peace with Israel, and the PLO leadership had to come to terms with that. It was our collective desire for the same freedom and dignity that other nations enjoyed that lured Arafat out of his underground lair and forced him to come to terms with Israel and the Jewish people.

With that settled in my mind, my attention turned to *A Tale of Love and Darkness*. Over the years I'd gotten to know Amos Oz at peace rallies, demonstrations, and debates between Palestinian and Israeli intellectuals. We first met after Lucy and I visited him at his home in the Negev in 1978. His autobiography impressed me for the sheer beauty of his language, but what made it particularly poignant was his description of his childhood in the 1950s.

Born the year Hitler invaded Poland, Oz was nine when the Jewish-Arab war began in 1947. His descriptions of a parallel city on the other side of the conflict startled me.

As a boy, Oz sat on the floor of his parents' small, dark apartment devising complex military strategies to defend the Jewish people. But in his boyhood imagination, animated by the buzz of fighter planes and bold forays across enemy lines, he knew nothing of the ancient cobbled lanes of the Old City, or of the Haram El-Sharif, or Noble Sanctuary, where Mohammed had touched down with al-Burak. (Jews and Christians know it as the Temple Mount.) Nor could he have had an inkling of my mother's pervasive sense of having been terribly wronged by the same Zionist movement to which Oz owed his life. In fact, there were hardly any Arabs in his story, and not a hint of the world I knew as a child. Russian and East European literature, yes, along with Jewish scholars and historians, and Nietzsche, Marx, and Freud—just not the foreboding creatures beyond the barbed wire of a divided city. Uppermost in the Jews' minds were the Nazi death camps they had narrowly escaped.

I was raised no more than a hundred feet away from where Oz lived out his childhood, just on the other side of the fortified "No Man's Land" established in the wake of the first Arab-Israeli War.

When I thought about the absence of Arabs in Oz's childhood experiences, I had to think about my own upbringing. What had my parents known of his world? Did they know about the death camps? Weren't both sides of the conflict totally immersed in their own tragedies, each one oblivious to, or even antagonistic toward, the narrative of the other? Isn't this inability to imagine the lives of the "other" at the heart of the Israeli-Palestinian conflict?

I set the book down and let my thoughts wander—to my childhood, to my twenty-five years in politics, to all the carnage produced by senseless hatred, and finally to the Crusader knight I had abandoned in front of the Holy Sepulcher more than thirty-five years earlier, not knowing the secret that could release him. It suddenly occurred to me that I could conclude the fairy tale, and thus release the Crusader knight, only by taking the story originally conceived as a journey into the dream world of the past, and turning it into a journey into the dream world of the future. The secret I wasn't able to come up with thirty-five years earlier now came to me in a bright flash. It was empathy and the simple work of human hands.

I took out my laptop and began to type. My tale now had four central characters: Abdul, the son of the doorman who opens the door to the Holy Sepulcher; Louise, the little English girl; Amos, a Jewish boy;

and a wizard who lives in the former home of a very wise Sufi sage near the Ecce Homo Arch.

The secret to awaken the knight lies in the sweet smell of honeysuckle. A fortune-teller leads Louise first to Abdul, and then to Amos. The three march off to the Ecce Homo Arch to have an audience with the wizard, who reveals to them the secret. The three must work as one, tilling the soil until the flowers of the honeysuckle blossom and their liberating scent spreads out over the city.

With the fairy tale completed, I moved on to this book. The idea of writing about my life and the life of my family came to me by sheer accident. I was trying to open a computer file containing my fairy tale when I mistakenly selected a different file. It was a memoir my father had written about the 1947–1948 Israeli-Palestinian War. Unbeknownst to me, my son Buraq had scanned the original mimeographed text and put it on my computer.

I hadn't looked at the manuscript since my father died, twenty years earlier, and sitting in my office at the Radcliffe Institute, I was even more astounded at his account of the war. Father had a long public career after writing it—he was the Jordanian minister of defense, governor of Jerusalem, and ambassador to England. But the book captured him in his prime, before seeing his dream of helping establish a modern liberal Arab nation in Palestine shattered by war.

If I have any ambition in writing my memoir, it is the same as that behind my father's decision to write his. His sense of hope was his greatest legacy, and it is for this reason I dedicate this book to him. Over the past few years I've seen my share of smashed dreams, but like my father, I believe that human life is much more than the sum total of all our mistakes. Rubble, he used to tell me, often makes the best building material.

Chapter One

The Key

WHEN I WAS A CHILD it seemed that everywhere I went I came across traces of my family's history in Jerusalem. My father once told me that we Nusseibehs came from a long line of thieves. All family dynasties, he explained with an expression between earnestness and jest, can trace their histories back to some act of brigandage. I think he said this because of the pride Arabs often take in their ancient roots. You have to live in the present, Father lectured to me over and over when I was a child. Whereas I never pinned down precisely who the thieves were, I had no trouble finding old gravestones with names chiseled into the eroded limestone that in my imagination magically connected me up with 1,300 years of forbears, all the way back to the hot sands of Arabia.

My family's story in Jerusalem begins with Mohammed's Night Journey. By the time the Prophet took his legendary pilgrimage to Jerusalem, he and his few companions had already been forced out of Mecca to Medina. It was on the outskirts of this desert town that he was met by his first followers: fourteen tribal leaders who pledged their allegiance to him and to Islam.

Surprisingly, given the way the contemporary world views the role of women in Islam, four of the fourteen tribal leaders were women, and one of these was Nusaybah, from the warrior tribe of Khazraj. (She was also called Umm Umarah al-Maziniyyah, which is short for Umm-Omara alꞋ Maazinia al-Khazrajiyyah min Bani-Amir alꞋ Ansaria.) After the Prophet returned from his Night Journey, he and his followers, including Nusaybah and her clan, directed their prayers toward Jerusalem.

Nusaybah, the progenitor of my family, was a fierce fighter who, on horseback, skillfully defended the Prophet with life and limb. In one battle she lost two sons and a leg, yet continued fighting. Islamic chronicles tell us that Mohammed was so taken by her bravery that he promised that she and all her offspring would always have a place in heaven.

When dealing with more than 1,300 years of family history, there are bound to be some fuzzy points. Much of what I breathed in as a child as irrefutably true is no doubt an innocent mixture of fact and fiction. But in Jerusalem, the source of the magical relation between man and city is precisely the beautiful mosaic of tales rooted in events both real and imagined.

One of my favorite childhood yarns is the story of the caliph Omar's entry into Jerusalem in A.D. 638. By then Mohammed had already died, as had his first successor and hence first caliph (*caliph* meaning "successor to the Prophet"), Abu Bakr. Omar the Just was the second caliph. Humble, pious, and ascetic in his living and his style of dress, he was also a general on par with Alexander and Napoleon, and led armies to one conquest after the next. Following his lead and the banner of Islam, the hitherto chaotic bands of Arabian raiders and camel herders swept across the lands of Persia, Egypt, and Byzantium; with a mixture of bravery, strategy, and brutality, they brought old civilizations under the control of Islamic armies. Damascus, Baghdad, and Cairo fell. Peoples and religions were coming to terms with this dynamic force shaking up the ancient world.

Eventually Omar's army reached the walls of Jerusalem. Panic broke out inside the city. Less than a century earlier, Persian hordes had sacked Jerusalem, burning most of its churches and monasteries and slaughtering thousands. Invoking similar atrocities in their imaginations, people feared the worst.

For me, the most intriguing part of the story when I was a child was how Omar took the city. Like every boy, I liked tales of noble riders bearing arms cutting and slashing their way through hapless foes. But Omar's conquest of Jerusalem was different.

Omar's Muslim faith led him to consider Jerusalem unlike any other place. It was there where his teacher, the Prophet, was miraculously transported on the Night Journey, and he had prayed with Abraham, Moses, and Jesus next to the Rock of Ascension. This was no city conquerable by man's sword. Violence and bloodshed, which had worked wonders elsewhere, were not to defile Jerusalem.

Thinking that their lives were at stake, the people of Jerusalem endured a long siege. But after two years, with their supplies running out, and faced with the specter of starvation, they asked for the terms of surrender. Omar, fighting skirmishes in the north at the time, sent back his reply. He requested that Sephronius, the Byzantine bishop of Jerusalem, meet him outside the gates. Meanwhile, at Omar's instruction, the armies ringing the city walls refrained from all attacks.

At the determined time, Sephronius, dressed in the gilded raiment of his office, came out to meet Omar, expecting to find a royally armored conqueror. He was surprised to meet a simply dressed man leading a camel mounted by Omar's manservant. The two had traveled together from the north, taking turns riding the camel. The humbly attired commander of the Muslim army promised Sephronius that the people, property, and holy sites of the city of Jerusalem would be spared. Moved by his pledge, the bishop handed Omar the keys to the city gates, and to the Holy Sepulcher.

Sephronius ushered Omar to the Holy Sepulcher, the holiest church in Christendom and a repository of divine history. Adam, the first man, was buried there. This was the place of Christ's empty tomb, and it was there that Helena, the mother of Constantine the Great, had discovered the true cross and the crown of thorns. For centuries, legends of the salutary effects of a visit to such sites—just a touch of the sacred stone of the tomb was said to cure deadly diseases—had been luring pilgrims throughout the world.

As the story goes, when the time came for the Muslim prayer, Omar refused to pray in the church, for fear of setting a precedent. If he prayed there, he feared later Muslim leaders might be tempted to turn the glorious church into a mosque. Instead, the caliph chose a spot outside the church to perform his ritual.

Omar then asked the bishop about the site of the Holy Rock and of Solomon's Temple. The bishop didn't know exactly where the temple was, as the plateau where it had once stood was now a vast garbage heap. There were piles of bones and human dung, animal skins, and—most shocking of all for Muslims and Jews—pig carcasses.

Out from the nearby crowds, says Muslim legend, a Jew stepped forward. It was he who now offered to help Omar locate the site of the temple and the rock. And so the two burrowed their way through the rubbish until they came to the spot. "It is here," the Jew said to Omar. "This is the place you seek."

Omar began digging with his own hands. Once he had cleaned away the debris and wiped the Holy Rock clean with his robe, he performed a prayer.

One of Omar's companions to Jerusalem was Nusaybah's brother, Ubadah ibn al-Samit. Before leaving the city, Omar installed him as the first Muslim high judge of Jerusalem, and handed him the key to the Church of the Holy Sepulcher. He then charged Ubadah, along with five other heads of families, with keeping the Holy Rock clean. (As a child, I liked visiting Ubadah's tomb, in the southern corner of the wall enclosing the Holy Sanctuary.)

Ubadah's sons were the first Nusaybahs (now spelled Nusseibeh) born in Jerusalem. Over time, the family became wealthy, with vast landholdings. Centuries run into one another here: for long stretches, our family is not much more than a list of names and titles neatly divided into judges, Koranic scholars, Sufi sages, and landowners.

The family's political fortunes have always depended on the particular empire that controlled Jerusalem. Whether in favor or not, though, the family has fastidiously performed its duties of dusting off the Holy Rock and safeguarding the key.

Keeping the rock clean soon got easier. Within a few decades of the Muslim conquest, the construction of the Dome of the Rock was begun. The Islamic caliphate had moved to Damascus in A.D. 661, setting off an architectural revolution. The Umayyad caliph, Muáwiyah, wanted to construct a magnificent mosque on the site of the Holy Rock. But unlike other mosques, it was not to be designed to face Mecca. As the place of the ancient Temple of Solomon and of Mohammed's Night Journey, it didn't need to point anywhere. Some storytellers say that the son of the Jew who pointed out the Holy Rock to Omar was the architect charged with the mosque's design. As a Jew, the storytellers say, he constructed the new house of God, the Noble Sanctuary, or Al-Aqsa, with the original temple in mind. The Dome of the Rock was completed in A.D. 691.

As control of the church of the Holy Sepulcher was the main bone of contention between Latin Christians and Muslims, possession of the key was a matter of supreme diplomatic importance. And so, over the centuries, my family performed its duties: an ancestor opened up the door, the Christians filed in, at night they left again, and the door was locked until the next morning.

During the Crusades, with the Franks in control of the city, the Nusseibehs yielded up the key. The clan's only survivor from the Crusaders' conquest of Jerusalem was thankfully pregnant, and she fled to the north of the country. A century later, in 1187, after the Kurdish warrior Saladin drove the Crusaders out of the city, her offspring returned to Jerusalem.

Back in Jerusalem, the leader of my family clan, Sheikh Ghanim ben Ali ben Hussein al-Ansari al-Khazrajy, took up a leading post in government. For the first few years after the defeat of the Crusaders, there was no need to unlock the door to the Holy Sepulcher, because Christians weren't allowed back in Jerusalem. In 1192, the Muslim governor of the city returned the key to the Nusseibeh line after Sultan Saladin and King Richard the Lionheart concluded an agreement to allow Christian pilgrims to visit the city.

These were the salad days for the family, especially during the reign of the Malmuks in Damascus. The clan lived off vast tracts of land that Sheikh Ghanim had received from Sultan Saladin. This may have been where my father came up with his story of the Nusseibehs having been "thieves." Peasants worked the soil and paid tithes to us, their feudal masters, who in turn used some of the proceeds to benefit the Dome of the Rock.

Financially, the family fortunes slid precipitously after the Turks expelled the Malmuks in 1517. One of my ancestors wasn't happy at all about the new overlords and decided to join up with a Malmuk prince in his hopeless guerrilla campaign. Both he and the prince lost their heads, and the Nusseibeh family lost its lands and most of its rights. The one major property they kept was the Suq al-Khawajat, the Goldsmith's Souk, one of the main markets within the ancient walls of the city.

A few years ago my cousin Zaki, the family historian, stumbled across a good example of our declining fortunes. It is in a four-hundred-year-old document painted in gold on deerskin and sealed with the sign of the Turkish sultan, declaring that henceforth the Nusseibehs had to share the rights to the key with the Joudeh family, a local clan on far better terms with the Turks. And so it was. For the last half millennium, a Joudeh has brought the key to a Nusseibeh at 4:00 a.m., and the Nusseibeh has proceeded forthwith to the church.

Chapter Two

The Pan-Arab Nation

I SHOULDN'T GIVE THE IMPRESSION that ancient history lurks in every corner of our lives. Quite the contrary. I was raised by a modern, forward-thinking man who adored ancient and modern Arabic poetry equally, and was as pleased with my elder brother's stellar marks at Cambridge as he was with my sister's pursuit of painting in Paris. While proud of our ancient matriarch's desert exploits, Father always kept an eye on the here and now.

A modern sensibility first began to stir among aristocrats in Jerusalem in the late nineteenth century. Times were changing, not least because the Ottoman Empire had by then become the "sick man of Europe." As with every despotic system, the first signs of weakening set off political grumblings in every corner of the empire. Urban groups were demanding the rights and freedoms enjoyed by Europeans. Inspired by the Italian Risorgimento, in 1909 the Young Turks (officially known as the Committee of Union and Progress) captured the Sublime Porte in Constantinople, sent the sultan packing, and set up a new administration. The Young Turks tried to snap the empire out of its lethargy by promising the rule of law, industry, and progress.

In Palestine, the movement for more European-style liberty was particularly intense because the place was already shot through with European influence. By the time my grandfather's generation came onto the scene, in the 1880s, the scramble for Palestine had begun.

Ironically, it was the ancient legacy of the Holy Land that brought much of the change. In Europe, a new romantic sensibility regarding the Holy Land—you can sense it in George Eliot's *Daniel Deronda*—was combined with photography and cheap package tours to stir up interest in the area. It was common to see eccentric English explorers traveling the country with a Bible stuffed in their saddlebags. A good example of the craze was the way the war hero General Charles Gordon, one of Lytton Strachey's half-mad "eminent Victorians," discovered what he swore was the Garden Tomb.

Governments, organizations, and entrepreneurs were equally caught up in the fashion. In Jerusalem, Czar Alexander II built the Russian Colony to accommodate the flood of Russian pilgrims streaming into the city. (The Israelis later turned it into a prison.) Not to be outdone, the German kaiser built the Benedictine abbey on Mount Zion. Protestant churches threw up schools and hospitals by the score. The Catholics appointed their first Latin patriarch since the Crusades, and Baron Edmond de Rothschild erected windmills for a colony of Jewish farmers.

Among Arab Jerusalemites, the movement for political reform was indirectly emboldened by this building and missionary frenzy, in part because many of the reformers were exposed to modern notions in schools run by Europeans.

Students at the Arab College, and later at my alma mater, the Anglican-run St. George's, discovered Pan-Arabism, a movement spearheaded by Arab Christians in Beirut and Damascus, and by figures such as Abduh and Afghani in Cairo. These intellectuals, many of them fine poets and thinkers, frowned on old local loyalties of clan, tribe, and sect as leftovers of the feudalism that had arrested Arab scientific and cultural development.

In Palestine, a main source of the nationalist fervor among Jews was Zionism. As seen in the legends surrounding the Dome of the Rock,

Jews had always been an organic part of Islamic Jerusalem. (My cousin Zaki, digging through ancient documents buried for centuries in an old synagogue in Egypt, once discovered letters praising caliph Omar for allowing Jews to move back to the city after centuries of Roman and Christian prohibitions.) Around the end of the nineteenth century, most of the Jews in the city were either East European ultrareligious Jews, or Arabic speakers who had lived with the Arabs for centuries and felt themselves to be a part of Arab culture, language, and life.

The Zionist movement had very different roots. Theodor Herzl, a journalist and failed Vienna playwright, was an assimilated Hungarian Jew. At the time he wrote *The Jewish State*, Herzl hadn't even visited Palestine; he knew it only through books. What he envisioned was a future state for those Jews who would not or could not assimilate into European societies. Arabs, he was convinced, would have nothing to fear. "The Jews have no belligerent Power behind them," he wrote, "neither are they themselves of a warlike nature."

Arabs were unconvinced. A decade after Herzl wrote *The Jewish State*, the Palestinian journalist Najib Nassar published, as a wakeup call, *Zionism: Its History, Aims, and Importance.* Fears of a European Jewish "invasion" made the rounds. The mayor of Jerusalem, Zia al-Khalidi, was so alarmed that he sent a missive to his friend Zadoc Khan, the chief rabbi of France. "Who can contest the rights of the Jews to Palestine?" he wrote. "God knows, historically it is indeed your country." Nevertheless, the "brutal force of reality," namely that the country was already thickly inhabited by Arabs, precluded mass resettlement by Jews. "In the name of God," he concluded, "leave Palestine in peace."[1]

In terms of power and social prestige, by the nineteenth century, the Nusseibeh family stood in the shadow of other aristocratic clans in the city, foremost among them the feuding Husseini and Nashashibi families. The decline in our political fortunes that set in with the Ottomans was probably a blessing in disguise. Generally speaking, it forced the Nusseibehs to adopt distinctly bourgeois attitudes. Women shed their veils, while both men and women picked up European languages. Like other patrician families, the Nusseibehs began to move out of the Old City and into the manorial residencies in Sheikh Jarrah and Wadi el Joz. As a sign of the family's forward-thinking attitudes, one of its members modernized a medieval fortress outside the city walls. In family folklore, the four-story house was called Al-Kasr, or "The Castle." (The Israelis blew it up in 1948.)

Another example of the family's modernity was its cavalier attitude toward the past. My great-grandfather, for instance, was perfectly willing to give up his part of the key for the sake of the amorous appeal of a younger woman. One day, he announced to his wife that he wanted to take on a second wife, still common practice among the wealthy at the time. She wasn't thrilled with the idea, and putting her disapproval in a language her husband could appreciate, she demanded compensation. She wanted the key. It was an erotic variation on the story of Jacob offering the porridge to Esau. In our case, the "birthright" now belonged to her children and not to the children of my great-grandfather's new wife, who was my great-grandmother. Thus Great-grandfather's amorous desires led him to establish a new branch of the family, leaving the key behind.

My grandfather, an offspring of his father's second nuptial bond, never missed the key. He had more important things on his mind, such as investing his inheritance in new business ventures, or spreading it freely as acts of charity, or social climbing, which, judging by his nuptial preferences, was a skill he certainly mastered. His first wife belonged to the Khalidi family, famous for scholarship. She died, and Grandfather's second wife, my grandmother, came from the powerful Husseini clan. When she died soon after giving birth to my father, his next and final wife was a Nashashibi, a family that rivaled the Husseinis in wealth and influence. In a matter of a few years Grandfather had managed to stitch together four ancient Jerusalem families, two of which were bitter rivals.

Chapter Three

Promises, Promises

W ORLD WAR I brought the 1,300-year-old political system of caliphate rule to an end, ushering in a time of great hope for Arab nationalists. In this respect my father, who came into the world in 1913, was born at an auspicious moment. One childhood photograph shows him dressed and posed like a young noble. He was still too young to realize that the Arab movement he was to embrace his entire life was about to be strangled at birth.

With the coming of war in 1914, the relatively tolerant prewar years became a thing of the past. The Turks made the mistake of supporting the Axis powers, and the Turkish governor, Jamal Pasha, whose not-so-subtle nickname was "the Butcher," ruled over Palestine as if it were his personal fiefdom. He brooked no dissent, and as the war dragged on and Arab sentiment turned against the masters in Constantinople, the vengeful Turk handed out death sentences with the flippant ease with which a later generation of police would write up parking violations. Water was scarce, as was food. Then came the locusts. By 1916 most Arabs secretly longed for an Allied victory. Pan-Arab intellectuals pinned their hopes on the English and French.

Well aware of the mood, the British stoked these hopes whenever they could. T. E. Lawrence (Lawrence of Arabia), a British liaison officer, joined in common cause with Faisal al-Hussein, the Arabian sheikh and member of the powerful Hashemite dynasty, to destroy the Turkish army. Lawrence, speaking in good faith on behalf of his government, assured Faisal the support of the British Empire. Once the war was over and the Ottoman defeated, the Allies would help Faisal unify the Arab provinces of the Ottoman Empire into a single kingdom, with Faisal as king.

The first promise of a free Arab Palestine came from the sky, when British airplanes dropped leaflets bearing the message, COME JOIN US FOR THE LIBERATION OF ALL ARABS FROM TURKISH RULE SO THAT THE ARAB KINGDOM MAY AGAIN BECOME WHAT IT WAS DURING THE TIME OF YOUR FATHERS.[1]

While the English made their promises to the Arabs, they and the French were making contradictory plans, in the Sykes-Picot Pact, to divide the booty of the war between them. Meanwhile, Lord Alfred Balfour, the British secretary of state for foreign affairs, wrote to the Zionist leader Chaim Weizmann pledging support for "the establishment in Palestine of a national home for the Jewish people." He addressed a similar letter to Walter Rothschild, whose family were supporters of a Jewish state, informing him of his government's support, with the proviso that the establishment of such a state "not prejudice the civil and religious rights of existing non-Jewish communities." It was a strange promise for many reasons, not least because the proud citizens of the future "Arab kingdom" described in the flyer dropped from British airplanes were now reduced to a "non-Jewish community." It was also an unusual promise to make when the Turks were still in charge of Palestine. Moreover, this generous pledge was made by a man who, in 1905, had pushed for immigration limits to prevent Eastern European Jews from entering England.

In 1917, with General Edmund Allenby and his Mule Corps closing in from the east, Jamal Pasha surrendered to the British. Like a scene from a Brecht play, the Turks slipped out through the gates in the middle of the night and gave the letter of surrender to the mayor, who ripped a sheet in two, attached half to a broomstick, and wandered down Jaffa Road until he found his first British soldier.

In 1917, the city of Jerusalem witnessed the entry of armies from the European West for the first time since Saladin tossed out the Franks. When standing victoriously inside Jaffa Gate, General Allenby did not fail to remind his troops of this historic fact. Even as he did so, the Arab crowds cheered him on. For the pan-Arabists, this was the moment they had been waiting for. With the Turks expelled, it was time to realize their dreams.

None of the Arabs gathered at Jaffa Gate knew that Allenby's entry was but the first step leading to Jerusalem's being wrested from Arab hands. Once the Sykes-Picot Pact and the Balfour Declaration became public, Lawrence, having tasted British perfidy up close, returned all his medals to the British government. The Arabs of Palestine were the most directly affected by these secret agreements. With admirable candor, Lord Balfour confided to fellow politicians back in London what the Arabs could expect from the agreement:

> In Palestine we do not propose even to go through the form of consulting the wishes of the present inhabitants of the country . . . Zionism, be it right or wrong, good or bad, is rooted in age-long traditions, in present needs, in future hopes, of far profounder import than the desires and prejudices of the 700,000 Arabs who now inhabit that ancient land.[2]

He didn't say this to the Arabs. The official line, duly echoed by the Zionists, was that the rights of the Arabs would be safeguarded. At every opportunity, the Zionist leader, Chaim Weizmann, declared with hand on heart that the Zionists would vouchsafe the rights and property of Arabs.

At first Arab fears in fact seemed overblown. After the war, Faisal Hussein became king of Iraq, and his brother Abdullah the king of Transjordan. Palestine wasn't in Arab hands, but neither had it turned into a Jewish state. The British made a number of improvements in Jerusalem. They finally completed a water system for the city begun by King Herod 1,900 years earlier, and they solved the locust problem, using stockpiles of poison gas brought over from Flanders. The main thing the English imported was an efficient administration, along with the very thing the inhabitants of the region had never known: law, order, and a sense of justice.

Administration was a more accurate term than an enemy *occupation*, because no one wanted the Turks back. Gone was the despised system of forced conscription, which had been little better than slavery; gone were the absurd taxes that kept the population poor; gone was the never-ending and necessary *baksheesh* (bribery).

The new British Mandate economy was a boon to professionals, merchants, and government civil servants. The Arab middle classes built their homes in Qatamon, Talbieh, and Baqʾa, while Jaffa Road grew into a busy commercial strip, lined with banks and shops, mostly belonging to Arab Christians.

The general mood was upbeat enough in 1921 that Musaa Kazim al-Husseini, the president of the Arab Higher Committee, asked the Palestinian people to "put their hope in the government of Great Britain, which is famous for its justice, its concern for the well-being of the inhabitants, its safe-guarding of their rights, and consent to their lawful demands."[3]

Father's education can serve as a good gauge of the mood among the children of Jerusalem patricians. With the exception of general hostility toward the Balfour Declaration, the Jerusalem elite fit into the social order imported by the English as if tailor-made for it. The men belonged to the same gentleman's society, and in private, English officers tended to prefer them to the Russian Jewish upstarts streaming into the country.

As a child, Father lived in a wonderful jumble of worlds. On top of the social pyramid sat the British governor, perched high on his white horse. He ruled from an administrative building on top of the "Hill of

Evil Counsel," where in New Testament times the Jewish High Priest had his home. (In Arabic we call the hill al-Mukabber, because when Omar first set his eyes on Jerusalem from its crest, he was so moved to tears that he asked the muezzin to call for prayer.) Then came the ornamentally dressed representatives of the various religious orders, led by the Haj Amin Husseini, the grand mufti of Jerusalem and the most important Muslim leader in the city, and the various Christian archbishops and bishops. Next were families like ours, still living off real or imagined past glories, whose children wore pressed suits with creased trousers and typically carried a volume of modern Arabic verse or *Robinson Crusoe* under their arms. Their version of cowboys and Indians were Islamic warriors and Frankish Crusaders. Below the notables was the emerging class of urban professionals, mainly administrators, teachers, and merchants. Finally, down on the bottom, were the hardworking peasants, or fellahin, of the villages and countryside, proudly clad in the bright colors of their traditional dress. Rounding out the scene were Bedouin in long flowing desert djellabas, leading their camels through the streets, which now had a few private cars. (Cousin Zaki tells me that my grandfather imported Palestine's first Buick.)

Father's upbringing was something out of a Victorian novel. For starters, he was the only child of a mother who had died giving birth to him, and after Grandfather remarried, he promptly put Father in the custody of a widowed aunt. This aunt was obsessed with the memory of her late husband, who was a fine Arab poet and had left behind a body of work his widowed wife memorized and recited back to my father every chance she got. It was thanks to her that Arabic poetry became for him a source of inspiration and pride, even as he was busy imbibing Latin and English literature at his thoroughly English school.

It was a measure of the traditional religious tolerance in Jerusalem that the members of the Muslim haute bourgeoisie all attended Christian schools. The Arab College, where my father went and later taught, was one of the best schools in the Arab world at the time. Its head under the Mandate was Ahmad Sameh al-Khalidi. Khalil al-Sakakini, a poet whom my father held in high regard, was one of the school's luminary professors. There he mastered the canon of European learning, and when he wasn't beating English officers at their own game—he learned to play an excellent game of tennis—he was practicing the piano. Another sign of tolerance was Father's favorite holiday: the yearly pilgrimage south of Jericho to the shrine of Nebi Musa, or Moses the Prophet and Lawgiver to whom God spoke, a custom that dates back to Saladin and takes place during Easter. The shrine, as Father liked to joke, contained nothing more edifying than the worm-eaten remnants of a wandering Bedouin tribesman. As a boy, my father loved the pilgrimage because the ceremony was accompanied by singing, dancing, lots of clowning around for the children, and, for the adults, horseracing.

My father and his fellow students at the Arab College also picked up Arab nationalism, and in far greater doses than their parents.

With the downfall of the Ottoman Islamic regime, Pan-Arabism was fast becoming second nature to the young generation. They had never identified with the Turks in the first place, and they harbored high hopes for the "Arab spirit," now set free from the Ottoman yoke, to rejuvenate the glory of Arab civilization. Anyway, for a student body of Christians and Muslims tied together by class, education, and language, religion was becoming a vaguely private affair. Language, not religion, was the creative domain for young poets and intellectuals. It was for this reason that my father and his friends preferred fraternizing with the like-minded in Beirut and Alexandria to adhering to the dusty system of inherited privileges, rank, family name, and symbols in Jerusalem.

The reigning spirit of the age was without question one of hopeful change, and yet when my father was still an adolescent, an event occurred that presaged the catastrophes that would accompany him all the way to his death. As a sixteen-year-old, he witnessed how the three-thousand-year-long Jewish spiritual attachment to the Western Wall (we call it al-Burak, after the Prophet's steed) turned into a nationalistic slogan, which in turn produced a nasty backlash among the Muslims. Overnight, Islam, a religion my father was raised to consider inherently humane, turned into a lethal stick with which to club opponents. Even worse, by unleashing a murderous mob on defenseless men, women, and children, the village clerics equally attacked Father's luminous pan-Arab vision of a free, tolerant, and open society.

It's remarkable how sacred sites that can arouse in us a sense of the ineffable mystery of life can also spawn a bare-knuckle brawl. This is a mystery only a metaphysician or psychotherapist can make any sense of. I won't try.

In 1929, anti-Jewish rioting started after a few hundred young supporters of Zev Jabotinsky (the Jews nicknamed him their "Duce") marched to al-Burak hollering, "The Wall is ours!" Amid waving flags, Jabotinsky's followers sang the "Hatikva," the Jewish national anthem.

Our hope is not yet lost
The hope of two thousand years.
To be a free people in our land
The land of Zion and Jerusalem.

An English journalist living in the city at the time described the scene this way: "The young heroes who passed a while ago were guarded heavily by the police; mounted officers in front of them and behind them, with policemen on foot marching alongside. The material for an awful three-cornered fight. What an exhibition of imbecility the whole thing is!"[4]

Among Muslims, rumors spread that the Jews were trying to take over the Noble Sanctuary, the traditional spot of Solomon's Temple, and a mob stirred up by the mufti went berserk. The next day, screaming "Islamiya," Muslims raided the Wall and tore up Jewish prayer books. Then a Jewish boy was stabbed to death after a quarrel in a soccer field.

In Hebron, sixty-four Jews were slaughtered, all of them from an ancient religious community that had always lived in peace with its neighbors, and had nothing to do with the secular nationalism of the Russian Zionists. But the mob, inflamed by an insanely simplistic nationalism, no longer made any distinction between Jews and Zionists. It was a black-and-white proposition: them against us. An awful precedent.

The English responded to the "al-Buraq Revolt," so called because it started at the Western Wall, by flooding the country with soldiers. They also did something that would be repeated innumerable times in the future: they sent in clueless "experts" to find a solution.

The anti-British sentiment created by the Balfour Declaration and by the heavy-handed response to the rioting didn't prevent my grandfather from, out of defiance and pride, sending Father off to Cambridge to study law.

It wasn't long after he returned to Palestine with his degree in 1936 that he met my mother, at her father's estate in Wadi Hnein (now the Israeli town of Nes Ziona). Her father was a wealthy landowner and political activist who regularly opened his home to political leaders and literary figures. The estate in Wadi Hnein stood amid vast tracts of orange groves that stretched all the way to Gaza. His palatial home had a swimming pool and enough guest rooms and servants to accommodate visiting effendis or even the occasional prince, king, or prime minister. King Abdullah was a frequent guest. My father showed up ostensibly to acquaint himself with the illustrious political milieu there, but in fact he wanted to set eyes on the beautiful young woman his cousin had told him about.

I've been told that for my parents it was love at first sight, which was hardly a traditional Muslim way of doing things. But given the social and even blood ties between the families (my maternal grandmother was also a Nusseibeh) it might as well have been an arranged marriage. These two children of wealth and position seemed fated for a life of ease and happiness. The world stretched out before them like an open garden.

After my parents met, my father returned to Jerusalem to start a legal practice. He must have picked up some Victorian attitudes in England, because he wasn't about to start a family without having established himself professionally first. His ancestry, education, and his powdered wig and the black cloak of a barrister guaranteed his rapid ascension up the professional ladder. He had no doubts that he and my mother could soon marry.

But catastrophe stood in the way. Father would soon find himself using the English legal code he adored to defend people who were doing everything in their power to evict the British from the Holy Land. In the months leading up to the rebellion, when Father was not in the courtroom defending people hauled in under the draconian security laws passed by the English in their effort to suppress a new uprising, he taught courses at the Arab College. His fellow professor, Khalil al-Sakakini, a Christian, represented what was best about the Arab Awakening. Cultured and deeply proud of his Arab heritage, he lived in the posh neighborhood of Talbieh, where he had turned his home into a literary salon for poets and intellectuals, and a meeting place for a circle of literati who called themselves the Party of the Vagabonds (*hizb al-saʾaleek*). Al-Sakakini's Pan-Arabism was reflected beautifully in his verse. (Father adored his poetry, and often quoted it to me when I was a boy, in particular the poem lauding the individual's resolute defiance against the world.)

In his free time Father played tennis, and over the years collected enough trophies to fill several shelves. He also took long rides on horseback with Thomas Hodgkins, an English officer stationed in Jerusalem and a closet Marxist who sympathized with the Arabs. They sometimes traveled for days through the desert.

Before it became too dangerous, that is. In 1935 political tension, building up for years, exploded into the open. The catalyst was the mass immigration of Jews fleeing for their lives from fascist Europe. Unlike in 1929, it wasn't the mufti who stirred up trouble but instead a village cleric named Sheikh Izzeddin Qassam, who found his followers among farmers who had lost their livelihoods when absentee landowners sold their land to a Zionist organization.

Sheikh Qassam (Hamas's crude handmade "Qassam" rockets recall his memory) started a guerrilla campaign in the tradition of the mountain fedayeen from the Ismaili sect, who came from the Syrian mountains to terrorize the Franks centuries earlier. Qassam and his band hid out in caves, only venturing out at night to attack the British and the Jews. But Qassam's strategic vision, like that of many subsequent Palestinian leaders, fell sadly short of his nationalistic ardor. In one of his famed exploits, he wanted to lay siege to the British navy at Haifa, with two-score of his followers armed with antiquated World War I–era rifles. In no time he was caught, and he and his followers were duly hanged. "Martyrdom," which always feeds base instincts, became a staple ingredient in the conflict over Palestine.

The sheik's uprising may have been something straight out of the Three Stooges, but for various reasons neither the British nor even the grand mufti understood the forces the simple village cleric had released. English officers, born and bred to rule, naturally dismissed Qassam as a crackpot. For his part, the mufti was embarrassed by Qassam's call to arms, because at the time the mufti was trying to get the British to crown him Palestinian leader.

In truth, the grand mufti's real fear was competition. The crudely woven kefiyyeh of the Palestinian peasant farmer in the countryside was threatening to replace the tarbush, the red felt hat (similar to the fez) with silk tassels, worn by the urban leadership. This was a classic case of a conflict between the simple man's fanatical commitment to a cause, and the diplomatic ambiguity of sophisticated and self-serving politicians. Both methods, as it would turn out, would be equally futile.

The following year, nobles tried their hand at an uprising. The 1936 uprising, called the Great Rebellion, began as a harmless fistfight in Jaffa before quickly escalating into brigandage. Arabs held up cars, robbing some Europeans and killing two Jews. There were reprisals and counter-reprisals, and the violence threatened to spin out of control.

The reason it didn't, at least initially, was because the Arab elite of the country took charge, and conducted their protest campaign with the civility of European-educated gentlemen. The Arab Higher Committee, with six members led by the grand mufti of Jerusalem, comprised political and civic leaders throughout the country. Nationalist clubs and groups put out newspapers and erected public banners calling for a stop to Jewish immigration, and in support of a freely elected representative assembly. Such an assembly would be based on majority rule, along the lines of Iraq and Transjordan, and aligned with the British but no longer governed by a policy aimed intentionally at undermining pan-Arab ambitions. Zionists, who claimed to represent Western values, logically rejected free elections in which they would have been badly outvoted. They fought ferociously, and effectively, against all efforts to weaken the Balfour Declaration, an antidemocratic document if there ever was one.

Politically, one royal delegation after the next trooped through the country, all with the solemn expressions of well-meaning professionals trying their best not to think about the impossibility of reconciling Arab national demands with the Balfour Declaration, which the British were not prepared to abandon. Divided by the cold facts of demographics, Jews and Arabs were at loggerheads.

To show the British that they meant business, Arab leaders organized strikes and demonstrations. (In a prime example of their ill-conceived strategies, they shut down Jaffa Port, which only encouraged the Jews to build a port of their own.)

In 1937, the English responded with a tri-council plan, which was actually more of a power-sharing scheme that envisioned the country ruled equally by Jews, Muslims, and Christians. Arabs unthinkingly rejected the plan. A stalemate set in, and the English came up with more committees and more papers and more plans. The one thing they weren't prepared to do was abandon Balfour.

This largely peaceful movement quickly degenerated into a three-year guerrilla war. It began in the north of the country when some local Arabs attacked and killed L. Y. Andrews, the acting district commissioner for Galilee, after church one Sunday. The English overreacted by pinning the moral blame for the murder on the Arab Higher Committee, which they now banned. The main members of the committee had their properties confiscated and were expelled from the country. The mufti escaped from Jerusalem dressed as a woman.

Mother's father was one of these expelled nobles. One day British soldiers showed up at the front door of the villa and arrested him.

Operating under the new security laws, the British Mandate administration stripped him of his lands and home and sent him off to the Seychelles without a trial. My grandmother and all of her children, including my mother, moved into a small house in Ramle, which was in fact the site of the tomb of one of the family's patriarchs, a Sufi Muslim mystic who had lived there in the fifteenth century. (Sufism is a mystical form of Islam with an ecstatic belief in unity with God through love.) As a child my mother had watched with rapture during an annual religious festival as various members of Sufi orders congregated at the house before marching off into the city streets. Now it was her home.

My father clearly stood on the side of the rebellion, even if he considered the grand mufti of Jerusalem—who at the time was an avid admirer of Hitler—to be a disastrous leader. Father's nuanced view of Zionism never conflated it with the Jewish people or with Judaism, both of which he held in great esteem, even after his leg was shot off in 1948 by Fighters for the Freedom of Israel, an underground Jewish faction. His conception of Pan-Arabism was of a pluralistic and vibrant society composed not only of Muslims and Christians, but also of Jews. The Pan-Arabism he believed in was not yet the chauvinist or exclusivist ideology it later became.

Father ended up supporting the rebellion because he had come to the conclusion that the Eastern European Zionists arriving by the boatload had no interest in fitting themselves into Arab culture and society. In the Russians he saw ideologues with no understanding of the country, and without the slightest intention of respecting the culture or rights of the Arabs living there. Most of all he saw very determined men and women with scientific, industrial, and political ambitions to create a Jewish state. The attitude that frightened him the most can be summed up in Chaim Weizmann's words: "Palestine shall be as Jewish as England is English, or America is American."[5] These were public words. In private, Zionist leaders spelled out their plans. In 1936, in a letter to his son, David Ben-Gurion wrote nakedly, "We will expel the Arabs and take their place."[6] It would be hard to think of something more antithetical to Pan-Arabism.

The British committed an enormous blunder when they arrested my grandfather and his colleagues. The latter were political leaders, not terrorists, and most of them had probably never fired a gun in their lives. So now, instead of a secular leadership as represented by my grandfather and his colleagues, the British made way for the creation of a guerrilla war fueled by militant followers of Sheikh Qassam.

Only after the British sent in twenty thousand troops did the Arab leaders finally agree to call off the boycott of Jaffa Port. But the country would never be the same. After 1936 only the blind refused to see that what people were now calling the "Arab problem," it being national and not economic in nature, was not about to go away. A memorandum delivered to the British Mandate and signed by hundreds of high Arab officials and judges spoke of the "repellent" government policies and threatened the British with the "rage of the Almighty God."[7]

With the onset of World War II, the British brooked no more dissent. They were the ones who had encouraged Arabs to conduct guerrilla attacks against their Turkish overlords during the previous war, but they were not about to allow the same thing to happen to them. The British army outdid itself in its brutally repressive tactics. Its main target was the Palestinian countryside and the compliant fellahin. Stories of British brutality are still recounted in Palestinian villages to this day.

With the country full of British, Australian, Irish, Scottish, Greek, African, and Indian soldiers, there was no point in putting up a fight, and the uprising ground to an end. Ironically, when the British first set up a law college my father got a part-time teaching job. Many of his best students were German Jewish refugees, whose presence in the country had triggered the uprising in the first place. One of his star pupils is now my lawyer. Now retired, his only remaining case is fighting attempts by the Israeli government to shut down Al-Quds University, which I now head.

Chapter Four

The Herod's Gate Committee

M Y PARENTS FINALLY GOT MARRIED in 1943, and because of my father's position as itinerant court judge—the active life of a lawyer, judge, and later politician suited him more than teaching—they shifted residences from Jerusalem to Jaffa to Tiberias to Ramallah. Within five years, my father had a permanent position back in Jerusalem, and my parents and their two girls and one boy lived in a house across the street from the American Colony Hotel. (Munira and Saedah, my sisters, were born in 1944 and 1945, and my brother Zaki in 1946.) Life seemed to be returning to normal, when new disasters occurred. I, their fourth child, was born shortly after the tragedy called by Palestinians the *Nakba*, or the "Catastrophe."

The year of my conception, 1948, witnessed the collapse of the Palestinian dream. It was a year that left Father fighting for his life in a Beirut hospital from bullet wounds in his legs; my mother huddled in a cramped Damascus apartment, where she eventually gave birth to me; and her family along with seven hundred thousand Palestinians driven from their homes. An ancient way of life had come to an end.

Throughout my youth I heard innumerable accounts of my father's role as "Defender of Jerusalem" in the war of 1947 and 1948. But it was only after Father died in 1986 that I stumbled across the unpublished firsthand report he wrote in 1949 detailing precisely the part he had played. In Cairo recovering from his wounds, and running the offices of the so-called All-Palestine Government, he composed a sixty-thousand-word personal account of the battle for Jerusalem and for Palestine. As I read it, I imagined him typing away, doing his best not to think about the leg that had been blown off by the Stern Gang, the British name for the Fighters for the Freedom of Israel, and the fact that soon he would have yet another hungry mouth to feed. What I found more difficult to imagine was the role this paragon of bourgeois respectability—a judge, governor, and ambassador—had had in the battle for Jerusalem, when he donned a powdered wig and gown for his day job, then moonlighted as a gunrunner by night.

During the war the British finally permitted my grandfather to return from exile in the Seychelles—just not to Palestine. They moved him to Egypt. It was only late in the war, after eight years in exile, that he was finally allowed to join his family in their cramped quarters in Ramle. There was no returning to the estate in Wadi Hnein; the British had burnt it to the ground. With his wealth and properties confiscated, by day he ran a small shop, and by night he read, prayed, and chanted mystical Sufi songs.

In 1946 the British legalized the Arab Higher Committee. Almost immediately the local inhabitants of Ramle honored Grandfather by installing him as their mayor. But his health was broken, and the next year he died of a heart attack at the age of forty-eight. He was buried in Ramle in the tomb of a Sufi master and sage.

At the time of Grandfather's death, the country was descending into civil war. To stop the now-daily terrorist attacks, the British went back into the business of meting out draconian sentences. Mere possession of a weapon or ammunition was a capital offense. As in 1936, my father again had his hands full defending Arab nationalists in court.

In Jerusalem political tensions lay close to the surface. My father used to visit his friend Raouf in his office behind the King David Hotel, where the two of them sat and drank coffee and where my father often overheard the bloodcurdling threats that Raouf and a Jewish colleague traded under their breaths. As professionals, the two men respected each other, but because of the nationalist conflict, they greeted each other with a combination of friendly hellos and threats. "What kind of madness was this?" my father asks in his memoirs. The two men were hardly to blame as individuals. After all, what could Raouf and his Jewish colleague have done to stem what must have seemed to them the inevitable tide of history pulling their respective peoples apart? They continued to work as colleagues, and after clocking out they returned to their respective tribes, each preparing for a war everyone felt was inevitable.

My father's memoirs turn on one date: November 29, 1947, the day the United Nations General Assembly voted in favor of the partition of Palestine. The same British who had endured the Nazi Blitzkrieg had had enough: terrorism and the cost of pacifying the country were driving them away.

The preceding year saw a massive upsurge in organized, systematic terrorism. Initially, most of it came from the Jewish underground for simple, logical reasons. The Arabs had never recovered from the 1936–39 uprising: their political leadership was fragmented, and most of the old guerrilla leaders were either dead or still in prison. Moreover, the Arabs had no compelling reason to attack the British. Time seemed to be on their side, as the British were clamping down on Jewish immigration from Europe—and without a massive influx of immigrants, everyone knew there would never be a Jewish state.

By contrast, immigration was the main factor triggering Jewish terrorism. Fueled by a potent mixture of desperation, ideology, and political calculation, Zionist forces were resorting to terrorism to pressure the government to allow survivors from Nazi death camps into the country.

Father describes many of the acts that finally led to British capitulation, many of them perpetrated by the Stern Gang, the most active Jewish terrorist organization and the group who later took Father's leg. The group's founder, Abraham Stern, is described in my father's manuscript as an ex-student of the Hebrew University: "He was a very nice, quiet, studious type of fellow," my father wrote. Members of his group kidnapped two British soldiers, executed them, and hung their booby-trapped bodies from a tree in a eucalyptus grove. "When the rescue party came to lower them to the ground, a bomb wired to the corpses exploded." Then there was the machine-gunning and killing of British soldiers asleep in their camp in Tel Aviv.

An attack my father describes in great detail was the bombing of the King David Hotel, in July 1946, one of whose wings housed the nerve center of the British colonial administration. On the day of the attack, a milk delivery van drove up to the service entrance of the hotel from the Jewish neighborhood of Yemin Moshe. Three men got out of the van, each carrying what appeared to be milk cans but were in fact bombs. When the bombs went off, the whole area dissolved into black dust. The explosives brought down the southern wing of the hotel, killing more than a hundred civil servants and senior officers. A close friend of Father's (a British officer he affectionately called "Blenks") was among the dead.

For the British it was a losing battle. Restricting immigration to the victims of Nazism was a hard policy to defend at a time when bestselling books such as Arthur Koestler's *Thieves in the Night*—in Father's estimation a "very ably written work"—cast the Stern Gang and Irgun, another militant Zionist group, in the same glamorous light as the underground fighters who had fought against the Nazis. Fed up, the British submitted another partition plan, which both Arabs and Jews rejected. Terror and British retaliation continued until London announced that it would hand over the problem to the newly created United Nations, which came up with its own partition plan. In it, the Jews, with a third of the population and ownership of only 6 percent of the land, were to occupy more than half the territory, including the fertile coastal strip, parts of the Galilee, and all of the Negev, while the ancient Jewish biblical heartland, the stony hill country, would go to the Arabs.

Bracketing out the palpable injustice of divvying up a country without asking the opinion of those living in it—needless to say, Arabs were not invited to vote on the deal—the plan required so much goodwill and imagination that no one in Palestine, Jew or Arab, believed it could work. The plan called for an "economic union" between the two states, a silly thing to expect in a country that, since 1936, had had no common economy, where economic and communal separation was an overwhelming fact of life, and where each side used economic weapons whenever it could to bring maximum harm to the other.

The United Nations plan also guaranteed the rights of the Arabs in the Jewish portion. But Arabs would make up half the population (and with a much higher birthrate.) How could a Jewish state possibly exist with this built-in fifth column? Judah Magnes, the American-born president of the Hebrew University, was certain that partition was bound to lead to war. Even if the Jews could "lick the Arabs"—and he had no doubt they could—the irredenta produced by two squabbling mini-states was guaranteed to spark one war after the next.[1]

To make matters worse, at least for the Arabs, the British made it clear that they wouldn't enforce the terms of the UN's partition plan because they knew it wouldn't work.[2] "Arch intriguer in the sordid drama," Father writes of the British decision to wash their hands of the problem, "the guardian who had failed in her duty toward her ward and who, in order to cover up his failure, had condemned her ward to death."

The UN Member States accepted the plan, with Joseph Stalin and Harry S. Truman as its chief backers. For the sake of a clean conscience, the British abstained, even though they were relieved that on May 15, 1948, they would no longer be in the thankless business of controlling two hostile populations.

In Palestine, the Zionist leadership voted to accept the plan, with stiff opposition from Jabotinsky's followers, who considered it a betrayal of the Zionist dream of controlling all of Palestine, including the east bank of the Jordan. Meanwhile Ben-Gurion, while championing the plan in public, privately assured his followers that the real borders of the state would be defined by the army.

It was predictable that Arab leaders in Cairo, Damascus, and Baghdad would reject partition out of hand, and they issued one martial statement after the next vowing an armed response. Many leaders, under pressure from the mufti Haj Amin Husseini, went so far as to declare a war to rid Palestine of the Zionist interlopers. In fact, the "united Arab opposition" was anything but united, with the Syrians and Jordanians making plans to carve out a piece from the Palestinian carcass for themselves. Amir Abdullah, now king of Transjordan, is said to have made a secret deal with Ben-Gurion, hammered out with Golda Meir, to take over the West Bank, making it part of Jordan.

Local Arabs were far more united in their opposition. "Why should we pay for what the Europeans did against the Jews," ran the argument. Father also rejected the plan, though for a different reason. Partition wasn't just about a piece of real estate to be haggled over at the UN; what was at stake was his heritage, stretching back well over a millennium.

Another reason for his opposition was his belief, widespread at the time, that the Zionist leadership had no intention of fully complying with the terms of the partition requiring them to respect the legal rights of Arabs living in the Jewish state. He believed that they were paying lip service to the proposal only because they wanted legal recognition by the world at large of an independent Jewish state. However, they knew that the state as proposed was unviable, and feared more than anything that the Arabs would accept it. So while on the one hand the Zionists backed the plan, on the other they did all they could to whip up Arab opposition to it. "When Arab resistance to the partition plan seemed to be flagging, the Jews stirred it," Father wrote. They did this by using the same instrument that had proved so effective against the British: terror.

Most of the action in my father's memoirs takes place during the interregnum between the UN decision, in December 1947, and the technical end of the British Mandate, the following May. When the UN made its decision, the Jews spent the whole day in jubilation, and local Arab leaders ordered a countrywide three-day protest strike in response. On the first day of the strike Father was sitting at home when his younger brother told him that there was a demonstration on Mamilla Street, a major commercial area where my father had his law practice. The two walked over to the demonstration, and instead of a mass protest saw "fifty odd urchins" standing around with hands in pockets, not knowing what to do. There was no leadership, no organization.

Father went up to his office and watched how an "uninspiring" protest turned into mayhem. It started when the "urchins" beat up the only Jew they could find, a journalist for *The Palestine Post*. The demonstrators next sacked the commercial center. They "indiscriminately looted Arab and Jewish premises alike," carting off from shops and buildings whatever they could carry, everything from the shops' inventory to their doors, window frames, and toilets. "Nothing was spared." They used TNT to blast open locked shops, and by the time they had finished, the commercial center had been reduced to "dust, noise and chaos."

The British police, for twenty years enforcers of law and order, looked on with their hands in their pockets. It was now a battle between Arabs and Jews, with the British as unwilling umpires. Beyond defending themselves when attacked, "they cleared the ring and composed themselves to watch the fun."

While the Arabs were so disorganized that they couldn't even stop street rabble from looting Arab shops, the Jews had a well-oiled quasi-governmental apparatus. The Hebrew University president Judah Magnes was right about the Zionists "licking" the Arabs. It was never a fair fight, nor could it have been. The Jews had created a highly organized community with an admirably disciplined leadership, who knew what they wanted and set out systematically to achieve it. They had statelike institutions, such as a Hebrew educational system, including a university on Mount Scopus in Jerusalem. They had their own bus service, health system, and, more pertinent to the first Arab-Jewish War, a crack underground army.

In his memoirs, Father surveyed the respective strategic and military forces of that time. His fellow Arabs went into the fray with a great store of illusions and misplaced pride. "The Palestinians . . . had no shadow government ready to take over, no leader, no weapons, no armed forces." There were hundreds of villages and cities to defend, and nearly no one to do so. Even more fatally, they had no clear understanding of what the fighting was all about. In the earlier rebellions against the Turks, territory was never the bone of contention. The Turks didn't take over a village in order to drive out its people and replace them with settlers. With the Zionists, the struggle was for every inch of soil.

The only forces that could have put up a fight were the British-trained and -equipped Arab Legion, and the Arab Liberation Army. At the head of the Arab Legion was John Bagot Glubb, known by the Arabs as Glubb Pasha, an eccentric Englishman who spoke fluent Bedouin Arabic. Glubb was a military expert who knew that without British troops in the way, the Jews would easily overrun the whole of Palestine.[3] But the orders he got from London forbade him from crossing into Palestine until May 15, and even then he could do so only to occupy those parts included in the Arab section of the partition plan.

Until May 15, the only force in a position to put up any resistance to the Jews was the Arab Liberation Army, comprising 2,800 mostly Syrian and Iraqi volunteers. Poor leadership, however, doomed it to be disastrously ineffective.

Arab leaders in Cairo, Damascus, and Baghdad, assuming that the Jews would be pushovers, were already arguing over who would take the credit for their glorious triumph. They passed over local Palestinian leaders, most notably the grand mufti's cousin Abdel Kader el-Husseini, and handed joint command of the army to the Syrian Fawzi al-Kawekji and the Iraqi general Ismail Safwat.

Both were "phenomenal failures," Father comments. "Kawekji and Safwat never even set foot in the country which they were charged to rescue throughout the period of operations. Often it was even difficult to locate them . . . Delegations from the National Committees of the various Palestine Arab areas used to make a tour of all the capitals of the

Arab States seeking them. They would go to Damascus, only to be told that the Pasha Generals had left for Cairo, and so on, in an interminable circle."

A friend of Father's from Haifa knew the city would fall if it didn't get help from the Arab Liberation Army. He and some of his colleagues succeeded, after many attempts, in tracking down General Safwat in Damascus. The friend pleaded to the general for troops and weapons. "The great man listened to all this with the tolerant patience of a trained brain specialist watching the curious antics of a mental case gone past the tertiary degree of decomposition, and when it was all over, he, the specialist behaved in rather an extraordinary manner.

"'Hello,' he said, picking up his telephone and addressing the mouthpiece. 'Hello, is this the Skoda Arms factory? Would you be so kind as to send me the following weapons of the best and latest variety.' He followed with an impressive list. Replacing the receiver the General turned around to his audience and blurted: 'You want guns? Right.' Clawing the air with his right hand he placed imaginary guns at the feet of the importunate delegate."

When the local Palestinians warned the general that their towns could fall if they didn't get the support of the Arab Liberation Army, the general said there was no need for alarm. "Let Jaffa fall," he told my father's friend. "Let Haifa fall," he added, warming up to his theme. "Let Acre fall, let Safad fall, let Jerusalem fall, let Nazareth fall, these towns are of no strategic importance whatever, and we can always take them back."

The Jewish leadership, by contrast, knew precisely what they wanted. They had a plan, and the discipline necessary to carry it out. Counted together, the various military groups such as the Haganah and Irgun had thirty thousand well-trained men working together in coordinated attacks. Theirs was a Spartan army, steeled by the horrors of Europe. It was also far better equipped than the local Arabs, as it had access to large numbers of weapons that had been smuggled into the country from Europe or stolen from the British during the war. Small factories were making armored cars, mortars, and bombs.

As for their plan, it was offensive rather than defensive. The idea was to expand their borders and thin out the Arab population by taking the battle far beyond the UN-sanctioned partition borders. They set out to grab as much territory as a fait accompli before the Transjordanian army arrived on May 15.

In the months leading up to the end of the Mandate, while the British were still technically in control of the country, the same story repeated itself throughout Palestine. Just as Glubb Pasha had predicted, in villages and cities, organized groups under either the Haganah or the various underground Zionist organizations, attacked poorly defended Arab areas. A large number of Arab towns and cities designated by the UN plan as part of the Arab state fell under Jewish control. Jaffa, Haifa, and other Arab towns and villages "were sacked and ravaged." By May 15, hundreds of thousands of Arab refugees clogged the roads heading east away from the coast. My father's memoirs tell a grim story of an entire people fleeing out of fear.

There was a lot of expulsion at gunpoint, though just as many Arabs left their homes willingly, as people often do to escape a battle or a natural disaster, assuming that they would return the moment calm again prevailed. This was another case of people not knowing what they were up against. Ben-Gurion had come to the conclusion that expulsion was both necessary and, under the cover of war, possible. Rational political and military planners, not hate-filled thugs, ordered these expulsions. Their primary aim was to make their state demographically viable.

This tragedy was something Father experienced firsthand. One day a peasant farmer came to his office. He was from a small village in the south, near the Jewish town of Rechovot. His modest house had been blown up, and his village lands had been taken by Jewish forces. His only son had been killed, and he himself had been shot in the leg and was in danger of losing the limb.

Father didn't recount this man's adventures with the detachment of a historian, but rather with the flare and skill of a tragedian. "Jaffa is the home of 200,000 Arabs," he writes about their expulsion by Israeli forces. "And its loss means the dispersion of these people. The loss of Acre, Nazareth, Safad, Ramle, Lydda, and all the other towns and villages of Palestine mean more than red dots on the map. They mean the warm hearths and proud homes of an old established community. The hearths have turned to ashes and homes ground to dust and the life that once throbbed within them throbs no more."

The partition plan designated Jerusalem to be an international area outside both the Arab and Jewish states. The British had divided the city into security zones before May 15, and their policy was to keep the warring tribes confined in their respective districts.

Like the rest of the country, the cosmopolitan city rapidly descended into civil war. Father's is a nightmarish account of normal life disintegrating into madness and chaos as professors, doctors, and shopkeepers on both sides manned checkpoints and traded fire with people who under different circumstances would have been houseguests, not targets. The moorings of civilization were uprooted, and military logic governed the thinking of two otherwise peace-loving peoples.

In my father's story, the battle for Jerusalem began with a bombing at Damascus Gate, a fifteen-minute walk from his home. A few days after the UN vote at the end of 1947, three members of the Jewish underground dressed as Arabs drove in a taxi to Damascus Gate in Jerusalem and deposited what seemed like two tar barrels among the market stalls. Just as they were driving off, my father's brother Hassan was heading out of the Old City. Approaching Damascus Gate, Hassan heard a faint, dull thud, like a badly backfiring car. Within minutes he saw a torn human limb, bloody and shapeless, stuck to the wall of the Old City. Suleiman the Magnificent's thick walls prevented the bomb from injuring people inside the gate, to my uncle's good fortune. Those outside, however, were defenseless against the shrapnel of the homemade bomb.

A few days later Uncle Hassan came under direct attack. He had inherited Al-Kasr, the massive old stone fortress just outside the Old

City walls, which belonged to our family. He had recently renovated it—indoor plumbing, hot and cold running water, a heating system, the works—to fit the modern tastes of his new bride. One night, Father heard a loud explosion. He got dressed and rushed downstairs to see what had happened. His cousin arrived within minutes and said to him cryptically, "Long life to you." It was an ominous remark.

"Who's dead?" my father asked.

"No one, but they blew up your brother's castle."

"And my brother?"

"Thank God, he's safe. He's with his wife's people in the Old City." Alive thanks only to a Jewish neighbor who warned him of the attack, Uncle Hassan didn't end up blasted to smithereens like his castle. The next morning the Jewish underground, as echoed in *The Palestine Post*, justified the attack as a necessary operation to eradicate "snipers' nests."

Shortly after this, Father prudently decided to send his wife and children to Lebanon for safety. He rented them a beautiful villa in the Lebanese hills.

In the months leading up to May 1948, Jews and Arabs traded attacks and counterattacks. One day, what looked to be an armored police car drove down Jaffa Road, turned around the traffic island, and parked outside some stores. It aroused nobody's suspicions because the area, a busy trading center for Arabs, was often patrolled by police cars for security reasons. A few moments later the car drove off again. Before anybody realized what was happening, a huge explosion was heard. The militants in the vehicle opened up with automatic fire on both sides of the road and sped back in the direction of the Jewish quarter of Rechavia. More than two dozen people died in the attack.

Father also describes the constant sniping coming from the roof of a synagogue in the Jewish quarter of the Old City. The snipers targeted Muslim worshippers at the Al-Aqsa mosque and the Dome of the Rock.

Arab counterattacks were no less bloody. There were bomb attacks on the building housing *The Palestine Post*. At one point three trucks loaded with dynamite, escorted by what appeared to be an armored police car, stopped on Ben Yehuda Street and exploded.

Through all this, my father divided his time between defending nationalists condemned to the gallows by the British and defending the Old City against the siege. In the spring of 1948, wave after wave of attacks chipped away at the granite blocks of Herod's Gate. The din of exploding bombs was too much for many of the middle class, who left the city until things calmed down.

My father and a group of other leaders were concerned that if they didn't put up an effective defense, the Old City would be lost. The time had come to take things into their own hands and form a defense committee. Father named it the "Herod's Gate Committee." "There were about thirty of us, each with a family and home to think about, and all rather scared."

Father's manuscript mentions some members of leading Arab families who participated—the Husseinis, El Khalidis, Darwishs, and Dajanis. But most of the defenders had neither social status nor education. It was the chauffeur and not the pasha in the backseat. In my father's words, they were "heroic, stupid, or just plain commonplace" men fighting with antiquated weapons.

The Herod's Gate Committee made its first move when it decided it needed to compete with the Haganah, which was smuggling in prodigious amounts of weaponry from Eastern Europe. They needed guns. And to get them Father and his friends did what normal people often do when they need public funds: they held a public raffle of old clothes from their closets. The two hundred people who showed up for the raffle gave enough donations to purchase a total of one rifle and a few rounds of ammunition. "When compared with dizzy figures which the Jews were said to be collecting from New York alone," my father writes, "our modest effort seemed puny and pathetic, guaranteed to discourage the most optimistic."

Their first meeting was held near Herod's Gate, but a few hand grenades tossed over the wall convinced them to move to the home of

Sherif Sbouh, a retired inspector of education whom my father considered the most outstanding character on the Herod's Gate Committee.

Originally from Nablus, Sbouh spoke in the thick dialect of his native town, and was almost entirely self-taught. By dint of hard work he had pulled himself up from humble village origins, all the way to the top of the educational ministry. Father's manuscript describes him as "a slight figure of five feet six inches, balancing himself elastically on two bow legs, like a cowboy in town clothes, his eyes blinking myopically from under steel-rimmed spectacles, a broad and determined grin on his withered face, waving his lean, eloquent hands to give point to his momentous decision."

His main job was to mind the account books. "He was usually poring over some neatly written figures with a Waterman black fountain pen poised in one hand and a string of maroon-colored beads in the other. We would discuss the latest news and our campaign for the evening, then sally forth to inspect the various posts and collect money from the residents for our meager treasury."

The fact that a retired inspector of schools with a constant head cold and a knack for numbers should be the Herod's Gate Committee's most important man says something about the group. Its members laid no bombs, planned no attacks. Their group was defensive in nature, and their chief preoccupation was scraping together weaponry.

This was my father's job. In one account he went home for lunch one day to find the mulberry tree near the front door of his house overloaded with an odd assortment of pistols, bandoliers, and rifles. They had been dispatched by the Arab Higher Committee in Cairo.

> The Arab Higher Committee . . . bought whatever arms they could find, whenever and wherever they could find them. The Western Desert was said to be littered with the arms that had been left behind by the various armies in the ebb and flow of battles. It was necessary only to collect the weapons . . . We had the English, German, Italian, French and Canadian varieties of weapon and a few others whose identity was difficult to establish.

Exposure in the Western Desert had made most of the guns useless. None had spare parts, and even the weapons that functioned lacked sufficient ammunition. To get the weapons operational, the committee turned to Raouf Darwish, whom Father immortalizes in his memoirs as the "nearest living approach to Falstaff I know . . . Built on rather a generous scale, red of face and witty of tongue, I have known him to put a quarter-full bottle of bad whiskey to his mouth and, for a bet, only remove it when he had drunk the last drop."

Darwish was the Herod's Gate Committee's night supply officer. He cleaned the sand-jammed guns and, "like a hawk in an oriental bazaar," sorted through an assortment of finger-shaped cartridges, handing out the appropriate type and caliber to waiting guards.

The climax of my father's story occurred six weeks before the end of the British Mandate. The situation in the city was growing more and more desperate. "Jerusalem, during those last tense days of the Mandate, was like a worn-out water hose, repaired in one place, only to burst in two more. Day and night the patching continued, with everyone taking part." To save the Old City from capture, Father met frequently with Abdel Kader el-Husseini to discuss the security situation.

My father had known Abdel Kader since both were children in Jerusalem. And in fact, on my father's mother's side the two were related, due to unfortunate circumstances. (Several generations earlier, two Nusseibehs, both tax collectors, were on their way from Jaffa to Jerusalem with a small force of gendarmes. At one point, near the village of Abu Ghosh, a band of Husseinis appeared and murdered them in cold blood. Afterward, the Husseini family made peace with my family by giving the sister of the then mufti in marriage to the surviving brother of the two victims.)

Back to 1948—Abdel Kader el-Husseini had quit his senior government post and taken to the hills to oppose the British policy of partition. His headquarters was at the village of Birzeit, north of Ramallah. Because the British had put a price on his head, he came to Jerusalem only on very rare occasions and under conditions of the strictest secrecy.

Abdel Kader, my father, and the other committee members decided that to save the city, Abdel Kader's forces would have to win back al-Castal, an old Crusader fort that the Jews had captured in a surprise attack. Al-Castal's position, on top of a high hill, gave it immense strategic importance. It was there that most Jewish Tel Aviv–Jerusalem convoys supplying West Jerusalem had come to grief under Arab attack.

Abdel Kader, accompanied by my father, headed immediately to Damascus to try to persuade Ismail Safwat, the commander of the Arab Liberation Army, to provide some support. At one point, Safwat turned to them and said, in what my father describes as a deliberately insulting tone, "I hear, Abdel Kader, that the Jews have occupied al-Castal. Do you want to go back and recapture it or do you wish me to order the Liberation Army to do this for you?"

Abdel Kader rejoined that it would be impossible to recapture the fort using the antiquated assortment of Italian rifles his men were fighting with.

"I am afraid we cannot spare you an army," Safwat announced imperiously while sipping tea.

"I'll recover al-Castal then," rejoined Abdel Kader, "but frankly I think that you have no wish to save Palestine"—at which point he and my father left the room. "I have no hope left," Abdel Kader said to Father. "We'll either go and hide ourselves in Iraq or return to die at al-Castal." They headed back to fight.

It was on their way back from Damascus to Jerusalem that Father made a slight detour to look in on Mother in Beirut. This was the last time my mother saw her husband in one piece. They had an amorous reunion, resulting in what would become their fourth child: me. Meantime, Abdel Kader continued on to al-Castal.

The following day, Father arrived home and headed directly to the makeshift offices of the Herod's Gate Committee. There he learned that the fighting in al-Castal had begun, and that Abdel Kader was leading the attack. Father decided to visit the scene of the decisive battle. In his typical fashion, he left only after finishing up some office work.

It wasn't until after lunchtime that he and his younger brother Ahmad set off from Jerusalem by car. Before long, a sniper forced them to abandon their vehicle and continue on foot. It wasn't until dusk that they arrived at a hilltop not far from the battle site.

From there they watched the Arab attack: "The people in our sector started going forward, warily keeping to the edge. Bullets whizzed all around . . . One fighter," my father writes, "jumped forward very much in the manner of a grasshopper. Throwing all discretion to the wind, he hopped along kneeling down every now and then to point his rifle and fire at his objective."

On the third day of the battle, Father was there to experience the victory: Abdel Kader and his band of fighters had put Safwat to shame by recapturing the strategic mountaintop. As the first sign that the supposed victory was the harbinger of catastrophe, however, Father learned that Ein Kerem, another village on the outskirts of Jerusalem, had come under attack, and many villagers were wounded and without medical help.

Father immediately decided to return to Jerusalem via Ein Kerem. His brother Ahmad, a medical doctor, said he could help. They both decided to stay the night at a Franciscan monastery in Ein Kerem. As Ahmad tended to the wounded, Father went around the village to take stock of what the residents needed. At a local café he was surprised to meet up with a group of Arab irregulars whom he had earlier seen at al-Castal. From them he heard the devastating news: Abdel Kader had been shot dead.

While he was still reeling from the shock of his friend's death, even more disturbing news began to arrive. Another village, Dir Yassin, was now under attack. Father immediately returned to Herod's Gate Committee headquarters for an assessment of the worsening situation. The battle for Jerusalem had taken a sharp turn for the worse.

That day, after the Arabs retook al-Castal, Jewish fighters decided to do something to maintain their morale. In collaboration with the Haganah, 132 Stern Gang and Irgun soldiers, led, respectively, by the future Israeli prime ministers Yitzhak Shamir and Menachem Begin, launched an assault on the village, butchering more than 250 villagers.

That night, Father collapsed from exhaustion in his office. Events were rushing along at increasing speed—the futile meeting in Damascus, the attack on Ein Kerem, the death of Abdel Kader, and now the blood-bath at Dir Yassin—leaving him despondent.

The Herod's Gate Committee's troubles rapidly multiplied. With the massacre at Dir Yassin, people in neighboring villages began a panicked flight from their homes, crowding into the Arab-controlled parts of Jerusalem and occupying convents, churches, mosques, and empty fields. The Jewish forces were throwing fresh consignments of matériel and trained soldiers into the battle. The Jerusalem neighborhood of Katamon fell, and all its residents were expelled.

On one occasion my father escaped from a courthouse in a spotted peasant headdress just before the Stern Gang blew up the building. He also narrowly avoided being kidnapped.

At this point the Arab defenders of the Old City numbered three hundred trained and armed volunteers, many from the British Mandate police corps. But as May 15 approached, attacks grew fiercer and the situation more desperate. Father knew that once the British Mandate formally ended, the committee would be facing twelve thousand well-trained Jewish soldiers hammering away at the city's gates. Unless he managed to get the help of the Arab Legion in Amman, the city would fall. King Abdullah was their last hope.

Father traveled across the Jordan River to meet the king. First he visited Glubb Pasha, who made it quite clear that if the Arab Legion ever entered the country, it would do so as a British unit, in order to support British policy.

From that meeting, Father continued on to the palace, where he kissed His Majesty's ruby ring and told him that Jerusalem was anxiously awaiting the Arab Legion. "It had once been sacked in the Crusades," he explained, "and judging by Dir Yassin, there was no reason to anticipate better treatment at the hands of the Jews once they succeeded in storming their way in." Father pleaded with the king to allow the army of the Arab Legion to defend the area allotted to the Arab state. "If this isn't done, the Jews will occupy all Palestine in a few hours, regardless of the UN boundaries." His Majesty assured him that he would never allow the Holy City to be sacked by a new set of Crusaders.

On May 13, Father bought some ammunition and inspected some new Soviet-made weapons for sale on the black market. The next day, Abdullah ordered his troops to Jericho in preparation for the march up to Jerusalem.

On May 15, the British Mandate ended, and Russian-born David Ben-Gurion announced that after two thousand years, the "foreign rule" of Palestine was over, once and for all. Jewish forces immediately took over the Arab neighborhoods of Talbieh, the German Colony, and Baqᵃa. There were also attacks at Jaffa Gate, New Gate, and Zion Gate. For four days the ragtag Arab forces held out. Arab radio stations broadcast appeals for help in Jerusalem, but the only volunteers came from a small village near Haifa, arriving in Ramallah eager to "save the Holy Sepulcher and the Mosque of Omar from Zionist desecration," according to one of my father's colleagues, a Christian physician.[4] My father declared to the motley band of volunteers, armed with primitive weapons and lacking all military leadership and training, "we will march with you and we will be in the front line." Four of the five were unarmed; one carried a tommy gun.

With ammunition running dangerously short, Father went to Ramallah to meet with the commander in chief, but he wasn't there. Father and four others then visited the Jewish settlement Nabi-Yacoub, which had been abandoned, its defenders having fled to Hadassah Hospital on Mount Zion. Local Arabs were ransacking the place, carting off everything they could.

It was in the car on his way back to Jerusalem that he was shot in the thigh. The bullet came from the Mount Scopus Police Camp and hit the main artery of the leg above the knee. He was rushed to the Nablus Government Hospital, but with the loss of blood, gangrene set in. Without any anesthetic, doctors amputated his leg, abruptly cutting off his pursuit of tennis, his favorite sport.

Chapter Five

The Pepper Tree

I CAN PICTURE MY FATHER with his typewriter set on his bandaged stump, looking for the causes of a disaster that had led to what he described as the "dislodgement and dispossession of nearly a million Palestinian Arabs." When I read his poignant description of the refugees created by the war—he called them "unwanted outcasts, wretched people wandering about homeless and jobless, living mainly on the handouts from the West"—I understood the emotional source for his subsequent decades of labor defending their rights.

There was plenty of blame to go around, starting with the Zionists who did the expelling and the Arab leaders (he dubbed them "grinning apes") who didn't lift a finger to stop them. Father also blamed himself for never having taken the trouble to understand his foe.

My fault lay in my overweening conceit and in this I speak of myself as the average man. I underestimated the strength of my enemy and overestimated the strength of my own people . . . I thought too much in terms of the past glories of my people and willfully blinded myself to present shortcomings. My approach to Palestine's problem has been effort-saving and therefore fundamentally dishonest—and again I speak of myself as a type.

But my father's privileged family background, his ancient Arab roots in Jerusalem, along with his self-esteem as a Cambridge man, gave him the inner resources to brush off disaster, spring back, and barrel ahead. He liked to call his attitude "Kismet," which for him wasn't fatalistic submission to the "will of Allah" but an attitude described by one of his collection of favorite English mottoes: "There's no use crying over spilt milk." Kismet gave him the knack of springing back up after a fall, of rolling with the punches, and of maintaining his dignity and self-confidence while others mourned their losses and decried their fate. Father was a master at spinning gold out of dross.

Compared with the hundreds of thousands of stateless refugees living in camps, my immediate family suffered relatively few material losses in the war. Arabs had maintained control of the eastern half of Jerusalem, where most of the family properties were, though Father lost some properties in Israeli-controlled West Jerusalem, as well as land near Lydda, the spot where Ben Gurion International Airport now sits.

What happened to my mother's side of the family was a more typical refugee story. By 1948 the family was already impoverished, having lost its holdings to the British. After my father was shot, my pregnant mother left my older siblings with relatives and went to the hospital in Nablus to look after my father. She then returned to Ramle to take care of her widowed mother.

In June, the Israeli army showed up. Yitzhak Rabin, at the time a commander of the Haganah, recalled with perfect frankness in his memoirs the events that led to the expulsion. Once his forces had established control over the area, he asked Ben-Gurion what was to be done with the population. Having concluded a decade earlier that expulsion was a necessity, Ben-Gurion waved his hand in a gesture as if to say, "Drive them out!" Expulsion was a popular move among Zionist politicians.

Chaim Weizmann, hitherto a man who had vowed a thousand times to re-spect Arab rights, now, giddy with joy, called the mass exit of the Arabs from the coastal plains a "miraculous simplification of Israel's task."[1]

Some of the dispossessed Arabs were given transport in trucks or buses. Most, like my family, had to travel on foot back across the demar-cation lines and into Jordanian-controlled East Jerusalem and the West Bank. My mother, grandmother, and the rest of the family left behind centuries of memories. They feared they would never again see my grandfather's grave, in the tomb of the Sufi master.

The blisteringly hot summer sun took its toll, and many people died along the way. My family managed to survive the foot journey east. Mother made her way to join my older siblings, Munira, Saedah, and Zaki, now in Damascus. At first my grandmother joined her, then eventually moved to Cairo with her children. Ironically, Cairo was where her dead hus-band had been exiled, and now she began her life as a refugee there. The one thing she didn't dare do was head back to Ramle. Israeli shoot-to-kill orders prevented people—the Israelis called them "infiltrators"—from returning to their ancestral lands.

After his recovery in a Beirut hospital, Father returned to the divided land, where he was asked to join a new Palestinian "government," to be established in Gaza under the leadership of the grand mufti. Soon after its establishment, this "government" moved to Cairo, as did my father. In a pathetic sop to Palestinian national sentiment, the League of Arab States, formed in 1945, offered this "government" a few shabby offices with broken furniture in its own headquarters. This was where Father spent the following two miserable years, almost penniless and increas-ingly annoyed at the fictitious Palestinian "government" he was a part of, and at the mendacious Arab leaders who had set it up. With little else to do in his empty office, he composed his memoirs.

But he refused to be defeated by circumstances. (He loved the hoary English motto to "pull yourself up by your bootstraps," which he often inserted seamlessly into long monologues in Arabic.) Many years later he recounted to me a story that for more than half a century had remained untold. With Israel now firmly established, the Palestinian "government" languishing ineffectively in Cairo, and concern growing over the remaining Palestinian territories now under Jordanian control, the earlier ideological rejection of the UN partition plan started to seem rather misguided, to put it mildly. There had always been those among the Palestinian elite who believed that the partition plan should have been accepted, but the grand mufti, the towering figure in the leadership, had always been against it. Mother tells me that her own father, though a member of the leadership at the time, had been in favor of partition.

From the vantage point of his Cairo office, where the prospects for the future looked bleak, Father concluded that the time was ripe to raise the issue of partition again with the mufti. For the mufti, the alternative was to allow his rival, King Hussein of Transjordan, to absorb the West Bank and Jerusalem into his kingdom. True to character, Father phoned the mufti and persuaded him to send him to London as a secret envoy, with a written statement signed by the mufti declaring his acceptance of the plan.

Carrying this top-secret document in his pocket, Father flew to London. It was a highly sensitive mission fraught with potential dangers, for the slightest indiscretion could totally unhinge the plan—and could cost him more of his remaining limbs. He had promised the mufti that he would initiate contact with officials from the British government only if there was utmost secrecy.

Upon his arrival in London, the "cat," to use another of Father's English idioms, was "out of the bag." A newspaper report hinted at a furtive Arab rapprochement with Israel. Father felt personally threatened by the report, and with the specter of vitriolic Arab attacks against him should his mission be discovered, he headed back to Cairo with the document still in his pocket. Father came to think that Israel had leaked the story, as the freshly created Jewish state was in no rush to return to the borders prescribed by the United Nations in exchange for peace with the defeated Arab side. The secret deal they had made with King Hussein had given them far more.

"What happened to the statement?" I asked Father when he recounted the story shortly before he died. "Do you still have it with you?"

Gazing into the distance, Father smiled. "As soon as I returned, the mufti immediately demanded it back, and as soon as I handed it over, he tore it to shreds."

Back in Cairo, Father was finally convinced that the All-Palestine Government was a sham product of internecine Arab squabbles. In fact, the pseudogovernment was an attempt at undermining King Abdullah, the only Arab leader who had benefited from the war.

The secret agreements the king had made with Ben-Gurion had secured him a sizable piece of new territory. Ben-Gurion proved a reliable partner by preventing a number of young Israeli generals from having their way and conquering the West Bank, which they could easily have done. Abdullah and his British-trained Bedouin army controlled the West Bank and Jerusalem. The fortified No Man's Land running through the middle of Jerusalem was, for Abdullah, a source of comfort. With a strong and reliable Israeli state at his back, he could more easily incorporate his war booty into his desert kingdom, and at the same time fend off the poisonous darts coming at him from his Arab brethren. Now owning both banks of the Jordan, Abdullah changed the name of his kingdom from Transjordan to Jordan.

Meanwhile, my pregnant mother was in a cramped apartment in Damascus with her three children, her mother, and all her siblings. As fate would have it, I came into the world during a record cold snap, when Damascus was covered with a thick blanket of snow. It seems that I didn't stop crying from the moment I was born. I still didn't have a name, but jokesters in the family found a provisional solution. The Russian scenery outside, combined with the fact that *Crime and Punishment*, *The Idiot*, and *Notes from the Underground* were being passed from one family member to the next, inspired the family to give me the temporary name of "Dostoevsky." And so it was: for a few precious days, until word got to my father, I was named after the darkly metaphysical Russian novelist.

The wire from Cairo eventually arrived. *"Mabrouk"* [Congratulations], began the telegram, "on the birth of Sari." Father chose the name both for its linguistic association with Mohammed's Night Journey and because it had been the name of the dead son of Khalil al-Sakakini, the a celebrated literary figure and teacher at the now-defunct Arab College. I would like to believe that al-Sakakini's poem on the individual's rebellion was on Father's mind when he came up with my name.

Father soon decided to put an end to the Cairo charade. Weighing the options of working for a powerless government in exile and living as an ordinary citizen back home in Jerusalem, he opted for the latter. He was hardly alone in his disgust at Arab politics. Young Egyptian army officers led by Gamal Abdul-Nasser, incensed at the Egyptian king Farouk's apparent apathy for the Arab cause, were already cooking up a plot to overthrow the monarchy. In Palestinian circles, young activists and students inspired by the young Yasir Arafat were also planning to get rid of the mufti and the old regime of notables.

By the time my parents returned to Jordanian-controlled Jerusalem in 1951, it no longer was made up of the rich fabric of a cosmopolitan British-governed city. Gone were the English and Arab aristocrats, the free-wheeling parvenus, middle-class tradesmen, and the demimonde catering to soldiers; gone were the bohemians, servants, and British clerks; gone too were the rich blend of cultures—the bishops, Muslim clerics, and black-bearded rabbis crowding the same streets.

What was left was a tired provincial city with barbed wire snaking through its center, and much of its political life drained off to the desert capital of Amman.

Without the British court system providing a semblance of good legal practice, Father decided to set up his own law offices. He soon found work as a lawyer for the United Nations Relief and Works Agency (UNRWA), defending the rights of refugees.

On the political front, Father only had two options: either to accept Jordanian domination, or to leave politics altogether. That year, King

Abdullah organized the "Jericho Conference," in which Palestinian notables and leaders declared their loyalty to the king and their acquiescence to a union between lands straddling the two banks of the Jordan River. Wishing to further solidify his rule over the West Bank, the king approached Father, a bona fide war hero, with an offer he couldn't refuse: he promised to make him minister of defense. Father hadn't attended the Jericho Conference, and he agreed to the king's proposition only because he assumed the union was a transitory measure, pending the restitution of Palestinian rights. Soon after accepting the post, Father was elected as Jerusalem representative to the Jordanian parliament. This launched him into a fifteen-year career of frenetic political activity.

This is important to point out because it meant that I barely got to know him as I was growing up. Fitted with a metal leg, he spent his days rushing to meetings in Jerusalem, Ramallah, Amman, or farther afield. The evenings when he was home, he was huddled with his brothers, friends, and colleagues in heated political debate.

Success as a parliamentarian soon led to an offer to lead the kingdom's Baath (or "Renaissance") Party, a pan-Arabist movement created by Christian nationalists in Syria and Iraq. But the Baath Party's mixture of Arab nationalism and socialism, so redolent of European fascism, made Father suspicious, and he demurred. He did something far more ambitious instead: he started the Constitutional Party. His aim was to create a liberal, open system that could help bring the splintered Arab states together, much as Jean Monnet was trying to bring together postwar Europe. (Monnet, a French diplomat from a family of cognac merchants, pushed the idea of European union as a way to prevent future wars.) And for him, the linchpin to Arab unity was the constitutional rule of law.

Father became fully immersed in Jordanian politics. It was he who greeted the young King Hussein in 1954 when the latter returned from the Royal Military Academy Sandhurst. Three years earlier, his grandfather King Abdullah had been assassinated, after Friday prayers on the steps outside the Dome of the Rock. That day the young prince, wearing a medal Abdullah had given him, stood proudly next to his grandfather. The assassin had intended to kill them both; what saved the prince, now king and forty-second direct descendant of the Prophet Mohammed, was the medal pinned to his uniform. Since King Hussein was only fifteen at the time, a regency ran the country until he finished his studies at Sandhurst. (His father had become king but abdicated within a year due to mental illness.) His English teachers there addressed him as "Mr. King Hussein sir."

Even if he disagreed with many of his policies, Father always retained a paternal fondness for the new king, who was twenty years his junior. (King Hussein was born in 1935.) But Father's primary loyalty was neither to the king nor even to himself: it was to his principles, a sure guarantee for a checkered political career.

I was raised in a house on Nablus Road in Jerusalem, not far from where my uncle's "Castle" once stood. The home had an old-world feeling to it, with Persian carpets, gold-embossed academic degrees on the wall, crystal decanters for after-dinner drinks, and dozens of finely buffed tennis trophies. Across the street was the American Colony Hotel, once the home of a Turkish pasha and his three wives. Next to that was a small private cemetery, housing the graves of the Husseini family.

My first memories of my father are of a distant man who would occasionally take my brothers and me up to the Noble Sanctuary for Muslim festivals, or to funerals or other occasions. As a Nusseibeh, he had to practice a tolerant ecumenicalism. He made sure we all fasted during Ramadan, and like clockwork every Friday, he was in the Al-Aqsa mosque for his prayers. On Christian holidays he visited church dignitaries, as they visited us on our holidays. Once a year, members of our extended clan joined the high clergy dressed in robes and carrying golden crosses to circle the Church of the Holy Sepulcher seven times. Of all the religious ceremonies, my brothers and I liked this one the most because the Christian girls were by a long shot the prettiest in town.

Religious ceremonies may have played a prominent role in Father's public life, but in private he always believed that creeds had to serve man, and not the other way around. To quote from his manuscript, "religion, being essentially universal and one, should be made to serve the end of uniting the world rather than separating it."

Mother ran the household and raised the children. (Her fifth and sixth, Hatem and Saker, came along in 1955 and 1961.) She was the perfect complement to a man who hadn't the faintest idea how to relate to children. Holding a child was for my father like carrying a weapon: he preferred leaving it to the professionals. For Mother it came naturally, and the home she created was always so full of love that she diffused sibling rivalries and jealousies before they could arise. She also instilled in us loyalty to our extended families. Each year she sent us to Cairo to spend our school holidays with her exiled family, and when the widowed aunt who had raised my father fell ill, Mother took her into our home, where she stayed until her death. I still can picture this melancholy octogenarian lying on her bed, reciting endlessly with a haunting voice the elegiac poetry of her deceased husband.

I've often suspected that Mother's intuitive grasp of the art of nurturing children might have stemmed from her father's Sufism. Whatever the source, the Islam she inculcated in us was a religion with minimal miracles—Mohammed's nocturnal ride on his magical steed is one of the few I can think of—and a cornucopia of rock-solid humanistic values. For her, Islam taught dignity, honesty, self-worth, simplicity, kindness, and of course love. Endless love. It was also flexible enough to change with the times. With the conclusion of the Ramadan holiday, on the first day of the Eid, she allowed my father and uncles to break out the beer and whiskey. In her Islam, there was also no competition among faiths. My mother, a pious Muslim, had no problem telling us that the Via Dolorosa was the path of Christ's Passion, or celebrating Christmas with a Santa Claus and a brightly ornamented tree.

Some of the sweetest memories of my youth are of cold Ramadan nights when my aunts and great aunts would visit us from Damascus or

Amman or Lebanon. After breaking the fast, we would sit by the fireside, roast chestnuts, and listen in near rapture as our aunts mesmerized us with fables and tales.

Islam was thus no different for Jerusalem families like ours than Catholicism or Anglicanism was for our Christian friends, or as I would later learn Judaism was for Amos Oz a couple of hundred feet away, just beyond No Man's Land. We had our rites and feasts; religion added a bit of spice to life, but it didn't go much beyond that, and certainly never came between us and our education. The only place to meet the sort of wild-eyed fanatics who pose as Islam's spokesmen today would have been in old musty stories of Sheikh Qassam, or in St. George's library collection of Victorian-era horror novels.

One thing I should mention about my mother was her almost religious respect for the wash ladies and drivers and cooks and peddlers who came in and out of our home. Here we were at the top of the pyramid in a class-conscious society, a society in which those with position and power liked to lord it over those with less, and yet I never saw my mother treat a beggar with less regard than someone of her own class, and sometimes with more.

Looking back on my childhood, I can say that Mother's tolerance had only one limit—and yet, as we shall see, even this was provisional. She made no bones about her dislike of the Jews. When Mother spoke about the "Jews," she didn't mean Jews in New York or Argentina, or even the tailors, greengrocers, or managers of the Edison Cinema in West Jerusalem she'd liked so much before 1947. She meant the Zionists who plotted to take over her country, who'd shot her husband's leg off, and whom she held responsible for her father's early death, the uprooting of her ancient roots on the coastal plain, the despoiling of her homeland, and the exile of her mother. Even her dear father's grave was now in inaccessible enemy territory, and, as far as she knew, plowed under by land-hungry kibbutzniks.

I call this provisional dislike because her compassion was able to surmount it. One day my older sister Saedah, thirteen at the time, fell into an uncontrollable fit of tears. She had brought home from school a copy of *The Diary of Anne Frank*. She cried and cried in anguished identification with this Jewish child hidden in an annex, terrified at being found out by the killers of her people. It was a paradoxical identification for the daughter of a mother who had suffered so much at the hands of the Zionists. But without a word, my mother gently wiped Saedah's tears away, and furtively wiped away her own.

My first political recollections are of screams. It was in 1956, and a new war had broken out. It was my first war.

Politics was the real gravitational center of family life. Even after nearly half a century, I recoil with dread when I think back on the interminable discussions between my father and his brothers about King Abdullah, or Ben-Gurion, or President Eisenhower, or the Soviet Politburo, or General Nasser. I was seven when the Sinai War broke out. The living room was filled with dense smoke during long evening debates. I picture a red face, impassioned shouting, and the spittle of indignation flying from the mouth of an uncle who was otherwise the model of soft-spoken civility. My brother Zaki, a precocious ten-year-old, watched the debates with large, round, curious eyes, absorbing every word as if his brain were a complex calculating machine.

When Mother talked politics, she shifted Jekyll-and-Hyde–like from being a paragon of love to an unyielding victim. Her words were about the idyllic innocence of a magical dreamland. She told me about oranges I envisioned as the sweetest on earth growing on a plantation stretching all the way to the gently swelling waves of the Mediterranean, a sea I'd never seen because of No Man's Land but that, like the oranges, I pictured as the noblest on earth. Then came the intrusion by the foreigners, the struggle with the British, the depredations of the Zionists, and the terrorized flight on foot.

I never liked these long-winded political discussions, and when I could, I would retreat back to my room. Perhaps I wasn't mentally astute enough to follow all the arguments and counterarguments, the dialectical loops and turns, the rousing monologues and heated spats. It must have been my own shallowness that caused me to prefer playing soldiers with matchsticks. My brother Zaki, by contrast, couldn't get enough of politics.

It set in early, this feeling of being lost. I can't pin it down to a month or a year. As far as I can tell, I have always been puzzled with the world around me. You'd think that with 1,300 years of history backing me up I would have known who I was. I didn't. From the moment I was cognizant about the world, everything was a riddle, now dark and foreboding, now as luminous as a Sufi song. How could it have been otherwise in a place where the prosaic sights of barbed wire were juxtaposed with the myth-shrouded mount of Solomon, Omar, and Mohammed, or where Christ's Garden Tomb was opposite the main bus station? In some ways, growing up in Jerusalem was like being in a fairy tale invaded by Detroit and modern armies, though its magical quality remained, and the dangers merely added to the mysteries of a city I feel I belong to.

Out of the large window of my bedroom I could see the spires and crosses towering over the Notre Dame Pontifical Institute, just opposite the New Gate. I could also look down on a shoot-to-kill zone that separated the Jews from the Arabs. It was a good perch from which to spy on the other side. From street level it wasn't so easy to peer into enemy territory because the Jordanians had built a high wall to separate the two sides. Cousin Zaki (for some reason my father and uncle both chose the same name for their sons) told me that Israeli snipers used to take random shots at people, seeing them as plastic ducks in a shooting gallery. To disrupt this macabre game, the Jordanians had erected an unsightly concrete barrier.

Our house bordered what UN and security negotiators had inelegantly dubbed No Man's Land, an expanse of wasteland between our section of East Jerusalem and Mea Shearim, a neighborhood inhabited by the religious Haredim (literally "the Awestruck Ones.") Between the back of our garden wall and the State of Israel were: one lonesome, semi-destroyed and bullet riddled cement structure; a UN observation and border-crossing station; and scattered rocks and thistles growing among the odd land mine. There was also a grapevine that had managed to survive all the fighting. In springtime I used to stare for hours at the vine's new leaves, and in the fall I watched the juicy grapes grow big.

The wall at the end of the garden defined for me the beginning of a forbidden territory. For this reason it intrigued me, as did the men with the long wizard's beards whose black coats and dangling curly side locks I could make out from my bedroom window.

Hardly a day would go by when I didn't spy into the streets beyond No Man's Land. Sometimes I saw strange-looking buses and vehicles plying their way along the narrow streets. Sometimes a knot of black-clad men appeared from behind a corner and walked a short distance along a narrow street before disappearing again around another corner. Sometimes the bearded creatures looked back at me. It was almost like being in a dream.

Hearing about all their fiendish acts and then staring over at the other side stirred my imagination. What did I know of the Other Side? People who lived in the city before the war told me about the elegant shops on Jaffa Road, the Gary Cooper Westerns at the Edison Cinema, the villas in the old neighborhoods, and how from the hills to the west you could see the Mediterranean. (Our section of Jerusalem backed up to dust and desert.) What about the people? I concluded that they must be super-evil beings to have given the Arabs such short shrift.

Fed no doubt by the steady stream of adventure books I was filling my head with, I imagined that one of these long-bearded phantoms could actually be inhabiting the trunk of a large pepper tree just outside the front door of our house. Plainly I had to be on guard! Each morning, as I successfully dashed past the tree on my way to school, I felt that I had managed to foil the efforts of a dark claw reaching out from inside the trunk and snatching me into nothingness.

In 1959, my sisters Munira and Saedah were in high school. Both liked to draw and both hobnobbed with the children of diplomats and UN officials. Zaki was already reading and writing like a scholar; he won one academic prize after the next, read avidly, wrote poetry, and was popular with the girls at the Schmidt Girls' College, down the road. I was in grade school at St. George's School. With my siblings occupied with their various pursuits, I began to make forays into the surrounding streets. I was gaining in confidence, for the dreaded villain in the pepper tree had never managed to snag me. The world seemed safe enough for me to venture out and discover a landscape more magical than that of Sinbad the Sailor and beautiful Sheherazade.

There was no television in those years, only some radio signals from the Arab capitals and the Israeli Hebrew stations. But it would never have occurred to us to tune in to the Hebrew stations. The sound of Hebrew was just as much an anathema as the sound of the word "Israel"—we always called it "the Zionist entity" or "enemy." Cousin Zaki, who lived down the street, was one of my playmates. Among his more grisly capers was to hunt birds with slingshots and cook them over burning leaves in his backyard. I preferred a more innocuous pastime, such as playing in the abandoned Jordanian bunkers. Another ritual Cousin Zaki and I shared was to make our way on December 25 over to Mandelbaum Gate, Jerusalem's Checkpoint Charlie. Christmas was the only day of the year the gate was open, to allow pilgrims from the other side to attend services at the Holy Sepulcher. It was dizzying to see a hermetically shut door suddenly open.

It was just as mysterious to come to sudden dead ends. Often alone or with Zaki I walked to the shrapnel-lashed Damascus Gate and into the labyrinth of streets and alleys, and then all the way to Jaffa Gate, which had been sealed shut after the war. Did the gate lead nowhere or everywhere? Maybe both.

Other jaunts took me into the warrens of the Old City, full of smug shopkeepers with their golden pocket watches, old women hawking wares, and sweaty rooms of praying men or, if I was lucky, some whirling dervishes. The cafés resonated with the bubbling sounds of people smoking water pipes. I could spend hours skulking around the graveyards outside the Lion's Gate, or among the sacred sites on the Noble

Sanctuary, and then out again on the other side. There I entered the dense, tangled streets of the Moroccan Quarter, dating back seven hundred years to the age of the Ayyubids and Mamluks. Saladin's son built a mosque there in 1193, and I got a thrill each time I saw it, because this was the spot where the Prophet had tethered his wondrous steed before his ascension.

To walk through the city was to journey through family history. There was the Goldsmith's Souk, a street of shops in ruins since the great earthquake of 1927. One uncle kept his donkeys and a camel there. Then of course there was the Church of the Holy Sepulcher. Amid the cramped domed streets surrounding it on all sides, the church struck me as almost infinitely large, a rococo collection of every architectural fad since the Romans, with each new age having added its own mark. Nothing seems ever to have been taken away, such as the famous wooden ladder outside a second-story window. (Generations ago, it was used to haul food up to Armenian monks locked in the church by the Turks.) The church was like the closet of an eccentric relative that gets more and more cluttered as time goes on, but also more mysterious.

I remember hearing about a spot in the church that is the cosmic center of the world. When the Greeks switched religions eons ago, the center of the world shifted from Delphi to a spot in the middle of the Church of the Holy Sepulcher. A large urn marks the spot. Pious Muslims insist that the center is in Mecca, but as a child, I preferred the local address: a five-minute walk from my house.

Another of my favorite spots was a crack in the Rock of Golgotha that was said to be the passageway for Christ's entry into the underworld after his crucifixion. There, in the flaming fires of Hades, he rescued the righteous souls.

For Father, possessing the key to the Church of the Holy Sepulcher simply was an affirmation of familial pedigree, but for others in the clan, having the key was like operating the front gate to one of the world's great founts of legend and sacredness. It was our job to keep the Church of the Holy Sepulcher from falling into the wrong hands. Weren't the Crusades started because of troubles at the church? Wasn't the Crimean

War ignited by a dispute between the French and Russians over the Church of the Nativity in Bethlehem? Nothing of the sort was going to happen on our watch!

As I've said, because of the erotic indiscretions of my great-great grandfather, the key was in the possession of a distant cousin. Each morning someone from the Joudeh family would show up at my uncle's house shortly before four in the morning and toss a pebble at my cousin's window. My cousin would come down, take the key, then make his way to the church. There he'd slip the foot-long skeleton key into a keyhole in a small door and tug it, and the four-inch oak door would groan and open. A priest on the other side of the door would put his head out the door, greet my cousin, and hand him a ladder. Cousin Nusseibeh would then mount the ladder to reach a second keyhole in a larger door. He'd turn the key and pull hard. "Peace," he'd say to the priest once the door had opened. "Peace," the priest would reply.

In 1963, after various stints as Jordanian defense minister, education minister, vice premier, and minister of development, Father accepted the king's offer to take up the post of governor of the Jerusalem region, which at the time extended all the way down to Jericho. It was the most powerful position in the West Bank.

By this point, Jerusalem had recovered much of the life it had lost in 1948. As it had done time and time again throughout the ages, it had reasserted its role as the world capital of religious pilgrimage. The Jewish half was closed off by a wall. But since nearly all of the ancient sites were located in our half, tourists flooded in. Pope Paul VI's historic visit in 1964 sparked a speculative building boom.

With the Zionist threat gone, centuries-old patterns reasserted themselves, and the old noble families were back on their feet. The Husseinis, Nashashibis, the Islamic scholars, and the Christian bishops now set the tone for the city. If you could ignore No Man's Land and the refugee camps, it was as if nothing had ever happened.

The hautes and petites bourgeoisies and the merchant class were building and buying and talking about a brighter future. Jerusalem was turning into a boomtown, with Saudis spending their oil wealth there during summer vacations. My uncles on my father's side wanted to be in on it, and so for all their talk of tradition, they razed the grandest of my grandfather's villas to make room for a five-star hotel with one hundred rooms. Nearly overnight, the elegance of the Ottoman-era house made way for a prosaic piece of masonry.

My father had a big role in fostering the city's economic and cultural recovery. His administration recalled the best of the British Mandate era: it was corruption-free and stood on the rule of law. Property was safe from undue meddling, pickpockets were rare, and religious fanaticism was unknown. All that was missing were the proud men in arms that any self-respecting capital had. My father did his best to conjure back to life an Arab army in the West Bank by creating a National Guard modeled on the Swiss militia. He also introduced khaki uniforms and military drills in school.

As Father's political power increased (his brother Hazem was the foreign minister and later the ambassador to the UN), so did the frequency of my parents' dinner parties, which inevitably concluded with everyone retiring to the living room to talk politics.

If in the world of religion and myth—the stuff behind the pilgrimages—Jerusalem was front and center, politically it was a peaceful backwater. The convulsions elsewhere in the world only seeped into our world through the newspapers and BBC radio, or, in our case, the nightly family salon. These salons were right out of a Russian novel, where the dinner guests at a prince's distant estate engaged in furious discussions over the fall of the Bastille, completely unaware how this far-off cataclysm, stuff of an evening debate, would eventually bring their own world crashing down.

There was plenty to talk about in the 1960s. One of the most dramatic events close to home was a spat between my father and the archbishop of the Greek Orthodox Church, who presented Father with the

Order of the Holy Sepulcher. Father declined because the award dated the family's custodianship of the key to Saladin, whereas my father was convinced we had had it since Omar the Just.

Then came Khrushchev and Kennedy, the Berlin Wall and the Cuban missile crisis, Lee Harvey Oswald, and the occasional guerrilla who managed to cross over into Israel for an attack. General Nasser's rousing radio addresses always made for good after-dinner talk. Nasser had come to power in a coup against the decrepit Egyptian monarchy, and swept away the old powers with great bravado. Non-Arabs fled the country, and the Russians came in to modernize the army for the coming battle. With his saber unsheathed, the Egyptian liberator promised to restore Arab pride by defeating the Zionist Crusaders.

Mother listened to Nasser's speeches with as much relish as she did her favorite records of Umm Kulthum. Like most refugees, she hoped that the disturbed waters of the river of history, forcefully diverted from their natural course in 1948, would soon begin flowing again in the right direction. It was just a matter of time before justice would have to be done. Hadn't she been stripped of her homeland, her patrimony, her orange groves? Wasn't her father's tomb in a stranger's backyard, uncared for, forgotten, or perhaps even dynamited? Didn't the entire world agree that we had been grievously wronged?

My father was less sure about Nasser. I can recall the pained grimace on his face each time Nasser's name was mentioned, as if he had eaten something disagreeable. He didn't believe in Nasser's Arab socialism, and he had a loathing for his demagoguery. In Father's moral estimation, expelling from Egypt an old and established community such as the Greeks had landed Nasser in the same chauvinistic company as Ben-Gurion.

Age didn't diminish my dislike for these endless nightly political discussions, and I continued to retreat into my imagination. My father got the job as governor of Jerusalem just as I was entering high school at St. George's. During my subsequent high school career, I remained in the thrall and shadow of Father's unflappable self-certainty.

Too old for matchsticks, I moved on to books. There were plenty around the house, starting with Father's library, Mother's collection of modern fiction, my elder sisters' books, and those borrowed from the British library by my brother Zaki, also an insatiable reader. My reading ran the gamut from Arabic to Western classics, though one shouldn't get the impression that my literary habits were those of a precocious future scholar. My favorites were murder stories and mysteries and comic strips featuring such exquisite characters as Donald Duck, Uncle Scrooge, the Belgian Tintin, and, last but not least, the mighty Superman.

Father soon acquired a new hobby that brought us closer. He bought a farm in the Jordan Valley. Our experiences on the farm—we had tomatoes, bananas, and chickens—are among my fondest memories within the family. Thinking back on those days now, I'm certain that the ancient Roman ideal of the gentleman farmer must have inspired my father, because he wore a tweed jacket and a silk scarf each time we made the trip with the new Ford automatic. The car could barely fit through Suleiman the Magnificent's walls, but was ideal for zipping down the old Roman road into the desiccated wadis of the Judean desert. We were usually the only private car on a road we shared with military jeeps or, far more frequently, Bedouin goats and the occasional camel.

Sometimes my family drove and I took my bicycle. I rode down, down, down to the deepest ditch in the world, all the way to the Jordan River, then over the bridge. Along the Dead Sea, I explored Ottoman ruins, monasteries, and desolate canyons. Armed with long ropes and torches, my friends and I would sometimes venture into deep tunnels and caves, imagining we would discover hidden mysteries, such as a new batch of Dead Sea Scrolls buried in the bowels of the earth.

My parents had ecumenical tastes in education. My sisters went to a French school run by nuns, then to the Schmidt Girls' College, run by the Germans. My elder brother, Zaki, and I attended the Anglican St. George's, down the street. The school's proximity forced me to forgo a perk my predecessor had enjoyed: the son of the previous governor had arrived at school in a black Cadillac.

St. George's was for me yet another hint of Paradise. It has the look of any neo-Gothic public building at the height of the Victorian age, which in itself is a testimony to the wonderful eclecticism of Jerusalem at the time. A medieval city, Jerusalem didn't have Gothic buildings because the Crusaders were kicked out before the Gothic age got under way. So to see the Christian Middle Ages in architecture, it was necessary to visit the most modern school in town. St. George's was also surrounded by gardens full of flowering bushes and bougainvillea. In spring the sweet smells of jasmine and honeysuckle wafted through the classrooms.

The school combined a strong emphasis on a set canon with what you could almost call anachronistically a postmodern respect for cultural differences. A Christian institution with a split Christian/Muslim student body and staff, it had no choice but to be tolerant. In all my years in school, I never encountered the slightest whiff of ethnic or religious chauvinism. The school's religion lessons were restricted to a weekly sermon delivered by the English headmaster in the Anglican cathedral, attached to the school. The academic standards were exacting, the teaching staff dedicated, and the expectations high, and we were taught to think of ourselves as the future elite of the country.

To my parents' dismay, however, I showed less academic promise and less commitment to school discipline than my elder brother. I certainly betrayed no signs of special interest in the sciences or arts, and no inclination to go into engineering—a popular career choice at a time when the Aswan Dam was going up.

A favorite pastime was playing hooky to roam through the Old City, whose ancient bustling alleys seemed more enchanting than anything I could glean out of schoolbooks. I also liked soccer and playing with animals, mainly birds. My favorites were pigeons, and at one stage I had as many as two score of them living in our garden, each of whom I could describe in taxonomical detail. The pigeons would often greet me upon my return from school, and perch on my shoulders or head like a scene out of the life of St. Francis—which was only fitting for a boy who also showed no proclivity for martial pursuits. My father may have once been minister of defense, but I wasn't the warrior type. The fact that I assiduously gave the family political salon wide berth also seemed to preclude a career in politics.

Compounding my parents' worries was my sad habit of underperforming on exams, which must have had something to do with my inability to drum up interest in subjects requiring rote learning—physics, chemistry, math, and geography. My imagination needed to be activated, and this happened only in classes taught by teachers with a flare for narrative.

The best teachers in this regard were Arab nationalists, who spiced up history with emotion and imagination. In their hands, even the stories of Jesus and Mary—taught from Muslim sources—included a dash of pan-Arab nationalism. In the classroom, Jesus was a human, though Mary's Immaculate Conception was spiritual, even mystical. It came about through a breath from God's soul. Mary was a good mother who raised her son, a dyed-in-the-wool Palestinian revolutionary, to be a noble prophet of humanity. For their part, the Twelve Disciples were Palestinian-Arab nationalists *avant la lettre*, precursors, as it were, to the Central Committee of the Palestine Revolutionary Council.

The people who taught English literature classes were expatriates, adventurers, or pilgrims who had ended up in Palestine. The way they taught us, straight from their native hearts, implanted in me a love of literature. I was able to visualize Hamlet, existentially lost like me, and the three witches of *Macbeth*. As the son of the governor, I identified with the rowdy and rebellious Prince Hal, more at home in the taverns of London than at his father's court. The far-flung voyages and adventures of Ulysses by Tennyson captured my imagination, as did the metaphor of "drinking life to the lees" by seeking newer and higher worlds. Jane Austen evoked grand expectations of English life, all fated to be utterly dashed later, while Thomas Hardy took my mind to wooded mountains where a scholarly recluse hunched over a candlelit desk writing out lofty esoteric truths with his quill.

At its best, classes in Arabic literature produced similarly evocative images. The instructor, a Christian Arab who later took up a teaching post at McGill University, started us off on a rigorous regime of grammar and poetry, largely drawn from the Koran, a book that, like his fellow Christian and literary luminary Khalil al-Sakakini, he considered the source of his own language and culture. In his class I learned to see Omar the Just as a hulking but humble giant of a man who, with vast empires at his feet, slept unattended in the wilderness under a tree. And the burning love between black Qays and the aristocratic Laila, a tale reminiscent of Othello and Desdemona that had inspired tribal wars and epic poetry of Homeric magnitude, continued to play in my mind long after classes were done. I allowed myself to enter their world, and eventually to become lost in it.

Eventually this teacher supplemented traditional Arabic tales and poetry with the free verse of, say, Adonis. In him we were exposed to a magic carpet of words, wonderful sounds that seemed to dance on the tongue. A Syrian Shiite who fled to Beirut because of his political views, he changed his name from Ali Ahmad Said Asbar to Adonis, in honor of the Greek god of desire. To this day I can still hear our teacher recite "The Language of Sin":

> *I burn my inheritance, I say:*
> *"My land is virgin, and no graves in my youth."*
> *I transcend both God and Satan*
> *(my path goes beyond the paths of God and Satan).*
> *I go across in my book,*
> *in the procession of the luminous thunderbolt,*
> *the procession of the green thunderbolt,*
> *shouting:*
> *"After me there's no Paradise, no Fall,"*
> *and abolishing the language of sin.*[2]

Like every other big event at the time, the sixties rebellion made it to our section of Jerusalem by way of several detours, and by the time it arrived there was little of it left. There were no Arab hippies, no drugs, and the ethos of respecting your elders was as strong as ever. Of course, there were no antiwar protests; quite the contrary. If there was any stir of dissent, it was over the king's passivity toward the "Zionist enemy." But this, too, was largely derivative, aping the Pan-Arabism of Beirut. There, at least, Arab students were shaking off the dust and cobwebs of the past, liberating themselves equally from theocratic shackles and colonial oppression. In Beirut, a new nation was breaking out, and by marching boldly into the future, its avant-garde was recovering the powers of the past: such, at least, was the vision.

The Sturm und Drang of the age reinforced my ambivalent relationship with politics. On the one hand, my earlier ritual of staring out my bedroom window at the ultraorthodox gave way to a new hobby: that of beginning to pick up my elder siblings' taste for foreign music—Edith Piaf and Enrico Macias were my sister's favorites, but I soon picked up my brother's taste for Elvis.

Being the son of the governor, however, I couldn't ignore politics completely. Yet I was still in such dazed confusion that as a passive bystander, I followed from a safe distance as my schoolmates lined up behind the political program of Arab nationalism coming from the coffeehouses of Beirut, or from Nasser's oracular radio addresses. That the Beirut anarchists' visions and Nasser's Arab socialism were diametrically opposed ideologies didn't seem to bother anyone. Students wanted renewal, even at the cost of logic.

The West Bank and our section of Jerusalem were part of Jordan, and King Hussein made it clear he would brook no rebellious talk, which only increased the prestige of the students in their clandestine groups whispering slogans in an atmosphere of playful subversion. There were even a couple of demonstrations. I tagged along once or twice, then prudently stopped, after one of my cousins got grazed in the leg by a rubber bullet.

As occurs in many authoritarian societies badly in need of reform, the regime permitted an outlet for dissent. In our case, it was the evil Zionists just beyond No Man's Land. King Hussein had a live-and-let-live relationship with his former Israeli partners; he even preferred them to many of his other neighbors, whom he constantly suspected of expansionist designs. He certainly trusted Moshe Dayan more than Yasir Arafat, whose plans posed a direct threat to the Hashemite kingdom.

But a new campaign against Israel was popular on the street, and the king couldn't afford to suppress it. The first Palestine National Congress met in Jerusalem in 1964, laying down the structure of the Palestine Arab Liberation Army and drafting the Palestinian National Covenant, which among other things called Zionism "a colonialist movement in its inception, aggressive and expansionist in its goals, racist and segregationist in its configurations, and fascist in its means and aims." The only solution was the total liberation of Palestine through armed revolution.

Father was cynical about this new concoction of Palestinian leadership. He had experienced enough in 1947 and 1948, and he had had his fill while serving in Cairo in the Palestinian government. He sincerely believed that such bravado only guaranteed fresh calamities.

Father similarly shied away from the vulgar bombast of the Arab "revolutionaries" and their loose talk of "racism" and "fascism," which only served to intoxicate Arab thinking (an inebriation that allowed the Arabs to forget how weak their institutions were). To be sure, Father didn't mince words when it came to the Zionists. In his manuscript, he writes about their "will-to-power," which he linked up to the revolutionary spirit of France and Communist Russia. "When I see earnest, bespectacled young men patting each other on the back and talking of the utter stupidity, doleful incompetence, and shocking ignorance of the so-called older generation, I feel uncomfortable." Judaism was not at fault here, but rather a cadre of revolutionaries willing to wipe the slate clean in order to materialize their dreams.

I was fifteen when the Congress was convened, but so lost was I in the alleys of the Old City and the stories of the mind that I ignored the entire affair as just another gathering of blustering nobles in a hotel lobby up the road, much as they had been congregating in the family living room for as long as I could remember.

• • •

At the age of sixteen I was slowly, dimly, becoming aware of myself.

One particularly poignant recollection of my school days is walking in the evening with a school friend named Bashir. The two of us liked to march the two hundred feet between my house and his over and over until one of us got tired, or it became too late. Bashir was a Christian, and I a Muslim, but this difference never occurred to us, because it never seemed important to discuss our respective faiths. We had bigger fish to fry: existence. What was the universe made of? Where did it start or end? What role did we have in it? Could we choose our actions? Could we choose who we were? What was I doing here? Who was I really? And what if there was no God after all? We shuddered asking this last question.

One day we decided to take our questions to the British Council library. Scouring the shelves, we came across a volume by Bertrand Russell. The only dealing I'd had with philosophy up to that point was with the ideas Lewis Carroll buried in *Alice's Adventures in Wonderland*. But with Russell, philosophy wasn't tucked into a children's tale; it was right on the surface. You could say that reading Russell shocked me out of my intellectual stupor by giving me a taste of rigorous thought. Russell struck such a chord in me that I've never shaken the questions he raised in me the first time I opened up one of his books:

> There are many questions—and among them those that are of the profoundest interest to our spiritual life—which, so far as we can see, must remain insoluble to the human intellect unless its powers become of quite a different order from what they are now. Has the universe any unity of plan or purpose, or is it a fortuitous concourse of atoms? Is consciousness a permanent part of the universe, giving hope of indefinite growth in wisdom, or is it a transitory accident on a small planet on which life must ultimately become impossible? Are good and evil of importance to the universe or only to man?[3]

Russell's reminiscences put words to the questions and riddles I had been literally walking around with. Henceforth the focus in my reading shifted to the books of philosophy at the British Council library. There weren't many to choose from, but at least I now had an inkling of what to do with myself.

One question Bashir and I never asked during our peripatetic inquiries was about the moorings of the post-1948 order. No one understood, and I least of all, that the world we lived in was doomed to be swept away by new disasters. Our blindness was due to youth, compounded by the total security of our Brahmin homes.

Looking back on our life in Jerusalem on the eve of the 1967 Six-Day War, at the time nothing seemed realer than our tottering make-believe world. Sometimes the king visited with his retinue, flanked by colorfully clad Bedouin guards. The noble families continued to outdo one another with tales of ancient ancestors—it was extraordinary how many "direct" descendants of the Prophet lived in Jerusalem in those days. No Man's Land seemed as immutable as the desert at our back. The 1948 catastrophe was there as a reminder that cataclysms do occur, but no one expected another one. Nor was there much talk of reclaiming the "other side"; irredentism was coming out of Cairo, Damascus, and Baghdad, not Jerusalem. Father, using another cliché, sometimes said one had to "let sleeping dogs lie." I had long outlived the fear of a monster in the pepper tree. No Man's Land had become a benign presence, like Father's metal leg.

I was in my junior year at St. George's when the cold brutalities of power made a brief cameo appearance in my family's life. If I had to describe the family in 1965, I'd say that my father was the proud patriarch. Mother still had her wounds from the past, but she, too, was happy. She always seemed young to me. Only a few strands of gray hair mingled in with her jet-black curls. My sister Saedah had just gotten married, and was gearing up to move with her husband to Abu Dhabi. Munira was studying in Cairo, with her heart set on Paris. Zaki was about to begin his studies at Queen's College, Cambridge. My two younger siblings, Hatem and Saker, were in school.

Father had been serving as Jerusalem governor for the previous two years, and the only Jordanian soldiers I ever saw were friendly members of the army contingent housed along the border next to our home, or the officer with his anachronistic pointed helmet who directed traffic, or those who accompanied King Hussein when he dropped by the house for lunch. One day, as I sauntered back from school, I found our house surrounded by armed soldiers and armored vehicles. Slipping innocuously past the soldiers, I managed to enter the house.

There was a buzz of frenetic activity inside. Father was on the phone with his brother Hazem, who at the time was the minister of justice. My mother was racing from room to room like a passionate revolutionary. As I was soon to discover, Father, loyal as always to his principles, had infuriated the king, and the king had ordered the armed siege of the house because he thought he had a full-fledged Palestinian rebellion on his hands.

Compared with the other political crises that have plagued Palestine over the years, it may strike one today as ludicrously overblown, like the proverbial tempest in a teapot. As governor of Jerusalem, Father was tasked with overseeing the crossings at Mandelbaum Gate. Typically, consuls-general, religious dignitaries, official visitors, and UN officials were the only ones permitted to cross from one side of the city to the other. Once every two Wednesdays, an armored Israeli convoy headed up to Mount Scopus, the only Jewish enclave left on the Arab side of the border. And at Christmas, of course, ordinary people crossed over in order to visit the Church of the Holy Sepulcher.

Out of the blue, however, the guards at the gate had phoned Father's office one day and asked if they should open the gate to a prominent American Jew who was insisting that he had made personal arrangements with the king to cross through. The guards phoned because they normally took their instructions from the governor's office, but this time they had none, only the impassioned assurances given by the American.

Father made some phone calls and found out that the king had indeed been expecting the visitor, but he had failed to inform him. King or no king, Father felt that established procedures and simple human courtesy and respect had to be maintained—it was his decision to make, not the king's. He phoned the guards and told them to keep the gate closed.

King Hussein, needless to say, was outraged at this act of defiance and insisted that my father open the gate. "I will not," Father said, digging in his heels. A man of unbreakable will who had absorbed al-Sakakini's defiant verse to his bones, he maintained that it was the king who had made a mistake, and therefore it was he who must back down. Uncle Hazem tried to intervene, and in vain pleaded with my father to yield. The crisis was mounting. Now tanks rolled into our neighborhood and parked in our front yard.

As the news leaked out, crowds of protesters gathered in front of the house in support of Father's defiance. The already tenuous relationship between Palestinians and Jordanians edged toward rebellion.

The king's response was swift. He fired Father immediately from his post. Not wishing for a recurrence of Palestinian impudence, he appointed a Jordanian as his replacement.

For the following few days, the entire West Bank broke into nationalist demonstrations and confrontations with Jordanian soldiers.

Chapter Six

A Grapevine

As a sign of how theatrical the showdown was, the king never lost his respect for my father, and Father continued to have a paternal relationship to the young king, at the time barely over thirty.

Shortly after the mini-revolt, King Hussein made Father his ambassador to London. It was an act of gratitude, for Father had arranged for the king's first official audience at Buckingham Palace. So, in 1965, Father took up his post as Jordanian ambassador in London. Given his still-wobbly relationship with the monarch, no one knew how long it would last.

My own future was already laid out for me. I was about to graduate from St. George's, and it seemed logical to my parents that I would follow in my elder brother's footsteps by going to a prep school in England. The plan was for me to spend two years at Rugby, which Zaki had attended, before moving on to either Cambridge or Oxford.

The first part of the plan went without a hitch. I traveled by ship alone to Europe, first to Venice and then by train through the Italian and French countryside, all the way to the English Channel. Finally arriving at Victoria Station was thrilling for a teenager who had been cooped up his entire life in the desiccated hills of the Middle East.

But the excitement of what seemed like boundless individual freedom soon clashed with the reality of a highbrow public school, the breeding ground for English dukes and princes, but manifestly not for brown-skinned Arabs. Like Eton and Harrow, Rugby was overburdened with the heavy weight of tradition. Its suits and ties, coat of arms, formalities, upper-class pretensions, and impenetrable social snobbery were more than I could stomach. By comparison, St. George's had been a humble, lowbrow place. All I wanted to do was to slip my jeans back on and explore the world. Instead I found myself tethered to suffocating traditions of tailed jackets and caps, and the disciplined mannerisms of a class and a nation I didn't belong to.

"But how shall I behave if I sit next to Her Majesty?" I once asked Rugby's aloof headmaster as he huddled with a select number of students before a special dinner in honor of the queen. "You should just behave as one *normally* would," snapped the headmaster in a subtle but unmistakable reproach for my not having mastered the air of a young English gentleman. I gritted my teeth and did my best. The headmaster sat me as far away from the royalty as possible.

I wanted to leave Rugby, but my parents wouldn't hear of it. They assumed that the place would eventually grow on me, and that I would be groomed as the young gentleman they wished me to become. What they had yet to figure out was just how similar to my father I had become. Having determined to leave, nothing was going to stop me. And so, after my repeated requests went unheeded, I simply absconded. I packed my bags and headed for London. The path to university would now be longer and more arduous, but at least I wouldn't have to play-act any longer. An aunt with a flat near Kensington was kind enough to offer me temporary refuge.

It was the fall of 1966, and in London my father's boundless ambitions were beginning to take their toll on the family's finances. The Jordanian embassy's meager budget couldn't come close to covering his ambassadorial initiatives—he wanted Jordan to develop extensive diplomatic relations with the political and diplomatic community. He'd already had to sell one of his Jordan Valley farms to make ends meet. Finally, he added up the numbers and realized that if he didn't scale back his activities to mindless bureaucratic duties such as signing visas, he would go bankrupt. He resigned, packed everything up, and headed back to Jerusalem. As it turned out, it was a fortuitous move. Had he been away from Jerusalem in June 1967, we might all have ended up as homeless refugees.

I finally managed to take my A levels, and would have left it at that had Father not stepped in at the last minute and gotten Oxford to bend its rules by allowing me to take a late entrance exam. I was interviewed and accepted for the fall of 1968. My educational future was settled just as all the certainties of my past—my family, home, and city—began to totter.

By May 1967, Nasser felt strong enough to take some risks. After the 1956 Sinai War, the UN stationed an "emergency force" as a buffer between the two belligerent nations of Egypt and Israel. Now Nasser demanded that the UN withdraw from the Sinai. He left it to the Egyptian radio show *Voice of the Arabs* to explain the reason:

> As of today, there no longer exists an international emergency force to protect Israel. We shall exercise patience no more. We shall not complain anymore to the UN about Israel. The sole method we shall apply against Israel is total war, which will result in the extermination of Zionist existence.

Within a week Egypt closed the Straits of Tiran to all Israeli shipping and all ships bound for the Israeli Red Sea port of Eilat. The time had come for the great Arab nation to exert its rights, and Nasser felt legally justified to ban enemies from plying his waters. Choking off commerce to Eilat was for Israel an act of war.

What no one knew—that is, no one except the Israeli military—was that Nasser had no intention of attacking Israel. It wasn't war he was after—the troops he sent to the Sinai couldn't have come close to defeating the "Zionist enemy." His bellicose rhetoric was little more than posturing. "He knew it and we knew it," said the Israeli general Yitzhak Rabin in an interview he gave to *Le Monde* in 1968.[1]

Whereas in most of the West the antiwar movement was galvanizing students—even I trooped along to some demonstrations—Nasser's hypnotic radio addresses were turning young Arabs like me into warmongers.

Congregating daily in a cafeteria housed in a building belonging to the Egyptian Information Office, conveniently located across the street from my aunt's house, Arab students from across England were beginning to mobilize for the oncoming conflict. All of us assumed that the humiliating debacle of 1948 was about to be avenged, and our wounded Arab pride restored. After all, we had been reared thinking that war was inevitable. Like a religious sect anticipating the Second Coming, we knew it would come, we just didn't know the date. With Nasser as our leader and the Soviet Union behind us, war was going to be a cakewalk, a mop-up operation against a poor, badly equipped, internally divided, and outnumbered enemy, an enemy that didn't even deserve the appellation "nation." To us, Israel was an "entity," a thing, at most an impersonal thorn in the flesh.

All sorts of political groups were roaming around London. (Years later the film *Life of Brian* would remind me of the excitement, and the absurdities, of those days.) Thanks to two older friends, one a Trotskyite and the other a Maoist, I found my way to Café Troubadour, in South Kensington. The Troubadour, with its smoky atmosphere, avant-garde owner, and deafening music (Bob Dylan was the favorite), was a perfect setting for the meeting of young revolutionary minds. Besides Trotskyites and Maoists, there were generic communists, an assortment of hippies, and several varieties of anarchists.

At first I didn't know which group to join, and in the end I threw my lot in with the anarchists. The others reminded me of my parents and their dinner guests: too sophisticated and self-confident for my taste. What I liked about the anarchists was their hostility to institutions, and even more their favored black-and-red colors. Wearing the anarchist pin, my tattered jeans, my uncut and unruly hair, and an aggressive-looking beard, I tagged along with the anarchist contingent in their flag-waving protests against the System, institutional violence, villainous governments, and, in one case, inclement London weather.

One day at the Café Troubadour, as I was sitting around a table with the leaders of the Vietnam Solidarity Campaign, chain-smoking and pondering our next move, I heard that some of my older and wiser comrades were considering using the Vietnam Solidarity Campaign as a template for the Arab cause. It sounded like a good idea. After all, why shouldn't there be a Palestine Solidarity Campaign? There was general approval of the scheme, and henceforth, in our demonstrations in Hyde Park or Trafalgar Square, we carried the banners STUDENTS AND WORKERS: UNITE AND FIGHT; AMERICA: GO HOME; MAO WILL LIVE A MILLION YEARS; and JUSTICE FOR PALESTINE.

At the Egyptian Information Office, things were far more serious, as the sound of the war drums grew louder by the day. Arab students driven by national sentiment were seeking ways of participating in the war against Israel. All over the building, meetings were taking place, statements being written, committees being formed, radio broadcasts being carefully monitored. The place had the feel of a war room.

As we headed into June, and the armed conflict appeared more and more unavoidable, demonstrations grew in size and bathos, not unlike a rowdy boxing match. In Hyde Park's famed "Speakers Corner," brawls broke out between young Arabs and Jews. The opposing sides, both wearing identical faded jeans, traded insults. My brother Zaki, fresh from Cambridge, was an elegant debater who delivered a forceful defense of Palestinian rights. But the crowds rarely valued the subtlety of a finely trained mind, as more often than not the debates degenerated into shouting matches. We called them fascists, and they called us fascists. Sometimes the verbal sparring transmogrified into physical blows, and in one case an angry Israeli supporter rushed at me, fists bared and ready to strike. I stood there dumbfounded, and would have gotten a good beating if the attacker hadn't been pushed away by a fellow Palestinian student standing next to me. (Three decades later, he would be the dean of the science faculty at Al-Quds University.) That night we had to take him to the hospital to be stitched from a ferocious bite to the cheek.

During one demonstration, one of our Jewish counterparts made an extraordinary assertion. We Palestinians, he maintained with his umbrella pointed menacingly in our direction, were the real usurpers. We didn't belong in Palestine. When the first Zionists arrived, shovel in hand, the country had been empty, barren, and neglected, hardly fit for jackals. "My family arrived in Jerusalem long before the Norman invasion," I shouted back at him. "Why did you refuse the partition plan and go on to attack?" another protester shouted at me. The first protester nodded approvingly. "Answer him!" I heard someone else mutter. But I was too astonished to say a word.

Later, back in the café, I gave the incident some thought. Never before had I heard someone come out with the old canard that we Arabs had drifted into Palestine and as such had no deep loyalty or right to its soil. How could an educated man, as the man with the umbrella doubtlessly was, deny the obvious? How could he, with a wave of his umbrella, wipe away 1,300 years of my family history?

As the summer dragged on and the war drums beat louder, the atmosphere in London grew more hostile. Public opinion was increasingly against us, and Israel's supporters were winning the PR battle. One day, our beleaguered faction received a visit that printed itself indelibly in my mind. A well-dressed man walked up to my brother during the weekly Hyde Park row and invited him to address a sympathetic English audience. It was a thrilling offer. Finally, we thought, we could present our case in front of respectable people.

My brother went, and when he returned to our café he looked downcast.

"What is it?" we asked, worried that he had been lured into a Zionist trap.

"You wouldn't believe it," he started with an expression between laughter and tears. "The people who invited me to speak were Nazis. You know, fascist pigs." Our fervent belief in our cause wasn't shaken, but it was appalling to discover the brown tint to our only English "allies."

. . .

The one good thing that came out of all the 1960s histrionics was that I was politically engaged for the first time, even if it was in a barely conscious manner. I enjoyed the passion and commitment exhibited by both sides. Strangely, I didn't even associate all the war talk with real physical violence. All I knew about the military was the Boy Scout–like drills we had to do at St. George's and the flurry of activity around the house when the king's tanks rolled up to the front door. It wasn't hatred I felt, only the excitement of the moment, like at a soccer match.

It was during these heady days leading up to disaster that I was first recruited to Arafat's Fatah organization. (Spelled backward, *Fatah* is the Arabic acronym for the "Palestinian National Liberation Movement.") All I knew about it at the time was that it was a clandestine Palestinian national liberation movement whose mission was to lead the Palestinian people to freedom. My simple assignment was to collect donations. Holding the official receipt book in my hands and seeing Fatah's emblem emboldened on every page made me feel a part of some vast rumbling coming up from the depths of the Palestinian psyche.

My connection to Arafat and his Fatah movement has always been tenuous, often ambivalent. As someone who from childhood was repelled by political chatter, the movement attracted me because unlike the different flavors of Marxism, it was a national movement with a sober, commonsensical approach to ideology. And for all its flaws, over the years Fatah has more or less managed to adjust to new realities; steering clear of the endless babble of intellectuals and ideologues, it has opted for direct action.

Before Arafat's Fatah began to shake things up, the PLO wasn't very different from the All-Palestine Government in Gaza. It was set up by Arab states, and the people installed to run the operation were expected to follow the lead of the Arab governments. Ahmad Shukeiri (1908–1980), its first designated leader, was anything but a radical. He was a lawyer by training and a politician by profession: he had been the assistant secretary general for the Arab League. Most of the other top PLO leaders were upper-class intellectuals living in Jordan.

The 1964 Charter may have resounded with bluster, but with Nasser in charge, the PLO toed the line that "unity and a socialist revolution" had to precede the liberation of Palestine. In other words, the interests of the Egyptian and Arab states came before those of the Palestinian people. It was a strange set of priorities for a group calling itself the Palestine Liberation Organization.

Arafat's group was different. The first acquaintance I made with its ideology was in a crudely printed magazine, *Our Palestine*. From the first page, it was clear that the Fatah activists were not going to buckle to the interests of Arab leaders. Their first aim was "vengeance against the butchers of Dir Yassin."[2]

But Fatah went well beyond this by taking a swipe at Arab leaders. It told the Palestinian people they could not rely on the UN or on Arab states. "Did any of the slogans relieve your distress? You remained scattered, without honor, or personal or collective identity."[3] Theirs was an argument for self-respect and political maturity, a call to life for the Palestinian people.

And so as the others continued to talk, Fatah mounted its first operation inside Israel, a brazen guerrilla attack near the Arab village of Ailaboun, aimed at the economic infrastructure. The message to the Israelis was that there was a Palestinian force ready to fight. Pamphlets, leaflets, and various publications to that effect began circulating around the West Bank.

In my capacity as fund-raiser, I managed to raise only a few dollars before the start of the Six-Day War. With the first shot fired, Zaki and I lost all contact with home. The phone lines didn't work, and our telegraphs didn't get through.

News reports were sketchy at the time. On June 5, all we knew was that major battles had broken out. Rumors spread that the victorious Arab armies were marching unfettered into Tel Aviv, with the Israeli soldiers—

cowardly upstarts whose luck had finally run out—in frenzied retreat. An inimitable euphoria took hold of us in the cafeteria of the Egyptian Information Office. We all wanted to join the victorious Arab armies commanded by the new Saladin. At one point some friends and I rushed over to the Egyptian embassy, only to find it closed. Undeterred, we continued on to the Soviet embassy, thinking the Russians could use us. We were barely in the front door before Slavic guards twice our size kicked us out.

The BBC reports told a different story. The fighter planes in the Egyptian air force didn't even get off the ground before they were blown to smithereens by an Israeli preemptive strike. Most alarming for my brother and me, the BBC report stated that Israel had crossed over the border between it and Jordan, and hundreds of thousands of Arabs in the West Bank were fleeing before the invading army. Naturally, we were desperate to know the fate of our family. The telephone and telegraph lines had been cut, and there was no getting through.

By day three, we all knew that the glorious war was turning into an ignominious debacle. Egypt's fleet of Soviet T-34 and T-10M tanks was easy prey for the American Shermans. The entire Egyptian army was prostrate, crippled, helpless. In the West Bank, King Hussein had never wanted the war, and if it had been up to him, the No Man's Land dividing the city would have stayed in place until the end of time. But he felt he had to put up a halfhearted show of resistance, as a prophylactic measure against the inevitable Arab charge that he was cooperating with the enemy.

Symbolic or not, the shots fired by Jordanian soldiers went against the silent understanding that the king had had with the Israelis. The Israelis took the opportunity to decimate the Jordanian army, capturing the West Bank and Gaza, along with nearly a million Palestinians. In 1948 my father and his friends had defended the Old City with everything they could muster. This time, no one lifted a finger. In East Jerusalem, the Israelis blasted a hole through the New Gate and flooded the quarter with soldiers. Solders sang the "Hatikva" at the Western Wall, while a rabbi accompanying the troops offered a prayer: "Blessed are thou, who comforts Zion and builds Jerusalem."

The reaction throughout the Arab world was stunned silence. After 1948, revolutions had swept away the old leaders accused of backwardness and corruption. This time, with the revolutionaries in charge, whom could you blame? If mighty Egypt, with its charismatic leader, Soviet armaments, and vast army, could be defeated without even putting up a fight, was there any worldly force capable of regaining Arab honor? As a sign of the bankruptcy of Arab politics, there was an outbreak of mystical sightings in Egypt. Muslim peasants, in a strangely ecumenical mood, reported seeing visions of the Virgin Mary. Defeat also bred spurious rumors about the conquerors. One theory held that the Jews in Palestine were none other than tall, blond-haired, blue-eyed Germans or Vikings. Superhuman Wagnerian heroes, not fellow Semites, had defeated us.

Zaki and I had still had no word from our family. At the Egyptian Information Office cafeteria, nibbling our nails, we were like anguished fans watching our favorite boxer get hit with the opening swing, swoon, and then crash unconscious to the mat.

Then, suddenly, in one of those rare moments in the history of Arab politics, Nasser tendered his resignation as the only manly thing to do. Within minutes, an emotional current swept through the Arab world, reaching all the way into our crestfallen little band sitting unshaven and unwashed in our London café. At once, we leapt to our feet and raced off to the Egyptian embassy. We might have lost the war, but we weren't about to lose our leader.

From Fez to Baghdad, hundreds of thousands of ordinary men and women like us marched with the same purpose, begging Nasser to come back. *You may have failed us, but we still love you.*

It wasn't until several days after the war that word finally came that my parents were safe. Because our house and that of my grandfather, now belonging to my cousins, were on the border, the extended family had decided to sit out the first two days of the war in the basement of a shuttered-up Arab school just down the street. Our vacant house was an open invitation for Israeli soldiers to plunder. Sure enough, soldiers spirited away the family crystal and silver, my father's tennis championship cups, and his gold medals from the British, including Her Majesty's Knighthood of the Malta Order of St. John's Hospital. At least they didn't take his powdered wig. (My son Jemal, who's now finishing his law degree, has it.) All the family's papers and letters and photos were heaped into a corner, the beds had been slept in, and the stock of Scotch whiskey had been reduced to empty bottles. An officer found the keys to the family Volvo and drove off with it. (A few days later, the car was returned with a full tank of gas and an apology from an Israeli army official.)

My brother and I, relieved that our parents were safe, began to worry about our own fates. Our fear was that the Israelis would do as they had with refugees in 1948: block our return. The longer we stayed in England, the more we risked not being allowed back into our country.

My brother, being older and in a hurry to get on with his life after graduating from Cambridge, chose the adventurous option of clandestine return. He first flew to Jordan, and from there he made his way to the Jordan River. The borders at the time were still not hermetically sealed, and Palestinians stranded in Jordan were making their way back to the West Bank with the help of smugglers. It was risky business: once the river was crossed, Israeli soldiers might open fire; then safe encampments on the other side had to be found. Undeterred, my brother made the crossing successfully, together with a small group. He hitchhiked a ride up to Jerusalem.

A week back in the city was enough to convince him that there was no future for him in Israeli-occupied Jerusalem. He left for the Gulf to find work, never to return to his birthplace. "I prefer living with my childhood memory of Jerusalem rather than with what it's become," he later explained. He went on to become an Abu Dhabi citizen and a top adviser and friend of Sheikh Zayed, first ruler of the United Arab Emirates.

I dallied in London a few more weeks. When I finally began to seriously ponder a return, I chose a different route. Why not fly directly to Tel Aviv? I asked myself. Why not openly challenge the Israelis to see if they would allow it? With this in mind, I asked Teddy Hodgkins, the brother of my father's Marxist friend from the British Mandate days who wrote for the *Times* of London, to help me publish an open letter to the Israeli government, demanding that Israel not rob me of my patrimony and allow me to return home.

As soon as the letter appeared, I got an official invitation from the Israeli embassy in London to discuss the matter in person. Many of my Troubadour friends were certain I would tear the invitation to shreds, as no self-respecting Arab would ever step foot in an Israeli embassy, let alone ask a favor from Zionists. I went straight away. Within a few days, an embassy official stamped a visa into my laissez-passer, a travel document that, as a Jerusalemite, I continue to use to this day.

I boarded the El-Al flight to Tel Aviv in August. It's hard to convey properly the uncanny sensation I had upon stepping onto an airplane, with its mammoth Hebrew letters painted on the outside, that was the enemy's central symbol of statehood and power. Inside, I took my seat among a tightly packed group of Israelis going home, and well-wishing Jews and Gentiles traveling to a state that was suddenly enjoying near-mythic status. The experience of sitting among Israelis inside an enemy machine and being served by frankly gorgeous Israeli airline hostesses would leave a permanent mark on my approach to the Palestinian-Israeli conflict.

Things got stranger as we flew over the Palestinian Mediterranean coast. From my window seat, I looked down on the orange groves below, spread out in large geometric patterns. Were these the famous oranges I'd heard about from Mother?

At the taxi stand outside the airport in Lod, the Israeli name for Lydda, amid the pushing and jostling, I spotted only a handful of the black-bearded wizards I had been spying on since childhood. The other Israelis, too, weren't nearly as mighty or as Wagnerian as I had been led to expect. I was shocked most by their simple clothes and boorish gesticulations, like peddlers in the Old City bazaar. *How could such a badly dressed, ill-mannered people, who couldn't even stand in line for a cab,*

*defeat all the Arab armies in the same number of days it took God to cre-
ate the cosmos?* Their working-class appearance actually boosted my
spirits. Just as I had suspected since listening to the Beatles over enemy
radio waves, they were normal people just like us.

I soon found an Arabic-speaking Israeli cabdriver offering service to
Jerusalem. I got into the car, and for the first leg of the trip I barely
opened my mouth, so astonishing was the journey. It was like being
driven through a dream. It was uncanny enough just to drive east on
the badly potholed and winding Tel Aviv–Jerusalem road. Naturally, I
didn't recognize the landscape unfolding out the window; but what got
my heart thumping were some of the road signs. At one point we drove
through mythic Ramle. From the backseat I looked out eagerly, and of
course entirely in vain, for Grandfather's grave.

Along the road to Jerusalem there were few traces of Arab civilization. It could have been Southern California: no Arab villages, no donkeys, no camels, and no Arabs. Wiped clean. Among the first evidence
of our 1,300 years in the country was a ruined stone house adorned with
Ottoman ornaments near the steep climb into the Judean hills. Closer to
Jerusalem I saw a sign in English to al-Castal, site of the famous battle.

Finally, around dusk, we approached the Arab village of Abu Ghosh.
The driver suggested we stop for a coffee or a snack. To sip Turkish coffee after my absence in England was a real delight. The pit stop opened
my eyes to the fact that not all Palestinians had been driven out of their
homes in 1948; many had stayed. I also discovered that the owner of
the restaurant, a member of the Abu Ghosh clan, was in fact a distant
relative.

As we got back into the cab and drove on, I was once again lost in
thought. The one thing I hadn't anticipated when I planned the trip was
to feel at home among Arabs in the Jewish state.

Crossing over what had been No Man's Land was the highlight of the
trip. It was miraculous to see how the barbed wire and shoot-to-kill
zones, things I had lived with since childhood, were gone. It was only

then that it dawned on me how the war had ended the division of my country. *Defeat had given me back my homeland.*

Growing up, I had never doubted for a moment that my homeland started in Jerusalem and extended west to Jaffa. Amman and all the deserts to the east were always foreign to me. I never felt a part of the Jordanian system, and the fact that No Man's Land had now moved to the eastern bank of the Jordan River didn't bother me in the least.

I don't have to mention here just how misplaced my optimism was. As there was no crystal ball in the cab, I couldn't forsee the coming years of occupation, the thousands of corpses, or the twenty-foot-high concrete wall or the electrified fences now carving up my country. But in one respect my naïveté wasn't far off the mark. I believed then, as I do now, that the Palestinian Arabs and the Jews are natural allies, not adversaries. In 1967, I saw no reason why I couldn't live in the same democratic, secular state with the people who had cut in line for a taxi. In fact, I felt my fate was far more entwined with theirs than with the public school types at Rugby.

My parents and my two younger brothers Hatem and Saker were at home when the cab pulled up to the house. (All my elder siblings were abroad.) It was a festive reunion, like finding each other alive and well after an earthquake. Almost immediately, Mother announced her dislike for the new military regime. The way the soldiers had plundered the house had only confirmed her grimmest prejudices against "this uncivilized gang of thugs," to use her words. Father was more stoical. The war had only confirmed what he had long suspected about Arab leaders, who time and time again had made their countries pay a steep price for their blundering demagoguery. Father's words were few, but intuitively I knew that his political mind was spinning as furiously as a top.

I quickly got a full report on what had happened since the war. Father hadn't held an official post since leaving London, yet he was still at the center of things. Over the centuries, during other political upheavals, the family had always fallen back on its old role as protector of holy sites, Christian and Muslim. My father was following in this old tradition when he, together with religious and political leaders from throughout the West Bank, formed the Higher Islamic Council. His main partner in this was the new mufti of Jerusalem, Sheikh Saadedin al-Alami, who also became the head of the Higher Islamic Council. The mufti respected my father's political advice on whatever issue was at hand. Whenever the mufti needed advice, he would don his flowing robe and sweep through the streets from the *haram*, or holy sanctuary, to our neighborhood. My father was always ready to give the holy man levelheaded advice.

Father envisioned the council as a representative institution that could give voice to the people under the new occupation. A major concern on his mind was the preservation of the religious sites in the Old City.

In the meantime, Israel had moved quickly to impose its rule on the entire city. The new rulers shut down the Arab municipality, and sent the mayor of Jerusalem, Rauhi el-Khatib, packing, across the Jordan. Full control of public services therefore passed into the hands of the Israeli municipality in West Jerusalem. A couple of weeks after the war, the Knesset voted to annex our section of Jerusalem. We were not just getting a new ruler to tax and control us. We faced a state with a military and civil bureaucracy with claims to our land.

"None of this will ever hold up in an international court of law," my father commented with an open hand lightly rubbing his metal leg, after concluding his survey of developments. His confidence in the lofty and impartial hand of Justice, impervious to the machinations of mere men—or alternatively in the common humanity embodied in an international court of law or the United Nations, where the wrongs in the world could always be put right again—was as unshakable as ever. My father's faith in the supremacy and permanence of law never wavered, even as he lived to witness the daily mockery of legal standards by brute force.

It was already evening. After dinner, my parents launched into their customary salon discussions with friends and family. The scenario was a replay of 1948, when refugees believed they would return in a matter of days. After the current disaster, everybody in the living room assumed that Israel would soon be forced to withdraw, despite all evidence to the contrary, such as the widespread land confiscations, house demolitions, and new construction signifying long-range plans. How could the "thieves of 1948" now be allowed to gobble up the West Bank? Just as unthinkable was that the world would stay silent against Israel's "brazenly illegal actions." The wanton destruction of the Moroccan Quarter, the confiscation of property, the expulsion or house arrests of leaders, were all cited as examples of Israel's criminal intentions. I listened without comment.

The next morning I undertook the most astounding trek of my life. I leapt over the garden wall of my parents' house and ventured into No Man's Land.

It began with a few halting steps onto the rocky, thistly, perilous territory, with my eyes trained on the grapevine straddling a crumbling ruin. The vine had always been for me the undisputed king of No Man's Land. Each spring it rejuvenated itself under my watch, and then withered, untouched.

My heart palpitating with excitement, I picked a branch clean of the vine's fruit. Blowing off the dust, I popped a shriveled, raisinlike grape into my mouth. The taste wasn't the sumptuous burst of flavor I had long imagined. It was bitter, and I spat it out.

I forged ahead, toward the previously forbidden streets of Mea Shearim. With each slow step, I was trying to adjust myself to the new reality. At one point I looked behind me at the back of the garden, where I had stood, year in and year out, gazing westward.

A few minutes later, I reached the narrow street populated by pious Jews in their ink-black trench coats. This had been the limit of my vision into Israel as a child, but also a section of the city my parents had known well before 1948. A group of startled children dashed around a corner. Turning and taking a long and steady look back toward my home, I tried to imagine the thoughts of the people in Mea Shearim over the years. What had they thought when they saw an Arab boy looking out at them from the garden of a red-tiled house? Had *I* been the evil goblin in *their* pepper tree?

My behavior that summer caused just as much of a fuss among my parents' friends and associates as it did among the startled children of Mea Shearim. Here I was, an Oxford-bound Nusseibeh, and the ex-governor's son to boot—who in their eyes should have been sporting a blazer with a Rugby coat of arms stitched on the breast—with long hair and wearing sandals, just like the European hippies then roaming around the Middle East.

Over the rest of the summer, I took frequent walks to explore the ways the city had changed. My forays led me to Talbieh, Baqʿa, and Qatamon, all former Arab neighborhoods in West Jerusalem now re-populated by Jews. Life was thriving there. The prosperous inhabitants, so different from the people I had first seen at the airport, blithely went about their business, unconcerned and probably unaware that they were living in other people's homes. "Should I blame them?" I asked myself. I didn't have an answer. I still don't.

I didn't have any such muddle when I walked to the former Moroccan Quarter, whose destruction left me speechless and outraged. Its tangled and mazelike Oriental streets had been my favorite haunts as a child. Now it was all gone. Within days of the war, the sappers, wrecking squads, and bulldozers had arrived. The quarter's wretched inhabitants were given two hours to clear out, and the entire quarter was razed, including two twelfth-century mosques, to make room for a plaza in front of the Western Wall. It seemed monstrous to me to uproot a community and destroy its past for what resembled a featureless Soviet-style parade ground.

In my parents' nightly salons, the same issues popped up with predictable regularity, as they did anytime Palestinians discussed politics. Seeking consolation, people fantasized that the old status quo would magically reassert itself. The slightest incident spawned speculation that the Jordanian army was marching back across the river. Tales circulated of armed Fatah cells operating surreptitiously in various parts of the Occupied Territories. "Who are these people?" my uncle asked Father, who didn't have an answer. I knew, but I didn't say a word. Knowing more than the stalwarts of the salon was a milestone for me.

The house was always full of people asking Father for advice. An influential cleric, Sheikh Abdel Hamid Al-Sayeh, issued a fatwa forbidding Muslims from abiding by Israeli law. There was talk of a general boycott, a throwback to the glory days of 1936. "Should we cooperate?" people asked Father.

My father walked a fine line that maybe only he, equipped with an aluminum leg, could. Writing about the past is tricky business. With what we know now, it is easy to see how, already in 1967, the Israelis were devising wide-ranging plans to strip Arab Jerusalem of its character, its history, and its role in the cultural and political life of our people. There were signs of such an attitude, but there were just as many signs of a spirit of respect and cooperation.

With no crystal ball to consult, Father's first instinct was to extend his hand to the Israelis—not as an obsequious subject to new overlords, but as a proud pan-Arab nationalist who realized that we could overcome our weakness only by approaching the enemy with an unbending neck. To the Israelis with whom he had dealings—and there were many—he was amiable and polite, entirely free of the taint of hatred or ill will. At the same time, he wholeheartedly supported the boycott of Israeli courts and jurisdiction in East Jerusalem. His rejection of dubious legal practices was as immovable as solid rock.

I sat in on some of Father's meetings with Israeli officers, and I was astounded by his poise, as if it were he who had won the war, not they. A proud Arab believing in the immeasurable superiority of his heritage, in his defiant civility he infuriated—and, I think, impressed—his guests.

His political imagination was also working, fed, as it were, by an inbred ancestral duty to serve the City of Peace. Almost thirty years later, Yasser Amer, a member of the PLO executive committee and minister of education in the newly formed Palestinian Authority, told me about an exchange he had with Father in his law office shortly after the Six-Day War.

"Tell them," Father told Amer, referring to the leaders of the PLO, "to go straight for negotiations with Israel for a two-state solution." Father assumed, perhaps correctly, that in the wake of Israel's victory over the Arab states, a peace offer from the PLO might just bear some fruit. "And do it now. If you wait, the Israeli position will harden."

The PLO ignored the advice. "Your father," Yasser Amer explained, "had a far longer range vision than we did. Given the nationalistic mood back then, there was no way we could have listened to him."

Chapter Seven

Smashing Idols

I N THE FALL, I HEADED TO OXFORD. I was eager to study philoso- phy, but when I ran this past my father, he only grunted. The com- promise that he suggested, and I agreed to, was the preferred track for a "gentleman" seeking a career in public life. The course combined phi- losophy, politics, and economics. My college, Christ Church, has a ros- ter of alumni that includes kings, prime ministers, archbishops, and such luminous characters as John Locke and Lewis Carroll.

I must have been an unlikely sight when I first crossed the threshold of the college. What set me apart was less my long hair and thick beard or the antiestablishment pose I had picked up at Café Troubadour—in those days Oxford still had its fair share of Marxists and communists— than my dark Arab complexion. There was only one other Palestinian undergraduate student at Oxford at the time, Ahmad Khalidi, a mem- ber of Jerusalem's most illustrious family of scholars, grandson of the head of the Arab College, and son of Walid Khalidi, the eminent pro- fessor at the American University of Beirut. (Both my father and my un- cle Hazem knew Walid Khalidi well.)

Ahmad and I spent a lot of time together. Having been raised by a nationalist intellectual, he gave me a crash course in Palestinian politics. Among other things, I learned what stood behind the dizzying array of revolutionary acronyms, such as the ALF (Arab Liberation Front), the PLF (Palestine Liberation Front), the PFLP (Palestinian Front for the Liberation of Palestine), and the PDFLP (Popular Democratic Front for the Liberation of Palestine). Ahmad's favorite was a splinter group of the PFLP, led by the legendary Ahmad Jibril. Monty Python obviously had us in mind when, in *Life of Brian*, they depicted the "Judean Popular People's Front," the "People's Front of Judea," and the "Judean People's Front" competing for converts.

It was an exciting time to be a student. The year 1968 was the height of the student rebellion and the hippie age, and young activists worldwide looked to revolutionary leaders such as Fidel Castro and Mao Tse Tung. In Paris, "Red Danny" Cohn-Bendit was shaking up the stilted French establishment. In Yasir Arafat, we, too, had a firebrand to follow.

Arafat was the mysterious figure behind the vague rumors back home of guerrilla strikes against Israelis. I still knew little more about him or his Fatah movement than what I read in *Our Palestine*. Given the debacle of the war, what he had said about the Arab states sounded prophetic. In March came reports over the radio of a major battle between his fighters and the Israeli army. What riveted my attention was the site of the battle: it was in Karameh, where as a boy I drove a tractor at the family farm.

The Battle of Karameh was a bloodbath in which dozens of Palestinian insurgents died. But afterward, when Israeli units retreated over the Jordan River, Fatah proclaimed victory. The Israelis had given it their best, and many of our fighters had died, but the movement lived on. The Battle of Karameh went down in our mythology as the "Stalingrad of the Palestinians." Arabs weren't the only ones impressed by the heroism. Lady Fisher, wife of the Archbishop of Canterbury, was quoted as saying that the Arabs were "surely only doing what brave men always do, whose country lies under the heel of a conqueror."[1]

We were finally beginning to win some respectable allies. Another thing that attracted me to Arafat, even more than his scruffy bohemian appearance, was his vision of a unified democratic state of Palestine. I should add that he was a master of ambiguity and mixed signals—he dodged the issue of what would happen to the Jews once Zionism was swept away. I filled in the blanks. For me, a united Palestine was to include both Arabs and Jews. With no border, people would be able to mingle normally, and eventually a single state would emerge, without a shot fired. Half the Israelis looked as if they could be my cousins anyway. Many spoke Arabic because they came from Iraq or North Africa. We liked the same food and music and smoked the same tobacco in the same kind of water pipes. Why shouldn't we share the same state?

Thinking that this conformed with the vision behind Arafat's movement, I began to hand out Fatah flyers to audiences or students attending lectures on the Middle East by such eminent figures as Roger Owen, an old-school author of such tomes as *The Middle East in the World Economy, 1800–1914*.

At Oxford, Palestinian politics soon faded into the background for me, just as my social world began to expand. I mingled with students from different backgrounds and with different interests. One was an American graduate student named Jay, who liked driving around to pubs in his convertible Mercedes. We sometimes went to parties together, and when the weather permitted, we raced around the countryside with the top down. Politics and guerrilla wars seemed far away indeed.

It may sound strange, but I kept up my interest in politics only after meeting some Israeli students doing graduate work at Oxford. Though formal enemies, we had a lot in common, starting with a strong predilection for debating politics over hummus, our shared Palestinian-Israeli national dish.

My favorite sparring partner was Avishai Margalit, a philosophy student studying with the great Isaiah Berlin at Queen's College. We would often meet in the mornings at a teahouse run by a church on St. Aldates, across the street from Sir Christopher Wren's imposing Tom Tower. It was easy to discuss politics with Avishai because we both had sufficient distance from events back home to scoff at the bugle-blowing victors (his side) and the caviling complainers (mine).

Tooling around in a Mercedes and conducting my own political salon in a teahouse was giving me some much-needed self-confidence. At times I even suspected I was finally getting a bit of Father's backbone, and hence his unflappable strength of character. I was also beginning to put my political convictions on a better footing than they had been at the heated bull sessions at Café Troubadour. Unfortunately, serious inroads into philosophy proved exasperatingly elusive.

Troubles began with my first tutorials. As if by destiny, the first book I was given to read was none other than Bertrand Russell's *Problems of Philosophy*. A week later my tutor, to whom I still owe the deepest gratitude, pulled the rug out from underneath me, causing my seemingly incontrovertible world of ideas and facts to come crashing down. I was settled in the leather chair in his office and venturing forth into my commonsense epistemology when he let me have it. And when I tried to offer counterarguments, he finished them off, too. He did so with such remarkable ease that it seemed effortless. Making a cup of tea would have worked up more of a sweat.

The following week the same thing happened. After one more round of crawling out of his office utterly defeated, I had to admit that whatever certainty I had found over the previous year or two had gone. I was back to my familiar condition of floundering.

This condition was, in truth, considerably worse than the foglike state of my childhood. Now there was no safe harbor to which I could retreat. My Arabism was in shambles, and now my realism, too, was flat on its face. My hair became more disheveled by the day.

I nevertheless kept going back to my tutor, and as the semester wore on, it began to dawn on me that his ruthless attacks were not nearly as merciless as I had first suspected. His was a Socratic method of challenging set beliefs and assumptions, if necessary by tearing away safe moorings and hallowed orthodoxies and legends. He wanted to inculcate in his students enough critical reflection and steeled intellectual discipline to allow them to live and think consciously, to open up doors of the mind previously sealed shut. He went beyond challenging my conscious views; far more disconcertingly, he forced me to question hitherto unquestioned assumptions, and to jettison them if they didn't measure up. During one sitting, he quoted Francis Bacon's belief that the mind has idols in need of being shattered. I was immediately reminded of the story of Mohammed's triumphant return to Mecca from Medina, when he entered the Kaʾba armed with only his camel stick, and without further ado dispatched the pagan gods.

Although my readings concentrated largely on masters from the European Enlightenment, it wasn't long before my attention shifted over to the philosophy of language as conceived by Ludwig Wittgenstein and John Austin, the former a Cambridge man and the latter from Oxford. What was thrilling was the sense that this new school of thought was being reshaped even as I was studying it, precisely because of its local provenance.

Although he had died years earlier, John Austin's legendary intellect and sharpness of mind still reverberated in the corridors and cloisters of Oxford. (His book *How to Do Things with Words* had won over a generation of philosophers to "ordinary language.") Wittgenstein had also recently passed on, and like Austin's, his spirit was still fresh and alive. An Austrian aristocrat with ancient Jewish-Catholic roots, he threw security to the wind by giving away his fortune, and launching himself out into the world, trusting only in the powers of his mind. At one stage, Wittgenstein ended up as a schoolteacher in a peasant village high in the Alps. He was constantly on the outside looking in—at language, society, and himself. Somehow he found within himself an existential perch from which to observe life. Far more than Descartes in his barrel or Kant on his daily rounds in Königsberg, Wittgenstein struck me as an explorer I could follow, if only from a distance.

In the summer of 1968, I returned home. Given the painful new intellectual horizons opened up to me in my tutor's office, it was odd to return to a family, and a nation, in a deep rut. My family, with all its titles and honors, reminded me of aristocrats in exile from Soviet Russia. Father had even had his country estate confiscated—a two-hundred-acre tract of land in the Jordan Valley, seized by the Israeli authorities. The clan from Medina, with a name redolent of past glories, had turned into a small family of ex–civil servants, the children all gone or about to leave.

The Palestinian side of Jerusalem seemed moribund and uncertain of itself, just like me. It was neither under the boot of the Israeli military, like the West Bank, nor free, like the rest of Israel. A bizarre process had begun, of professionals boycotting their professions: Arab lawyers, for instance, had stopped working as lawyers because they refused to work within the Israeli justice system. The Arab municipality was gone, just as the social and economic fabric was in flux. Confusion had begun to set in as Israeli currency, license plates, transport systems, legal procedures, consumer products, and habits were all rapidly becoming ingrained into daily life.

Upon my return, I found Father actively seeking ways to undo the catastrophe of the latest defeat. UN Security Council Resolution 242, which called for an Israeli withdrawal from the territories it had conquered, had been denounced by demagogic Palestinian leaders the minute it was announced, and for the simple reason that with 242, Israel had won tacit legitimacy for the pre-1967 borders and hence for all the territories it had conquered in 1948. Article III calls for the "respect for and acknowledgment of the sovereignty, territorial integrity and political independence of every state in the area and their right to live in peace within secure and recognized boundaries free from threats or acts of force."

The official Israeli attitude toward 242 can be summed up by Ben-Gurion's disparaging quip about the UM (the Hebrew acronym for the UN): "UM-shmum."

Father never thought it was possible to undo 1948, and as such focused on the resolution's discussion of the more recently conquered territories. He liked 242's clarity on the "inadmissibility of the acquisition of territory by war and the need to work for a just and lasting peace in which every state in the area can live in security." In Father's mind, the UN was unambiguous: Israel had to move back beyond No Man's Land.

Father's indefatigable diplomatic activity drew a steady stream of foreign dignitaries, prime ministers, and journalists to the house. At one point he tried unsuccessfully to convince King Hussein of Jordan to negotiate a deal with Israel. The king, threatened on all sides by a rising nationalist Palestinian power within his kingdom and not wanting to end up gunned down like his grandfather, didn't dare. Father toiled on nonetheless. Eventually King Hussein had some secret meetings with Moshe Dayan and Golda Meir, but they foundered on the issue of Jerusalem. The king was willing to let the victors keep the entire area around the Western Wall in exchange for handing back the rest of the Old City and the West Bank. The Israelis weren't interested.

This didn't prevent Israeli dignitaries such as Moshe Dayan and Mayor Teddy Kollek from visiting the house. Kollek dropped by on Islamic holidays, and I can recall the sight of him and my father sitting across from each other, smoking the Havana cigars that my eldest sister, Munira, supplied the family from Abu Dhabi.

"Anwar, we're just about to introduce some innovations in the Arab school system," Kolleck said to my father, lazily blowing out a warm stream of smoke. "Why don't you find some way to get the local Arab educational leadership engaged in this effort? It's in your own interest, after all."

"Fabulous idea," Father responded in a serious tone, flicking some ashes into the tray. "But tell me, when are these innovations to come into operation?"

Kollek, not used to having an Arab respond positively to his initiatives, leaned forward, and excitement entered into his voice. "Why, as soon as the academic year starts."

Father, innocently pretending to calculate the months, shook his head and put on a befuddled look. "But that's in another five months. Surely you'll be gone by then."

Father also took up invitations to speak to Israeli audiences or to engage in debates with Israeli leaders. On one occasion I went with him to Petah Tikva, where he was invited to address a large audience of Arabic-speaking Yemenite Jews. Father drove, and I was supposed to read the map. Predictably, we got lost, and after driving in circles, an Egged bus driver, noticing our East Jerusalem license plate, waved us down to help. Father recounted the incident to his audience, adding that if only politicians were like bus drivers we would have peace. The audience roared with pleasure.

Soon after I got home from Oxford, I was surprised to see Israeli journalists lining up to see my father, either at the house or at his law office not far from Damascus Gate. I had been back a week when Danny Rubinstein, a reporter from the Hebrew daily *Haʾaretz*, came for an interview. Danny wasn't much older than I, and in contrast with my nonexistent Hebrew, he spoke fluent Arabic. After the interview, we chatted. I told him about Oxford and that I had befriended a couple of Israeli students. This must have impressed him, because he asked me if I'd like to see the Knesset. I told him I'd seen it from the outside plenty of times. "I mean from the inside," he explained. "Are you joking?" I said.

He wasn't.

Before the visit, I had had various mental images of the Knesset. I had heard, for instance, that on a massive flag hanging from the ceiling were images of the Euphrates and the Nile, a symbol of Zionism's voracious appetite to extend its territory from the suburbs of Cairo all the way to Baghdad.

Within a few days, Danny had made all the arrangements, and from the top gallery I got a close-up view of the Israeli government. I didn't see the flag, though I did make out Moshe Dayan's eye patch. Down on the government benches, I saw Golda Meir, David Ben-Gurion, and Prime Minister Levi Eshkol in what looked like a conspiratorial huddle.

By this point I was developing a strong desire to understand what made Israel tick, what gave it its dynamic energy. I was soon to get my first chance.

One day, representatives of the Higher Islamic Council showed up at the door to inform Father that the Israelis were beginning archaeological excavations in the vicinity of the Al-Aqsa mosque. They feared that the new masters would burrow under the *haram* in search of Solomon's lost temple. The gentlemen of the Higher Islamic Council wanted to enlist Father's support in protecting the Dome of the Rock from desecration.

Father and his fellow council members took me with them to the archaeological site. We made our way through the Old City until we reached the place of the dig. Me²r Ben-Dov, the leader of the archaeological team, saw us standing skeptically off in the distance. In perfect Arabic, he raised his voice and asked, "Do you want to see what we have found?" He waved us over to take a look at a pile of Islamic artifacts from the Umayyad period that his team had unearthed.

The Islamic scholars among our group looked at one another awkwardly, not knowing how to respond. Father finally asked who was doing the digging.

"Students from all over the world."

"Would you accept a Muslim volunteer to help in the dig?"

"Of course," went the reply.

My father, head straight up, left the puzzled clerics behind and approached the archaeologist. "Come," he waved me to him. I was to be his volunteer.

I'd seen Father's Kismet before, but never had I witnessed such a good example of his willingness to ignore peer opinions, step out of line, and snub his nose at prejudice, especially when knowledge was at stake. Naturally, in his mind, the destruction of the Moroccan Quarter had been a criminal abuse of power. But for this he blamed politicians, not archaeologists. Arabs, he knew, had nothing to fear from science, in particular the science of uncovering our ancient ossuaries and coins.

The next day, I showed up with my customary sandals, tank top, and jeans, and went to work deciphering the Arabic script from old coins. I didn't spend a lot of time at the site, but enough to ignite a minor controversy back in our part of town. People were not happy that the former governor's son was working with the devilish Zionists burrowing under the Holy Sanctuary. This was the first time I heard my name uttered in a political context, and little of it was flattering. It was good practice in ignoring what others thought. Even Cousin Zaki was irked with me.

With Father's encouragement and money, in that summer of 1968, I also signed up for an *ulpan*, a language school, to begin to learn Hebrew. I made an even more important step when I volunteered to work on a kibbutz.

At the time, the kibbutzniks were the darlings of the European left, and volunteers from Sweden to Switzerland flocked to kibbutzes to experience socialist ideals and, just as important, free love. To Arabs, the kibbutzniks were the shock troops of the Israeli system, merciless Spartan soldier-farmers on the front line of every fight. I wanted to see for myself where the swords of Zion were being fashioned.

Father made all the arrangements. He contacted someone he knew from Kibbutz Hazorea, in the Galilee, which belonged to Ha-shomer Ha-tzaír, or the "Young Guard," of the left-wing "Mapam" movement. This friend put the question of my visit to his fellow members, and they debated the issue over supper. They then put it to a vote, and decided to extend an invitation to me.

Kibbutz Hazorea was founded by socialist youths who had fled Nazi Germany. Expelled from school by Hitler's government, they emigrated to Palestine and built a communal farm. (*Hazorea* means "the sower.") Within an hour of my arrival, the kibbutzniks made sure I knew that before they showed up with their crude plows and immense energy, their land had been a swamp owned by absentee landowners. They showed me the black-and-white photos of the pioneering days. The empty desolation in the photos was in striking contrast to the forests on the hills, the lush vegetation, and the flowers I could see just outside the window. The white tents they had initially lived in reminded me of an illustration in a book I read as a child on the Prairie Indians.

Already on this, my first day in "enemy territory," I was getting a good sense of the high caliber of the people there. Nestled among the simple white bungalows was the Wilfrid Israel Museum, named after a German Jewish art collector who fell into Gandhi's inner circle during his travels to India in the 1920s, and who, in 1943, died while trying to rescue German Jews during World War II. In his will, Israel bequeathed his art collection to the kibbutz. I was amazed to see the ancient pottery and goddesses and Oriental art filling the museum.

I stayed for about a month with a kindly old couple who, after dinner in the evenings, told me about their lives. They loved listening to Umm Kulthum on Arabic language radio, they said, along with other great Egyptian singers. I also heard about their fears, stirred by listening to Nasser's ranting speeches on the radio. Unlike me and my colleagues in London, they had dreaded Nasser's promise to annihilate Israel.

Some evenings I spent with people my own age. With my rudimentary Hebrew, I tried my best to follow what they said. From the bits and scraps I was able to piece together, what impressed me most was their idealism. They earnestly believed that the kibbutz was forging the New Moral Man. Theirs was no less a political project than a humanistic one, in which all people, men and women alike, were to live a life of freedom and equality, without a trace of capitalistic rapacity, with wealth distributed according to need.

After a month, I left the kibbutz with even fewer certainties than before. The kibbutz was a microcosm of what was best about the nation that had rooted itself deeply in the same country I had been taught to believe was my own. The standard kibbutznik was a model humanist and socialist, a person I had no choice but to admire. At the same time, he was an elite soldier trained to fight my people, and me. Nor did this kibbutznik have any conception of the steep price we Arabs had paid for his freedom. What I took from the experience resembled the way I felt decades later reading Amos Oz's book: that at least until 1967, we had hardly existed in the minds of these fine people. This absence wasn't a product of malevolence or ill will. Physically, we simply weren't part of their world, with most Arabs having been cleared out twenty years earlier. Morally speaking, it was a case of out of sight, out of mind. Their humanism never had to face us.

The rest of the summer was rounded off with a summer fling, and evenings spent in a West Jerusalem café with members of the local leftist-revolutionary group Matzpen, Hebrew for compass. I also spent a lot of time thinking about the kibbutzniks. They were without question fine people, despite their blind spots. Didn't we have our own? I concluded from all this that ignorance, rather than some undefined evil intent, had to be at the core of our conflict.

The next academic year at Oxford (1969–70), Lucy came into my life. I had already heard of Lucy—*every* philosophy student at Oxford had heard of her. Her reputation around campus was as a free-spirited Renaissance woman: a brilliant classicist, a flutist, and a member of the famous Oxford choir, Schola Cantorum. To top it off, her father was the great philosopher John Austin.

The first time I set eyes on her, I was smitten by her fair skin and hair and her striking, tall elegance. It was at a party I was throwing with Ahmad, in my room at Christ Church. She'd dropped in for a few minutes with a couple of friends who knew Ahmad. But it was not until that summer that I really got to know her—and that was not in Oxford but in Jerusalem. She had come to join a dig in Gaza, and as luck would have it, she ended up (through a mutual Oxford friend) having lunch at my parents' house! From then on, each time I saw her back at Oxford, my attraction to her grew. Now I spotted her wearing tight pants and a trendy jacket, now it was a sexy skirt and high black boots; now she was in a pub, now in a classroom. I had to know her more closely.

It finally happened under unlikely circumstances. I was just leaving a Laundromat, and there she was, coming in! Waiting for her clothes to be washed gave us time to strike up our first conversation. Later I invited her to listen to some of my LPs. It was somewhere between Handel's "Hallelujah Chorus" and Jimi Hendrix's "Purple Haze" that we both knew we had hit it off. With that issue settled, we listened to Dylan.

We began seeing each other almost daily. We went to the cinema, took long treks in the surrounding countryside, picnicking or eating at old-world English pubs; we went on some camping trips and punt rides; and at the Trout Inn, a pub on the riverbank oozing with character, we talked about our lives. (They say that the pub helped inspire *Alice's Ad-*

ventures in Wonderland.) I became a religious devotee to the Schola
Cantorum choir and attended all of their concerts in the various Oxford
churches. On a whim, at mid-term, we drove in Lucy's Hillman to Scar-
borough, made famous by Simon and Garfunkel. I can still hear her
singing the lines as she drove:

> *Are you going to Scarborough Fair?*
> *Parsley, sage, rosemary and thyme*

With the academic year nearly over, I assumed I wouldn't see Lucy for
months. We had tried to arrange for her to come to Jerusalem on another dig, but it didn't work out. Then one day, I spotted her on the
street. I was sitting in the passenger seat of Jay's roadster, and I shouted
out a hello. She waved for us to stop, and once we did she told me
excitedly that she was heading to Israel for the summer, on a tour with
the Schola Cantorum. "You see, we are destined to see each other in
Jerusalem," she said in classic English understatement. I hadn't been so
pleasantly dumbfounded since my journey across No Man's Land.

It was the summer of 1969, and Israel had now occupied the West
Bank for two years. If the nobles, intellectuals, and pan-Arabists were still
wringing their hands in despair, the masses were taking the occupation
in stride. Tourists were flocking back to Jerusalem, many of them free-
spending Americans. The shops were full, and there was more money to
spend than ever before. Construction projects began again, just not on
my uncles' five-star hotel, which was still a hulk of naked concrete and
rusting rebar.

At the family salon the big news was my cousin Salim's arrest for
planting a bomb—a dud—in a bus station. Salim had grown up in the Old
City with his widowed mother. His father had died when Salim was a
boy, leaving him and his mother impoverished. As often happens, pov-
erty made Cousin Salim easy pickings for an ideology promising quick
revolutionary solutions. He joined the Palestine Front for the Liberation
of Palestine (PFLP) just after the Six-Day War, and was sent into the

hills of Hebron for training as an insurgent. He was only seventeen when the order came from the leadership for him to carry out the thankfully failed "operation" that would earn him a life sentence in prison.

Beyond this, there was the usual talk. No one in the salon said a word about peace with Israel, and everything I heard echoed what the Arab states had come out with during the conference in Khartoum in August 1967. (As if rubbing Aladdin's lamp, Arab politicians thought the three magical words "No! No! No!" could erase the humiliation of defeat: No peace with Israel. No recognition of Israel. No negotiations with Israel.) All talk was about reestablishing the cease-fire agreement that had existed between 1949 and the outbreak of the June war. They wanted the wall back; No Man's Land had allowed them to hide the reality of the Jewish state behind a veil of concrete, as one might hide an object of shame.

Arafat's name was now guaranteed to pop up at some point in the evening; King Hussein's almost never. I got a good laugh from an uncle one evening when he showed me a copy of a letter apparently written by a deceased great-uncle to his Jewish lover thirty years earlier. The great-uncle's letter promised his mistress a home in the Goldsmith's Souk, our ancient family property that had been destroyed by the earthquake in 1927. The promise may have been the great-uncle's commentary on their relationship. Less humorous was how my uncle got hold of the letter. It seems that the woman's Israeli relatives had unearthed it and were now claiming possession of the house.

With the old borders gone, a trip to the beaches of Tel Aviv was as simple as getting in a car or boarding an Egged bus. That summer was the first time I traveled inside of Israel with both of my parents. We drove the Volvo to Mother's childhood home in Wadi Hnein, near the Israeli city of Lod. When we arrived, my mother stifled a hurt cry, for the only thing left was the gnarled tree she used to swing from as a child, its unhappy boughs coated with an oppressive layer of dust. As for the villa, there wasn't even detritus left from the dynamited walls. The famous orange groves were nowhere to be seen. Surprisingly, Grandfather's grave in Ramle had survived amid the rubble. By its side in the same cavern, the ghost of the Sufi master had mysteriously protected it.

• • •

During the summer, two exciting but wholly unrelated events occurred, the first of which could have easily turned into the apocalypse. One bright sunny day, an Australian fundamentalist Christian named Michael Rohan tried to burn down the Al-Aqsa mosque. It took ages for the municipal firefighters to reach the mosque, so hundreds of volunteers tried to put it out themselves. I was one of them, as were Father and Mother. An angry crowd broke out in the chorus, "Down with Israel!" As I was carrying a bucket of water into the third most sacred shrine of Islam, I noticed a fellow Arab, blood running down his nose and face, swinging his arms at Israeli soldiers. "Who's that?" I asked a friend. "What do you mean 'Who's that'? It's Faisal Husseini." Faisal was ten years older than I and ran in different circles. I had heard from Father that he was working as an X-ray technician. Judging by his bloody nose, I also gathered that he carried within him a good dose of militancy, inherited from his father, the great Abdel Kader el-Husseini.

The maniac's fire destroyed a thousand-year-old wood-and-ivory pulpit that had been sent from Aleppo by Saladin. At his trial, Rohan justified the arson because, in his words, he was the "Lord's emissary." Declared criminally insane by the court, the "Lord's emissary," before being deported, was sent to an Israeli mental hospital, built on the ruins of the former village of Dir Yassin.

The other event was seeing Lucy. This time it was my turn to show her my city and country. My parents still didn't suspect that I was desperately in love with her. To them she was just the daughter of Walid Khalidi's friend, the famous Oxford philosopher.

In the fall of 1970, I began my final year at Oxford uncertain as to what to do with myself upon graduation. The atmosphere in England at the time was an unusual mixture of vibrancy and decay. There were the Beatles and the Stones, MG roadsters and Graham Greene novels, Pink Panther and James Bond movies. The BBC aired the first episode of *Monty*

Python's Flying Circus in 1969. But Britain was also a dying empire. Every year new countries emerged, while England was buffeted by strikes. When my father was a student in the 1930s, graduates saw the vast world open to them. There was still an empire to run. Now if students were lucky they could end up at one of the new red-brick universities in Leeds or Birmingham.

Lucy and I grew closer by the day, and we began to discuss marriage. On a whim—I think we were discussing Hegel—two weeks before classes started we decided to head to Heidelberg, in the Black Forest, where we felt we had to walk the Philosophers' Path.

I bought an old MG convertible for a hundred pounds, and despite the dire warnings of a local mechanic who said it wouldn't make it out of town, we drove it across Europe. We shipped the car to Ostend, and drove from there, mostly camping along the way. After Heidelberg, and with frigid air seeping in through the threadbare vinyl roof, we pushed the car up Alpine passes. It was somewhere in the mountains that we finally decided to begin spreading the word that we wanted to get married.

Falling in love changed everything. It wasn't only the heart palpitations that took me by surprise, it was Lucy herself—what she stood for, and what she stood against. I loved, and still love and admire, her spiritual depth, her fortitude, her sharpness of mind, determination, and sagacity, and her down-to-earth simplicity. To use a worn-out cliché, she was both my soul mate and my partner in crime.

Loving Lucy meant running headlong into family and cultural taboos specifically engineered to prevent mixed marriages. My family was far away and could thus be kept in the dark about our plans for the time being. Lucy's mother was a different story. An accomplished philosopher in her own right, Mrs. Austin taught at St. Hilda's College, and was far too sharp to miss anything. (I once went with Lucy to London to hear her mother deliver a paper at the Aristotelian society on "knowing one's own mind," so titled in response to the fashion at the time of writing on "other minds," and on knowledge more generally.) Lucy's way of introducing to her mother the subject of our marriage was to pit me against her mother, who had a formidable mind, in a discussion of philosophy.

It was a frankly frightening proposition, and I thought of a hundred ways to get out of it. Did Lucy really want to endear me to her mother, or was this a litmus test for a family of philosophers? With fear and trembling, and no choice but to go along, I agreed to this philosophical encounter.

Her mother's house was in a village called Old Marston. The house was set in a large park and close to a pond that attracted wild birds. Lucy sat smiling in a corner with her nose in a book, while I did my best to pass family muster. Whether by dint of conviction, or due to her daughter's unyielding determination, we finally got her mother's nod of approval.

One day, over the Christmas break, I passed by the pub where J.R.R. Tolkein and C. S. Lewis once upon a time met every Wednesday to discuss their fantasy books. It was there that I hit upon the idea of writing a fairy tale. One thing was for certain, it wasn't going be like *The Hobbit*, a Christological story of good and evil. My story was going to be about love: my love for Jerusalem and my hope that I could return to my country with Lucy and raise our children in a place where Jews and Arabs were equals. (I still thought there was a good chance of this actually happening.) Writing the fable injected me with such intense pleasure that I couldn't stop—that is, until I lost my way at the end and didn't know how to awaken the knight in front of the Church of the Holy Sepulcher.

One morning, back at school, Lucy came by the teahouse for a surprise visit and caught Avishai and me in the act: we were scribbling out some possible solutions to the Israeli-Palestinian conflict on napkins. What Avishai didn't suspect was that I was picking his brain for an elegant ending for my fairy tale.

Over my three years at the university most of my reading in philosophy was in the house specialties at Oxford: logic, continental philosophy, and the philosophy of language. Being engaged to the daughter of one of the greatest philosophical minds of the generation did wonders for my motivation. Lucy kept me on my toes.

I had no doubts about the greatness of European civilization. Nevertheless, as graduation approached, I began to think of ways of bringing together this European heritage with the greatness of my own heritage. Was there perhaps some hidden treasure buried in Islam comparable to the astounding intellectual feats I'd been studying about in Leibniz, Locke, Spinoza, and Descartes, to name just a few?

Another question dogging me since high school was about the sources of Islamic civilization. How did an austere religion conjured up by Mohammed, an illiterate tribesman, emerge in full gallop in the high culture of Baghdad? It took Christianity 1,200 years to come up with an Aquinas. Islamic culture produced a raft of comparable minds within two hundred years of Mohammed's death. Already by the ninth century, Muslim intellectuals were debating in Arabic the respective merits of Plato and Aristotle.

Politically, I was faced with a more painful question. How could a civilized nation rooted in Palestine for well over a thousand years be so easily plucked out and chased away at gunpoint? By now I knew this wasn't because of the inherently superior intelligence or even the malevolence of our enemy. What was it then?

I didn't have any answers. What I now had were some skills and tools I could use to find out. I began toying with the idea of studying Islamic thought, perhaps even the Koran. At Oxford there was no one who could guide me. The Philosophy Department swarmed with disciples of Wittgenstein and Austin, along with every other aspect of philosophy *besides* Islam.

One day I made a discovery.

Through a close friend I met a graduate student by the name of Fritz Zimmerman, a German specialist in the field of Greek and Syriac transmission of ideas and texts into Arabic. The first time we sat down to talk, I confided to Fritz some of my questions, and at once he invited me to accompany him to a seminar in London. The seminar was held at the

Warburg Institute, which was originally founded in Hamburg by an eccentric German Jewish genius and bankrolled by his rich brother, who also helped move the institute's library to London before the Nazis could seize it. Once every two weeks, Fritz attended a seminar there led by the Egyptian philosopher and historian of science Professor Abdulhamid Sabra.

On the train down to London, Fritz told me more about the Warburg Institute. He described Aby Warburg, its founder, as the quintessential Jewish cosmopolitan. The central idea animating the library Warburg created was that various cultural roots, mostly subterranean and thus invisible, continue to link up modern civilization with the medieval and ancient European cultures, and with the even older cultures of the Near East and the Mediterranean. The Warburg Institute Library embodied this unbroken esoteric tradition. For someone trying to come to grips with his own Islamic heritage, I was captivated.

When Fritz and I arrived at the Warburg, five or six people were sitting in a room reading a manuscript by a theologian from the eleventh century by the name of Abd el-Jabbar, who had composed treatises on subjects such as perception, epistemology, free will, and justice. El-Jabbar had belonged to a theological school called the Muʾtazilites, the impeccably dressed Professor Sabra explained. The Muʾtazilite school taught that human beings have a free will and are, as a consequence, entirely responsible for what they do. Adherents refused to use God's sovereignty as a cop-out. God didn't dispense rewards and punishment arbitrarily, independently of humans' deeds and misdeeds. According to the Muʾtazilites, God was no Oriental despot; nor was he a puppeteer sitting on a cloud and pulling our strings. This radical view of human freedom sounded distinctly modern to my ears.

The Muʾtazilite rationalists ran into opposition from the more traditionalist Ashʾarite school, whose adherents considered God so omnipotent that he could disperse rewards and punishments willy-nilly as he chose. The traditionalists won the day, and suppressed the rationalists and their writings with such inquisitional thoroughness that for more than nine hundred years all we knew about the former was what we heard from the very critics who had been instrumental in driving the Muʾtazilites into extinction in the first place.

Then, in the early 1950s, a group of Egyptian archaeologists working in a Yemenite mosque unearthed the manuscripts of the Muʾtazilite school. It was a cache of ancient texts, mostly theological but with enough philosophy in the mix to help explain the subsequent glories of the Islamic Golden Age. For the first time, scholars had direct access to Muʾtazilite writings.

The discovery intrigued me. All my life I had heard about the heyday of intellectual life in eleventh-century Baghdad, but like all versions of the Golden Age, this one was always long on reputed glory and short on detail. The dearth of extant documents made serious intellectual histories of the era little more than educated guesses. The discovery of these old writings now opened a window into the period. Flipping through the printed text, I felt myself standing up against a monolith of intellectual power, something I could sink my teeth into.

By the end of the two-hour seminar, I had discovered my entrée into Islamic philosophy. The Muʾtazilites impressed me with their extremely high level of clarity and rigor; at once I felt the power and depth of their argumentative method and analytical treatment of philosophical topics. Professor Sabra, likewise, came across to me as a penetrating scholar of vast erudition. He had studied under Sir Karl Popper (like Wittgenstein and Warburg, Popper was also a German-speaking Jew), and had picked up Popper's particular spin on logical positivism. This came out in Sabra's meticulous search for meanings and relations in the words and lines of the text, all of which immediately struck a chord in me. I resolved to ask him to supervise me in my further training.

Afterward, I introduced myself to Professor Sabra and told him I would like to attend his seminar on a regular basis. He agreed. On the train back to Oxford, I felt as if my future stretched out clearly in front of me. Lucy had one more year to go to finish her degree. I would study with the Egyptian in London, and Lucy would visit me on weekends.

. . .

Sure enough, I graduated, moved into my aunt's place in London, and enrolled at the Warburg.

The Warburg Institute was attached to the University of London, which I liked from the first, not least due to its radical heritage. It was inspired by Jeremy Bentham, who despised the aristocratic and clerical prejudices at Oxford and Cambridge, and believed that knowledge should be open to all. The university also had some old English eccentricities I liked, such as the fact that after his death, Bentham's body was stuffed and stored in a wooden cabinet. Dressed formally for the occasion, it was carted out at official functions.

Working in the library came as second nature to me. The books there were arranged to mirror Aby Warburg's underlying hunch that ancient mythic, artistic, and intellectual patterns survived into the modern world through transformation. Having been raised in Jerusalem, I was familiar with the idea that ancient patterns take on fresh life in new times.

It took only a few months, however, for my plan to study with Professor Sabra to fall apart. The Egyptian professor received a chair in the history of science at Harvard, and he promptly left for the United States. Once again, the line fastening me to my moorings had been cut.

What was I to do? Move back to Oxford with Lucy? Go back to Jerusalem? I decided to stay in London, where I had free rent and probably more Islamic texts at my fingertips than anywhere else in the world.

Reading a text and understanding it are two different things. More difficult still is, in the spirit of Warburg, to set it in the context of what preceded it, and what followed. Reading the texts was the easy part; they were in classical Arabic. But I found the arguments presented in them baffling, as if a different kind of mind had employed my native tongue in a totally incomprehensible way. Nevertheless, I set off on a journey into this strange literature, prodded on by the hope that if I could solve the puzzles inherent in these writings I could make sense of the rise and fall of the Islamic Golden Age. Maybe buried somewhere within these cryptic writings was a thread joining medieval Islam with the modern West. Could such a thread, and not politics or armed rebellion, be the key to a new Arab renaissance?

Over the course of that year, these writings became more and more familiar to me, and not because I learned the art of deciphering an alien way of thinking. It dawned on me that in their own way, these ancient theologians and philosophers were in pursuit of answers to the very questions that had been plaguing me since I first picked up Bertrand Russell. Is what we call "reality" something independent, or is it something we construct? Do we have free will? What is perception? What is justice? Can we expect any of it in this life?

I became a partisan in the battle of clashing philosophies, in feuds being slugged out among atheists, mystics, agnostics, and pious fanatics. During a single afternoon I could side with the freethinking Hellenistic philosophers, then shift my sympathies over to the theologians. It was an exhilarating clash.

The fight started during the reign of al-Ma²moun, the second Abbasid caliph (813–33). One night, al-Ma²moun met Aristotle in a dream. The Greek philosopher encouraged him to translate the great books of the world into the sacred language of Arabic. The caliph subsequently set Christian and Muslim translators to work. The lost wisdom of the Greeks began to come alive again for the Arab world, like a mummy rising from the dead.

Traditionalists weren't convinced this was such a great idea, and in the course of the tenth and eleventh centuries an acrimonious tussle broke out within theology over the influence of Hellenistic culture on Islam. The Mu²tazilites believed that Greek science had a universal validity, while their adversaries the Ash²arites insisted that since all knowledge was already contained in the Koran, all that was needed was a better understanding of Arabic and the exegetic methods. This battle between "Greek" reason and "Islamic" revelation looks at first glance like any fight between modernists and traditionalists, free thinkers and the fire-breathing Khomeinis of the world.

As I soon discovered, there was much more to this than meets the eye. At one stage in my relentless pursuit of Islamic philosophical texts, I zeroed in on the quintessential anti-philosopher al-Ghazali.

A giant in the Ashʿarite tradition, al-Ghazali knew philosophy as well as his opponents—maybe better. This can explain the bad reputation he earned among philosophers for launching his lethal assault against them. Al-Ghazali taught that philosophy had nothing to contribute to religious thought; even worse, he asserted that Greek metaphysical speculation was deleterious to religion. Philosophers had nothing to contribute to revelation, and should limit themselves to lower-order questions such as those in the field of logic. By pounding away at philosophy with such masterful skill, al-Ghazali sealed its fate. Pure philosophy eventually withered away and died in the Islamic world.

If this was the whole story, al-Ghazali should be ranked among the worst foes of free inquiry. But as I continued to dig, a far more sympathetic picture emerged. He was a professor and a judge, and as head of the University of Baghdad, he had one of the most prestigious jobs in the most glorious city on earth. At one point—I imagine him leaning back in his chair and staring out the window down at the Euphrates River—he realized that there had to be something more to life than prestige and honor and hashing out old philosophies. Aristotle bored him. A number of more existential questions tormented him, none of which could be answered by his living out his days in smug bourgeois comfort.

So he gave it all up—family, position, reputation—and launched out on a Wanderjahr in search of knowledge. He had the courage to stick his neck out and to give up everything for the sake of free inquiry. The journey eventually led him to a small ascetic cell inside the Dome of the Rock in Jerusalem.

In Jerusalem he wrote his mystical book *The Jerusalem Epistle*. Truth, he now concluded, could be obtained only through an ecstatic and visionary state. (Even if he didn't use the expression, what he was really talking about was the Greek notion of *Thaumazein*, the sense of wonder at the miracle of Being, and a miracle that can't be bridled by syllogisms.)

Logic was too weak a tool to grasp Being; only God, our limitless Creator, could contain it. In Jerusalem, al-Ghazali turned into a Sufi. He and Heidegger would have gotten along.

Intellectually, the way he arrived at his mystical conclusions was daring and rigorous, and the more I studied his work, the clearer it became that his so-called rejection of philosophy had actually opened up Islamic culture dialectically. The spirits of Occident and Orient came together in a room cheek by jowl within the Dome of the Rock.

I was most intrigued by two of his contributions. First, by ridding theology of Greek metaphysics, he didn't slam the door on thought but rather looked for different ways of conceiving theological knowledge. By separating imagination from logic, giving each its due, he taught that we can have access to higher truths only through analogy, metaphor, and intuition. Moreover, by restricting logic to the sciences, he helped pave the way for the first renaissance in the study of nature since antiquity. In spite of himself, he cracked open the door to allow Greek scientific thought to flood into Islam.

There was one other thing I learned about al-Ghazali: he invented a new way of conceiving miracles. The followers of Aristotle denied the possibility of miracles. If the essence of an object—say, a drop of water—is inherent and immanent, that is to say, if no matter how deeply you explore the drop you will always find "waterness," then there can be no way of turning water into wine. Or, to use a political example, if two sides of a conflict have essential differences, even God can't bridge their differences. If nothing else, as the creator of natural laws, God must be consistent. If Q inherently contradicts P, it will always do so.

To account for miracles al-Ghazali adopted atomism. Borrowing from the ancient Greek thinker Democritus (known as the "laughing philosopher"), he argued that the world and all the objects within it including our soul, are composed of discrete, featureless, and interchangeable "atoms." These atoms take on various shapes, so if God chooses to turn water into wine, all he has to do is shift the atoms around a bit. Or, going back to politics, hatred may seem as immutable as Dr. Johnson's stone, particularly in the Middle East, where blood feuds can keep it going for generations. Yet, emotions are not Aristotelian essences, but can be transformed through an act of will. It's up to us to turn hatred into understanding. No matter how hopelessly entrenched two parties seem, their feud can be solved through an act of human will.

Chapter Eight

Sunflower

WHILE I WAS DELVING EVER DEEPER into Islamic philosophy, and Lucy was finishing her degree in the classics, we did what many pious people frowned upon. We formally announced our engagement.

Lucy's mother was already on board when I set out to break the news to my parents. Father said nothing when I went back to Jerusalem. He preferred to watch the debate with Mother from a safe distance; as a man who chose his battles carefully, and knowing that Mother was engaged in a losing fight, he preferred to stay silent. Mother's resistance was weak from the beginning, and she gave the impression of someone fending off my arguments—that love was more important than tradition or background—less out of conviction than out of protocol; she had to put up a bit of opposition before embracing Lucy, which she soon did. So did Father.

Whereas arranged marriages were still the norm in Palestinian villages, in a city like Jerusalem, romantic love was accepted, so long as it was between people of the same religion and background. Even my parents, as enlightened as they were, thought it best that Lucy convert to Islam. If we wanted to return to and live in Palestine, they reasoned, conversion would make life easier for us.

Lucy agreed. Her parents were atheists, and as such the church didn't figure in her life, except as a musical institution. Stepping into Islam didn't, therefore, involve the problem of stepping out of something else. What helped was the painless simplicity of the conversion process: all she had to do was state that Mohammed was the Prophet—as was Jesus, for that matter—and that there was no other god but God, which to Lucy's thinking was a logical truism. If God really existed, she reasoned, how could there be another one? (Years later, the famed Harvard logician W.V.O. Quine jestingly assured Lucy that her reasoning had been perfectly sound.)

A far bigger hurdle for Father was financial. As a married man, I was becoming an adult. As such, I had to be prepared to stand on my own two feet, and to support myself. I, of course, concurred, as I wouldn't have dreamed of asking for my parents' financial help. In our culture, it would have been ludicrous and humiliating to do so. Father then reminded me of my lack of marketable skills. If I wanted a family, I would need to find myself a career. The time had come for me to get serious about my life.

My brother Zaki and my two sisters, Munira and Saedah, were all prospering in the distant sheikhdom of Abu Dhabi. My sisters' husbands worked in contracting, and my brother was becoming a confidant of the sheikh. These were prosperous years in the Gulf; fortunes were being made, and my siblings were reaping the benefits. "Come to Abu Dhabi!" they all kept saying. "Here you can have a fat salary, a new apartment, and a big American car."

It was an enticing offer. Life in London, with little money, no adviser, and an MG that no longer ran, couldn't go on, while a job in the oil business could prove I could support myself. And I knew so little about business and the real world that I managed to convince myself that I could spend a year with my siblings and leave with a million dollars in the bank.

Lucy and I decided that I would head off to Abu Dhabi alone, and that she would join me after the wedding. And so I packed my belongings and flew off Abu Dhabi, where I stayed with my brother in his apartment overlooking the Gulf. Zaki arranged a job for me in the Public and Government Relations Department of an oil company with offshore concessions.

The Yom Kippur War—in the Arab world it is known as the Ramadan War—broke out just after I arrived. It was October 1973, and I recall the dizzying atmosphere in Palestinian neighborhoods when news came of the heroic advances made by the Syrians and Egyptians; wild cheers erupted when Anwar Sadat's armies breached the ostensibly impenetrable Bar Lev Line. Initially it seemed like a reversal of 1967. This time our side sprang the sneak attack, and it was we who were advancing.

No one paid much attention to General Ariel Sharon's extraordinary counterattack, which cut off the entire Egyptian Third Army, or the fact the Arabs had to impose an oil embargo on the countries supporting Israel to get the Americans to stop the Israeli advance. Psychologically, none of this mattered. The war was like the Battle of Karameh on a gigantic scale. The Arabs had shown that the Israelis were mortals after all. We won by not losing.

The wedding took place the next summer. It was held at my parents' home and presided over by Father's friend the gentle Sheikh Sa'd el-Din el-Alami, the mufti of Jerusalem.

Crowds of family and friends thronged our garden. The first order of business was the guardianship. Tradition required that Lucy have a Muslim guardian to accept her into the faith, and Sheikh El-Alami agreed to do this. The conversion, clearly a perfunctory act, was next. Yes, she said with a straight face, there was no god but God. Minutes before the wedding, the grand mufti asked her to repeat her lines. It was over in five minutes. Lucy's mother and brother, standing with my parents in the front row, looked amused.

Another preliminary act was the legal contract stipulating a financial guarantee to Lucy in case we divorced. Traditionally, the bridegroom puts in writing that in case of divorce, his bride would get his house, his flock of goats, a car, an olive grove, or some other asset. It is an Islamic insurance policy.

And so the two of us stood before the mufti and announced our agreed-upon guarantee: one freshly plucked sunflower. The mufti's eyes opened wide in incredulity. Never before had he heard such a thing, and he asked us to repeat it. "I promise Lucy one freshly plucked sunflower," I stated again, this time loud enough for our guests to hear. Snickers broke out among some of my friends, who had expected me to pull some sort of prank.

After the ceremony, Lucy and I drove off to a hotel run by a church in a nearby village that had served in the past as a pilgrim's station. The hotel was set on top of a hill lush with cypress trees in the pastoral surroundings of Jerusalem not yet ravaged by the cancerous spread of Israeli settlements, bypass roads, power lines, and the security barrier. We arrived at that special moment when the sun is about to set, and its golden light spreads over the hillsides, rocks, and trees. We were served a simple dinner and a bottle of local Palestinian wine under the trees. We couldn't have been happier.

The next day the scene shifted from bucolic simplicity to a raucous beach party in Gaza. Some of my mother's family there were wealthy farmers with beachfront property. Tents were put up, servants placed the meat of slaughtered sheep on open fires, and a group of traditional musicians performed hypnotic songs. Lucy's mother had never imagined that such an Oriental carnival would serenade her youngest daughter into married life. There were no Oxford dons in tuxedos and tails on the beach that day, only gallabiya-clad Arabs reclining on the sand.

After a week's holiday in Beirut, Lucy and I, this time together, left for Abu Dhabi.

The best part about living amid the gilded tents of a sheikhdom was spending time with my brother Zaki, whose intellectual reach, expertise in music, love of books, political grasp, and facility with different languages and cultures were all woven through and through with extraordinary kindness. It was his humanity that prevented his successes from going to his head, for he seemed to me totally unaffected by the incredible network of social and professional relations he had built up with local sheikhs and foreign nationals alike.

As it turned out, the job with the oil company was the first and only one I would ever have in the so-called "real world." The 1973 war had been good for oil. Petrodollars flooded into the Gulf as a result of the oil embargo, and Western companies, eager to benefit, lined up to strike deals with oil-producing governments. It was an exciting time. Due to the war, changes were afoot in the relationship between oil companies and governments. The oil companies naturally wanted to maintain their total private ownership; by contrast, nationalists were calling for total nationalization. Wisely, the government decided to shift over to a more collaborative system that would keep the expertise of foreign companies in the country while ensuring that the wealth produced by oil benefited the country. I learned a lot about the give-and-take of the negotiations: being a fluent English-speaker, I was brought in to help broker deals.

Abu Dhabi was not Oxford or Jerusalem, but Lucy and I made the most of it. She worked as a columnist for a local English newspaper and started a radio program on classical music. It was amusing to hear Bach's Christmas cantatas carried over the waves of the sheikhdom's radio station. With our jobs we were able to buy a brand-new car, maintain a respectable apartment, and rub shoulders with the gin-drinking expatriates and foreign diplomats there. None of this meant—at least this is what we told ourselves—that we had succumbed to bourgeois comfort. We still found time to rough it on a foray into the oases at Al-Ain. To celebrate New Year's 1974, we camped on an island studded with ancient ruins off the Abu Dhabi mainland.

However interesting my job was at the time, I was obviously not cut out to be a businessman. My plans to make a quick million foundered on the iron laws of economics and logic. No one with my low level of material aspirations and total dearth of financial acumen could, or should, become a millionaire overnight. To my credit, at least it didn't take me long to conclude that I had no interest in business, and as such had to find a career alternative fast.

On one particularly sand-bitten and lonely day—it was my twenty-fifth birthday—I decided to treat myself to a gift. This was an important juncture: I was a quarter of a century old, married, and, on paper, a respectable employee at an oil company. But I was scared that in the world of business I was beginning to lose my inner self. What better way to regain my bearings, I told myself, than to take a couple of days off work, lock myself away, unplug the telephone, and spend long hours in quiet reflection, just like al-Ghazali in his room near the fabled Dome of the Rock.

In one go, with short breaks for meals and naps, I read all seven volumes of C. S. Lewis's *The Chronicles of Narnia*. What intrigued me about the books, and the reason I kept all in my apartment unread for months awaiting the right occasion, were things I had heard about Lewis at Oxford. C. S. Lewis came up with his fairy tales after an unexpected vision—and there's no better way of describing it—of what he called "mental images." One was of "a faun carrying an umbrella," another of a "queen in a sledge," and a third of a "magnificent lion."

Once again, legend served me well, for it was somewhere in the middle of reading *The Lion, the Witch, and the Wardrobe* that I came up with a plan to do my Ph.D. at Harvard with the Egyptian professor.

Lucy, who knew I was hankering to do more research on what I had started in London, promptly backed me up. With a higher degree, we also thought, I could probably get a teaching job back in Palestine, at some university—altogether a more suitable profession and location for us than the business world of the Gulf. I contacted Professor Sabra, applied, and was offered a place as well as a scholarship. Beginning in the fall of 1974 I'd be at Harvard. I quit the oil job and we spent the summer back in Jerusalem.

Shortly after our arrival back home, I paid a visit to my cousin Salim in prison. Ironically, days afterward came the exciting news from the *Voice of the Lightning Bolt*, a Palestinian radio program in Damascus, that there had been a guerrilla attack against what it described as a "strategic Zionist stronghold."

It seemed that a bomb had gone off at the studios of Israel Radio, the source of my rock-and-roll education before the war. The broadcast made it sound as if the attack had been a major blow to the enemy, and a first step toward taking over the Knesset. The Popular Democratic Front for the Liberation of Palestine (PDFLP) claimed responsibility for the "heroic and daring strike," which involved clandestine infiltration, strategic brilliance, and an audacity straight out of James Bond. The guerrillas had hit the enemy's communications nerve center at the Russian compound. It was from there, the former Russian monastery, that the Israelis broadcast their propaganda to the world. Now the PDFLP's heroes had silenced them.

The studios were housed across the street from the central prison where political prisoners were detained (over the years I would get to know this building well), and a short jaunt from my parents' house. A cynical friend from my Café Troubadour days rang me up and invited me to amble over to check out the ground zero of the attack.

We covered the distance in fifteen minutes. As we approached the explosion's epicenter, my friend let out a derisive guffaw. He pointed to a small huddle of soldiers standing around looking bored. Next to them was a chalk mark on the asphalt. I had to look twice until I finally spotted a small tear in the pavement at least a hundred feet away from the communications hub, which was not an imposing Brave New World monolith but an attractive turn-of-the-century stone building in the Arab style.

That night I told guests at my parents' after-dinner salon about the "attack." My father only shook his head. A wan grin spread over his face. Mother's expression hardened, as if we shouldn't be mocking an attempt, futile or not, at getting back our rights. Mother was already far more involved in street politics than my father. She had established a Committee for the Defense of Prisoners, was organizing demonstrations and getting herself arrested time after time, and on more than one occasion had ended up with bruises at the hands of baton-wielding riot police in street confrontations. With her thick black head of hair and effervescent dark eyes, she maintained that Israel would only yield by dint of force.

The conversation shifted over to the PLO. At Oxford, I had lost touch with Arafat's Fatah movement. I knew, of course, that the Palestinian Stalingrad, the Battle of Karameh, had helped Arafat gain control over the PLO in 1969. From that point on, Arafat was the chairman of the PLO's Executive Committee, which was made up of the heads of various Palestinian factions, all of which more or less recognized Arafat's leadership.

In 1970, King Hussein had expelled the PLO from Jordan, and Arafat began his exile years in Damascus and Beirut. Just as this was happening, the PLO started to reinvent itself. As of 1970, Fatah's official vision of liberated Palestine was that of a democratic state guaranteeing equal rights to all its citizens—Muslims, Christians, and Jews. The PLO also started reining in its earlier crank remarks, such as seeing a grain of truth in the anti-Semitic *Protocols of the Elders of Zion*. Much of the world didn't buy the new moderate line, however, because the PLO was blamed for the kidnapping and murder of the Israeli Olympic athletes in 1972. There was justified worldwide outrage after the 1972 tragedy and Arafat denied all responsibility.

My father wanted to know what I thought about the PLO and its claim—which Arafat repeated every chance he got—to represent the interests of the Palestinian people. Surprisingly for Father, the Arab states were ready to echo Arafat. In a meeting in Algiers in November 1973, just a month after the 1973 war, the Arab heads of state crowned the PLO the "sole legitimate representative of the Palestinian people."

I welcomed the declaration, and told my father why. Who else was going to represent our interests? In the Occupied Territories we had no leadership, no bar association, no legal strategy, no civil rights movement. Nothing. Do the Arab states know what we need? Does Jordan? Who gives a damn about us?

Father only shook his head in disapproval. He was still a pan-Arab nationalist, and as such did not believe in separate Palestinian politics. The Palestinian Arabs had not created the problem with the Jews, and it wasn't up to them to solve it. Anyway, he had no truck with the PLO tactics, and no faith in the ability of scruffy "revolutionaries" to sit down with the Israelis and negotiate a solution to our conflict. How could a shadowy organization constantly on the run from one redoubt to the next represent all Palestinians? Besides, how could the PLO represent us if it refused to allow contact between Arabs and Israelis? Even the word *Israel* had no place in their vocabulary.

Father was partly right. It would take years before PLO leaders figured out how to make use of international legal instruments, such as Resolution 242. And by then, vast swaths of our best lands had been lost.

Chapter Nine

Monticello

LANDING ON THE AMERICAN CONTINENT for the first time in my life, at Logan Airport in September 1974, was exhilarating. With the exception of Jay, the playboy at Oxford, I had never had any American friends, and psychologically I was hobbled by the reigning anti-American prejudices common in European and Arab left-wing circles. Even so, America's time-honored spirit of adventure, of making a new start, and of seizing opportunities had always held for me a secret appeal. Even before Lucy and I were out of the airport, I felt at home.

We quickly settled into a working routine whose intensity only increased with time. We got an apartment, bought some used furniture and an old VW Beetle—parts of the steel floor were rusted through, but this didn't keep us from far-flung camping trips, some in the dead of winter—and made our first friends. I was soon to learn, however, that I no longer had the carefree liberties of the undergraduate.

America, this vibrant and ramshackle democracy, was fun to watch. Nixon had just resigned. The Vietnam War was over but the images of returning POWs gave Americans a wrenching reminder of the lost war. To top it off came inflation, crime, and OPEC ministers jacking up the price of oil. I must have heard the wisecrack "you Arabs have us over a barrel" a thousand times.

In Boston, the school busing issue exposed how much raw racial tension existed in the city. The gunning down of Martin Luther King, Jr., a few years earlier seemed to have proven to black militants that if you wanted change you had to be armed—just in case.

Lucy and I immediately discovered Café Algiers, a local place just off Harvard Square, where students smoked through the night, giving the place the subversive feel of a Left Bank café. At Algiers and other cafés, and sometimes in a literature or philosophy class, students talked about the "downfall" and "crisis" of American democracy, as if the sixties hadn't ended. It was amusing for me to observe the future leaders of this massive imperial power talk about the downfall of an ascendant system of which they were a part, and which it would be their destiny to serve and eventually lead. Oxford represented the leisured life of literature and conversation in a dying colonial power. By contrast, the academic ambition at Harvard was palpable, with the muscular American empire needing the expertise of her best and brightest.

When Lucy and I needed a break from the intensity of Cambridge, our Beetle offered an easy escape from the excitement and turmoil of modern America. With a short ride to Concord, one could take a quick afternoon pilgrimage to Walden Pond, Thoreau's *Walden* and *Civil Disobedience* in hand.

I felt at home in America. As a child I had never felt like a citizen of the Hashemite kingdom of Jordan. In some vague sense I knew I was a part of the Arab nation, but that was only an ideal. In terms of an actual country, with a real flag, England had been the only place that exemplified the civic values I was raised with. Yet living in England had taught me that no matter how well I spoke the language, or how pure my wife's Anglo-Saxon bloodline, I could never become a part of English society. England was cramped and small, and its social system closed to outsiders.

It didn't take long for me to recognize how different the atmosphere in America was. I missed the eccentricities of Europe—at Harvard there was no stuffed Jeremy Bentham presiding over university functions. But neither did I sense invisible barriers to trip me up and keep me in my place. America was a place with lots of elbow room and as much opportunity as you could take. I immediately fell in love with the beauty of the country and the friendliness of the people, and the thought of settling there often crossed my mind.

One "mental image"—to borrow from C. S. Lewis—that illustrates what was so liberating about the country took place at the Blue Parrot Restaurant, where I worked part-time washing dishes. (I resolutely refused to accept money from my family.) One day, the Polish-born cook in the kitchen took me aside. He must have seen me sneak a cold French fry into my mouth and assumed I was broke. "Don't worry," he told me with his arm around my shoulder. "Okay, you're just a dishwasher now. But look at me! I started out as a dishwasher, now I'm a chef. One day I'll open my own restaurant. You can make it, too."

A different image comes from a trip along the Shenandoah Trail. Shortly after we arrived, Lucy and I decided to go camping, making a side trip to Thomas Jefferson's Monticello. I'd rubbed Monticello often enough on the backside of the nickel to know what it felt like under my thumb, but to see it for myself was a shattering experience. The first glimpse I had of it reminded me of an English country gentleman's estate. The architectural style Jefferson employed had been the rage among eighteenth-century aristocrats. I'd seen a dozen buildings like it in England. But the man behind this estate was the same contradictory figure behind the revolution against England and its aristocratic system of privileges.

I wandered through room after room thinking about this slave-holding, tobacco-growing member of the American gentry devising his rebellion. In my mind's eye, I pictured him in his library, a volume of Thomas Paine on his lap, conspiring to overturn a system of rules and laws made according to imperial interests rather than to the interests of the people living in the governed territory. Grandfather had turned against the British in the 1930s for the same reason, though he and his friends on the Arab Higher Committee never drew up a constitution, and they never founded a university.

From Monticello, Lucy and I made our way down to the original brick buildings of the University of Virginia, and there I pondered the additional fact that the author of the Declaration of Independence had also established a university. He called it an "academical village." What was so astounding for me about Jefferson, in contrast to Robespierre, say, or any of the Arab revolutionary leaders, was the systematic manner in which he went about putting flesh and bones on the conception of liberty by building free institutions. Just as impressive for me was Jefferson's philosophy of public education: "It is safer to have the whole people respectably enlightened than a few in a high state of science and the many in ignorance." Tears welled up when I read this.

The next stop was the obelisk marking his grave. Inscribed into the stone was more than his personal legacy, it was a clue to the internal strength of American democracy:

HERE WAS BURIED

THOMAS JEFFERSON

AUTHOR OF THE

DECLARATION

OF

AMERICAN INDEPENDENCE

OF THE

STATUTE OF VIRGINIA

FOR

RELIGIOUS FREEDOM

AND FATHER OF THE

UNIVERSITY OF VIRGINIA

Lucy and I stayed in America for four years. During our last year, we had our first son, Jamal. With our new baby, we moved to a graduate student apartment complex off Mt. Auburn Street. We now saw more of Walid Khalidi, whose kind wife provided us with clothes for our newborn son, as did his friend Stanley Hoffmann, the eminent German-born political scientist. Jamal spoke his first words in that apartment of ours. One was the Arabic word for *ant*, the other for *light*.

Raising a son, plugging away at my dissertation in my office at Quincy House, doing dishes at the Blue Parrot, and stalking the campus in my new part-time job as a security guard didn't leave me much time for socializing. Nonetheless, I did get to know some fellow Arabs, and sometimes we got together in the smoke-filled Café Algiers to discuss politics over Turkish coffee and cheesecake. Conversations ranged from the "Third World" liberation movements to Jean Genet's account of homoerotic forays into the gritty refugee camps in Jordan and Lebanon.

Unsurprisingly, I also ran across some Israelis. One was none other than Avishai Margalit in the philosophy department; another was Gedaliahu, or "Guy," Stroumsa, a French-born Israeli and a child of Holocaust survivors. We first met when we were invited to talk to some American students about Middle Eastern politics, and we ended up agreeing with each other more than we agreed with the views espoused by the students in the audience.

Over the four years we spent in America, Lucy and I returned to Jerusalem only once, after Jamal was born. In those days, it was too expensive. Even a ten-minute phone conversation could cost me a couple of hours of washing dishes at the Blue Parrot.

I did my best to keep abreast of events back home by attending the occasional lecture. When my father's friend Walid Khalidi—his son was with me when I first met Lucy—came to campus, I naturally showed up for his talk. An immensely witty and charming man with a piercing intellect, Professor Khalidi had just published a controversial and unprecedented article, "Thinking the Unthinkable," in which he squarely argued for two states: one Jewish, the other Palestinian. In his lecture, he laid out his position. A two-state solution was still an unthinkable proposition for me, and in the Q-and-A at the end, I unfurled the standard PLO vision of a single secular, democratic Jewish-Arab state. Wasn't that what progressives were demanding in South Africa? Why should Israel be held to a lower standard?

The other way I kept in touch with the Middle East was through the American media. Palestine was in the news a lot at the time, albeit cast in a less-than-flattering light. In the 1970s, Palestinian international terrorism went into high gear. By nature I've always recoiled from violence of any sort, even Cousin Zaki's barbaric bird hunts. At the same time, no one could deny that the world took notice of our plight only once passengers in first-class seats on airplanes began fearing they could end up in Beirut instead of Tokyo. Terrorism put the Palestinian issue on the map, and suddenly politicians in Washington and Moscow were discussing the issue.

The PLO and the Israeli government entered into a protracted period of trench warfare, with neither side prepared to take their dispute into the public forum of international law and justice. To fight the PLO, the Israelis used assassination and commando raids into Lebanon. On the propaganda front, their lobby scored a number of successes, notably in the United States. Their cause was helped along in 1976 when a book titled *The Arab Mind*, by the Israeli American writer Raphael Patai, appeared. (His *The Jewish Mind* followed the next year.) Included in its pages are such insights as: "Most westerners have simply no inkling of how deep and fierce is the hate, especially of the West, that has gripped the modernizing Arab." The book also claims that Arab males are full of twisted sexual hang-ups. (Years later, Seymour Hersh referred to the book to help explain the torture conducted at Abu Ghraib.)[1]

Given the circumstances, the PLO's successes were even more impressive. Militarily, it had bases in Southern Lebanon and parts of Beirut and Tripoli. But compared with what the Israeli forces had, these were minuscule. Its real success was diplomatic, not military. In 1974, the UN invited Yasir Arafat to speak. I recall the famous images of Arafat swaggering up to the podium with his scraggly whiskers, crumpled fatigues, and empty holster. "I have come bearing an olive branch and a freedom fighter's gun," he announced to the world. "Do not let the olive branch fall from my hand." He got a standing ovation.

In 1975, the United Nations General Assembly conferred on the PLO the status of Observer in the Assembly and in other international conferences held under United Nations auspices. The "PLO Observer Mission" promptly opened an office in Midtown Manhattan. The PLO soon began to speak, albeit in hushed tones and rarely without a fistful of caveats, the language of diplomacy and compromise.

It was during my final year at Harvard, in 1977, while furiously scribbling away at my dissertation, that an astonishing thing occurred. Anwar Sadat, a man who had once referred to the Jews as "contrivers of plots," embraced Menachem Begin, the revisionist hawk who had blown up the King David Hotel. Even more astounding for me were the words Sadat spoke in front of the Knesset. There is "a psychological barrier between us. A barrier of suspicion. A barrier of rejection. A barrier of fear and deception. A barrier of hallucination around any deed and decision." By his reckoning, the psychological barrier was "seventy percent of the problem."[2] I watched this momentous event on television while visiting Uncle Hazem, then Jordan's ambassador to the United Nations in New York.

Back at Harvard, the handful of members of the Arab Student Society, a "society" in name only, decided to debate the issue. We met only rarely, but given the political earthquake set off by Sadat's visit, we duly came together. All over the United States, Arab student societies were issuing statements condemning Sadat's visit to the Knesset as an act of treason to the Arab and Palestinian cause. The leaders of Harvard's Arab Student Society wanted us to do the same.

A friend of mine, an Israeli Arab named Shukri Abed, who had philosophical interests similar to mine, called me up and suggested we go to the meeting together. Once the meeting started, Shukri and I realized that the president of the society expected us to rubber-stamp a formulaic condemnation, most likely at the request of an apparatchik sitting in an office in Damascus or Baghdad. Both Shukri and I had actually been mesmerized by Sadat's audacity, and we were not about to blindly support the resolution. We piped up and said so, which led to a nasty altercation. At one point I suggested to the Arab students gathered in the room that we vote the Arab Student Society president out of office. He stood there agape, not quite sure how to react. And before he regained his mental footing, we called a vote and kicked him out. By nature not a very good citizen when it comes to such groups, I never attended another meeting of the "society."

I was in America to get my Ph.D. and not to squabble over silly resolutions. My first two years were spent taking courses and preparing for my general exams. I will always be profoundly indebted to the scholars I studied under. Besides Professor Sabra, who presented in his classes and scholarship a coherent picture of the Islamic theological, philosophical, and scientific schools, there was Muhsin Mahdi, an expat of encyclopedic intellect. Professor Mahdi was a student of Leo Strauss, and over the years he had established himself as one of the world's great authorities on Islamic political philosophy. I was still eager to deepen my understanding of general philosophy and logic, and the man who helped me immeasurably in this was the logician W.V.O. Quine. With him I explored my own father-in-law's philosophy of logic and language, as well as Frege's. I explored my old interest in the question of the will in a seminar paper I wrote for Robert Nozick. Professor Martha Nussbaum, newly appointed at Harvard, helped me understand the ways in which medieval Arab philosophers appropriated Aristotle. She still remembers (I stay in touch with her) her bafflement at my interpretation of Aristotle's *ousia* (substance). One essay I wrote for another seminar was on Wittgenstein and the role of jokes in philosophical discourse.

Meanwhile, Lucy did a master's in Middle East studies at the Middle East Center. She studied Arabic and Persian, and did research on the economy of the Israeli occupation of the West Bank. You could say she was preparing herself for her future life in Palestine.

After two years of coursework, I had to commit myself to a theme for my dissertation. I thought about the philosopher Abu Nasr al-Farabi (c. 870–950), especially after, at Professor Mahdi's prodding, I plunged into Leo Strauss's brilliant commentary: "We may say that al-Farabi's Plato eventually replaces the philosopher-king who rules openly in the virtuous city, by the secret kingship of the philosopher who, being a perfect man precisely because he is an investigator, lives privately as a member of an imperfect society which he tries to humanize within the limits of the possible."[3]

Though al-Farabi's wisdom would become a permanent fixture in my later life—especially the bit about quietly doing your best to humanize an "imperfect society"—my choice fell on Avicenna (short for Abu Ali Aa Hosain Ibn Abdallah Ibn Sina), a philosopher born in the year 980 near Bukhara, in Central Asia, where his father governed a village on one of the royal estates.

At thirteen, Avicenna went off to study medicine, and over time moved on to Greek thought. He was a polymath who wrote major works on logic, astronomy, medicine, philology, and zoology, composed poetry, and produced an allegorical autobiography called *The Living Son of the Vigilant*. (Lucy and I named our second son after Absal, a character in this fable that symbolizes the soul's search for knowledge.)

For months, I worked on my dissertation the way an artist chisels away at a piece of marble. In a work of love, you are so entirely absorbed in what you're doing that there is no longer a barrier between you and your subject. That was how I felt. I wrote with a manic obsession, sometimes eighteen hours a day. Much of it was conceived during the graveyard shift of my new job with campus security. All night I skulked around, lost in my internal debate with my medieval philosopher, while innumerable thieves no doubt took advantage of my preoccupation with arcane issues of knowledge, selfhood, Being, and Truth.

The fact that this early medieval thinker from a society that vanished centuries ago could speak so powerfully and directly to my own experience got me thinking. Maybe the intellectual giants of the Enlightenment, whose works had inspired me at Oxford to explore my Arabic tradition in the first place, could be better understood by bringing to light the Arabic tradition that underlay so much of Western philosophy. Despite Patai's *The Arab Mind*, maybe there was a hidden symbiosis at work between two civilizations that seemed to have radically diverged and were often at loggerheads.

I really thought I was on to something when Lucy's mother came for a visit. One of my compulsions since the Warburg was to show the common heritage joining East and West. Far from what would later be known by American neocons as the "clash of civilizations," our heritages are actually fed from common sources. Avicenna, went my hunch, was a prime instance of this. Lucy's mother had come to visit her new grandson, and I recall one day sitting on the back steps of our small apartment, explaining to her Avicenna's system of perception, when she quizzically asked if I wasn't really talking about Locke's distinction between primary and secondary qualities. While I pondered this, she added, "You know, I believe Locke taught himself to read Arabic," which wasn't surprising, she continued, given the fact that one of the major texts being studied when Locke was at Christ Church (my own college at Oxford) was Avicenna's main treatise on medicine.

For over a millennium there has been an element of mystery surrounding Avicenna, and philosophers and exegetes have fought countless skirmishes over his so-called "Oriental philosophy," an expression he used in distinguishing his own brand of metaphysics from Hellenism. Avicenna never spelled out precisely what he meant by it—hence a thousand years of philosophical head-scratching.

What was Oriental philosophy? As a lover of riddles, I probably spent a hundred hours wandering around campus at midnight with my flashlight, pondering an answer to this. The hunch that eventually formed was that Avicenna cleverly imbedded his "Oriental philosophy" esoterically in his books, which scholars have traditionally read as meat-and-potatoes commentaries on Greek metaphysics. Solving the puzzle required reading "between the lines" of his Greek works, the way Leo Strauss read al-Farabi.

My six-hundred-page dissertation attempts to do this. I should add here that the dissertation had a long afterlife, not as a book—I have not yet had time to work on making it publishable—but in my various efforts in the political arena. Much of my political work over the last twenty-five years leans on Avicenna's profoundly humanistic system. Call it a system of human freedom.

The most enduring idea that joyfully rubbed off on me is Avicenna's theory of the will, whether God's or the human being's, and how this relates to the nature of the world on the one hand, and what we make of it on the other. The upshot of my study is that the Oriental philosophy can be grasped only by exploring Avicenna's approach to the will.

Unlike philosophers before him, such as Plato and Aristotle—who held that things in the world are what they are by virtue of some essential property they possess—Avicenna took a position philosophers today associate with Leibniz: that our world is one of many possible worlds. Simplifying it a bit, Avicenna insists that the world does not have an inherent nature; rather, it is what it is by virtue of an entity that is inherently necessary: God. God has willed our world into existence; being free, he could have willed a different world, or ten million of them.

Avicenna goes further by insisting that our own conception of the world is similarly one of many possible conceptions. There is nothing inherently true about our epistemological system or logic. The human intellect, with all its seemingly immutable rules, is in truth a product of an external agency, namely the human will. Our knowledge is a construct of the will.

The commonsensical question naturally arises: If the world is one of many possible worlds, and our knowledge of it is one of many possible systems of knowledge, how is it that our system of knowledge fits the world hand in glove? Doesn't Avicenna's position contradict our experience, and lead to utter relativism?

Avicenna's answer to this puzzle is simply God's love and grace. Our knowledge of the world (one construct among many possible alternatives) corresponds with the world (one reality among many possible alternatives) by the grace of God.

But what does this "correspondence" consist of? It is here that the "will" takes center stage. While it is true that our world is one of an infinity of possible worlds, and our mental construct is also one of many possible constructs, knowledge in fact corresponds to reality because both are the best possible choices. Our world is the best possible, and our construct of it is the best possible because of the will. What God wills is the best of all possible physical worlds, and what human beings will as an epistemic construct is the best of all possible systems of knowledge. How do we know this? We do so through faith in the moral will of God, and in the moral will of man. A "true" epistemological construct of the physical world is hence one that corresponds to God's moral system. A moral vision is hence hoisted above scientific knowledge of the world. Ultimately, science takes its cues from morality and not the other way around, as logical positivists would have it.

If Avicenna wasn't taken up into mainstream Islamic tradition it was because he put his finger on a dangerous truth, and no amount of clerical *fatwas* can erase the fact that Islamic thought revealed man's radical metaphysical freedom long before Spinoza, Leibniz, or Hegel woke up the Christian West from its cumbersome Aristotelian dogmatism.

Avicenna's original ideas, easily glossed over by a superficial reading of his main work, have profound implications not only in philosophy but also in politics. For example, his rejection of inherent identities leads to a theory of identity as a dynamic function of the will, whether that will be the identity of the self or of the nation. Far from being a priori objects set in place by some natural or supernatural Prime Mover, we are responsible for our own identities and actions. The self and the nation come about as acts of conventions and personal choice. From this it follows that we can use our will to change facts and situations that may appear fatalistically predetermined. All we need is faith, love, and a moral vision.

It wasn't a coincidence that I was concluding my sojourn in America with Avicenna's moral theory of the will—the impressions I had formed at Monticello were still with me. More than anything else I experienced in America, Jefferson's home and university symbolized for me a special kind of will. It wasn't just the will to political independence that impressed me—even the most brutal political campaigns speak of independence. What stirred my imagination—and still does, especially after all the intervening years of violence and disappointment in my homeland—

were the moral assumptions at work behind the American Constitution. With all his failings and contradictions, Jefferson believed in the dignity of the moral conscience, and that human freedom was a good in itself, not needing the sanction of tradition or religious authority. A revolution must have at its core a belief in the moral integrity of the individual; otherwise it will inevitably degenerate into despotism.

This was an important intellectual breakthrough as I was preparing for my return to Palestine.

Chapter Ten

The Lemon Tree Café

IN 1978, I was approaching the age of thirty. I'd been away from Jerusalem for the last twelve years, and I wanted to go home. You could say I felt the urge to be in my own country the way an American does to be in his, free to wander among familiar sights, to watch the native birds, and to educate my son in an Arab milieu. Intellectually, who wouldn't have preferred the life of a scholar at a major university in the West? But I felt a duty to help educate Palestinians who couldn't go abroad. As long as the Palestinians were struggling for their freedom, my personal priorities came second. Once the problem got solved, I could follow more individual ambitions. That's the way Father had raised me to think.

This was also the reason that when Birzeit University in the West Bank offered both Lucy and me jobs, we accepted with alacrity. We were hired to teach in a cultural studies program in the Great Books tradition. An American-educated Palestinian philosopher ran the program, whose initial inspiration came from Hugh Harcourt, a professor at the American University of Beirut whose scholarship and dedication were an inspiration to us all.

My auspicious prognosis of the Palestinian-Israeli conflict—that a gradual and organic process would lead to a single Arab-Jewish state— led me to take up a suggestion made by my friend Guy Stroumsa, who had returned to Jerusalem the same time I had, to teach a course on Islamic philosophy at the Hebrew University.

Having worked on polyglot thinkers such as Avicenna, who easily bounced around the world picking up knowledge wherever they could find it, I relished the prospect of returning to a land of contrasts. I pictured Israel-Palestine (I jokingly dubbed it "Palest-El"), with its population of Muslims, Jews, and Christians, with its invigorating clash of opposites, as an ideal place to engage in the sort of open dialogue that had frequently churned up renaissances in culture in the past. And as a teacher at both an Arab and a Jewish university, I could rattle my students' smug certainties just as mine had once been shaken up. Like small ticking bombs set to go off, students—taught the secrets of self-thought, self-will, and self-creation—could help forge the Jewish-Arab state of my dreams.

"Fat chance," said Mother when I shared with her my vision, her Chesterfield cigarette lightly balanced on a crystal ashtray.

Lucy and I arrived in late summer to give ourselves time to settle in, living with my parents while scouting for a place of our own. Father, now sixty-five, was as much on the go as ever, traveling widely and speaking his mind. His was becoming a favorite address for Israeli and foreign officials seeking to figure out what Palestinians were thinking. It was the Camp David Accords that really put him back in the spotlight. In September 1978, Carter, Begin, and Sadat spent thirteen days in the hardwood forests of Maryland. The breakthrough in their talks gave the Sinai back to the Egyptians, while the Israelis got a peace treaty with the leading Arab state. What this meant for us was less clear.

The agreements hammered out by Carter, Begin, and Sadat raised expectations that serious talks between Israelis and Palestinians were imminent, and people assumed that in such a scenario, Father would be a key figure. Rumors circulated that Shimon Peres had given him a note to pass on to King Hussein regarding the "Jordanian option," namely that Jordan and the West Bank should be rejoined into a federation.

My father denied the rumor, and even if Peres had given him such a note, he probably wouldn't have delivered it. As I mention earlier, Father was a staunch pan-Arabist who believed in toeing the Arab line. The Arabs had designated the PLO as the "sole and legitimate representative of the Palestinian people" and my father, holding his nose, had gone along.

In an article he published in an Israeli paper at the time, he writes, "I think Israel should be the first to recognize the P.L.O., because you are the strong ones and have all the cards in your hands. If you will sit together with the P.L.O. for negotiations, this will automatically create mutuality, which will mean that the P.L.O. recognizes Israel's right to exist . . . Once and for all you must eliminate this complex of fear of the Palestinian state . . . I really believe that you could live peacefully with them in mutual cooperation, side by side."[1]

A far bigger fear lurking in the background during the after-dinner family salons was the promise of Palestinian autonomy in the West Bank and Gaza under the terms of Camp David. "In order to provide full autonomy to the inhabitants," ran the text, "under these arrangements the Israeli military government and its civilian administration will be withdrawn as soon as a self-governing authority has been freely elected by the inhabitants of these areas to replace the existing military government."

Most Arab commentators assailed Sadat for selling us down the river and then mocking us with empty promises of "autonomy" and local elections in place of sovereignty. Sounds being made by the Israelis only strengthened this impression. When a journalist asked Begin if he was prepared to negotiate on the future of the Occupied Territories, he snapped, "What occupied territories? If you mean Judea, Samaria and the Gaza Strip, they are liberated territories. They are part, an integral part, of the Land of Israel."[2]

The consensus at the Nusseibeh family salon was that talk of autonomy and nondeployment was woefully short on detail. Nowhere did the agreement mention a full Israeli withdrawal or possible sanctions if they refused. Sadat's deal had ensured withdrawal from Sinai, but autonomy only under Israel's rule for the Palestinians. The rest was left up to chance. The "redeployment" was to be to "specified security locations." Where were these locations? Was this up to the whim of the Israelis? Only after a five-year transitional period would the question of borders and a final status be raised. Who would guarantee that the Israelis wouldn't use that time to create irreversible realities on the ground? Most important, what was to happen to East Jerusalem?

Father dismissed the plan as patronizing and vague. In the same interview, he criticized it because "it includes no real element that will solve the basic problem: the right to self-determination for the Palestinians . . . It tends to freeze the process of giving self-determination to the Palestinians for many years to come . . . Are we children? Are we politically cripples? Why does Israel think that we are unable to manage our life on our own on all levels and that we need a guardian?" In a front-page article in the mass-circulation daily *Al-Quds*, Father writes in the spirit of Woodrow Wilson that it is basic justice for a people to be free to exercise their sovereignty, an aspect of which is the full control over their land. Autonomy as offered by Israel ran roughshod over these rights. (Moshe Dayan admitted as much when he stated, "If the Egyptians understood Israel's real intentions on this matter they would not sign the peace treaty."[3])

Mother contemptuously ignored Israeli plans and promises. She had by now known too many politicians in her life, Jewish and Arab, and had come to the understandable conclusion that people with a sense of decency avoided most of them like the plague. As always a person more of actions than of words, around this time she started a school for girls whose families couldn't afford their education, called the Young Women's Muslim Society. The school started with seventy pupils, and over the years has grown to more than a thousand.

Lucy, Jamal, and I soon moved to an apartment owned by an uncle of mine, around the corner from my parents' house. It was there that Lucy gave birth to our second son, Absal. An omen for the kind of strong-headed boy we had on our hands occurred just after his birth. Smiling happily at the successful delivery, our doctor, a kindly man and old friend of the family, held Absal up by his feet. Absal responded to the doctor's good work by peeing directly in his face. Absal was destined to be a defiant child.

Soon afterward we moved into the snarled lanes of the Old City. We would have rented a place close to where Mohammed hitched his legendary al-Burak, if it hadn't been turned into a parade ground. The next best choice placed us in the center of two mystical traditions. Our new home, which had once upon a time belonged to a wise Sufi sage, was on the Via Dolorosa, less than a hundred meters from the Antonia fortress where Jesus was brought to trial before Pontius Pilate. We were now straddled between the fortress and the Ecce Homo Arch, the second Station of the Cross, where Pilate, pointing to Jesus as he came out from the fortress, exclaimed, "Behold the man" to the roaring crowds. (*Ecce Homo* also happens to be the title of my favorite book by Nietzsche.)

Our new home was part of the Muslim quarter, where for centuries pilgrims from Avicenna's hometown of Bukhara stayed when they came to Jerusalem to pray at the *haram* where the Dome of the Rock sits. The Sufi's empty bedroom, an extension of our apartment, sits on the top of a Roman-built arch.

From its place buried in a box of my old papers, the unfinished fairy tale had somehow worked its magic, because Lucy and Jerusalem were a perfect match. (The magical donkey in the story transported her to the very spot, to the inch, where we now lived.)

Installed as a resident for the first time, Lucy was enchanted by a place that retained much of its Oriental charm. Camels still grazed in empty lots, peasants dressed as they had done for centuries, and the old stone buildings were redolent of distant epochs. Our main sitting room, which had once served as an Islamic court, had a high, wooden ornamental ceiling. Next to the courtyard at the back of our house was a medieval minaret, and next to that was one of the gates to the Noble Sanctuary. Sitting in our courtyard, we would look over a maze of domed houses to the Hill of Gethsemane to the east and the Hill of Evil Counsel to the west. This was where tradition says caliph Omar caught his first glimpse of the Holy City. In the evenings, Lucy and I liked to climb to the roof to catch a view that was just as grand: into the Noble Sanctuary compound, at the majestic Dome of the Rock.

Our third son was born in this house. Not surprisingly, given where we lived, he got the name al-Burak, after Mohammed's legendary steed.

Jerusalem equally worked its familiar charms on me. At times something as banal as walking down the street can transport you into a different realm. Just as Avicenna said, with a shift in perspective the concrete world, so immutably familiar, can become animated by the will, as if the inner and outer worlds, instead of being opposed to each other, join into one. That was how I felt strolling the streets of the Old City with my family. Places I had passed a thousand times as a boy took on a fresh tone and hue.

I adored the smells of cardamom, sage, and thyme in the souk, and the sight of old men in their Crusader-era cafés sucking up fumes from the burning coals set into their bubbling water pipes. It was here that rumors were hatched or spread. Occasionally Lucy and I caught a vaguely tantalizing taste of the old Jerusalem of oud players and poets.

We especially loved our house, whose meter-thick walls, at least in our imagination, were alive with intimations of whirling dervishes. One day, we even managed to bring the dervishes to life. In Muslim tradition, upon his return home from his *Haj*, his pilgrimage to Mecca, a pilgrim deserves some sort of festive reception. After my parents came back from theirs, Lucy and I decided to throw a party at our house. I managed to track down some Sufi sheikhs and dervishes, some of whom knew and loved Father.

On the appointed day, our home was full of Koran-reciting sheikhs, whirling dervishes, and the resounding echo of beating drums. Family members and guests packed into the courtyard, and the melodious sound of religious songs traveled along the Via Dolorosa and the surrounding alleys. No one enjoyed it more than Jamal. He ran around in the midst of dance and song as if in religious ecstasy, and then leapt into the lap of his grandfather, who for the first time in his life learned how to hold a child.

Almost immediately after moving in we decided to open up a café and art gallery in an abandoned building next door belonging to my uncle. We called it the Lemon Tree Café, after the lemon tree growing in its inner courtyard.

We had a European model in mind. It was to be a café and hostel where backpackers could mingle with the young Palestinian intelligentsia. The hope was that some of the free-spirited free-thinking of the Europeans would rub off on our youth, and that the Israelis and Europeans would also get to know one another.

Bir zeit in Arabic means "container or well of olive oil," which makes sense because the Greek Orthodox village of Birzeit (a few miles from Jerusalem in the West Bank) has lived off its olives for millennia. The Nasir family, a local Christian clan, founded a school for local girls during the British Mandate. Under the Jordanians the school evolved into a junior college whose graduates typically continued on to the American University of Beirut. After the Six-Day War, Palestinians could no longer easily sally back and forth to Lebanon, which led the directors of the junior college to think about turning it into a full-fledged four-year liberal arts school.

The university first got going in 1972. Musa Nasir, the founder, had a résumé similar to my father's: he had been a governor during the British period, and under the Jordanians served the king as his foreign minister. When Nasir died, his son Hanna, a physicist by training who had been educated at Purdue University, returned from the United States to become the school's president. As university president, Hanna Nasir fostered a devoted faculty with a strong commitment to teaching and to the development and future of the Palestinian people. His vision, shared by many members of the faculty, was to create the Palestinian version of the American University of Beirut.

President Nasir was engaged and liberal, giving weekly lectures to faculty and students on democracy, dialogue, and the significance of protecting people's rights to their opinions, however unpalatable. But his notion of a renaissance of a free Palestinian people put him on a collision course with the military governor—which was no surprise given the attitude of one of Israel's chief consultants for Arab education, who is quoted as saying, "It is good for us if the Arabs are hewers of wood and carriers of water." The first closure at Birzeit took place in 1973, a year after it opened. The following year the Israelis expelled Dr. Nasir from the country. Thinking the exile would be only temporary (it would last twenty years), no one was named as his replacement, and the university was led by its vice president, Gabi Baramki.

Most mornings, Lucy and I drove to Birzeit together. Between lessons we often wandered through the mesmerizing countryside. We took in the scents of the flowering plants, the feel of the earth in isolated wadis, and the sight of old men plowing fields with mules. Like a siren song, the ringing of the old church bell in the village told us it was time to head back to class.

My other walking partner was Bashir, the boyhood friend with whom I once wandered Jerusalem and discussed Russell and who was now a professor of chemistry. He and I took up our old habit of peripatetic musings about the unanswerable enigmas of metaphysics. The intervening years hadn't changed our questions, only our vocabulary. We joined hands now in writing a paper on subatomic particles and matter's indeterminacy.

There were a number of faculty members at the university who would over time assume important national positions. The best known is perhaps Hanan Ashrawi, a Christian who got her Ph.D. in medieval literature from Thomas Jefferson's University of Virginia and later became official spokesperson for the Madrid Negotiating Team. A number of other Birzeit colleagues would later work with me in politics. During the intifada in the late eighties, Israeli interrogators would torture two of them, Sameer Shehadeh and Izzat Ghazzawi, in an effort to get them to cough up information on my clandestine activities.

One of the most eccentric characters (our fates would later be fatally linked) was an American Protestant missionary, Dr. Albert Glock, an archaeologist. Dr. Glock grew up in a strict German American midwestern home and within a fundamentalist sect that maintained that the Christian Bible was the inerrant word of God, down to the last punctuation mark. At Birzeit he swapped a religious crusade for Palestinian nationalism.

Dr. Glock realized long before we Palestinians did how ancient history was being used by the Israelis to cement their moral hold on the territories, and he made it his mission to preserve the Arab archaeological record before roots-seeking Israeli generals effaced it. He had in mind Moshe Dayan, who with the obsession of Captain Ahab had dug up the countryside searching for traces of ancient Jewish settlements. The military governor had done the same. A big swaggering man with thick arms, he had ignored the international ban on conducting digs in the Occupied Territories.

When asked by an Israeli newspaper reporter in 1979 about my experiences at the Hebrew University, I confessed that as an intellectual, I obviously preferred its first-world standards to those of Birzeit.

I didn't leave it at that. I unpacked my theory that living, thinking, and even struggling with the Israelis was actually a good thing for Palestinians. This went along with my hopeful prognosis of a future "Palest-El." Life was no bed of roses under the military regime, I pointed out with a chuckle, but neither was it as bad as it appeared from a distance. "In the U.S. or England, every new wave of arrests or every stone thrown makes it seem that the West Bank stands on the verge of an explosion. No doubt, there are problems, and some very serious ones. On the whole, however, one senses optimism everywhere."

Next came my point about why I had chosen to pursue my academic career in the West Bank rather than at an American or European university, where it would have made more sense. If the West Bank were returned to Jordan, I told the interviewer, "I wouldn't stick around even for a day. Nor will I stay a minute if the Palestinians get their state. But I will remain as long as we are under occupation."

"In this," the journalist summed up, I was "acting as the true son of his father." The title of the article was, appropriately, "The Son of Anwar Nusseibeh."

It was also in the spirit of my father that at Birzeit I did my best to keep education and politics separate. In politics, an untrained mind—Father liked to say in English—"is like a bull in a china shop." Trying to convince students that they first needed a solid education before pursuing their revolution was no easy matter. The students were on the whole more politically active than the faculty, though professors also tended to join one faction or the other. Of the politically active professors, most were associated with one or another of the leftist groups, such as the PFLP or one of the Marxist factions. Arafat's Fatah movement was small and ineffective, and was generally dismissed as overly conservative.

Among students, the situation was precisely the reverse. The strongest faction was Fatah, for it attracted poor students from refugee camps and the countryside. The second largest group was the emerging Islamists, and in a distant third place came the leftists and communists, attracting students from relatively well-to-do families. The more privileged the family, the farther left the politics.

It was standard practice for the factions, like fraternities in America, to woo new members, but when they came knocking on my door, I politely demurred by telling them that I needed time to think about it. I hoped they would get the hint and drop the issue. Socially, I got along with the leftists the best, whereas politically I still inclined in the direction of Fatah, as I had since my London days. My gut instinct was to maintain my independence for as long as I could.

This caution came in part from natural inclination, in part from witnessing the bare-knuckle workings of politics at the university. Soon after I arrived I was dragooned into a heresy trial. A professor, the American-educated political scientist Nafez Nazzal, had transgressed the national ethos that considered Sadat a traitor and the autonomy deal he had agreed to at Camp David a sellout by meeting with American officials at the American consulate to discuss the Camp David Accords. A faculty meeting was convened to take him to task for it. As I entered the hall, I saw Nafez standing on the stage, microphone in hand, absorbing rhetorical blows from all sides. He couldn't get a word in, so loud was the inquisitional clamor. "If I ever try to get my ideas across," I said to myself, "I'll have to figure out a different way of doing it." Professor Nafez, isolated and harried, served as a warning.

My focus was on teaching. Besides the cultural studies course, I worked with some other faculty and with Lucy to expand the course offerings in philosophy, until we succeeded in developing it into a minor concentration. One of my earliest contributions in this area was to introduce a badly needed introductory logic course.

Birzeit wasn't Oxford, and most of my students hadn't had the privilege of playing hooky at St. George's or dropping out of Rugby. Besides a smattering of students raised in well-off Jerusalem or Bethlehem families, most came from working-class families, the farmhand milieu, or refugee camps. In the classroom, I was determined to get my students to go to the ultimate root and cause of things rather than to skim the surface, which in my experience was what most political conversations tended to do. Besides, they didn't need me for their revolutionary politics; they were getting enough of it from their clubs and factions.

At first the students didn't know what to do with me. I stood in front of the class like all their other teachers, just without the customary tie, and with my uncombed hair. My socks often didn't match, which they could see because of the sandals on my feet, which also clashed with the image of the respectable schoolmaster. This put me in the category of the communists, the only other professors so slovenly dressed. Even more puzzling for them was the climate of intellectual confusion I intentionally or unintentionally fostered.

To be sure, in philosophy I tried to keep their minds firmly nestled in problems of logic, and in their cultural studies, my students read the prescribed syllabus of Great Books, from *Gilgamesh* to Albert Camus. But instead of lecturing to them about the meaning of the texts, I tried my hand at my don's method by steering clear of straight answers and easy facts. They must have thought I was just as lost and confused as they, if not more so. "Why do you believe what I just told you is true?" I said once, chewing out a student I had caught taking notes during one of my lectures. "How do you know it's worth writing down?"

Students were to think for themselves, without kowtowing to the opinions of their fathers or Muslim clerics or priests or professors like me. I wanted them to deconstruct their inherited mental horizons, to disassemble the myths they'd accepted wholesale, and reconstruct their thoughts so that they could discover their own identities and their own ways of thinking. My job as teacher wasn't to dish out precooked, easily digestible truths; it was to break the students' logic, the way a physician breaks a bone in order to reset it.

From the first day in the classroom I encountered a lot of bewildered students, and those who simply wished to collect data in order to pass their exams made a wide berth around my classes. But even with those who stayed, I was battling the effects of a badly constituted Palestinian educational system, which typically expected students to recite information, as if naked facts alone, in a sort of spontaneous generation, sufficed to prove a point. At most, students thus "educated" might be able to analyze past events; constructing scenarios for possible futures, however, was unheard of, and questioning established beliefs, even if only to understand them critically, carried with it a hint of heresy. Whether in religion or in politics, students were prepared only to imbibe received doctrines, memorize them, live by them, and defend them. Minds coming out of our high schools were either frozen or boiling hot. Almost never were they cool and balanced. And as I would later witness countless times during political demonstrations, they had a tendency to overheat and explode.

For the first few months I couldn't have been happier. At the Lemon Tree Café, Lucy and I organized concerts, discussions, and even self-published a couple of art books for some friends. The café was the only spot in the city, if not in the country, where young Palestinian and Israeli intellectuals could meet so freely. It attracted writers, musicians, European backpackers, and, alas, the occasional drug peddler. On occasion, some foreign visitors dropped by for a drink. One was the legendary Oxford philosopher of law H.L.A. Hart, an old friend of Lucy's father. (Later with the philosophers Isaiah Berlin and Peter Strawson, he published an open letter in the London *Times* protesting my imprisonment by the Israelis.) Hart came for a visit after climbing up the Mount of Temptation, outside Jericho.

One of the highlights from this period was a trip Lucy and I took to the Israeli town of Arad, in the desert hills overlooking the Dead Sea. We went there to visit the novelist Amos Oz for the first time. Along the lines of "know thy enemy" (and future countryman), since 1967 I had been soaking up Israeli fiction and poetry. With Amos, I read everything of his I could get my hands on, partly because of his genius and partly because my Israeli friends had always spoken very highly of him as a man of integrity and the conscience of the Israeli people. So I phoned him, and without hesitating he invited us to his modest, unassuming desert home.

Teaching at Birzeit had its challenges. Whenever I felt I was at the point of despondency at students fidgeting in the chairs while discussing al-Farabi or coming up with some outlandish comment on Kant, I always had the Hebrew University. Compared to Birzeit's two thousand students and Spartan conditions, the Hebrew University was in every arena—the libraries, the facilities, and the level of academic distinction—a first-rate research university.

Once a week I made my way to the main campus. The library there was large and the students less agitated—older after their two-year army service—and more demanding academically. Besides Guy and Sarah Stroumsa, Avishai Margalit was on the faculty. More important for me academically, the university had excellent scholars in the field of Islamic philosophy and thought. Guy introduced me to perhaps the world's best: the eminent scholar and linguist Shlomo Pines. With Guy and Lucy and a handful of others, I attended his biweekly seminar, in which we explored various translations and readings of Plato's *Laws*.

Within a year, my optimism for the natural evolution of "Palest-El" started to crumble. It was becoming unmistakably clear to me that the nature of the Israeli occupation would systematically and intentionally undermine any kind of natural, peaceful, evolutionary development.

This was a major change for me, and it started with a dose of humility. Probably the biggest lesson I learned my first year back was to respect deeply the feelings and traditions of my people, a people I barely knew after so many years abroad. Finally, in a sadly delayed reaction, my parents' immense admiration for the "man on the street" finally started to take hold in me.

In some respects I knew less about Palestine than my colleague Dr. Glock. To be sure, I could have written a tome thicker than my dissertation on the inner lives of Jerusalem patricians. Where Dr. Glock had an advantage over me was in his knowledge of traditional village life.

I quickly developed close ties and friendships with some of my students, who were for me a window onto the life beyond the narrow confines of urban Jerusalem. Whether in discussions with them in the cafés or at their village homes, where Lucy and I were often invited for a meal, I got a glimpse of pristine, unspoiled village kindness, tradition, and wisdom. Hospitable, dignified, and with unlimited capacity to offer respect and affection, they contrasted sharply with the city's überbourgeoisie, politicians, businessmen, and evolving sector of professionals and academics. It was from among the ranks of villagers and the denizens of camps that young men and women would later step forward to defy tanks and Uzis, and end up wounded, killed, imprisoned, and tortured. Such people I had—and have—as much to learn from as to teach.

One of the most important tutorials for me in the village life of Palestinians took place by way of shame. I was driving to Birzeit one morning, running late as always, hair disheveled, socks mismatched, when an older woman, clad in her local peasant clothes, suddenly jumped in front of the car to catch a bus that had just stopped on the other side of the street. I wasn't driving very fast, but in spite of throwing on the brakes, I hit her. She fell to the street with a thud.

Getting out of the car to see what had happened to her, I saw that she had luckily sprung back on her feet again. I tried to ask her how badly she was hurt, and whether she needed to be taken to a hospital. "I'm fine," she kept saying, pulling herself away from me. She still wanted to catch the bus, and began a quick dash across the street. I managed to give her my card before she disappeared.

I didn't hear from her and soon forgot all about it.

Three months later, Father returned from a trip abroad. He rang me up and asked to see me. Loosely translated, the first words he came out with were "What the devil have you been up to?"

I stuttered out something, because I didn't know what he was talking about. "What happened with this old woman?" he wanted to know. Someone from her family had contacted him.

It finally dawned on me what he was referring to. I explained that the accident wasn't my fault, that the woman hadn't been hurt, and that I had given her all my contact information. Father listened, nodded as if he understood, and finally said—again loosely translated—"This time you've really blown it."

I stood there speechless. Disappointing Father had always been my greatest dread.

"You failed to do the main thing," he went on. "By not apologizing, you impugned the honor of their family and ours."

He told me a story to illustrate the point. During World War II, Fakhri al Nashashibi, a prominent Jerusalem patrician, was murdered in Baghdad. An Arab news source accused Ahmad Nusseibeh, my father's distant cousin, of the murder. Nusseibeh was a "henchman of the mufti," said the report, and a member of a clan "long addicted to crime." Without a shred of evidence against him, the police in Baghdad arrested the cousin forthwith and threw him into a dungeon.

No one believed the newspaper report, and, anyway, the Nusseibeh family was related to the Nashashibis by marriage and the two families were on the best of terms. Nevertheless, Father went with Uncle Hassan and their cousin Ali to visit the Nashashibis on the evening following Fakhri's burial. Whether their distant relative Ahmad was guilty or not was irrelevant: the family had to honor the family of the victim.

My father at the time was like me: young and "modern," and he had to bite his lip to keep from laughing when he saw the reactions of the young Nashashibis who ushered them into the house. Here were young people like him, all living in the middle of the twentieth century, yet they were being controlled by observances that logically should have been extinct long ago. He managed to contain his laughter, though, and by paying his respects to their family, prevented an act of revenge against his.

Father told me this tale just to make sure I understood the seriousness of *Sulha*, our tribal system of justice. In Palestinian tradition, the individual isn't really an individual. If you steal something, or are even accused of doing so, you and your entire tribe become culpable. They are responsible for you. The wronged family or tribe has the right of revenge against any member of your tribe or family. What prevents revenge and bloodshed is a form of conflict resolution. The two sides set up a *Sulha*. Within a three-day period, intermediaries will go to the family of the injured party to set up a meeting.

If someone gets run over and killed, the person who drove the car (or someone on his behalf), guilty or not, must go with his family to the family of the victim to apologize and to offer compensation. The father of the victim may say, "We want fifty million dollars, even though there is no price for my son's life." Once the driver's family accepts the terms, the victim's father starts dropping the price. "For the sake of Allah, I'm prepared to give up on ten million"; "for the sake of Mohammed another ten," and so on until a reasonable price, or no price at all, is reached. *Sulha* is less about money than about honor.

In my case, we took a big convoy of one hundred family members to the old woman's village. The entire village showed up for the ceremony.

In great solemnity, we gave our apologies and offered compensation. Just as Father had predicted, the other family accepted our show of respect, and waved off the compensation. We had done our duty, and they showed us respect by refusing to take anything.

Many years later, addressing an Israeli audience, I repeated this story. It doesn't matter whether you set out premeditatedly to cause the Palestinian refugee tragedy, I told them, the tragedy did occur, even as an indirect consequence of your actions. In our tradition, you have to own up to this. You have to come and offer an apology. Only this way will Palestinians feel that their dignity has been recognized, and be able to forgive. But by denying all responsibility, besides being historically absurd to the point of craziness, you will guarantee eternal antagonism— a never-ending search for revenge.

This lesson of respecting the feelings of my own people also led me to a better understanding of what was happening right at my back door, in the Old City of Jerusalem. Once I began to observe and listen to the so-called "commoners," I realized that under the surface people were growing desperate. The occupation was strangling them.

My moving into the Old City was never a popular idea with my family. Had I been a bachelor, they would have dismissed it as a whimsical attachment to the landscape of my childhood. But to drag my blond English wife and my sons into those dodgy streets was sheer madness.

The Jewish Quarter, of course, was booming. Over the years it had been greatly expanded in size, overflowing well beyond its historic borders. More than six thousand Arabs had been driven out of their homes, and Israeli law had made sure they wouldn't go back. An enduring stain on a generally admirable institution, a 1974 Israeli Supreme Court ruling upheld a rule forbidding Arabs from living in the quarter.

By contrast, the decay of the Arab city's social fabric was astounding. The drug dealers around the corner from the Lemon Tree were signs that social rot had entered the life of the city, sapping it of its old strength.

Drug culture and the crime that comes with it had been unknown in the city I lived in as a boy. As had been the rats now scurrying in and out of tipped-over municipal garbage cans, which were almost never emptied.

Intentional neglect wasn't limited to the Old City. There were plenty of signs of decline outside the walls. My uncles' half-built hotel in the heart of East Jerusalem was still a concrete eyesore, mainly because the Israeli municipal authorities had thrown up bureaucratic obstacles to prevent its completion.

Arabs complained to Mayor Teddy Kollek, who just pointed his finger back at them, blaming them for much of the downfall of the city. And he had a point. I was quick to note that Palestinian leaders barely did a thing to defend their rights in the Old City or to promote its development. By boycotting municipal elections, they willfully relinquished the most potent democratic weapon available to them for pushing economic and social development.

But this didn't make Kollek's accusation any less of a self-serving excuse. It didn't take a Machiavellian genius to figure out the political dimension of the unraveling of the city's elaborate tapestry. From Omar all the way to the Herod's Gate Committee, the Old City has been a natural political and cultural center for the Palestinians. You see this in our literature, our symbols, and our language, in the city's architecture, its climate, its cyclical ups and downs, and in the dusty hills. All of these formed us as a people.

My first clue that deliberate Israeli policies were at work behind the collapse came from the local chatter in the cafés I was now frequenting. In 1967 the Israeli soldiers patrolling the streets were met with benign or even welcoming indifference. Now the old men puffing away on their pipes despised the Jewish occupiers far more than they ever had the Jordanians. It was as if the common people, having given the Israelis the benefit of the doubt, were now drawing other conclusions: they were up to no good.

This universal hostility had many sources, some as simple as the tipped-over garbage cans or the endless hassles with permits. A bigger source was the policy of building Jewish neighborhoods around the Old City and hence cutting it off from its hinterland. What was once a seamless web of city and villages was becoming chopped up and fragmented.

After 1967, Israel used a British Mandate land ordinance to expropriate agricultural land around East Jerusalem. With new expanded borders, it used a range of planning and zoning laws to build Jewish neighborhoods, the aim being to bring as many Israelis into East Jerusalem as possible. The creation of Ramat Eshkol (1968), Ramot (1968), East Talpiot (1970), Neve Ya²akov (1972), and Gilo (1973) led to a demographic shift in the city.

This, combined with the fact that it was nearly impossible for Arabs to get building permits, led me to conclude that the long-term Israeli plan was to degrade Arab Jerusalem into a ghetto of a greater Jewish city. Lacing our part of town with so many Israeli institutions dedicated to repressing Palestinian nationalism, notably the ministries of interior and the police, was engineered to keep the population docile. Meanwhile, Palestinian institutions and thus the financial, social, and political elite running them, were driven out and kept out, partly through diktats such as the dismissal of the municipal council in 1967, and partly through intentional neglect. I felt as if I was watching a slow act of homicide, the killing of a city that constituted the soul of my family and of my people.

Shuttling back and forth between the first world on the main Hebrew University campus and the third world at Birzeit was becoming a difficult balancing act. It had been easy when I believed that a natural process was going to lift the latter to the level of the former. The minute I concluded this wasn't happening, it got much harder. Doubts soon led to my resignation from the Hebrew University.

There had been a lot of grumbling at Birzeit regarding my job at the Israeli university. The administration said I had to choose between "them" and "us." At first I ignored their objections as just more of the same boycott thinking that had long outlived its usefulness. I couldn't honestly teach my students not to obey the village elders blindly if I buckled under such pressure.

Still, in the end, I quit. I felt ineffective at the Hebrew University, as if my words had no real influence there. It came to me one day at a checkpoint, after an eighteen-year-old soldier pushed his gun through my car window demanding I produce my ID. *This soldier could be one of my students,* I thought. I imagined a highly intelligent student eagerly debating the intellectual power and elegance of Islamic philosophy one day, and the next day going off to do military service in the territories and treating my people—or me—like animals. It was a contradiction I found impossible to bear.

Chapter Eleven

The Salon

HOWEVER ODD IT MAY SOUND, in 1980, at the age of thirty-one, it finally began to dawn on me that my fairy-tale childhood world had been reduced to ruins, that the city I had been raised to love was gone forever. Maybe the reason it took me so long was due to my natural disinclination toward politics, coupled with the social privilege that, like the young Buddha, had shielded me from the truth of the violent world I had returned to.

There are moments in life when frustration or anger gets the better of you. I had always tried to look beyond the soldier's khaki to see another human just like me. But having that gun pushed through my car window that day, all I could see was a churlish soldier standing on his side of the checkpoint facing me, an Arab under occupation.

My decision to stop teaching at the Hebrew University was also an admission that my previous assumptions had been dead wrong. Allowing evolution to take its course was bringing the opposite of justice and equality. Far from bringing the sides closer together, occupation was turning Palestinians into a permanent underclass of workers whose land, resources, and basic rights were being systematically violated and stripped away by a litany of regulations.

What I noticed was a strange process. On the one hand, the country was becoming unified, just as I had expected. Following the conquest of the West Bank, the Israeli plan was to integrate the new territories into the Israeli economy; and sure enough, after just a few years of occupation, Israelis were employing half of all Palestinians. Palestinians were relatively free to travel across the old Green Line, and on weekends, hordes of Israelis descended on Arab villages for hummus and fresh vegetables. The peoples seemed to be merging.

At the same time, an invisible no-man's-land was being created, this one by ideology and psychology rather than by concrete and barbed wire. The Israelis expected the Palestinians, paycheck in pocket, to forget about the nonsense of national identity. As a rule, Israelis didn't deny that there had been Arabs in their Land of Israel when they got off the boat from Kiev; we just were not a people with the same national rights to territory and independence that the Jews claimed for themselves. In Golda Meir's unforgettable words, "It was not as though there was a Palestinian people in Palestine considering itself as a Palestinian people and we came and threw them out and took their country away from them. They did not exist."[1]

This may help explain much of what the Israelis were doing to us, and why, for example, they began to build settlements in East Jerusalem without bothering to consult us. The Vienna-born mayor of Jerusalem, Teddy Kollek, was not a bad man; from what I gathered during his chats with Father, he was a decent cigar-smoking fellow with a good sense of humor and without any of the overweening arrogance displayed by so many Israeli generals and traffic police. Yet, decent though he was, his actions trampled upon our history in ways the Turks had never dreamt of. When he lobbied his government to build the neighborhoods Ramat Eshkol, Neve Yaʾakov, and Gilo, he didn't set out to harm our national rights. He simply didn't factor them into his plans. Building Jewish neighborhoods in East Jerusalem was in his eyes a matter of supreme national importance and a real estate deal that had brought construction jobs to an otherwise disorderly aggregation of Arab individuals who happened by historical accident to find themselves in the City of David. Giving these Arabs work and an income was doing them a favor, Kollek thought. Why, it was the chance of a lifetime for them to live in a fast-growing modern metropolis. He couldn't understand why we would make a fuss about it.

What the mayor couldn't appreciate was how the laborers, merchants, and peasants he thought were benefiting from his plans shared a collective identity no less human and no less deserving of recognition—and no less riled when it was spat upon—than Kollek's own Jewish Israeli identity.

In the classroom and Old City cafés, I became cognizant of what might be called a bad case of national schizophrenia. While at one level economic and administrative integration between Israel and Palestine was proceeding apace, throwing off the impression that all was well, at a more fundamental level a separatist Palestinian nationalist identity was growing stronger. Arabs were becoming self-consciously "Palestinian." The more the Arab "body" became immersed in the Israeli system, the more the Palestinian "soul" struggled to transcend it.

I was pondering all these shifts and dialectical conundrums in my mind one day when it hit me like a bolt from heaven: the solution to our conflict with Israel was not more economic integration or a better elementary curriculum, or nicer military governors, or a more humane form of torture. Nor was it to make bad Israelis better. The occupation simply had to end—lock, stock, and barrel.

In 1980 two years had passed since my return to Jerusalem. At Birzeit I still passed my time between classes either strolling dreamily through the nearby countryside or joining students in the heated discussions in the university cafeteria, or at one of the cafés in the village. Otherwise, I sat in my office correcting papers, working on my book on logic, or trying to write articles on Avicenna.

Meanwhile, the stream of politicians and journalists going in and out of my parents' house continued uninterrupted. Autonomy talks went nowhere, and probably were never intended to do so. (Begin told the Knesset, "We do not even dream of turning the territories over to the PLO, . . . history's meanest murder organization except for the armed Nazi organization."[2]) Far from giving up control in East Jerusalem, the Israelis did their best to expand it, and into every area.

The East Jerusalem District Electricity Company, the largest employer of Palestinians in the area, was facing a crisis. The company had a long-term concession from British Mandate times to provide electricity to the entire Jerusalem district stretching south to Hebron, north to Nablus, and east to Jericho and the Jordan River. All the municipalities served by the company had representatives on the board of directors, and the mayor of Bethlehem, Elias Freij, was the chairman.

The crisis broke out between the company's workers and Mayor Freij. Ostensibly, the cause was financial, as the company, unable to provide its own power generation, had to rely more and more on Israel's government-run power company. This increased the company's debts, and hence threatened the long-term job security of its employees. More important, it gave Israel greater say in the affairs of the company—especially as the company's concession was coming to an end. It was uncertain whether Israel would renew it, or if, as an occupying power, it had the right under international law to make the relevant decision in the first place.

To make matters worse, Israel refused to allow the company to provide power to the areas in which Israel was now busy building settlements. Given the electric company's growing debts, it made no financial sense—went the Israeli argument—for the company to provide the settlements with electricity. Israel's concern, needless to say, wasn't the financial well-being of the company but the security of the settlements. If Arabs controlled the electricity, they could, of course, shut it off at will.

In our part of the world anything can be political. A misplaced stop sign can spawn a hundred rumors. In this case, a power company became the impetus for the first full-blown nationalist protest movement. The company's Arab workers didn't want anything to do with Mayor Freij, whom they suspected was too close to the Israelis.

This was the first time the PLO, through Arafat's second in command, Abu Jihad, officially sought my father's help. Would he accept becoming chairman of the board and CEO of the company? Father agreed, and the workers threw their support behind him. Before he could take up the post, however, there was a technicality to surmount. To be a board member he had to own shares in the company. A veteran friend from the Herod's Gate Committee stepped in and transferred the necessary shares to Father's name.

Father's superhuman defense of the company—there's no better word for it—was to be his final battle, for it was at that time he was diagnosed with thyroid cancer. Exhibiting a stoic equanimity in the face of this slow-working disease, he threw himself into a dozen legal, financial, administrative, and political battles to save the company from a concerted Israeli attempt to undermine it.

One day Father got a call from someone in the company who nervously reported that a large contingent of Israeli police had raided the main offices and kicked out the employees and were now rummaging through the file cabinets. Father drove to the headquarters at once. As if he were the Israeli prime minister, he barked out orders to the police that they should evacuate the building without delay. Mysteriously, the police followed his orders, and without a murmur of dissent. The company employees stood around with dropped jaws.

Such was the mysterious inner strength my father was able to tap, and the respect he commanded, that when Israel's minister of energy, Moshe Shahal, his nemesis in the legal tussle over the company, visited him as he lay dying, I detected a striking deference. Shahal, representing youth and power, spoke to his one-legged, bed-ridden opponent with a demure air. It was for me as if the roles had been reversed, and it was Shahal, not my father, who had found himself in the weaker position.

In the summer of 1980 a main topic at the family evening salon, besides the situation at the electric company, was assassination attempts against some of the West Bank mayors. Perhaps irrationally, Father felt partly responsible. Already in 1967 he was urging Israeli leaders to allow for municipal elections, and Moshe Dayan finally permitted elections in 1976, for the first time since the occupation began.

It is hard to say what the Israelis were expecting, but what they got were nationalist mayors in all the major West Bank towns and cities. All but two were associated, directly or indirectly, with one or another of the PLO factions. Some of the mayors, together with other figures associated with the PLO, formed what was called the National Guidance Committee.

This was ironic, because Fatah still regarded itself foremost as a clandestine military organization, and as such was slow to take advantage of the political opportunity afforded by the elections. It was the Communist Party, historically not an armed military movement, that came to control the NGC.

Not long after the NGC got off the ground, the Israelis tried to crush it. In 1979 the authorities detained Bassam Shaka'a, the popular pro-Syrian mayor of Nablus, for "supporting terrorism." In May 1980 the mayors of Hebron and Halhoul, moderates as well, were picked up and deposited over the border. A few months later, Military Order 830 put a final end to Palestinian local democracy by doing away with the elections of municipal councils. Seven members of the NGC, including two mayors, were rounded up and tossed into jail.

They were lucky to be behind bars, because members of a Jewish messianic underground group with ties to the settler movement Gush Emunim, the "Block of the Faithful," tried to finish off those NGC leaders who weren't. Shaka'a, who had just been released, lost both legs in a bomb attack; the mayor of Ramallah lost his left foot.

The forcible sidelining of the National Guidance Committee set into motion deep changes in Palestinian political life, even if the Israelis didn't yet realize it. The old class of nobles and dignitaries, along with traditional tribal and clan leaders, were on their way out, replaced by military and civic networks organized by young activists throughout the West Bank and Gaza.

Another subject of endless salon discussion was the settler movement, and the threat this represented to any hope for a future Israeli withdrawal. Israel's Labor Party had built the first settlements after the Yom Kippur War to counter another sneak attack. If Kollek spearheaded the East Jerusalem settlements, it was now Shimon Peres who was serving as patron for the West Bank settlement of Beit El, built on the expropriated land of the Palestinian village of Beitin. The wheel was set in motion.

But it was the Likud Party, in the shadow of Camp David, that launched the construction of the largest settlement blocks. Prime Minister Begin believed that the captured territories were integral parts of Israel because they were the God-given Holy Land, the birthplace of the Jewish people. He was willing to grant limited autonomy for Arabs living there, just not national rights. National rights implied control over a territory, and this was what he was determined to deny us.

Settlements started sprouting up everywhere. Shilo, Neveh Tzuf, Mitzpeh Yericho, Shavei Shomron, Dotan, Tekoa, and a number of other settlements all share the same basic storyline: one morning you'd spy a caravan perched on a hill, the next there would be two or three. Before you knew it, like dividing cells in a Petri dish, caravans covered the entire hillside.

When I was a boy, Jerusalem was the nerve center of Palestinian political and cultural life, and the debates and meetings raging in my father's salon gave one a feeling of what was happening in the entire country. As the occupation put down deeper and deeper roots, the Jerusalem elite's traditional leadership role became emptier and emptier, until it was little more than hollow pretension. The political battles shifted over to the West Bank and Gaza villages and cities that now had to deal with decisions made by occupation authorities. Whatever the occupation touched produced a steady stream of new grievances, new stories, new heroes, new leaders, new experiences, a new reality.

It was from these far-flung battlefields that students were beginning to arrive at Birzeit. The university now had thousands instead of hundreds of students, and the cozy, intimate village setting couldn't facilitate the booming growth. In 1980 the university started moving locations to modern buildings in a new nearby campus. The new campus, largely financed by wealthy Palestinians living in the Gulf, was on a hillside. Growth meant more students, lower academic standards, and a growing demand to shift over to Arabic rather than English as the main language of instruction.

I was still learning more than I was teaching. On most afternoons my office—or, better, my "salon"—was a hummus restaurant in the village, where my students and I sat, talked, and chain-smoked. (I took to smoking Omars, the cheapest brand on the market, and the only cigarettes available to our political prisoners in Israeli jails.) As strange as it may sound, once I began to get to know my students I experienced a far greater intellectual intensity than I had known at Oxford or Harvard. Occupation made ideas as palpable as hunger or thirst or pain.

These salon and classroom conversations grew out of the quotidian reality of my students living in squalid camps and villages, and were then fertilized by the Great Books. At universities in the West, good students are meant to plow through a stack of material before they acquire the confidence to hazard their own take on a given subject. My students didn't feel they needed any authority other than their own experiences. They didn't need to read about what death was, or what rights were, or about freedom and identity and the difficulty of making choices. In every village, in every camp, in every town, almost every Palestinian was going through experiences just as profound as those to be found in the canon.

We would be discussing *Hamlet* in class when a student would come out with a puzzling comment. He would either have been recently released from an Israeli prison or have just come from a camp or a village where he had had a grueling encounter with the Israeli military. His comment, with this in the background, would cast a different light on the Danish prince's behavior.

One text we read in class was the Athenian historian Thucydides' account of an exchange between the Athenians and the Melians during the Peloponnesian War. We debated the relative merits of an aggressively expanding maritime power and a group of islanders wishing only to be left in peace. The islanders, as the weaker party, defended their position using moral arguments, divine right and the like. The Athenians retorted that the peaceful islanders had to wake up to the fact that the only laws of history were those of might, of power, of the stronger lording it over the weaker.

In a classroom at Harvard, Thucydides' account would have been part of a clever academic exercise, with no real relevance outside the classroom. To my students, Israel was Athens, Melos their village or camp. In their imaginations, the Israeli army officers who came to their village to speak with their elders were the cynical Athenian overlords issuing diktats from a position of power.

At this point our discussions gained more traction. If might makes right, as the Athenians/Israelis obviously assume, isn't it only natural to resort to armed rebellion, instead of coming out with useless moral arguments that will only be scorned by the masters? If international law is a sop, and the real world is created on the battlefield, as the masters believe, shouldn't we fight them using their own instruments of power and force?

Another classroom favorite was *The Wretched of the Earth*, an essay on the Algerian war by psychologist Frantz Fanon. Once again, the students saw themselves in the role of the Algerians fighting off the French army and the settler population it had been sent to protect. Moral arguments didn't prevent the Athenians from slaughtering the islanders. The people of Algeria, by contrast, heroically fought off the settlers, and gained their independence. The message for my students was obvious.

To give my students a different perspective more in line with my own position, I once invited to class the Palestinian Christian Mubarak Awad, a crusader for nonviolence and a proponent of Gandhi's civil disobedience. I had known him from my school days at St. George's; he was in Zaki's class. Awad had a hard time selling my students on Gandhi's nonviolence. How could white flags and tax boycotts chase Israeli tanks back across the Green Line? How could peaceful protest get the Israelis out of their hair? How could nonviolence prevent arrests without charges, land confiscations, house demolitions, searches without warrants? Only one person at the talk openly defended Awad's ideas: Lucy. (She later joined forces with him in creating the Palestinian Center for the Study of Non-Violence, in Jerusalem.)

Mubarak Awad was unfazed by his cool reception; he was used to it. He went on preaching and practicing his ideas until the Israelis expelled the pacifist gadfly from the country in the mid-eighties. They accused him quite absurdly of using nonviolence as a cover for the "armed struggle for liberation." In truth, as I would experience firsthand, the Israeli authorities often feared men of peace far more than they feared the terrorists.

Another book we read in class that generated continuing debate and interest was *Gilgamesh*, an old Akkadian legend dealing with immortality and the gods. Some of its stories, like the Flood, later showed up in the Bible. One raging debate set off by *Gilgamesh* was whether the received religious texts were really from God, whose very existence was now less than certain for some of my students. This theological question, which if debated at all at Harvard would have had less urgency than the outcome of a Celtics game, had a burning relevance in my classroom. Many of those who believed that justice would willy-nilly win out over occupation, right over might, fell back on God to prop up their hopes. This quietist tack was taken by the Islamic contingent. As strange as it sounds, this group, which eventually morphed into Hamas, was initially opposed to violent confrontations with Israel. Salvation, in their pious thinking, would come about only after we all went back to the unsullied Islamic way of life. People who would later praise suicide bombings as a sure ticket to Paradise were still strict pacifists in the early 1980s.

Those persuaded by the Athenian argument—or Fanon's—vigorously objected, insisting that God was irrelevant and monotheism was no more than a fairy tale. Marxists of all stripes belonged to this camp. God for them was either an illusion or, if he existed at all, the source of all our troubles, certainly not the solution.

I normally tried to stay neutral in the theological spats, and the only time I made an exception I got duly and roundly attacked. One day, at a poetry contest for students at a small Catholic university in Bethlehem, a student read out a poem attacking God. The accused blasphemer was like Dostoyevsky's Ivan Karamazov. He came from a camp and used his poem to vent all his rage and frustration. The university, fearful of being regarded as harboring anti-Muslim agitators, expelled him.

One of my friends from the Café Troubadour days, who was also teaching in Birzeit, told me about the student and his expulsion, rightly assuming I'd be indignant at this infringement on the liberty of speech. When he suggested that he and I write an article for the *Al-Quds* newspaper, I agreed. It was titled "Freedom of Opinion," and appeared on the front page the following day.

No sooner was it published than a tirade of angry responses arrived, one of these written in fire and blood by a sheikh who later became the mufti of Jerusalem. After six consecutive articles denouncing us, we responded with another article. (I would later use these articles in a course I gave on freedom.)

This is an example of how I began to adjust my teaching to the conditions of occupation. It was during one of the aforementioned discussions with my students that it suddenly hit me that I couldn't—to turn Plato on his head—stay outside the "cave" and expect the "cave-dwellers" to ignore politics, because their "cave" resounded with it. If I wanted to reach them, I had to enter into their "cave" by understanding their experiences. Only then would the Great Books or Great Ideas come alive to them.

In Western society, a liberal education can often be little more than a rite of passage or a sign of a proper upbringing, like eating your salad with the right fork. For us, it's a matter of life and death. Education is a tool to prevent people from passively stewing in their own resentment, and either giving up by submitting or lashing out by tossing bombs.

Hence my long conversations with students over Omar cigarettes and hummus. Students taught me what the occupation was doing to my people, and thanks to them I began to consider the kinds of intellectual skills they needed to outsmart a highly intelligent enemy. Rather than a Fanon-style gun-slinging romanticism of violence, we needed to think strategically.

The students I had less success with were the religious zealots, who were still a minority. In my courses on Islamic philosophy I never came out against Islam, and given the type of religion Mother raised us with, I had no reason to. I only explained to students that al-Farabi and other Muslim philosophers weren't traditional theologians. When al-Farabi wrote about human government (and he did so only esoterically), he didn't go along with the traditional line that describes the ideal government as one run by God or his prophet. Al-Farabi's ideal government was run by a wise and learned ruler; whether he was religious or not was secondary. A good ruler, of course, had to be able to read and write, but he also had to be educated in all the existing sciences, and above all to know his Plato and Aristotle. Sure, he also had to be moral. But for this he didn't need God. He could find his moral principles by reading Aristotle's *Ethics*.

The pious students clustered in the back row, their lips pursed in tight circles, didn't like the sound of this. Few of them knew the slightest thing about Islamic civilization, beyond what they had picked up from their village imam. But they knew enough to think that I was attacking Islam.

My preferred method of teaching—that is, rattling them a bit to make them think critically—only made matters worse, because I played devil's advocate by defending what for them were outrageous opinions. They saw the likes of al-Farabi and me as a danger to Islamic tradition.

"What do you say about the Prophet?" one righteous student called out, his beard quivering. "Isn't it true that he was the receptacle of true and complete knowledge, and he had no need for Greek or for Aristotle."

"Well"—I began pacing the front of the classroom—"you should recall that Mohammed couldn't read or write, and was but a messenger. Ditto the Angel Gabriel, who only transmitted the truth to Mohammed. Al-Farabi teaches us that when a person uses reason to figure out the truth, he possesses it in a far deeper manner than one who's merely a vessel." The Holy Rollers gasped. "It is the man who uses reason," I continued, "that al-Farabi, like his teacher Plato, singles out as the wisest ruler."

"Wiser than the Prophet?" four students asked at once.

"You got it!" said one of my Marxist students.

"Exactly," I continued, still pacing, playing with an unlit Omar in one hand. "Take any example in life. Someone who knows English is better at reading Milton than someone who doesn't. Someone who knows about banking is better at running a bank than someone who can't even decipher numbers. Isn't someone who drives a car better at getting from Ramallah to Bethlehem than a mule-driver?"

I had gone too far, and the religious students were fuming. In their tendency to personalize the exchange of ideas, they had heard me say that I—who was literate, had a checking account, and drove to work every day—was claiming to be better than the Prophet.

I was already in hot water with the religious community because I had defended the Bethlehem student poet. And to many, the way I acted seemed so utterly untraditional that they assumed I was antireligious. Didn't I consort with Marxists and PLO secularists? Didn't I have liberal views? And what about the sandals, the English wife, the long hair, and the conspicuously missing moustache? They added it all up and concluded that I was their sworn enemy.

A group of them went to Father to complain about me. "Get out of my house!" he barked at them after they called me a blasphemer. The new mufti of Jerusalem, at their next address, agreed with them, however. The mufti lashed out at me during his next Friday sermon at Al-Aqsa mosque. My young inquisitors were so irate that they put out a leaflet in broad black letters: THERE'S A NEW PROPHET AT BIRZEIT. It accused me of heresy by thinking I was better than Mohammed. The leaflet, meant to be a threat, actually was amusing. I rather liked the designation "prophet," because for me a prophet is less a magician than someone who thinks clearly and logically enough to detect future trends and patterns. I framed the leaflet and hung it on the wall in my office next to a photo of the Dome of the Rock.

Chapter Twelve

Military Order 854

There always comes a time when one must choose between
contemplation and action. This is called becoming a man.

—ALBERT CAMUS, "THE MYTH OF SISYPHUS"

How I issued from father's loins I'll never know. Since I was a boy, I've preferred analyzing a situation to rolling up my sleeves and getting my hands dirty. The thought of being burrowed for days in library stacks or chain-smoking Omars over a pile of notes in a café has always been far more alluring to me than jockeying for position and power. This is the reason I've always admired Hannah Arendt's definition of political action as "leaving one's private hiding place and showing who one is by disclosing and exposing oneself."[1] Who enjoys "exposing" himself? In my book you should do it only when your conscience forces you into a corner, leaving you no choice.

My entrée into politics came about through a paradoxical realization. By instinct an antinationalist with an aversion to flags and histrionics, I was becoming convinced that Palestinians had to pass through a stage of nationalism. Only a successful national movement could free us from the dangerous embrace of nationalism.

I still felt I could do my part in this as an educator rather than as an activist. Anyway, activism went against my nature, and it would have sapped what little time and energy I had left over after teaching. I had my own philosophical puzzles I wanted to solve, puzzles that had nothing to do with liberation.

It was while poring over one such puzzle during a break between classes (inclement weather had forced me to forgo my daily walk through the fields) that I got a visit from my childhood friend Bashir, who cracked open my office door and peered in with a mischievous grin. He was followed by several of my colleagues, one of them was Hanan Ashrawi, who was also smiling. My friends were up to something.

My broom closet–size office didn't have enough chairs for them all, so in contravention of the traditional Palestinian warm-up of coffee and a smoke, they immediately got down to business. Bashir, acting as spokesman for the others, said I couldn't "just sit there" as if everything were okay. "We need you to become involved."

He was referring to a brewing conflict between the administration and faculty members. At the time, our miserly salaries weren't even coming on time. But there were many other irksome problems besides money. Lucy had to set up a nursery for the children of faculty because none existed. We didn't have university health insurance, and we had no say in the university's governance. Faculty members wanted a union to represent their interests, and the people crowded into my office thought I was the one to create one.

A friend of mind had tried to set up a teachers' union at Birzeit back in 1977, and was immediately given the boot. The administration, to forestall any future agitation, craftily introduced into its bylaws rules for a faculty association that gave us a representative structure, while maintaining ultimate control. Now, five years later, the delegation in my office explained how the main political factions on campus—PFLP, the communists, and Fatah—had agreed to nominate one independent person to take over the faculty association and, from the inside, try winning concessions from the administration. Since I was one of the few faculty members not belonging to a faction, process of elimination had landed them at my door.

"Why not?" I told them without giving it much thought. No sooner had those words passed my lips than I felt bewildered, and for good reason.

Without knowing it, this flippant *why not?* was about to catapult me in the midst of the national political fray.

Within the matter of a week, I saw myself with the title of president of the faculty association. My first impulse was to dismantle it. How could it represent the will and interests of its members if the ultimate power over its decisions and actions lay with the authority before which those interests were to be brought in the first place? The association was a sham. Another trick the university administration used was to separate the faculty and nonfaculty employee associations. An action by either one of the two would be far less effective than a combined action.

What was needed was a change in the rules. The first order of business thus was to merge the two associations, which was easy to do because the head of our nonfaculty counterpart was the defiant feminist novelist from Nablus, Sahar Khalifeh. The two of us began what we called our "White Revolution." (We would later recycle the expression during the intifada.) We then jointly declared the formal death of the two associations and the birth of a union that henceforth would represent the interests of faculty and nonfaculty members alike. Pending new elections, the elected executive council members from the two associations became members of the provisional executive of the new union.

The administration, led by Gabi Baramki after Nasser's expulsion, was stunned. In a single act as decisive as a karate chop, we had exploded all previous efforts to prevent the unionization of the university.

More was to come. At An-Najah National University in Nablus, a pro-Fatah mathematician named Adnan Idris was spearheading a drive to create a labor union. We soon began talking about ways to cooperate. Wouldn't the muscle of our respective unions be greatly strengthened by forming a single nationwide structure? We could all benefit from union actions at any of the campuses. And why stop at universities? Why not involve teachers from vocational training centers?

Driving between Nablus and Ramallah for consultations and negotiations, we came up with a basic charter for the union we called the Federation of the Union of Employees in Palestinian Universities and Institutes of Higher Learning. According to our bylaws, each chapter would have independent elections and the autonomy to call individual actions depending on local needs. At the same time, the umbrella organization would have an overall strategy and unity of purpose.

Circumstances and events have their own logic, and one thing now led to another. What about student unions? The various universities and colleges already had student councils, and each council tended to mirror the political factions of the country. Some were pro-Fatah, others pro-Communist, pro-PFLP, pro-PDFLP, and so on. Couldn't we forge an alliance between our union and the councils?

In the meantime, we needed office space for our union at Birzeit. The direct approach of asking the administration for space on campus led to a predicable no. Now the student union, led by some of my pupils, adopted an even more direct method. We took over an empty room, hung a sign on the door, and moved in. We were already well ensconced by the time the administration found out, and the fact that all the political factions backed me—not to mention the young, burly Fatah activists posted outside the door—prevented our being evicted.

The following is a list of some of our successes: we developed a health policy for the employees through direct agreements with doctors, dentists, and hospitals; we negotiated salary disputes; and most important, together with the student councils, we fashioned a democratically legitimate political force of astonishing power. Soon enough, this power would come into conflict with both the PLO and the mighty Israeli military.

Our union can be seen as a good example of civil society at work. Though most members belonged to various PLO factions, or were sympathetic to them, the union was independent and democratic, and as such had none of the mystery-mongering and secretive cell structure of a guerrilla movement. As an open movement with nothing to hide, we put out a booklet describing our bylaws, budget, goals, and achievements.

The often raucous meetings in which elected representatives of student and union bodies sat to discuss policies and strategies—or sometimes stood on chairs and shouted—were a breath of fresh air in a society long run by aristocrats. As president, I spent hours in wearying union deliberations trying to persuade colleagues to accept my point of view; when I lost, as I often did, I had to play the spokesman for a view I had until then vigorously opposed.

At first we never thought to coordinate our policies and strategies with the PLO leadership. The legitimacy we needed came from our own experiences. If it hadn't been for the Israelis and the hubris of the military establishment, we probably never would have established links with the PLO, and the union would never have become a potent nationwide force against the military occupation.

The military had various repressive instruments to keep people in line. Its repertoire included closures, administrative arrests, house arrests, torture, and if these failed, there was always expulsion. The Soviet Union had Siberia; the Israelis had Jordan and Lebanon.

The single largest center of resistance to occupation was the university campus. Israel called Birzeit "the hotbed of Palestinian nationalism," and in the early 1980s it was. Other centers sprang up. In the 1970s a number of colleges were established in various parts of the West Bank and Gaza through private local initiatives, all propelled by the same needs that the founders of Birzeit had felt, namely to provide higher education to students who could no longer travel abroad. More campuses attracted more attention abroad, more international faculty, and among the students and faculty, more meddlesome nationalist activism. All of these were worrying developments for a military and occupation administration long used to unfettered control.

The military came up with what it must have considered an elegant solution. Soon after the occupation began, Israel placed the West Bank and Gaza under the control of the Israeli defense minister, who in turn appointed a military governor, investing him with all the prerogatives needed for ruling over a population. Mayors could be dismissed, trees could be uprooted, houses could be demolished, entire areas could be confiscated or redefined as military zones. In theory, paying lip service to international conventions, the governor ruled in accordance with preexisting law, which in the case of the West Bank had been Jordanian law. In truth, to carry out Israel's expansionist policies, he relied on the issuance of military orders that had to be ratified by his superiors in the Ministry of Defense.

The military governor now figured out a way to control the universities and colleges. There were no Jordanian laws governing universities in the West Bank, simply because there hadn't been any universities before 1967. In 1980 the governor promulgated Military Order 854, which placed universities under the same rules that the Jordanians had used to run government kindergartens and elementary schools. Such a creative application of the old law granted near absolute power to the Israeli authorities over faculty appointments, student admission, and curriculum. It gave the army the right to vet students before they gained admission or faculty before they were appointed, and every course or book taught required the stamp of the military governor.

As an adjunct to Military Order 854, the military governor demanded that all foreign professors, whether Palestinian expatriates or internationals, apply again for work permits, and that they sign a loyalty pledge, specifically stating they would not engage in opposition to the military government or have any dealings with a "hostile" organization as defined by the Israelis, namely the PLO.

Here it should be added that by "foreign" the government meant anyone who had been physically absent from his home in the West Bank at the time Israel took over, even if he had been born and bred there and had been on vacation in June 1967.

It was a calculated move to undermine our academic freedom and prevent a full-fledged civil society from taking root by threatening hundreds of professors teaching at West Bank universities with deportation if they engaged actively in politics. We in the union decided to mobilize the entire country in what retrospectively came to be known as the "mini-intifada," a dress rehearsal for the explosion of dissent in 1988.

The Israelis threatened to shut down all the universities if we refused to abide by the new order. The administration at Birzeit, not wanting to take the risk, agreed to go along. Many members of the faculty, and in particular the internationals and expatriates most threatened with expulsion if there were any trouble, sat with bated breath, not knowing what to do. Entire careers were on the line. This only increased the pressure on those of us in the union, as it was our decision whether to compromise with the occupation and submit, or put up a fight everyone believed we would lose.

We in the union and the various student councils debated it, put it up to a vote, and decided to thumb our noses at the Israelis and mobilize supporters throughout the West Bank and Gaza. It was not just academic freedom at stake, but our civil society and our political future as a nation. Collectively, we gave the occupiers the finger.

The Israelis repeated their threat to shut down the university, and we continued to refuse to sign the loyalty oath. The administration now weighed in, demanding that we submit to the order. We told the administration what we told Israel: forget it! We incited no violence and threw no stones. We simply ignored the order, and to everyone's amazement, mine included, the Israelis did nothing. And shy of actually shutting down entire universities, there was little they could do.

Like magic, a disciplined organization with a single will managed to run circles around a powerful state with a ruthlessly determined security apparatus. In mobilizing public support for our position, we published studies of the implications of the order in newspapers, distributed leaflets, and organized lectures at town hall meetings and on campuses. We came up with contingency plans to continue teaching if the Israelis carried through on their threats and padlocked the universities.

To drum up support in the countryside, union leaders spread out north to south, carrying our message to the villagers and their elders, explaining to them the significance of the military order and the reasons we needed to combat it. The foreign and Israeli press began to take notice once we began to hold press conferences. A number of Israeli academics showed up on campus to express solidarity. Menahem Yaari, today the president of the Israeli Academy of Science and my partner in the Israeli-Palestinian Science Organization (IPSO), headed up a commission of Israeli academics to investigate the legality and morality of Military Order 854. Yaari came to my home in the Old City for a chat, and his subsequent report backed our decision to resist his government.

It was for me an intriguing glimpse into Israeli psychology that only after the first hint of violence did they act. One day an Israeli officer dressed in civilian clothes walked onto campus, went directly to the administration building, and demanded that the university hand over lists of student activists. Word leaked out that he was there, and students began to crowd around the administration building. Nearly the entire student body showed up, shouting at him and demanding that he leave. As he walked out and down a narrow staircase, one of the students pushed him, and he fell to the floor. We all rushed to ensure he could leave the campus without getting ripped to shreds. He left in one piece but the damage had been done.

The following day the army ordered the campus shut for three months. Seventy professors from various West Bank universities were promptly picked up and deported.

By this point, our grassroots network was strong enough that by closing us down, the Israelis only spread the confrontation to the towns and villages throughout the West Bank. There were confrontations with soldiers in every village where the students returned home. In *The Washington Post* the front-page headlines read: "Israeli Troops Wound Nine in Protests on West Bank." Gabi Baramki's fourteen-year-old daughter was one of the wounded.

As soon as the university opened up again, the battle over Military Order 854 resumed. We still refused to sign, and once again the Israelis did nothing.

For me it was an extraordinary moment. For thirty-five years every shot we took at the occupiers had ricocheted back at us tenfold: more land was seized, more people expelled, more of our future trampled upon. It was a losing battle, because they had a strategy, whereas we had only emotions. Now, for the first time, we were discovering our strength. The Israelis had nothing in their repertoire to defeat a dedicated non-violent campaign of civil disobedience.

It was at this moment of euphoria that a baffling message arrived from PLO headquarters in Amman, insisting that we submit to the Israeli dik-tats. The seventy deported professors had arrived in Amman, and many of them were demanding that the PLO force us to comply. The various university administrations, with Birzeit's leading the chorus, said much the same thing: the PLO should show some mettle by reining us in.

We held an emergency meeting at Birzeit. Union and student coun-cil representatives from all over the West Bank and Gaza attended. The choices we debated during this tumultuous gathering were paradoxical but clear: either we submit to the PLO, against the PLO's best interests, or we continue our defiance. We opted to stick to our guns. At the meet-ing, I was charged with the disagreeable task of presenting to PLO lead-ers in Amman the national consensus on the issue—indeed, our vote was the closest thing to a democratic consensus Palestinians in the Occupied Territories had ever had.

So began a series of trips to PLO headquarters. At the time, contact with the PLO was treated as a criminal offense, carrying with it steep prison sentences. As a precaution, written materials had to be smuggled across the bridge into Jordan. Prisoners in Israeli jails had developed the best method, which only an X-ray would reveal. It was the "capsule." Messages were written in minuscule script on both sides of very thin pa-per. The message was carefully folded into a small tight roll, often no bigger than half an inch in width and two inches in length. This was then wrapped in a layer of protective paper taken from the inside lining of a cigarette packet. Finally, it was rolled up into a piece of plastic cut from a shopping bag. Once the message was properly wrapped, the skillful smuggler lit a match, blew it out, and used the glint from the dy-ing flame to melt the plastic together at both ends. Now the capsule was ready to be swallowed. The message could be safely moved across the bridge in the intestines of the messenger.

On my trips I took along Ali Hassouneh, a student affairs officer at Birzeit. Like me, he had a Jerusalem ID and could more easily obtain permits to cross the bridge into Jordan. In total we made five trips together, each time with capsules swimming around in our entrails.

The first meeting ended disastrously. I arrived in Amman with a strong résumé as the head of a coordinating body of all unions and students of all universities in the Occupied Territories, and cofounder of the Federation of the Union of Employees for the entire West Bank. I was also carrying in my stomach signatures of hundreds of union and student leaders backing our position.

In Amman we were met by Hamadeh el-Faraʾneh, an amiable fellow working for the PLO's educational department. Hamadeh belonged to the Marxist faction of the PLO, the PDFLP. Both Ali and I felt immediately that Hamadeh was on our side, and this created the mistaken impression that the sailing was going to be smooth.

Hamadeh started out by taking us to a number of meetings that had been arranged, some with the expelled professors. It was awkward to address them, for we naturally sympathized with their unenviable fates. They had lost their jobs and were separated from their families. At the same time, in our eyes we were fighting to preserve the very institutions they had been ordered to leave.

Soon after arriving at Hamadeh's home, we discovered the real reason we had been summoned to Amman. We were sitting around smoking and drinking coffee when we heard a car pull up outside. A man dressed in an expensive-looking suit—Ali swore it was an Armani—stepped out of a waxed and buffed Mercedes limo. He was the special representative in Amman of the Executive Committee of the PLO. What's more, the man was the head of one of the PLO armies, a brutish-looking character accustomed to inspiring fear and respect.

He had scarcely walked into Hamadeh's living room when he began talking down at us with an officious tone. Father had not raised me to suffer such arrogance easily.

"I have been asked on behalf of the Executive Committee of the PLO to order you to sign the anti-PLO pledge and the military order concerning universities." After delivering his message, he looked down at the untied laces of the tennis shoes I was wearing. I saw him roll his eyes.

The self-importance of his voice triggered an automatic response in me. Putting on my own officious act, I countered: "And I was asked on behalf of the entire network of unions and student councils in the Occupied Territories to deliver to you and to the Executive Committee the message that, no, we will not sign."

To hear a professor who couldn't even tie his shoes properly tell him no came as a jolt to this man. He had expected compliance, not a debate, and merely repeated his orders. I did the same.

"It is impermissible for you not to obey us," he said.

I was about to correct his grammar when Ali spoke up. "But what we are doing is precisely in the PLO's best interest. What you're asking us to do is to drive a nail in the PLO's coffin."

"I have a letter from Arafat ordering you to sign," snapped the professional revolutionary in his tailor-made suit.

"Let's see the letter," I requested.

"What, you don't trust me?"

"Yes, of course," I assured him. "It's just that I want to see what the chairman's signature looks like. I've never seen it before."

He pulled out a letter from his satchel and passed it to me. Scanning it, I saw that it only stated that Arafat considered higher education in Palestine a matter of great importance, and that he feared that foreign professors could be expelled from occupied Palestine.

"This letter says nothing about signing the order," I said, handing the letter back to him. "We, too, are concerned about the professors from abroad. Who isn't?"

The officer began nervously shifting his weight from one foot to the other, and with a red hue of anger in his face he told me that no one had ever spoken to him in that way. He was now gaping at me, as if stares alone could get me to comply with his demand. After a few seconds of awkward silence, he swiveled on his heel and left the room.

The next day the head of the Jordanian intelligence service rang me at my hotel and asked me to come to his office. When I arrived I saw an oversize, dark, and unsmiling figure sitting in a chair—like a photocopy of the officer from the previous day, only with a cheaper suit. With his thick jowls, he muttered out a greeting. Sitting next to him was an American, obviously a CIA agent. The Jordanian security man echoed what the PLO man had said the previous day: that it was best for us to sign the oath. I repeated the union's position.

My first brush with the shadowy world of security was not a very edifying one. Never in my wildest dreams would I have imagined that Israel, the United States, Jordan, and the PLO would have a common interest in Palestinian professors denouncing the PLO.

The same pattern repeated itself over the course of several cross-border trips, each time with me carrying new capsules. The PLO made demands, and we refused to comply. We got our way only after I met Abu Jihad for the first time.

Abu Jihad, the nom de guerre for Khalil al-Wazir, was Arafat's second in command. His intelligence and grasp of strategy made him a hated and feared figure for the Israelis. Just talking about the weather with him could have landed us in the Israeli prison camp.

Like Mother, Abu Jihad had been expelled from his native Ramle in 1948. He finished high school in Gaza and went off to Alexandria to study architectural engineering. It was in Kuwait where he met Arafat.

Abu Jihad was the only top PLO official who believed in creating viable political structures in the territories. While others were shoring up diplomatic ties, planning hijackings, or creating weapons stockpiles in Lebanon, Abu Jihad was designing a national education policy for the Occupied Territories as a way for the Palestinians to assert themselves against the Israelis.

We met during an encounter with the PLO in Amman that started out as yet another fruitless round-robin of demands and refusals. Finally, I pulled out one of our union leaflets and held it up to them. At the bottom was written, "The PLO is the sole legitimate representative of the Palestinian people."

"What does *representative* signify here?" I asked them as if they were undergraduates. "Does it mean that the PLO does what it wants, or what the Palestinian people want?" From their expressions, I knew they weren't following me, so I spelled it out for them. As leaders of the union, we represented the people who elected us. If we agreed to sign the military order, our voters would elect someone else who wouldn't.

I was there with Ali Hassouneh and another activist, Sami Khader. The three of us must have seemed a strange team to Abu Jihad. With confidence, and indeed with faith, we maintained that holding out against the Israelis would not, as some people feared, lead to the closure of institutions. The Israelis were bluffing, and we had the strength to call their bluff. By contrast, if we succumbed, we might as well shutter up the universities—because they would then cease to be true places of critical and humanistic thinking.

I could see Abu Jihad's mind at work, weighing the options the way a spice dealer apportions his products. No one said a word, and I was getting nervous because I knew we would have no option but to go along with his decision. Finally, he banged his fist on the table and told us to keep up the good work. I must have left a good impression on him, because from that point on, right up to his murder by Israeli commandos in 1988, we remained in close contact.

Winning the backing of Abu Jihad didn't mean I hadn't collected enemies during my forays back and forth over the Jordan. On my last trip, feeling elated at having won over the PLO, I made my way back toward the border. At the bridge, a Jordanian officer looked at my passport and flung it back in my face, accusing me of belonging to the Marxist "Popular Front-General Command" faction of the PLO. He pointed in the direction of the West Bank and ordered me never to show my face in Jordan again.

We won over the PLO by winning over Abu Jihad, who in turn persuaded Arafat to back us. This taught me something about the PLO. With some determined pressure, the main leaders came around to our position, and as such they demonstrated a willingness to adapt to popular pressure from their constituency within the Occupied Territories. Not that they had much choice. Sitting in Amman or Beirut, they didn't have the physical means to apply thumbscrews. It was this practical reality—the PLO on the outside, us on the inside—that initiated a change in the relationship between the people and their leaders. You could say that Israeli border installations helped create a division of power that allowed a Jeffersonian spirit to begin taking hold.

Which of course didn't solve our problem with the Israelis. They continued issuing threats to shut down campuses, and we continued to ignore them. In time, our strength and support increased. Not only did we win a special resolution from the UN calling for Israel to back down from Military Order 854, we also managed to win the support of the International Commission of Jurists, which stated, "Implicit in the right to academic freedom is an atmosphere in which the attitude of government toward academic institutions, teachers, students and research activity is favorable if not benevolent. Unfortunately, however, no such atmosphere exists in the West Bank."[2] Finally, and with Israeli academics supporting our cause, the Israelis backed down. They suspended implementation of the order for one year. They never formally retracted the law; they just chose not to enforce it.

We couldn't really savor the triumph, because just as the occupation authorities were backing away from Military Order 854, they began promulgating Military Order 752. The "Village League" called to life by 752 was the brainchild of the West Bank's new master, Ariel Sharon.

Sharon appeared on the scene after the Likud Party won the 1981 parliamentary elections by a bigger margin than anyone had expected. As if he had heard a voice from heaven, Begin interpreted the election sweep as a mandate to pursue an even more aggressive policy in the West Bank and Gaza. To execute this, he handed the Ministry of Defense over to Sharon. Defense Minister Sharon now had a free hand to shove "autonomy" à la Menachem Begin down our throats.

Among Palestinians, Sharon was best known for his role in a massacre in the West Bank village of Qibya in 1953. He was the commander of the infamous "Unit 101," whose mission was to retaliate against Arab attacks. In Qibya, Sharon and his unit showed up in the middle of the night, and by morning had reduced the village to rubble. The houses had been blown up and sixty-nine Arabs, two thirds of them women and children, were dead. Major-General Vagn Bennike, a UN commander, reported that "bombs were thrown through the windows of huts in which the refugees were sleeping and, as they fled, they were attacked by small arms and automatic weapons."[3]

Never a man without a vision, Sharon set out to translate Begin's mytho-political dream into facts on the ground. He began by replacing the previous military governor Benjamin Ben-Eliezer with Menachem Milson, an Orientalist who shared Begin's messianic ideal of a Greater Israel. Sharon and Milson promptly went to work. One of their first acts was to outlaw the National Guidance Committee, and to remove all the remaining mayors still left from the 1976 election. To replace the deposed mayors with a new civilian administration more to their liking, they came up with the Village League.

The Village League is a good example of *divide et impera*. Sharon and Milson made the correct assessment that while two thirds of the Palestinians lived in the countryside and in camps, only one third lived in towns or cities, home to the secular Palestinian leadership. Even the mayors who made up the National Guidance Committee belonged to the educated urban Arab elite, and as such lacked deep roots in the countryside, where the fellahin lived out their days with neither the time nor the inclination to get mixed up in the secular nationalist thinking seeping out of the cities and universities. Sharon's hope was to find, or if necessary buy or otherwise compel, local leaders, who would then win over the traditionally minded masses. Not having a national overview—went the reasoning—these more religious characters would be content to live in the fragmented chunks of the West Bank the Israelis left to them. "Autonomy" Likud-style envisioned a mass of Arabs happily bartering away national aspirations for the right to pray and mix cement for a contractor building the next Jewish settlement.

Sharon used the full weight of the army and the Israeli security service, the Shin Bet (the Israeli FBI), to help the Village League get off the ground. Milson set to work propping up the local leaders who agreed to cooperate. Some of the leaders they came up with had shady criminal backgrounds.

One of the docile local leaders Sharon and Milson decided to support was a quadriplegic cleric in the Gaza Strip by the name of Sheikh Ahmad Yassin. Already in 1978 the Israeli government had begun to prop up the sheikh as a way of undermining the PLO. The government allowed Yassin to start a newspaper and a charity he called the Islamic Association. Now, through the Village League scheme, Yassin's Islamic Association began receiving funds for new mosques, schools, hospitals, and medical clinics. The Israelis also allowed the sheikh to raise tens of millions more from Arab regimes opposing Arafat.

Meanwhile, Prime Minister Begin and Defense Minister Sharon picked up the pace of settlement construction. To increase the Jewish population, they appealed to Israelis with no ideological ties to Gush Emunim. The government offered low-interest mortgages and other economic perks to prospective settlers, and most of the people who took up the offer were secular.

Beit El, which had been a bare mountaintop when I arrived in 1978, now buzzed with buses, schools, shops—all within eyeshot of the squalid refugee camp of Jalazun. Begin and Sharon broke ground on the East Jerusalem settlement of Pisgat Ze'ev, named after Zev Jabotinsky, Begin's mentor and the man who had inspired the flag-carrying youths who sparked the 1929 riots at the Western Wall.

To facilitate and protect more settlers required more roads, electricity, and water, and more soldiers. With more settlers needing protection, new diktats were required. In the end we got a mountain of them governing all the details of Palestinian life. (Military Order 1015, for example, prohibited the planting of any fruit tree or more than twenty tomato seedlings without the agreement and adherence to the conditions of the military governor.)

Force of circumstance was pressing our union into the wider national struggle. Starting with the struggle for academic freedom and national rights, it was only natural that we would take up a leadership role in combating the Village League. We had a well-oiled organization, an effective means of communication, and a nonviolent strategy already in place. In the fight against Sharon and Military Order 752, the youth movement took a decisive role.

Shabibah, the Fatah youth movement, grew out of the student movement and quickly emerged as the most potent force in the Occupied Territories. One of its founders was Samir Sbeihat. Samir had completed a five-year prison sentence before ending up in my logic class, where he couldn't sit still, constantly interrupted me, refused to take things at face value, even when they came from W.V.O. Quine, and was in general the sort of student I loved having in class. Helped out by his self-confidence and prison credentials, he rose to the top of student council. But his ambitions—doubtlessly a by-product of sharing a cell for nine months with Marwan Barghouti, another charismatic figure, who in time would become the most powerful Palestinian leader of his generation—went far beyond Birzeit. He wanted to organize all the Fatah students in the West Bank and Gaza.

Samir and I had long discussions at the hummus salon in the village, and soon the basic concept and rules of operation developed. More important, once called to life, Shabibah spearheaded opposition to the Village League.

Samir and his fellow student activists employed the same strategies as before: a confrontation with soldiers at the university would erupt, followed by the school's closure, followed by a planned spreading out of students throughout villages and towns to mobilize for a more general strike. By fanning out to their hometowns, villages, and refugee camps, the student activists succeeded precisely where the Village League failed, and by doing so they exploded the Sharon-Milson theory that the country-side, being less nationalistic than the cities, was more amenable to Israeli expansionist plans. As it turned out, the countryside was more incor-ruptible and nationalistic than the educated urban cliques that Israel had sought to bypass. Just as threatening to the Israelis was the fear that this evolving grassroots movement was making use of our "assertive nonviolence" to throw a spanner into Israeli plans.

The Israelis quickly traced the source of the trouble back to Birzeit and did their utmost to stop us. There were closures, roadblocks, and the occasional violent flare-up. Inevitably, every time the army patrols came onto campus, rocks began to fly. The first student was shot dead when soldiers resorted to live ammunition instead of tear gas. After that, the university was shut down for six months.

Nothing worked, and Military Order 752 eventually went the way of its predecessor, 854. The Village League failed to gain any popular support.

Chapter Thirteen

Masquerade

Over the water, a destination; under the sky, a culmination.

—KIT WILLIAMS, *MASQUERADE*

T HE LONG HOURS SPENT puffing away on Omars and debating with students over fine points of a particular strategy gave me a reputation on campus. They must have thought that I spent my free time at home reading the medieval philosopher al-Farabi before spinning out my next political stratagem. I assured them that the Israeli-Palestinian puzzle wasn't the only riddle on my mind. After putting the kids to bed at night, I liked to exercise my imagination by grappling with other puzzles and paradoxes.

For Christmas in 1981, Lucy and I, needing a break from the tensions at Birzeit, visited her sister in Glasgow, bearing gifts from Bethlehem. Her sister, knowing I liked puzzles and children's books, gave me Kit Williams's *Masquerade*.

The book is a collection of pictures surrounded by letters, with a short narrative. It is the story of how the Moon, besotted by the Sun, talks Jack Hare into taking her a bejeweled treasure, but the hapless Jack loses the treasure en route. The riddle is the location of the golden hare. You have to look at the picture, read the narrative, and look for a clue to the exact location.

Within the pages of this book there is a story told
To solve the hidden riddle, you must use your eyes,
And find the hare in every picture that may point you to the prize.

The treasure is as likely to be found by a bright child of ten with an understanding of language, simple mathematics and astronomy as it is to be found by an Oxford don.

For readers all over England, the treasure hunt was on. All at once, seemingly normal middle-class people were seen climbing up cliffs or burrowing into someone's garden.

I read the book in one sitting. Still in England, I ran out to buy some detailed survey maps to take back to Jerusalem. Over months of nightly labor back home I untangled bits and pieces of clues to come up with a theory. I traced the hare to a spot in Sussex overlooking the Isle of Wight. On the survey map, I located a column in a park. At full moon in the middle of August, ran my hunch, the shadow of the tower should point to the spot where the hare was buried.

I was elated to have succeeded where a million native Englishmen and just as many European adventurers had failed. At once I phoned Bashir's brother, who lived in England, and persuaded him to meet me at Heathrow. Having grown up together in Jerusalem, he was used to my whims. "And please bring a shovel, pick, and flashlight." I persuaded Lucy's sister to pick us both up in her car. From the airport we sped off to Sussex. Luckily, it was a cloudless sky, and the full moon was slowly reaching its zenith as we reached the designated spot. Shortly before the stroke of midnight we got out of the car and walked to the park, only to find it padlocked and encircled by a high iron fence. My friend thought it best to return the next morning. But by the time he got the words out of his mouth, I was already scaling the fence. I needed to get to the column at the top of the hill at the stroke of midnight.

"There it is," I exclaimed. Lo and behold, the shadow of the pillar I had identified on the map pointed off into the grass. Taking turns, we dug and dug, and it wasn't until nearly dawn that I admitted to my friend, now looking on with bemusement at his crazed childhood friend brown with dirt, that like all the other treasure hunters scouring England, I had failed to ferret out the hare.

Trying to sort out puzzles kept my mind agile enough to figure out the far more dangerous riddles at work in our battle with the Israelis. My instincts told me that the essence of the struggle wasn't what it seemed to be. The fact that "assertive nonviolence" could slow down even Sharon proved that we weren't dealing with fascist Latin American–style thugs but with a democracy priding itself on its membership in the club of Western nations. Civilized, intelligent actions work because Israelis, generally civilized and intelligent themselves, are hesitant to answer nonviolence with death squads. Israelis are governed by a strong legal system and will open fire only if they think they can get away with it—for the most part, that is.

As with *Masquerade*, I was coming to realize that the nature of our conflict couldn't be grasped by sticking to the surface, or taking leaders' words at face value. Union work had shown me at close range how leaders may swear solemnly on Bibles and Korans and Constitutions, but still drop their ostensibly sacred positions in a flash if they feel that their underlying interests are threatened. They draw battle lines, sound the trumpet note, declare their bottom lines with hands on heart, and do the precise opposite if conditions require it. In other words, the problem affecting both sides was *a basic lack of honesty*.

This was where my riddle-mongering came into play. What was the truth that both Palestinians and Israelis did their best to hide from? What were our real rather than our pseudo interests?

As the chairman of a highly politicized nationwide union in partnership with a legion of crack student troops, I was constantly coming out with political statements and leaflets. More important, I was getting to know people from all walks of life and every corner of Palestine. Over time it finally dawned on me that most Palestinians, regardless of the lip service they paid to the slogan of a multinational secular state in place of

Israel, wanted an independent Palestinian state. Walid Khalidi, with his "Thinking the Unthinkable," had been right all along. As a democrat I had no choice but to substitute my old dream of "Palest-El" with the banner of an "independent Palestinian state, under PLO leadership with Jerusalem as its capital."

I concluded from these reflections that the essence of the Israeli-Arab conflict wasn't terrorism or settlements, or even Zionism. It was the simple fact that Palestinians wanted control over the territory conquered by Israeli in 1967, and that the Israelis didn't want to give the territory up. Few people wanted to state this openly, because it involved too much cognitive dissonance, for both sides.

Once I realized where we were heading as a nation, I began to prick up my ears. No one likes cognitive dissonance, especially not religions or revolutionary movements based on clearly articulated creeds. Palestinian leaders didn't openly tell their people where we were heading, because the two-state solution flew in the face of a generation of ideology. The old vision of a single, secular, democratic state negated the Zionist project of a Jewish state and sought to reverse the defeat in 1948, whereas the dream of a Palestinian state next to Israel meant making peace with Zionism.

I noticed that PLO leaders continued to pour forth their bloodcurdling rhetoric and bravado. "We will never compromise with the Zionist entity," was the standard line used for public consumption. "We'll fight to the last man." Behind the scenes, the same defiant leaders were a lot more pliable than anyone could have imagined. To be sure, there were plenty of people who still preferred shooting to talking. But the top people, from Arafat and Abu Jihad on down, took a pragmatic approach to freeing the Palestinian nation from occupation.

Israeli leaders were particularly deceitful, though not in the way anti-Semitic hacks claimed. They were even more dishonest than our leaders—itself quite an accomplishment—because the Israelis had morally dealt themselves a bad hand. They didn't admit that the conflict was essentially over lands conquered in 1967, just as they didn't dare annex what they called Judea and Samaria, because they knew the world would never support them if they did. Not only did international law bar the expropriation of territory conquered in war—this was the least of their worries—but stripping a people of 78 percent of their land, pushing most of them into exile, and then a few years later taking the remaining scraps from them flew in the face of what can be called fair play. "How much longer is the world willing to endure this spectacle of wanton cruelty?" wrote Bertrand Russell a few hours before he died in 1970, referring to Israel's behavior vis-à-vis the Palestinians. The last thing Israel wanted was for such opinions to become widespread among thinking people.

Violence was therefore the key. Israel often used violence as a tactical step to provoke a violent reaction, which it then used as an excuse for further violence in pursuit of its political end. The Israeli leaders wanted to create the impression that theirs was a life-and-death struggle against a band of ruthless terrorists (Begin's "history's meanest murder organization") committed to the genocidal destruction of the Jewish state. "Terror" was why the Israelis were in the territories, and terror was the reason they were building "defensive" settlements. In 1982, a government official confessed to a reporter for *Ha'aretz* that it was a "catastrophe" that the Palestinians were turning away from terror. It would be preferable to Israel for the PLO to "return to its earlier terrorist exploits, to plant bombs all over the world, to hijack plenty of airplanes and to kill many Israelis."[1]

Keeping the focus on the guerrillas provided the perfect cover for preventing a functioning government from developing in the West Bank. The war against PLO "monsters" permitted a permanent state of emergency. All civil dissent within the Occupied Territories was therefore cast as an extension of the international terrorist war of extermination against the Jewish state.

This analysis explained for me why it was far easier to win over a man like Abu Jihad to dialogue and nonviolence than Israeli leaders, who liked talking about democracy while relying exclusively on military means to suppress a people. The PLO had far more to gain from a nonviolent struggle than the Israelis, for whom a switch to dialogue would have meant having to defend the indefensible and would thus have necessitated an eventual full retreat from the Occupied Territories.

My analysis also made sense of the temptation, at times overwhelming, of luring the Palestinians into violence. Often it seemed that the Israeli military occupation fought terror only to promote it, because their real enemies were moderates—such as Mubarak Awad or the mayors. There arose a strategy of blaming moderates for the acts of extremists, crushing the moderates, and leaving the extremists intact—just in case they needed them as an excuse to smash the next crop of moderates in the future.

I felt as if I had figured out the most baffling riddle in our conflict with Israel, and soon enough I sat horrified and intrigued as the Israeli government provided the perfect laboratory to test out my hypothesis. In the summer of 1982, General Sharon persuaded Begin to intervene militarily in southern Lebanon. "Operation Peace for the Galilee" got under way on June 6, 1982, the fifteenth anniversary to the day of the Israeli conquest of French Hill in Jerusalem and Ramallah in the West Bank.

It was an odd time to launch a war against "terrorism," because not a single bullet had been fired over the Israeli-Lebanese border during the preceding twelve months. The casus belli wasn't even in Lebanon but in London, where the Israeli ambassador had narrowly survived an assassination attempt. Israel claimed that the PLO had done it, and the PLO denied all responsibility. The real catalyst for the invasion, however, was on the diplomatic front and in the conflict in the West Bank.

Over the months before the invasion I was becoming increasingly optimistic about the PLO. In 1981, fighting broke out in southern Lebanon between Israel and Fatah guerrillas. President Reagan sent an envoy to negotiate a cease-fire. Both sides agreed on its terms, and there was finally quiet on the northern Israeli frontier. Various forces high up in the PLO wanted to go well beyond a cease-fire by shifting tactics altogether from military strikes to diplomacy. Abu Jihad in particular dropped the militaristic language of armed liberation and began talking peace. Even Arafat seemed to go along with a new moderate tack. Desperately wanting U.S. recognition, he announced his willingness to continue the struggle through more peaceful means, just not at any price. "We are not Red Indians," he told David Ignatius of *The Washington Post* during an interview in Beirut.[2]

Pressure on Israel to hold direct talks was increasing. But a PLO willing to sit and negotiate wasn't something Begin or Defense Minister Sharon could easily countenance. Even worse for the Israeli government, our West Bank strategy of civil disobedience and nonviolence was gaining traction, and had turned Birzeit University into the Palestinian Berkeley circa 1968. The student movement was spreading to other universities. Moreover, the Palestinian human rights organization Al-Haq ("The Law") began issuing statements in English on human rights abuses. Their materials were finding their way into foreign newspapers and reports by Amnesty International. The moral high ground Israel had managed somehow to occupy since 1948 was suddenly getting more slippery.

My optimism was mixed with increasing alarm at the growing Islamist movement. While Military Order 854 and the Village Leagues hadn't worked as planned, the occupation had managed to foster the Islamists through the indirect support of the quadriplegic guru Ahmad Yassin. Yassin initially did precisely what the Israeli overlords expected: he and his Islamists went after secular nationalists who weren't "pure" and therefore impeded rather than hastened salvation. As time went on, their anger with the secularists grew. These bearded students came into my class with a glimmer of righteous anger in their eyes.

The ideological competition between the PLO and Islamists had begun. At universities in Gaza, Nablus, and Birzeit, verbal quarrels turned into fistfights.

Thus, with the nationalist movement in the West Bank increasingly opting for nonviolent means to carry on the fight for liberation, and the Islamists opposing them, General Sharon launched his invasion. Sharon sold his war as a necessary step in securing the border against terrorist attacks. Yet despite the talk of "terrorism," the true scope of Sharon's ambitions soon became clear. The invasion was a part of a much larger strategy to destroy any hope of our independence.

The war was planned long before the assassination attempt of the Israeli ambassador in London. For several months military fortifications were being prepared in northern Israel. A month before the invasion, obviously aware that a war in Lebanon would arouse violence, Military Order 1143 created a new prison near Nablus called Al-Fara. To help fill up the new facility, the "Order Concerning Organizing Guards in Settlements" gave vigilante groups operating out of Jewish settlements the right to "detain any persons who are acting suspiciously."

The initial phase of the war was swift and effortless, and once again the Arab world was left wringing its hands. For the Palestinians, watching the Israeli war machine chase four hundred thousand Lebanese and Palestinians from their homes in villages and refugee camps was a sobering sight, as were the warplanes that pulverized parts of Beirut. Defiant PLO statements coming out of basements of bombed-out apartment buildings didn't fool anyone. The rounds of Arab gunfire accompanying the PLO's evacuation belied the total disarray of the movement.

Under the cover of war, Sharon pushed through a number of military laws that vastly increased the scope of the occupation. Some of his actions went back to the defunct Village League, which the notoriously tenacious Sharon was unwilling to let die. He ordered his people in the West Bank Civil Administration to give some compliant local leaders massive support. More support flowed into the coffers of Sheikh Yassin's "charity" in Gaza—and just as the sheikh's ideological brothers in Iran were looking for ways to extend their influence into Lebanon and occupied Palestine.

In June, Military Order 994 allowed the head of the West Bank Civil Administration to assume all the power of local Palestinian authorities if he was convinced that even a single member of the municipal council was being uncooperative. In July another new law forbade Palestinians from living on their own expropriated land: "Any person occupying state property without permission will be prosecuted." In August, Military Order 1147 went a step further by prohibiting the planting of fruit trees without first obtaining the permission of military authorities. In September, Military Order 1020 gave military commanders the right to designate certain areas as closed military areas. In October, the "Order Concerning Provocation and Hostile Propaganda" made it illegal to "support a hostile organization by holding a flag or listening to a nationalist song." In theory, anyone within earshot of a radio tuned to any of the Arab stations, excluding Cairo, could be locked up.

In the summer of 1982, our life was busy with two children and a third on the way. The Lemon Tree was doing well enough, considering the Old City's continuous downward spiral. We normally had a full house, and the evening discussions often reminded me of Café Troubadour. It became a common sight to see an Arab student leave the café shaking his head, his smug nationalist presuppositions having been shattered by a conversation with an Israeli humanist, of which there were plenty at the Lemon Tree.

The day the war broke out, Lucy and I took the kids over to visit our Harvard friend Guy Stroumsa. "What will come of this war," I asked him, "besides a few thousand dead?" Guy was just as aghast. Neither of us was a prophet enough to foresee how the war would spawn demons such as Hezbollah, Hamas, and a twenty-year Israeli occupation of southern Lebanon.

Indeed, initially the venture backfired badly for Begin and Sharon. The day the invasion began, my friend Daniel Amit at the Hebrew University transmogrified his Committee in Solidarity with Birzeit University into the Committee Against the War in Lebanon. The committee's first demonstration attracted a few thousand protesters. Peace Now, which until then had been a small clutch of leftists led by the likes of Amos Oz and my friend from Oxford Avishai Margalit, followed the committee's lead, and a few days later a mass demonstration drew ten times as many.

Then came the massacre at the Sabra and Shatila refugee camps, in mid-September. With Sharon's army outside sealing off all the roads in and out of the camps, the Lebanese militias aligned with Israel methodically cut the throats of hundreds of old men, women, and children. The killing took place across the street from the national sports stadium, Beirut's second most popular recreation site after the beach.

Outrage over the massacres at Sabra and Shatila swelled the numbers of Israeli opponents to the war, and soon more than one hundred thousand chanting people were crowded into a square in Tel Aviv. Protesters demanded the resignations of Begin and Sharon and the establishment of a judicial commission of inquiry to investigate the massacres. More important for the region, Sharon's reckless war gave birth to Peace Now as a mass movement. Over the years, I would learn many things from Peace Now, for it was the first peace movement in Israel-Palestine that succeeded in mobilizing masses for nonviolent protests.

The massacres at Sabra and Shatila were, from the Palestinian perspective, the grim culmination of weeks of wanton destruction in Lebanon, and Sharon's heavy-handed tactics in the West Bank. At Birzeit the union responded with more assertive nonviolence, strikes, demonstrations, and the like.

The occupiers soon had plenty of new inmates at Al-Fara prison. Try as we could, television images of apartment buildings in Beirut going up in flames made discipline impossible to maintain. Fierce rioting erupted all over the territories. Stones flew; burning tires blocked roads; walls were covered with nationalist graffiti; and of course Palestinian flags defiantly popped up everywhere.

The army cracked down with lethal force. Soldiers closed Birzeit indefinitely after a confrontation one morning left two Muslim students dead. Lucy and I were in our car waiting at a checkpoint at the entrance to the university when I heard the news. At once I realized that a pivotal juncture in the conflict had been reached. With the shooting of its members, the Islamic faction would change its tune. No longer would it regard the PLO as its true enemy; Israel would increasingly get this role. Regardless of what its leaders said, the youth now regarded the occupation as their real enemy.

Outrage over the shooting that morning soon turned into incandescent vitriol. It increased when vigilantes from the settlements went onto the campus of the Hebron Islamic College in Hebron and sprayed a crowd of students with machine guns. Three students were killed and twenty-eight wounded. With the shooting, the mass arrests of activists, and the repression, a more radical student leadership developed. Sheikh Yassin, buoyed by the example of Iran, began winning more disciples, especially in Gaza. Patiently building his organization, Yassin still steered clear of anything smacking of anti-Israeli resistance.

For Fatah activists, time in prison became a rite of passage. By the war's end nearly every male under the age of thirty had either been in prison or had had a friend or family member who had been. Sometimes prison was a revolving door; other times it was more of a one-way trip, or a trip with a very delayed return. Some of my students vanished for years into this far-flung penal colony—without charges, without trial. Gone, just like that.

The long closures at the university forced us professors to improvise. Lucy and I held courses privately at home, in restaurants, at the Lemon Tree, at my father's office in Salaheddin Street—wherever we could.

With the revolving door of the prison system, my improvised courses on political ethics or the Great Books inevitably led to long discussions of my students' experiences. I learned from these talks to see in prison a paradoxical parallel reality in which something established on the basis of oppression could actually be the best proof that nonviolence was the only effective instrument against our nation's jail keepers.

An organized prisoners' movement grew up after 1967. After their arrest, dissidents and trained guerrilla fighters were stripped of the guns they had thought could win them basic rights. Incarceration forced them to adopt a disciplined and nonviolent strategy to get what they wanted. What evolved out of this necessity was a well-organized leadership with an elaborate system of communication (mainly capsules passed while prisoners embraced their wives during visits) linking them with the outside, and with inmates in other prisons. It was astounding for me to imagine these wretched and forgotten men, guilty mostly of defiance rather than of terrorism, organizing themselves and, through intelligent and coordinated action, prying concessions from authorities. Over time, hunger strikes pressured the jailers into giving their prisoners soap, books, and writing materials, and permission to listen to the radio.

I was even more astounded by my students' accounts of their interrogations. Given the situation at the time, it was hardly surprising that they brought back harrowing tales of sadistic manhandling like something out of Solzhenitsyn's *Gulag Archipelago*, or the Brothers Grimm. I heard about electric shocks to the genitals, beatings with truncheons, savage attacks by dogs, and what the Israelis called "shaking," in which the interrogator, with a physician's pliant help, clutched a prisoner by the lapels and shook him violently into unconsciousness.

It wasn't always easy to estimate just how truthful such accounts were. What I accepted more or less at face value was what I heard from the students closest to me. From their total absence of shame, I knew intuitively that I was getting the truth.

They described in detail the lice, rats, and rancid food, the excrement-smeared walls, the cold showers, and the vomit-filled black hoods pulled over their heads and padlocked around their necks. The accounts of prisoners forced to strip naked brought to mind the obsession with Arab male sexuality in Raphael Patai's *The Arab Mind*. The most hair-raising story was of a student who was nailed into a casket for days.

But the details of one torture technique or another were secondary for me. It was the psychological dynamic of the interrogation process that I found intriguing. These village boys, who before their arrest couldn't make heads or tails out of Kant or Sartre, returned from the interrogation room with a deep understanding of freedom. As paradoxical as it sounds, they reemerged from the Israeli prison camp emotionally, intellectually, and spiritually freer than they were when they went in. As far as I could gather, all the skill and brutality of the Israeli security system rarely achieved the desired results. If the harvest in information was meager, the unintended consequence was to turn these students into the full-fledged human beings I had tried with spotty success to produce through formal instruction. These young men exercised their wills by defying their interrogators, and in so doing the students became the teachers. I was again learning from them, not they from me.

I imagine an eighteen-year-old from a refugee camp sitting opposite his interrogator. The prisoner hasn't slept for days. Hungry and cold, frightened and alone, he has no lawyer, no legal system behind him, and no one to speak up for him. No one really knows where he is or why he was arrested. Parents and friends are as far away as the moon. And the interrogator, twice his age and trained to break the will of those under his control, goes to work. He wants information, and from one direction and then another he probes the prisoner's defenses. His logical tools, more effective than the medieval rack, hammer away at the prisoner's mind.

But the teenager refuses to submit to the will of the interrogator. By overcoming his natural biological instinct for survival, he becomes aware of his own freedom—because he is no longer a slave to his physical needs. Somehow he finds the inner strength to say no. His body wants food and warmth and sleep; he wants to be back with his family and friends; he wants to live. Still, he refuses.

Chapter Fourteen

Murder on the Via Dolorosa

P ONDERING THE STORIES OF PRISONERS reminded me of Avicenna's notion of the will. It brought me firmly over into the existentialist doctrine of taking control of your existence and of creating yourself.

At Oxford, I had picked up the Rousseauian philosophical assumptions that regarded every man as free by virtue of merely being. It was a technical freedom, a theoretical postulate that regarded freedom as a natural condition willingly sacrificed to avoid the dangers of nature or of other men. According to this bourgeois myth, people gave up their native liberty and joined together in a society in exchange for property and security. The tales I heard from my pupils went directly counter to this: people stripped of every scrap of worldly freedom were becoming free. This would have made a lot more sense to Sartre or Albert Camus than to John Locke or for that matter my stuffed friend in London Jeremy Bentham.

"The prisoner"—I said in a lecture presented at Pavia University in Italy, shortly after the outbreak of the intifada—"first develops a consciousness of the need to rebel, to reject, to refuse to submit his will to that of the interrogator."

This is the revolution of consciousness, where he develops the consciousness of the necessity to rebel . . . A person, a human being with a distinct individual identity, with a distinct personality, with a distinct individual will, is the total sum or collection of those acts of his which reflect the supremacy of his will, of his inner freedom. A person has identity to the extent that he has made his inner existential decision, and has decided to become master of himself, and has acted upon this decision. A person therefore is a function of his freedom acts, and personal identity is a function of freedom . . . We make our own essence; existence is prior to essence.

I realized that the interrogation room was really a contest of wills, and that if Palestinians as a nation refused to be broken, we would prevail over the interrogators. Once we chose to exercise inner sovereignty, we would prevail over the diktats of the military government.

With the frequent closures and the attendant difficulties of teaching on campus, those of us who lived in Israel's "Eternal and Undivided Capital" increasingly shifted our teaching, but also our political activities, to restaurants, cafés, and our homes. During one of the closures, I set up my temporary office in Father's law office on Salaheddin Street. There I had my classes, received visitors, held meetings, and pondered my riddles.

A course I came up with, together with a fellow Birzeit philosopher, deserves mention. Called Freedom, the class attracted some of the brighter students and activists. With tear gas circulating through the students' lungs, we didn't analyze freedom autopsy-like, as in a survey course; we hopscotched from topic to topic, unpacking freedom by identifying its most salient features for people living in a repressed, and repressive, society.

When we talked about freedom of speech, for instance, students didn't start off with J. S. Mill, Nietzsche, Sartre, and Isaiah Berlin, as their peers at Harvard do. We gave them local newspaper articles, such as the broadsides that appeared in *Al-Quds* after I had defended the blaspheming student poet. We did the same thing in discussing academic freedom. Instead of asking the students to crack open thick tomes on the subject, we presented them with Military Order 854, and an anthology of homegrown pamphlets and leaflets put out at Birzeit in our various and sundry protests. Then we moved on to sexual freedom, a taboo topic if ever there was one in our culture.

My own classroom for the topic of freedom was Jerusalem and its environs. There were days I spent hours wandering the city, smoking water pipes in my favorite café—my "grapevine"—and listening to the locals, merchants, professionals, artisans, and day laborers. I established contact in particular with a group of cabdrivers, who gave me the latest word from the street and who also told me about their troubles with Teddy Kollek's municipality, as well as with the tax authorities and the police.

Already immersed in the grassroots resistance throughout the West Bank, I started paying closer attention to the ways Israel was imposing its laws and procedures on the daily lives of average people, especially around Jerusalem.

This was brought home again and again just by driving around the countryside during university closures, visiting students and friends. In my red '77 Peugeot with yellow Jerusalem plates and my harmless look of a luftmensch, I usually breezed past the checkpoints erected along new highways tailor-made for Jewish settlements. The city of Maᵓaleh Adumim came into being when the government seized the grazing lands of the Jahalin Bedouin tribe, ostensibly for use as an army firing range. Bulldozers started working in earnest in 1982. (It was a common trick to declare an entire area a closed military zone, clear the people out, and then later turn it into a settlement.) At the opening of a new settlement in October 1982, Begin's minister of energy, Mordechai Zippori, explained the logic of settlement construction as "the backbone of the Zionist movement in the West Bank" and as the "only means to defeat any peace initiative which is intended to bring foreign rule to Judea and Samaria."[1]

The appalling transformation of hills and valleys by Israel's settlement activity made me think. I once mistakenly believed that the organic flow of events would inevitably lead to "Palest-El." Was I now just as naïve in assuming that the mutual recognition of basic interests would inevitably lead to a two-state solution? Was it possible that people could willfully ignore the dictates of logic and reason? Of basic common sense? It seemed so.

I'll start with the Israelis. The specter of nearly half a million Israelis calling for the resignation of the war's architects shook up the political elite. An investigation was ordered, and the subsequent "Kahan Report," in February 1983, pinned the indirect blame for the massacres at Sabra and Shatila on Sharon. Begin and Sharon resigned.

General Sharon was unrepentant about his failures in the West Bank or about the needless war that had cost thousands of lives. After resigning he was back at work almost immediately, launching his next career: building Jewish settlements in vast numbers.

As unrepentant as Sharon, Begin retreated back to his home, where he would live out the rest of his days gazing out on his handiwork on an opposite hill: the former village of Dir Yassin, now a mental hospital.

Yitzhak Shamir, a smart, scrappy veteran of the Jewish terrorist underground, took over until the new elections. (My father had witnessed this gnomelike man at work in 1947.) But Shamir lacked Begin's hypnotic power over the masses, and he failed to muster enough votes to put together a government. In 1984, Likud and Labor decided to form a curious cohabitation called the Government of National Unity. Under the rotating agreement, Shimon Peres became prime minister, Shamir was vice prime minister, and Yitzhak Rabin took over from Sharon as defense minister.

This shuffle in the government was a signal to the public and the world that things were going to change. In fact, in the West Bank, conditions only worsened. Both societies were becoming inured to a high level of violence.

A more radical generation of settlers, having been raised to believe that their ancestral home was Judea and Samaria, grew more and more brazen. A few days after Begin stepped down, one of his supporters threw a grenade in the middle of a Peace Now demonstration, killing a peace activist and injuring several others.

The so-called Bus 300 Affair was another sign of just how bare-knuckle the conflict was becoming. In spring 1984, Shin Bet agents arrested two Palestinians who had hijacked a public bus. The agents took the Palestinians into a field and beat them to death, death squad–style. South America had finally reached the region.

In Palestine, violence was also on the rise. When Lucy and I first arrived in the village of Birzeit to teach, the setting was pastoral and the people friendly to the point of naïveté. Traditional religion and tribal law kept human aggression under raps; far from being sources of aggression, tradition preserved a simple, peaceful way of life. Sectarian killings were unheard of, violent crime a rarity. Now, as in the Old City in the 1970s, violence was taking root in the villages and cities of the West Bank, and the traditional authorities were powerless to contain it.

As resentment among Palestinians mounted, so did the level of anarchy and lawlessness, and none of the political factions was able to exert broad authority. In 1983, Lebanese-like terror had reached Israel in the form of a bus bombing. The number of Israeli victims of terror shot up sevenfold between 1982 and 1985, from two to fourteen. (When I signed a declaration condemning the stabbing of a Jew, the Israelis said it was a PLO propaganda ploy. "Can a cockroach write a statement at all?" the chief of the military asked when he heard about it. "Only on strict telephone orders from Arafat, the terrorist magician," replied the intelligence specialist on Arab affairs, no doubt with mirth.[2])

One factor in the increase in violence was the growth of the Islamic movement, greatly bolstered by the successes of Hezbollah and other fanatical groups in Lebanon. Suicide bombings in Lebanon, which with deadly effect killed hundreds of Marines whom President Reagan had sent to help end the civil war there, entered into circulation as an odious new paradigm for "conflict resolution." Hezbollah Radio broadcast reports into Palestine of their "glorious martyr operations."

Sheikh Yassin's charity had by now fully morphed into the Muslim Brotherhood, the local Palestinian franchise of the secret Egyptian society responsible for Sadat's assassination in 1981. But Rabin and his colleagues in the Shin Bet continued to regard Islamic groups as a foil to the secular nationalists.[3] Incredible as it may sound today, they continued to believe that Islam could be used to fight Palestinian nationalists, which, before the killing of the two Islamist students at Birzeit, they did. With their coffers full and with more or less a free hand to operate, the sheikh and his minions began to challenge the secular nationalist groups. Their hope was to dominate politics in Palestine, just as the Hezbollah had replaced the PLO after the Israelis drove it out of Lebanon.

In 1984, I noticed a change among some of my students. All the humiliations of their brief lives, tossed into a religious cauldron, had turned village boys, and sometimes girls, into implacable fanatics, hostile to the sort of liberty I was trying to teach them to love. It was the opposite process from the prison interrogation: instead of self-liberation and identification with the finest fruits of humanity's thought, ideological inebriation locked them into a narrow, unbending frame of mind. I feared that the Brotherhood could win over the masses—they were far better organized than Fatah, were supported by the military government, and were busy setting up a social network to help people whose lives had been shattered by the occupation.

While I had no doubt that Palestinians needed and wanted their own independent state, I was becoming equally aware that in the duplicitous world of politics few people dared to openly say so. It was still heresy among many people in the PLO to talk about a two-state solution. At the very most, a PLO member would demand the "unconditional" establishment of a Palestinian state. As for the Israelis, they were doing everything in their power to forestall such an outcome, even though it should have been crystal clear to them that such a state was in their own best interest.

The more I mulled it over in my mind, the more I realized that both Israelis and Palestinians were refusing to talk about a two-state solution because it implied mutual recognition of the other's rights as a nation, and because it meant having to admit squarely there was a price that had to be paid. As for me, I could talk about national freedom as much as I wanted, as long as it was just a monologue or a conversation with my students; without active dialogue with Israelis, it would go nowhere.

It became clear that much of what I had unwittingly bought into was an illusion. Nearly all of the leaflets and statements I was busy endorsing and signing called for the "unconditional" creation of our state. What on earth does *unconditional* mean? I asked myself. Ali Hassouneh, my friend and travel partner to Amman, explained to me one day, with a jocular but slightly patronizing lilt to his voice, that *unconditional* meant, of course, unconditional: without negotiations. No strings attached. No conditions. "Nonsense," I retorted, with just as friendly a grin. I was thinking aloud when I said to him that if a Palestinian state were to come into being, it could do so only through negotiations with Israel. And negotiations required serious dialogue, not with Europeans or a handful of Israeli anti-Zionists who already agreed with us, but with committed Zionist politicians from within the Israeli power elite.

Two American Jewish visionaries soon left me no choice but to "put my money where my mouth was," as Father liked to say. They were Professor Herbert Kelman, a Harvard psychologist, and his lovely wife, Rose. The Kelmans realized long before almost everyone else that Palestinians and Israelis would eventually have to sit down and negotiate a deal. And since no one else was fostering dialogue, they decided to start. Herbert and Rose organized joint meetings, slowly and quietly bringing Palestinian and Israeli public figures together.

One day Kelman rang me up and asked me to take part in a meeting at Harvard. Representing the Israeli side, he told me, would be leftist but staunchly Zionist members of the Knesset, such as Yossi Sarid. Joining them on our side was my father's friend Walid Khalidi, which didn't surprise me given his long-standing views. Far more unexpected for me—but fitting well into my riddle—was the participation of prominent figures in the PLO, including Afif Safieh, a longtime director of Yasir Arafat's office and now a PLO rep in Washington, D.C. Abu Jihad and Arafat, who had met Kelman more than once already, had also signed off on the meeting.

I was ready to go, but as the head of the union I couldn't. Up to this point Palestinian politicians had held official meetings only with anti-Zionist Israelis, such as the great Hasidic sage and master Joel Teitelbaum, leader of an ultraorthodox religious sect. Anything else was considered illegitimate. On one occasion Father invited the Israeli president, Herzog, to our winter house in Jericho for lunch, and he asked me to join them. I declined because of my position with the union. The Harvard meeting was no friendly lunch but the first step toward real dialogue, and I knew I had to go. I equally knew that the members of my union would lynch me if I went to Harvard as their representative. This left me two options: either to turn down the invitation and continue my work in the union, or to quit.

It was hardly a soul-twisting existential dilemma. Fully convinced that it was in my nation's interest to brush aside a worn-out taboo against open dialogue with our occupiers, I tendered my resignation from the union and set off for Cambridge.

The meeting with Sarid and his Israeli colleagues was a lot more pleasant than the mess I faced when I got back home. Around campus, my participation in the meeting changed people's perception of me. In the eyes of close friends and colleagues, I had ceased being an independent gadfly with strange ideas and had thrown in my lot with the "right-wingers" surrounding Fatah's official leadership, and more specifically with Arafat himself, who was increasingly thought to have charted a "sell-out" course in order to curry favors with the Americans. The most heated ideological skirmishes I had back at Birzeit were with my best students, who, like good students everywhere, despised bourgeois compromise.

One of these students, a leader of the PFLP faction, came out against me in an anonymous leaflet he signed in the name of his faction. I knew he had written it; I had read enough of the faction's leaflets to spot his style a mile off. Holding the incendiary tract in my hand, I smiled proudly at his effective use of metaphor and at a polemic carefully crafted so as not to sound bombastic. I visualized the concentrated features on his face—the raised eyebrows and the folds in his forehead—as he penned it. Another inflammatory leaflet floating around campus, also anonymous and also in the name of the writer's faction, was written by another student and colleague of mine named Marwan Barghouti.

By this point I, too, was skilled at the art of cranking out leaflets. I typed one up explaining the logic behind my new course of dialogue, signed my name to it, and sent it into circulation. Nearly bent over from bursts of laughter, Marwan commented to me as I was handing the flyers out that my leaflet was the first in Palestinian history to have been signed by the author rather than by his faction, as if I were a faction unto myself. At the time it felt like it.

It hadn't taken Marwan long after his arrival on campus to establish himself, together with Samir Sbeihat, as the undisputed leader of Shabibah, Fatah's student movement. We first met in my political theory class. He was a twenty-five-year-old who had just been released from a seven-year sentence in an Israeli jail. He would go on to a brilliant, if checkered and unfinished, career. He now sits in an Israeli prison serving multiple life sentences on terrorism charges.

On the surface, his story sounds interchangeable with that of thousands of others. His forefathers were fellahin who for hundreds of years had lived in villages near Birzeit. Marwan was educated at a UN refugee school set up in the village, where he joined a PLO cell. He was soon locked up for throwing rocks at soldiers and shared a prison cell for nine months with Samir Sbeihat.

Marwan stood out. Short and stocky, as if he had grown out of the rocky soil of his native countryside, he had a flare for polemics coupled with a quick mind that easily sifted and absorbed information. His unflappable self-confidence made him a strong leader. If his mind wandered while reading John Locke in class it was because of his soaring national ambitions.

What intrigued me most about him was the way he spoke about his previous Israeli captors. In prison he had learned Hebrew, and in his various interrogation sessions, he developed enormous self-respect by not bending to the will of his enemy. He also learned not to hate the Israelis but to glimpse the humanity lurking behind their uniforms. They also, it seems, discovered his.

A good example of Marwan's authority took place several years after we met. Repression by the authorities, along with the frequent closures (once for six months at a stretch), invited angrier, more violent protests, which in turn led to more repression. In the spring of 1985, tensions at the university were riding so high that a mob of students attacked the American consul general's car while he was visiting the campus.[4] The consul general escaped from a lynch mob only after Marwan rushed to the center of the crowd, put his hand into the air, and snapped his fingers. The screams and shaking fists stopped at once. No one dared to lay so much as a hand on the man. "My name is Marwan Barghouti," Marwan said to the shivering consul general, who had just watched his life pass before his eyes. "I am the chairman of the student council here."[5] Later that year, the military authorities placed Marwan under administrative detention for six months. Two years later he would be deported from the country by the Israeli authorities, as was Samir Sbeihat.

History famously likes playing tricks. Hegel talks about its "cunning," its "capers" and its "pranks." Military governments are especially susceptible to history's law of unexpected consequences. In our case, the Israelis used every means they had to suppress the nationalist movement in the West Bank, and all they succeeded in doing was to encourage boomerang-like political activists to conduct business in the very place where Israelis most wanted to cement their rule: Jerusalem. The tighter the squeeze on the West Bank, the more Jerusalem returned to its pre-1948 status as the center of an Arab political movement. And in Jerusalem the government couldn't so easily throw us into a dungeon, or nail us into a casket, without an outcry from the Europeans and Americans—or increasingly from our Jewish friends in Peace Now, many of whose leaders also lived or worked in Jerusalem.

The cold war spread a glimmer of mystery and danger over a city already suffused with the atmosphere of a spy novel. Agents from various

Western and Soviet bloc security and diplomatic services met for cloak-and-dagger meetings. With some luck, at the American Colony Hotel, across the street from my parents' home, you might see men with dark glasses in the corner or the ubiquitous Mossad Man whispering to an Arab collaborator working as a waiter.

I experienced my first murder in the dead of winter 1983, when I also took up the habit of rubbing worry beads. The killing took place on my doorstep under the Ecce Homo Arch.

Problems at the Lemon Tree Café had been mounting, and in yet another paradox, the more dealings I had with Israelis, the greater the ills besetting the hostel and café—such as the time Shin Bet agents tried to recruit one of our sexy Scandinavian waitresses to work for them as an informant. On another occasion a security official summoned me to police headquarters in the Russian compound and intimated that if I didn't "make a deal" with them they might "accidentally" find heroin in the place and charge me with running a drug ring.

The murder took place on a cold and drizzly evening. On my way home to our apartment on the Via Dolorosa, I dropped by the café as usual for a quick double espresso. It was late, and business was slow. At a table across from me sat a European couple talking quietly, seemingly unruffled by the tensions poisoning the city. The man, a German backpacker with a frame as big as an ox, had arrived at the hostel several days earlier, but had had to book a room at a different hostel because ours was full. Now he was back with a dark-skinned woman who appeared to be his girlfriend.

They got up and left before I did. On my way home I passed them. They were ambling slowly, arm in arm, and kissing.

Within five minutes I was upstairs in our living room getting ready to watch the evening news on television. The room had two large windows looking out to the Via Dolorosa, an old cobbled lane with no cars and, on this bone-chilling evening, no people.

Just before switching on the TV, I heard a muffled sound followed by a heavy thud. Lucy, who had just put the children to bed, came into the room. "What was that?" she asked referring to the strange noise. We both moved toward the window, and in the silence of the night, we heard the distinct sound of footsteps walking quickly up the alley at a right angle to the Via Dolorosa. Putting my head out the window, I saw the German man from the café lying facedown on the steps of the Catholic convent across the street, with a stream of blood oozing out of his neck.

"Someone's been shot." I turned to Lucy in fright.

"I'll call the police," she said. "You go downstairs."

In seconds I was standing above the dying German backpacker, unsure of what to do. I heard the sound of someone shouting and running in our direction. Looking down along the Via Dolorosa, I saw it was a lone policeman. An Arab.

"What should we do?" I asked him when he arrived short of breath. The officer felt the man's pulse and assured me that he was still alive. "Help me carry him to the hospital," he said, pointing in the direction of the Austrian Hospice down the road.

Together the two of us, who together weighed as much as the wounded man, tried to carry or half drag the German several blocks to the hospital, then three flights up to the emergency ward. By the time we got there he had bled to death in our arms.

Fiction may not always imitate life; in this case it did. The events surrounding the death of the German tourist baffled me. When later, sitting in solitary confinement, I thought about trying my hand at writing a political mystery, the first chapter I sketched out had the title "Murder on the Via Dolorosa."

The riddle over the slaying started with the Israeli police investigator who took my statement the following morning. He jotted down some notes in a cavalier manner, as if entirely uninterested in solving the crime, and then bid me good day. I asked him what he thought had happened.

"Oh, you know, some Arab terrorist probably did it," he stated in the tone people usually use to talk about last week's soccer match.

"He had a girl with him," I told the officer. "What happened to her?"

The officer explained in his flat, uninvolved manner that she was the victim's girlfriend. She had been scared witless after the shooting and had screamed frantically for help, but no one came to her assistance.

"I didn't hear her," I informed him, puzzled that she would lie about such a thing. From my apartment I can hear the scuffle of a rat in the tipped-over garbage bins down the alley. Far from screaming, the girlfriend had slinked off as silently as a mouse. "She didn't scream."

"Yes she did," the officer assured me with the same abstract tone of voice. "She told us she banged on all the neighbors' doors but no one opened up for her. Finally she ran up to the police station at Jaffa Gate to inform us of what happened."

"But Jaffa Gate is in the opposite direction of the footsteps I heard tiptoeing away."

My interlocutor was no longer taking notes and was manifestly uninterested in continuing. Wrapping things up, he said dryly that the woman had been so rattled by the experience that she took the first flight back to Germany.

Something was fishy. The following day, a short item appeared in the newspaper stating that a German tourist had been shot dead in the alleys of the Old City, and that the police suspected Arab terrorists.

I didn't buy the story about the terrorists. A killing, especially of a Western tourist, normally would bring the entire weight of the Israeli police apparatus onto the Arab Quarter. Why the apathy? Why had the police allowed the girlfriend to leave hours after the crime? Who was this "girlfriend" anyway? Later, a moneychanger on Saleheddin Street filled in some intriguing details for me. The moneychanger's cousin managed a hotel, and the girl had been staying at this hotel when the murder occurred. When asked by the manager what she was up to in the country, she said that she was heading down to Eilat to look for her boyfriend. Most intriguing of all, she said all this in Arabic. Her passport was German but she spoke Arabic like a native. The suspicious manager—many Israelis speak Arabic—asked her about this, and she explained that she had worked for some German consultancy group in Saudi Arabia.

As scattered pieces came together, I was beginning to get nervous. I naturally didn't believe the tall tale of the Arab "terrorists." Did this mean that the Israelis had had a hand in the murder? Was it a coincidence that the victim was in my café fifteen minutes before the man's death? Who was he, anyway? Why had the "girlfriend" disappeared? Months later, the newspapers carried a story about the arrest and conviction of a local Arab for the crime. But years later I learned, from other Palestinian prisoners, that the man had confessed to not having been the murderer, and that he had been planted in jail as an Israeli spy on other Palestinian prisoners.

One thing was for certain, however: the shadowy world in which I now lived wasn't the innocent Jerusalem I knew as a child.

Chapter Fifteen

Faisal Husseini

T HE MURDER WAS THE LAST STRAW. The city's rapid decline, the unsolved mystery behind the slaying of the German, and the threat to plant drugs in the café did the trick. In life one has to choose the right battles, and keeping the café open, and continuing our defiant experiment to live in the decaying city, didn't strike us as the right one. In 1984, Lucy and I shut down the Lemon Tree and moved out of the Old City.

Our new apartment was in Abu Dis, a village on a hill just beyond the Mount of Olives. Our neighboring village was Ayzariyah, the Arabic name for the biblical town of Bethany, where Mary, Martha, and Lazarus lived. (You can hear Lazarus's name in the Arab name for the village.) We didn't feel as if we really had left the Old City, for from the balcony of our new apartment we could see in the distance the luminous splendor of the Dome of the Rock.

Living outside the city walls didn't change a thing for us politically or socially. The center of our lives was now East Jerusalem, which had come to displace Birzeit as the center of nationalist politics. Just as the Old World patricians had been displaced by the National Guidance

Committee, which in turn gave way in the early 1980s to the network of grassroots groups organized by student and union activists, a new power center was growing up. This one was located in the Arab Studies Society, in what would become known as the Orient House, and its central personality was Faisal Husseini. We didn't always agree on analysis or strategy, but disagreement never prevented me from seeing Faisal as more of an elder brother than just a collaborator or co-conspirator. Faisal fondly dubbed me "the revolution's philosopher."

Faisal could spin out yarns from his family history that were a lot more impressive than mine. His ancient roots went right back to Mohammed's Mecca, and, alas, in the starkest contrast to my clan, his was fabulously wealthy with land, businesses holdings, and connections throughout the Arab world.

Where he really had a leg up over a Nusseibeh was in being part of political legend. He was the grandson and great-grandson of mayors of Jerusalem, the grandnephew of the grand mufti of Jerusalem, and distant cousin of Yasir Arafat. Most of all, he was the son of the fabled Abdel Kader el-Husseini, the military hero who worked closely with Father and the Herod's Gate Committee before dying during the siege of al-Castal. Faisal, an eight-year-old at the time, was expected to take up his father's legacy.

After undergoing some training in PLO guerrilla camps, Faisal returned to East Jerusalem after the Six-Day War. Like my elder brother, he waded across the Jordan River, braving trigger-happy soldiers. Once word got out in Israel that he was in Jerusalem, a note of panic sounded. "It was as if the son of Ho Chi Minh had come to live in New York City," said one Israeli, comparing Faisal's father to the nettlesome revolutionary leader.

Arafat had also waded the river, and while trying to build up a local military cadre, he often hid out in Faisal's house. Arafat gave Faisal a gun, which Faisal took but never used. Not long after my first encounter with him, at the Al-Aqsa mosque during the fire in 1969, he was arrested, the gun was found, and he was expelled from the country.

In the late seventies the Israelis allowed him to return to Jerusalem. Not wanting to get exiled again, he kept a low profile, working odd jobs and steering clear of trouble. No one knew it at the time, but his mind was actively scouring the political landscape, looking for the right place to invest his energies and intelligence. Eventually he grasped something that only the indefatigable Dr. Glock—still zipping past West Bank checkpoints with his yellow Israeli plates in hot pursuit of our past— was thinking: that cultural memory was becoming a major battlefront in our fight for independence.

Faisal first started the Arab Studies Society in the neighborhood of Musrara, along the seam line between East and West Jerusalem. A couple of years later, it moved to a wing of the Orient House Hotel, which his family owned.

At its founding, the society must have appeared to the Shin Bet as a harmless hobby for an underachieving scion of a powerful martyred figure. I can imagine them pitying the poor fellow who had fallen so short of his family's expectations. What they didn't properly appreciate was how thickly his father's blood still ran in his veins. His enemies soon found out just how formidable a foe they had on their hands. For the occupation eager to portray opposition as inherently terrorist and bloodthirsty, Faisal was highly intelligent, urbane, and moderate. No guns, no half-shaven face, no revolutionary hubris. And he spoke Hebrew.

Fatah activists in the territories figured out what Faisal was made of long before the Shin Bet did. Activists regarded him as their natural leader. When Marwan was coming up with bylaws for Shabibah, he sought out Faisal's advice, as did Mubarak Awad when he wished to market his Gandhian nonviolence. Whatever the issue—settlements, arrests, house demolitions, or the latest administrative arrest—Faisal presented our views in clear, cogent terms. But he didn't just talk. After a press appearance where he'd denounce the latest outrage you'd find him arm in arm with the man whose house was about to be bulldozed or whose son had just been killed, or with the wife whose husband had just been arrested. He won the hearts of Jerusalemites by always being on call for their troubles. For Shamir, Sharon, and others of their ilk, who had no interest in dialogue, Faisal was the most dangerous enemy out there.

At the Arab Studies Society, Faisal invited such colossal Jewish intellectuals as Yeshayahu Leibovitch to address Arab audiences at the Orient House. This put him in the dialogue camp, and made the Arab Society a natural home for me.

Faisal and I first began working together shortly after my return from the controversial Israeli-Palestinian meeting at Harvard. Leftist members of the Knesset, led by the formidable Shulamit Aloni and Jossi Sarid, wanted to hold open meetings with some Palestinian public figures, at the American Colony Hotel. I agreed at once. Faisal also got PLO backing for him to take part.

The other Palestinians who participated were all associated with Fatah, either loosely or in some kind of leadership role. There was Raymondah Tawil, a fiery lady who during the days of the National Guidance Committee hosted the mayors at her political salon in Ramallah; she was also Arafat's future mother-in-law. Hanna Siniora and Ziad Abu Zayyad, two editors of the pro-Fatah daily *Al-Fajr*, also attended.

This being the first public meeting in Jerusalem of Fatah and Zionist members of the Knesset, Faisal and I prepared a statement affirming our allegiance to the PLO and to an independent Palestinian state. Hanna Siniora printed it up on the front of *Al-Fajr*.

The encounter at the American Colony was a breakthrough in many respects; most important, it finally shattered the dishonest silence over the issue of dialogue. The public now knew that Fatah was interested in talking with the Zionists. The Israeli presence similarly sent the message to average Palestinians that at least some Zionists were prepared to publicly accept the PLO and its call for a Palestinian state.

The American Colony meeting also created a template for joint Israeli-Palestinian committees and protests that eventually came to center around Faisal and the Arab Society. One idea we came up with was to commemorate the sixth of June, the day the occupation began, with a protest march along the former No Man's Land. Hundreds of Israeli peace activists and Palestinians held black flags and stood along the former border in a call for an open city of joint Palestinian-Israeli sovereignty.

For many of my student friends, holding a black flag was far from the sort of activism they had been raised in the Fatah clubs to admire. They still preferred more daring exploits, such as stoning tanks or writing graffiti. Still, a slow trickle began to warm up to dialogue. Once, as I was participating with Israelis in a sit-down protest at Damascus Gate, some Birzeit students came for a visit. I sat on the steps outside the gate, sweating copiously because of the heat and holding up a poster with some Arabic-Hebrew-English slogan, and a student who was an expert at stone throwing looked at me with resignation and said, "Is this what you've turned us into?" We smiled at each other. I handed him a poster, and he took it.

It didn't take long for Faisal's Orient House to become the power center of Palestinian national politics. Another step along the way came in 1985, when Ziad Abu Zayyad, Hanna Siniora, and I teamed up with an ex-Nasserite from Gaza named Zuheir el-Rayyes, and the mayor of Hebron, Mustafa Natsheh, to establish the Arab Council, founded, with Abu Jihad's backing, specifically to nurture formal contacts with Israeli Knesset members who agreed with us on the need for a two-state solution.

As a natural spin-off from the council, we started publishing a weekly newspaper called *Al-Mawqef*. Cousin Zaki joined the staff after being fired from *Al-Quds* over a labor dispute. At Marwan Barghouti's recommendation, we hired Hamzeh Smadi, a one-time Birzeit student from Qabatya, to be the paper's editor. Another colleague joined us after being released from prison: Fahed Abu al-Haj. Fahed was raised in a rustic rural setting, and he learned to read and write only after the Israelis locked him up for the first time at the age of sixteen. He finished school in jail.

My first conversation with Fahed in the office is unforgettable, because for me it was a metaphor for the decency, simplicity, and humanity that is as native to Palestine as is its prophetic religion. Freshly freed from years in the prison camp, Fahed had heard that our paper was an

Abu Jihad–supported outfit, for him the ultimate stamp of approval. So, he knocked on my door in search of a job.

"How much do you want?" I asked him.

"Whatever you want to pay me."

"Just tell me."

"Dr. Sari, whatever you want to pay me."

I suggested sixty Jordanian pounds, a pittance.

"Thank you, Dr. Sari."

"Will this be enough for you?"

"Dr. Sari, thank you."

I tried to press him on his needs, but each time, he responded only with gratitude. I ended up jacking his salary up to eighty.

Chapter Sixteen

Annex Us!

B Y 1986 THE MAIN ENGINE DRIVING the increasing levels of violence in the Occupied Territories was the settlement movement.
Back in 1983, General Rafael Eitan, Israel's highest-ranking officer at
the time, had drawn up blueprints for one hundred new settlements between Jerusalem and Nablus. "When we have settled the land," went
his prognosis, "all the Arabs will be able to do about it will be to scurry
around like drugged roaches in a bottle."[1] It seems the Israeli military
authorities enjoyed likening us to cockroaches. Just as General Eitan
predicted, three years later, settlements were springing up in every corner. Fortresslike suburban enclaves such as Halmish (built on the al-Nabi
Saleh forest, renowned for its dense stand of trees that astoundingly
managed to survive the Ottoman years) ringed the West Bank like a
necklace, or a noose. Sixty thousand Israeli settlers lived in the occupied
West Bank. It became an everyday sight to see, perched on a hilltop, settlements with swimming pools and sprinkler systems within eyeshot of
dust-bitten villages where people had to walk a mile for a bucket of
water—water, of course, pumped from West Bank aquifers. One settlement in the Jordan Valley was able to expand because the government,

having confiscated one of Father's farms after the 1967 war, had handed it over to them.

The situation in East Jerusalem was worse. When I arrived back in the Old City in 1978, I discovered that successive Israeli Labor governments under the municipal leadership of Teddy Kollek had allowed Arab East Jerusalem to decay, while building modern neighborhoods for a total of thirty thousand Israeli settlers. Now the number was one hundred thousand, and spiraling upward fast.[2] As a sign of our losses in Jerusalem, our family's saga of the Goldsmith's Souk took a new twist when some Israeli religious zealots clutching guns moved in and refused to budge. The police said it was a property dispute that only the courts could adjudicate. That the souk had belonged to the Nusseibeh family for centuries didn't impress them. Cousin Zaki then began to dig through four-hundred-year-old Ottoman documents to prove our ownership.

More settlements brought more rock throwing, more arrests, more rubber bullets, more abuse. Amnesty International reported cases of prisoners being hooded, handcuffed, and forced to stand naked without moving for many hours at a time.[3]

In 1986, fifty soldiers toting machine guns broke into the home of Birzeit's acting president, Dr. Gabi Baramki, and dragged him outside. They drove him handcuffed to campus and proceeded to ransack the administrative offices there. Soldiers confiscated schoolbooks, magazines, and newspapers. From there they continued on to the student dorms, arresting dozens of activists.

In December 1986, a group of soldiers showed up at the campus to hunt down more students. Hanan Ashrawi closed the main gate to prevent them from storming the campus. A sniper, taking up his position, narrowly missed her. The bullet ricocheted off the paving stone in front of her, and she leapt backward just in time to avoid the next one. The sniper, agitated at her quick maneuvering, shouted out at this graduate of Thomas Jefferson's university, "You Arabs are all animals!"[4]

With more violence came more demagoguery on both sides. Anti-Semitic literature smuggled in from Egypt circulated in the refugee camps and in cities such as Hebron. On the Israeli side, a poll taken by the Van Leer Jerusalem Institute found that 42 percent of young Jews between the ages of fifteen and eighteen supported the Orthodox rabbi Meir Kahane's call to expel all Arabs.[5]

The solutions that politicians proposed to defuse the ticking time bomb were a singular mixture of wishful thinking and Sartre's *mauvaise foi*. President Reagan, in a good example of the latter, took up an entirely disembodied ideal then being bandied about by Shimon Peres, the man of a thousand masks, and his clique within the Labor Party: it was the "Jordanian option" linking Palestinian destiny with Jordan. But this was a case of too little, too late. By this point the nationalist genie was out of the bottle, and to most Palestinians it took on the features of Yasir Arafat.

Anyway, the Labor Party was not in power, and Likud was doing all it could to prevent any new division of the Holy Land. Many ideologues on the Israeli right were openly calling for annexation of the territories they lovingly called Judea and Samaria. While the government shied away from talk of open annexation, from our balcony in Abu Dis we stared out at the new mega-settlement of Ma²aleh Adumim, a daily reminder of Israel's unilateral plans.

As the two peoples rapidly moved toward all-out conflict, a handful of politicians and public figures on both sides agreed that the only viable way to avoid war was a two-state solution negotiated directly between the PLO and the Israeli government. The riddle for me was how to break this message out of the insular world of peace activists meeting at the American Colony. How do you drive home the message to average people that their leaders are leading them to disaster?

In the summer of 1986, I set up a workshop—mostly at my father's law office—to try to fashion a bombshell.

Father's thyroid cancer worsened, and over the months I followed the progress of his disease. Banned from Jordan because of my earlier indiscretions, I couldn't be at the Royal Hospital in Amman to witness King Hussein and Queen Noor kneeling at his bedside after his operation.

The operation kept him alive, but with the stubbornness of a blood-hound the disease wouldn't let him go. During Father's frequent trips to the Israeli Hadassah Hospital in Ein Kerem for iodization treatments, Mother was left alone in the house with her memories. In the summer of 1986, as the chances of his recovery were slipping away, she began to reminisce with me about her childhood and the bright, vital, young lawyer who had charmed her. Fifty years earlier the world was intact and whole, full of the sweet scent of orange blossoms. Then the troubles started. "I've never known a day of tranquility since then. It's been one disaster after the next." Cancer was the last of a long string of calamities shadowing her adult years.

Spending so much time within Mother's memories, juxtaposed with Father's refusal to live in a fantasy world or be a victim of hallucinations, helped give structure to the "bombshell" I needed to deliver. I was fed up with politicians saying one thing in public while secretly doing the opposite. The sort of public service my father embodied had no room for such dishonesty, and I decided to do something about it. My "bomb-shell"—inspired by the medical profession, I also likened it to shock therapy—was to be my tribute to my father's titanic integrity, and his willingness to step on toes by saying the truth.

The trigger happened one afternoon when, after visiting Mother, I retraced my childhood walks through the streets of the Old City and came to the Goldsmith's Souk. As I stood there, I struck up a conversa-tion with one of the Jewish students who had taken it over, with the patronage of Ariel Sharon, meter by meter. Judging by his Brooklyn accent, I concluded he was an American.

I explained to him that the souk belonged to my family. "Do you think we *want* to be here?" he asked, moving his hand in all directions. At first I was encouraged by the question. I half expected to dive into an existential heart-to-heart between two people trapped in an impossible situation not of their choosing.

I was wrong.

"We are *destined* to be here," he said. It was as if he was telling me that divinity—the same force that once upon a time told humanity thou shalt not steal—was compelling him to dislodge us from our ancestral land, not because he *wanted* to do so, but because he *had* to. It was his mission in life.

I thought up my bombshell on a hot summer's day. Lucy and I wanted to take the kids for a swim and couldn't decide where. Broken and neglected, East Jerusalem lacked such public amenities as swimming pools, which left us with the YMCA. "How about Maʾaleh Adumim," I finally suggested. Lucy at first looked surprised, and then grinned once she surmised that I was cooking something up.

I had always been curious about life on the other side of the barbed wire and the locked gates of this Forbidden City built on Bedouin land. I had heard that to encourage new settlers, one of the first facilities the community had built was a large swimming pool.

We set off on our adventure, with towels and sunblock and loads of curiosity. At the entrance to the pool, we bought the cheap government-subsidized tickets. Jamal, Absal, and Buraq dashed off to swim, while I sat on the edge enjoying the trickle of water on my feet. Then my bombshell hit me. "How wonderfully diabolic!"

I was smiling at myself, my feet splashing playfully, when an attendant walked up and asked me with almost effusive friendliness if I was enjoying the pool.

"I most certainly am," I replied in my rusty Hebrew.

A charmingly wide grin spread over his face. He wanted to know where I was from.

My answer—Abu Dis—was calculated to shock, and the grin on his face froze. As if by remote control, he turned his head away from me and with automated, clocklike movements darted off without saying another word.

I returned to my plot. Here I was swimming in the settlement, and thanks to my Jerusalem ID, not even Sharon could do a thing about it. They could ignore me, walk away from me as the pool attendant had, they could even despise me as bigots tend to do to lesser humans, but they couldn't boot me out. What would happen, I asked myself, if one fine day Palestinians simply turned their political aspirations inside out? Instead of seeking independence in a new state, why not seek equal rights *within* Israel? After all, Israel is controlling our land, resources, and lives, and our taxes helped build the swimming pool in the first place. Why shouldn't we just demand to be annexed? *Demand to be Israelis?* Wouldn't it pull the rug out from underneath the Jewish state? One thing was certain, such a demand would bring the complacent Israelis back to their senses. In no time they would forget all about their settlement projects and their bogus schemes for Palestinian limited autonomy, all their silly talk of Judea and Samaria, and at full gallop would throw themselves into the arms of Yasir Arafat as a savior, embracing the two-state solution as a gift from heaven. In my mind's eye I saw the settlers in the Golden Souk hightailing it back to Brooklyn.

Still splashing and grinning, Lucy came and offered me a soda from the concession stand. I told her what I was thinking, and she predicted that my fellow activists would call for my head. After all, we had been issuing declarations by the armload accusing the Israelis of illegally trying to annex our lands, calling it unethical, abhorrent, cruel, and dozens of other hoary adjectives. And now I wanted to stand up and ask for annexation! Crazy! Lucy said all this with a twinkle in her eye, which assured me that it was my best idea yet.

The article I wrote in our *Al-Mawqef* newspaper the following week posed a thought experiment. Looking objectively at the essential Palestinian interest in freedom, I asked which scenario was preferable: autonomy or annexation with full equal rights in Israel? Answering my own question, I said that it stood to reason that as citizens of Israel we would wield far more power in shaping our destiny. A member of the Knesset elected from Tulkarem, say, would not only help pass laws for his home town, or for those areas in the Occupied Territories on which settlements were being built, but he would also participate in legislation for Haifa and Tel Aviv. The ballot box would give us what armed guerrillas never could: control over our own lives, *and over theirs.*

Within days, my article catapulted me onto the front pages of Israeli newspapers. Then came an invitation for me to participate on a popular Israeli political TV show. "Would you be willing to appear on the same talk show with one of the leaders of the settlement movement," asked the producer?

"Are you kidding me?" I replied, amazed at the effect of my bombshell.

I turned up at the studio with my hair uncombed, wearing sandals and my favorite T-shirt, old and a bit tattered but the most comfortable one I had. To the chagrin of the producer, who wanted to see sparks fly (police and a medic stood in the back just in case), I adopted an easygoing and chatty pose, and the conversation with the settler was friendly. But with each answer I gave, I could almost hear the squeaking sounds of a rusted mind opening to dangers it had never imagined possible.

"Are you saying you would actually run for the Knesset, and become a member?" asked the interviewer.

"Sure, why not?" I replied with a lilt in my voice.

"Are you trying to tell me you would accept the Knesset's national symbols, the flag, the national song?"

"I'd have to. But don't forget, Israel *is* a democracy, *isn't it?*"

He looked nervous and asked me what I was driving at.

"Just that if we Arabs were the majority in the Knesset, if we wanted to we could change the symbols, couldn't we?"

From the audience I heard the loud noise of people stirring in their chairs, following by some indecipherable voices and catcalls.

"And would you accept to be part of the Israeli army?" crowed my interlocutor, this time at a high pitch.

This was one of the questions whose response I had already rehearsed. "What are you talking about? To be allowed to wander around like the soldiers I see, slinging an Uzi over my shoulder? Any day!"

The shock many Arab viewers felt when they saw me banter with a notorious leader of the settler movement isn't easy to describe. The pro-Jordanian daily *Al-Nahar* came out with the headline "Arab Wants to Convert to Judaism." Another of the newspaper's headlines read, "Sari Nusseibeh Wants to Join the Israeli Army."

Newsweek ran a full-page interview with me on the subject of annexation. Israeli newspapers lined up to interview me.

The bombshell began to work. Sure enough, the left-wing faction of the Labor Party began invoking "a demographic threat" to boost its position that Israel needed to move fast to find a solution with the Palestinians. Gad Ya'acobi, the minister of economics and planning, realized that by calling for annexation I was tearing up the foundations of the Greater Israel movement. "Sari Nusseibeh," he wrote in the *Jerusalem Post*, "is not more moderate than his interlocutors, the advocates of Greater Israel. He's just smarter. He knows that annexation will eventually lead to the establishment of a Palestinian state throughout the Land of Israel."[6] Another commentator considered my ideas more dangerous than "PLO terror and the specter of an Arab military attack." A journalist for the Israeli daily *Ma'ariv* cited the Israeli representative of the UN: "If Palestinians begin to think like this, then we've really got something to worry about." One phone caller went so far as to deliver a blunt warning to me at home: "If you keep this up, you're a dead man." This was the first of many death threats.

The general mood around the Birzeit campus was that the philosopher had lost his marbles. (One of my closest colleagues dismissed my ideas as an "infantile fantasy.") But the main student and teacher activists, whose minds had been trained in the interrogation room to separate lies from the truth, rallied around me. Marwan, Sameer Shehadeh, and Samir Sbeihat caught on immediately that my ruse was a tactical move aimed at waking up the Israelis. Either we get our state, or they will have a battle for equal rights on their hands.

My students were not alone in figuring out what I was up to. I continued my morning routine of passing by my parents' house for breakfast. I didn't even have to explain to Father what I was up to. "It's all tongue in cheek," he explained to stunned relatives and friends.

The Israeli Shin Bet began to worry. Perhaps they thought the PLO had put me up to it; an even more threatening possibility was that a new and hitherto unidentified nationalist leadership had hatched the plot. The security men started to keep an eye on me.

One day a member of the Shin Bet, now doubling as a reporter for the Hebrew daily *Maariv*, rang me up and said he wanted to do a special report on some of my students and me. A few days later this agent-cum-journalist met Marwan, Sbeihat, and me at the *Al-Mawqef* offices.

Our interviewer had his worst suspicions confirmed. He spent several hours with us, and by the end he was shaking his head in disbelief. Savvy as ever, Marwan and Sbeihat let him know, and in Hebrew no less, that my annexation initiative made sense. Nonplussed, he asked them what they knew about Israeli life, only to discover that they knew as much as he did about football teams, radio shows, and folk singers.

From that point on, Marwan, Sbeihat, and I formed a sort of annexation club, and our frequent talks over cigarettes and coffee normally culminated in hilarious scenarios. Sbeihat excelled at conjuring up new and wonderful possibilities. "Big changes are afoot," he assured us. One day, he brought to my attention something Shimon Peres had just said in one of his speeches: While Israel holds the key to the present, Peres averred, Palestinians hold the key to the future. Being a Nusseibeh, talk of a key piqued my interest, and I took note. A fair exchange, Peres said, would be between what the Israelis presently hold, our land, and what the Palestinians will come one day to hold, a demographic majority. What he seemed to be saying was that Israel, to preserve the Jewish state, had to relinquish its grip on the Occupied Territories.

My bombshell had been designed to rattle the Israelis, not the Palestinians. Despite Lucy's warning, I hadn't expected such hostility, because in my eyes the call for annexation was nothing more than a repackaged version of the mantra of One Secular State that had long been chanted by various factions. The animus got me thinking. The hostility was toward the means, not the goal: heroic-minded "nationalists" still wanted unconditional victory over Zionism, and the idea of using the Israeli system to gain our rights was anathema.

One afternoon in my father's office I sat down and composed an essay for *Al-Quds*. This time around, my aim was to analyze the root cause of some of our nationalistic blindness. The article was deeply personal, addressing a problem I had been vaguely aware of as a teenager but that over time I had come to regard as debilitating for Palestinians. It was the fatal heroism of the defeated, whose victory lies far out of the realm of political power, and only in the secure regions of the imagination.

Mother had raised me looking off toward her beloved Wadi Hnein, hoping that the lost world would reappear as if by an act of God. The Palestinian past had been stolen from us; for justice to be done, *it had to be retrieved*.

Mother's longing, which had only intensified over the years, was less a longing for a place than for the innocent, unblemished moment before all was lost in 1948. If someone were to have handed her the title to Grandfather's orange groves, she wouldn't have known what to do with it. She wanted to *retrieve* the lost time of her youth, not physically go back to a piece of real estate gobbled up by a kibbutz.

In the article, I went on to describe what "retrieval" was in the Arab mind. I likened Palestine to a carpet that over the years following the catastrophe has become cluttered with skyscrapers, settlements, and strangers nestled in our land. For Palestinians, liberation meant grabbing the carpet by all four corners and shaking it to rid it of all that clutter. We could then replant all the lost orange groves robbed from us, and rebuild all the homes and villages that had been destroyed, or they would simply materialize by themselves.

Next I juxtaposed this silly notion of "liberation" with an immeasurably more realistic one, that of annexation and equal rights. Instead of emphasizing a return to the seized lands of the past, I asked, why not emphasize the liberation of the human being? Instead of a dreamlike search for a lost time—which by its very nature is a fantasy—why not focus on a realistic future dream?

We could start, I argued, by struggling for equal rights and the full rights of political self-determination within the State of Israel. Once achieved, we could also implement our right of return within the existing Israeli infrastructure, such as wading in the Maʾaleh Adumim pool. Rather than mentally erasing settlements or Tel Aviv's skyscrapers, we could physically move into those settlements and skyscrapers.

I should repeat here that I was still speaking tongue in cheek. Palestinians should only be playing games they can win, rather than pursuing futile and morally dubious tactics such as guerrilla attacks against the military system that the Israelis had perfected, or engaging in flights of fancy. What the article suggested was to operate openly within the democratic and legal systems of the Jewish state. By doing so, it would become obvious to us and to the Israelis that the present Zionist system was incapable of granting us full rights. Either the system has to be replaced, or the Israelis would have to grant us independence.

Father passed away on Mother's birthday, in November 1986. "It was typical of your father," Mother fondly quipped afterward, "not to give me a moment of peace."

He had had one last sojourn to the Hadassah Hospital before we took him home to die. Even in his weakened state, he maintained his sovereign sense of humor, and his civility. When the doctor came by, Father asked him if he had "found it yet."

"Found what?" the doctor asked, looking at him quizzically.

"Why, that tiny thing." Father raised his hand and rubbed his thumb against his index finger, as he often did when describing something abstract. "That thing that's been giving me all this trouble."

"Oh that." The doctor laughed, realizing that Father was referring to the Angel of Death. "No, I'm afraid we didn't quite find it."

When Father arrived home, he sat for a few minutes on the sunny

porch in his robe and pajamas. We all knew the inevitability of his passing, but nevertheless I wanted him to feel forty years younger. "Boy, it's
a lovely day," I began. "How about a cold beer?"

"Why not?"

I got a bottle of a local brew from a West Bank village, opened it up,
and poured two glasses. Father only had a sip or two before retreating
back to his bedroom. Later, Mother told me he wanted to discuss something with me.

As impervious to hallucinations as ever, he wanted to talk about his
death. "I'd like to tell you what to write on my gravestone." It was painful and awkward for me, and I tried to change the subject. He continued. "Just write Anwar Zaki Nusseibeh al-Khazraji. Born in Jerusalem
1913. Died in Jerusalem." The legacy he wanted to leave was the two
sources of his humanity: ancient Medina, where the family emerged in
the seventh century, and Jerusalem.

He died that afternoon, and we buried him within the confines of the
haram, the site of Dome of the Rock and of Solomon's ancient temple,
just inside Lion's Gate. Hundreds of people showed up at the house on
the morning of the funeral. Faisal, seizing the chance to turn the funeral
into a political happening, took me aside. "I'm thinking about piloting
the funeral procession past a new settlement inside the old city. What do
you think?"

It was a good idea, something Father would have enjoyed.

With Faisal, Jamal, Absal, and Buraq and me at its head, the large
crowd walked up Saleheddin Street, past the main offices of the Electric
Company that Father had run. In his honor, the company had shut
down, and all its employees streamed out to join the procession. As we
walked, we picked up more and more people, until the crowd turned
into the largest political demonstration in Jerusalem since the occupation began. We then proceeded through Damascus Gate and into the
warrens of the Old City. The crowd was like water from a fire hose
aimed into a maze.

On our journey to the *haram*, thousands of mourners filed past Ariel
Sharon's new house and a neighboring yeshiva, both provocatively set in

the Muslim Quarter. (Both had been paid for by a shadowy group set up by Sharon in 1982 called Ateret Cohanim, with the aim of "redeeming" properties in the Old City. The group also had a hand in the colonization of the Goldsmith's Souk.) Within earshot of the settlers, our silence broke into nationalist song. By the time we stepped into the *haram*, thousands were shouting pro-PLO and nationalist slogans. All the while, Jamal, Absal, and Buraq were at my side. They wept as I wept. A friend, seeing me cry, whispered in my ear, "You should hold your tears. It's not manly."

"It would be unmanly if I stopped," I replied.

When Father was laid to rest inside his grave (Muslims are not buried inside caskets), I climbed down into the hole and kissed him goodbye.

Chapter Seventeen

Sticks and Stones

FATHER'S PASSING LEFT an absence that will remain with me until my children bid me farewell. But like the funeral, sadness only encouraged more of my riddle-solving and bombshell-devising. The goal of Father's life was to help his people live in decency and freedom—freedom from foreign oppression, but equally from illusions and from what Kant calls "self-imposed immaturity." The longer that Israelis and Palestinians continued to ignore the existential facts of our situation, the bloodier and more tragic the conflict would become. Within a year the explosion did occur. And the intifada, as it came to be called, brought to light all the symptoms I now began to diagnose.

With the calculation of an inevitable rupture in mind, I went back to my workshop. The Israel settlement policy was creating a situation no one would freely have chosen, the Israelis least of all. The Israelis wanted land but certainly not a million rebelling Arabs. On the Palestinian side, no one wanted the occupation, and yet while dreaming of some magical liberation, we were willingly becoming inextricably caught up in it.

I decided to unpack this curious situation at a political forum held in the National Hotel in East Jerusalem. For some time, the Israeli intellectual and politician Meron Benvenisti (Kollek's deputy mayor of Jerusalem) had been arguing that the reality being created by Israel's settlement policy was irreversible. In my talk at the forum I picked up on that theme. One can't ignore the existence of two realities in the West Bank: that of Palestinians living next to a colossal infrastructure being put in place to support Israeli settlement life.

A system we had once regarded as alien was fast becoming a normal part of our lives. Palestinians worked as construction workers, gardeners, drivers, and deliverymen. With shekels in their pockets, they were becoming inextricably tied into the Israeli system of consumer goods. Ninety-five percent of what we consumed came from Israel. (By the mid-1980s we were the world's second largest consumer of Israeli goods.) Hebrew words such as *machsom* (roadblock) and *teudat zehut* (ID card) infiltrated our everyday Arabic. Our black humor made frequent use of the familiar Hebrew expression "mavet l'aravim" (death to the Arabs). The Egged bus, once an alien, awe-inspiring machine, had over time turned into a cheap and widely used form of transportation. Many of the bus drivers were now Palestinians. We had actually gone inside the once alien monster and taken control.

For most Palestinians, Israel had become more than the Shin Bet interrogator or the Uzi-slinging settler and their refrain "mavet l'aravim." It was also the Natanya beach facilities for Friday vacations, the Israeli trousers on sale in the Suq Khan el-Zeit in Jerusalem's Old City, and the special bus that arrived at dawn in the Tulkarem refugee camp district to pick up the women for their jobs at Israeli textile factories. Israel was Shamir with his iguana gape, but also Shulamit Aloni and Amos Oz commiserating with us at the National Palace Hotel. Israel was the Israeli brand of paint used to scribble our liberation slogans on walls.

Yet all this integration only seemed to increase our nationalism. I ended up by once again underscoring what I saw as national schizophrenia: our actions were making us more a part of the Israeli system, which only intensified our nationalist identity psychologically.

The body and the head, as I called them, could not stay in such glaring conflict much longer. Something would have to give. The mountain would either come to Mohammed, or Mohammed would have to go to the mountain—in short, we would either have to extract our bodies from the Israeli system or push for full absorption.

The business with annexation caught Shimon Peres's attention, and I soon received a call from his office inviting me to meet him at the Foreign Ministry. Joining me were Hanna Siniora and the prominent Palestinian lawyer Fayez Abu Rahmeh. As a foreign minister in his rival Shamir's Likud government, Peres wished to go behind his boss's back and jump-start a political initiative.

My meeting with Peres in the foreign ministry building was even more controversial than my talking to my old leftist Israeli friends at the American Colony. As chief promoter of the "Jordanian Option" and patron of the first West Bank settlement (the colony of fanatics in Hebron is partly his doing), Peres was far from being a proponent of a two-state solution and negotiations with the PLO. If I had nearly been pilloried after shaking hands with the arch-leftists Yossi Sarid and Shulamit Aloni, what would happen after a meeting with Peres? I asked Faisal Husseini what I should do, and he confirmed my inclination to accept the invitation.

Peres's manner was jovial and welcoming, and with broad and gracious gestures, like a king welcoming visiting dignitaries, he offered us sumptuous leather seats. Discussions revolved around the negotiation partner for Israel. My colleagues at the meeting toed the established PLO line by insisting that any political initiative begin with the PLO. Not about to break with the established government position that the PLO was a terrorist organization, Peres politely pushed off that possibility. My colleagues dug in their heels: the PLO had changed, they insisted, and the organization was now ready to recognize Israel's right to exist. Laughingly, Peres responded that "a tiger remains a tiger as long as he has his spots." ("Stripes, you mean," I wanted to chime in, but held my tongue.) "And if the PLO really is serious, it'll have to shed its spots, in which case the tiger would be a cat, and a cat is certainly no tiger." It was a wonderfully Talmudic argument.

"This guy isn't so bad after all," I thought to myself as I cracked a pistachio nut in my mouth.

"And what about you?" Peres turned to us, as if reading my thoughts. "What would be wrong if you were to take the lead and be our interlocutors?"

Hanna answered for me. "Who are we?" he asked. "We derive our legitimacy from the PLO. It is the PLO you need to talk to, not us."

By this point I had said almost nothing. I listened, reflected, and admired all the honorary degrees nailed up on Peres's wall. After half an hour of this I felt I had to say something, and what came out shocked me as much as it did my PLO colleagues.

"I'm ready to negotiate with you."

Jaws dropped.

"On condition that negotiation be based upon your willingness to withdraw to the '67 border, and we be allowed to establish an independent state with East Jerusalem as its capital." Peres eyed me suspiciously, as if I were hardly the sort of "spotless" tiger he had had in mind.

"Of course," I said, "if you declared this to be your intention, you could go down to the Damascus Gate and find a thousand people ready to negotiate with you." I made it clear that if he and his government refused to make a clear and unambiguous commitment to such a withdrawal, they had no other choice but to sit down with their archenemies, the PLO.

My point was that if he wished to have local interlocutors, he would have to agree beforehand on the terms of the solution. Failing that, he would have to address the PLO.

Peres said nothing, but his smile quickly bent downward into a hardened frown.

Word leaked out about the meeting, and it wasn't long after I got home that I heard the news from Birzeit: my former union had expelled me on the grounds that my behavior (i.e., just having met with Peres) had besmirched its reputation. The Fatah youth movement was also restive.

The next day Faisal decided to drive home the point that my presence at the Peres meeting had been a blessing from on high. He insisted

on accompanying me to campus and eating with me in the student cafeteria—"just so that they don't get the wrong impression."

Israeli coalition governments are strange beasts. Soon after the Peres
meeting, Faisal ended up under arrest (from this point onward, until the
Madrid talks in November 1991, he would spend more time in jail than
out), and one evening a self-declared maverick Israeli peace activist
dropped by my home. He introduced himself as "David Ish Shalom" (in
Hebrew, "David, Man of Peace"), though he confided to me that this
was a fake name. A man with wire-rim glasses and sideburns down to his
jaw, he told me that he had come to convey a message of mind-boggling
portent. It was of the utmost secrecy—hence the pseudonym—and I
had been handpicked to receive it. It sounded like a line from a fairy
tale, and I therefore paid close attention. "So secret in fact," the mysterious man continued, "that I didn't believe it at first." He promised me
that he had checked and double-checked his sources just in case someone was trying to "pull a fast one."

Briefly, the man's message was that within the Likud Party, Shamir and
a small group of leaders had concluded that peace had to be reached, but
negotiations were possible only "between the two parties that counted,"
namely, the Likud and Fatah. Only the two nationalist movements could
pave the way for reconciliation between the two peoples. "Ish Shalom"
was quick to add that he personally wasn't a "Likudnik" but only a well-
known supporter of peace who had been approached by a member in the
Likud's Central Committee to "sound me out." If I was willing, my
strange guest promised to set up a meeting with a "Likud bigwig."

This was a startling piece of news if I'd ever heard one. For starters,
I was surprised to hear that people in the Likud were pegging me as a
"PLO man." Since my union days, I had had little contact with the
movement, and more often than not the little contact I had was to fend
off criticism from them. My clandestine visits to Jordan during the Military Order 854 days left a bad taste in my mouth with regard to many

of the PLO functionaries. The figure I liked the most, Abu Jihad, had helped me keep faith that the movement could play a role in ending Israeli occupation. This vague hope, however, hardly qualified me to be the Fatah activist that my nocturnal visitor seemed to think I was.

Still, my mind whirled with ideas, the first being self-preservation. Even if what the man was telling me was true, the meeting with Peres had already placed me on a dangerous borderline beyond which any move I made would put my actions well beyond the pale to my fellow Palestinians. My next thought, pushing the first to one side, was that it was worth the risk if I could help avert the brewing war between our peoples. Without further ado, even before consulting Lucy, I called the messenger's bluff. "Well, Mr. Ish Shalom, I'd be happy to hear what your man has to say."

David Ish Shalom" introduced me to Likud's Moshe Amirav in July 1987. Amirav, once a leader of Jabotinsky's right-wing Beitar youth movement and now a member of the Likud Central Committee, was one of Shamir's closest allies.

In this first encounter, Amirav repeated what his messenger had said. A group of highly placed Likud leaders close to Shamir were seriously considering the prospect of a historical pact with the PLO. Fatah and the Likud were mirror images of each other. Both championed their respective public's nationalist sentiments, and if they could, both would take over the entire country, from the Jordan to the Mediterranean, at the drop of a hat. But since they couldn't, both parties had to give up on their dreams and split up the country equitably. And in a repartition of the Holy Land, only Likud and Fatah could strike a deal. Amirav added that, unlike Peres and his interminable grandstanding in international forums, Shamir preferred to work in secret, behind the scenes.

This was stunning news. Perhaps the ice really had been broken, I mused. Perhaps Shamir had what it took to make peace. In any event, I had never heard anything close to this from Peres, who was still hankering after his "Jordanian option."

I tried my best to conceal my excitement. "What's the deal being proposed?" I asked coolly.

Amirav answered that he was still working on the draft. In broad strokes, he said confidently, it was going to be a two-stage proposal. For the first five years, we would get "full autonomy" in all the areas that came under occupation in 1967. After that, a Palestinian state would come into being.

I had never liked the two-stage model. This was, after all, what had been discussed at Camp David, and had been roundly and rightly spurned by Palestinians. What I was hearing from Amirav, however, made the two-stage solution worth exploring.

Assuming wrongly that I carried weight inside the PLO, he thought I could act as a conduit. Since all contact between the PLO and Israelis was illegal (a law promulgated by the Likud), I asked him if he had Shamir's blessing. He assured me he did. In fact, he explained, Shamir dreamed of being a second Menachem Begin. He wanted to go down in history as the man who made peace with the Palestinians.

We were both well aware of the risks entailed in holding talks. One leaked word could destroy us. Amirav could end up in jail, vilified as a traitor, and I could end up in a ditch, with Lucy widowed and my children orphaned. We had to cover our tracks.

I made contact with Abu Jihad through the special channel we had established after my Amman visit. Word came back for me to press forward. Abu Jihad had gotten Arafat's enthusiastic endorsement for the initiative.

But for me that wasn't enough. I was familiar enough with the Fatah grass roots to know that I had to cover my back locally. Abu Jihad's blessing wouldn't prevent a local zealot from flinging knives in my direction. To shore up my support, I consulted Samir Sbeihat and Hamzeh, my editor at *Al-Mawqef* (both suspected the Likud might be setting a trap), along with two local Fatah operatives. One was Salah Zuheikeh, whom I had gotten to know at Faisal's Arab Studies Society.

I told them all about the mission, and that it had Abu Jihad's backing. Their job was to keep their noses to the ground, just in case word leaked out and there was a backlash.

Not only did they pledge their support—if Abu Jihad agreed, who were they to disagree—but Salah even asked to become involved.

Contacts with Amirav proceeded cautiously. Just to show how serious Likud was, he gradually divulged the names of the Likud inner circle. I could barely believe my ears, though at the same time it only confirmed what Mother had always told me about the duplicity of politicians. The so-called Likud "princes" Ehud Olmert, the present Israeli prime minister, and Dan Meridor were in on it, as was the right-wing youth leader Tzahi Hanegbi. (At the Hebrew University in the early eighties, he and his band of chain-wielding hooligans had beaten up left-wing and Arab students.) Just to prove he had their support, Amirav arranged a meeting at his house in Ein Kerem between Ehud Olmert and me, and on another occasion put me on the phone with Dan Meridor.

By the time Faisal came out of jail, I already had a fairly good picture of what was on Amirav's mind. A draft agreement would be worked out and signed in Jerusalem between us, and we would then take it along with us to Geneva, where Arafat was planning to attend a UN meeting of NGOs in September. There he would receive us publicly and give us his blessing. Because the first clause in the proposed draft stated the need for the Likud and the PLO to negotiate directly, the ball would then have been set rolling.

"Is this guy serious?" Faisal wanted to know. "Does he speak for the government?" I said I thought so, but even though I wasn't absolutely certain, I argued for calling their bluff.

Amirav, Faisal, and I had our first meeting at my home in August. Amirav started off by outlining what he called Likud's basic position. There could be no peace without Likud and the PLO. And any solution that did not recognize the right of Israel to exist or of the Palestinian people to have their own state, or that tried to ignore the PLO, would never work.

We all knew that this meant a two-state solution, and so that evening we launched into a discussion of the details of establishing one. Likud believed, Amirav explained, that such a state would have to come at the

end of an evolutionary, three-year confidence-building incubation period. During that time Israel and the PLO would mutually recognize
each other, and the PLO would forswear the use of violence against
Israel. For its part, Israel would cease expanding the settlements.

We liked what we were hearing.

Ten more meetings took place between July and early September,
with the venues alternating between Mother's house and the garden of
Faisal's Arab Studies Society. We were now working on the draft. Sometimes Faisal and I worked alone, and sometimes Salah joined us. On the
Israeli side, "Ish Shalom" dropped out of the picture, and a man Amirav described as a "professional journalist" took part "to take down the
minutes," as Amirav explained. In all of these talks we focused our attention on the specific stages needed to create a Palestinian state. While
Faisal and I agreed to the stage approach, we wanted some tangible
signs of independence in stage one.

This being the first time Palestinians were negotiating autonomy,
Amirav was remarkably forthcoming on all issues, short of sovereignty.
Faisal and I got—only on paper, to be sure—a Palestinian currency,
passport, television station, flag, and above all, East Jerusalem as the
capital of the interim autonomy.

The draft was exchanged between us several times, with Amirav
each time insisting on running it past his superiors. All in all, and with
surprisingly few bumps along the road, we managed to arrive at a final
draft. Now all that was left for Faisal and me to do was formally and cer-
emonially present the draft agreement to Arafat in Geneva.

Israeli coalition governments are strange creatures indeed. First it was
Peres who tried to win us over to his harebrained "Jordanian option."
Next came Shamir and his band of loyalists offering to sit down with the
PLO. And now Defense Minister Yitzhak Rabin arrived on the scene to
scuttle the deal. On the eve of our scheduled departure for Geneva, by
order of Rabin, Faisal found himself back behind bars.

I was floored. All my years of solving riddles hadn't prepared me for the crazy dynamics of the rotating Likud-Labor government, which was not one leadership, and not even two, but had multiple power centers, each jockeying for position. Had Samir and Hamzeh been right in their initial suspicions? Had I fallen for a trap designed from the start to lay bare our channels of communication with the PLO? Or to cut Arafat's support from underneath him by exposing him as another Israeli stooge? I went to the offices of the Arab Studies Society and faxed the draft agreement directly to Arafat's office in Tunis. Along the top margin I scribbled the news that Faisal had been arrested and that the initiative had been a ploy. My advice was to call off Geneva.

At the next level of a constantly ascending spiral of surprises, I got a phone call from Arafat's office. "The chairman wants you to proceed," I was told. "Too bad about Faisal, but we have to go on. Make your travel arrangements immediately."

When I called Amirav, I could tell by his voice that he was just as panic-stricken at Rabin's actions as I was. His first fear, he let me know, was that I would blame him personally. For this reason he was both relieved and shocked when I told him that the Geneva meeting was still on. "Arafat is ready to receive us in spite of Faisal's arrest."

Amirav agreed to meet me later that afternoon at Mother's house. Sitting face to face, I stared at a beaten-down, defeated man. "I'm afraid," he began with a quivering voice, "I can't make Geneva. Shamir killed the deal."

Months of hard work were down the drain because of Rabin and Shamir. Ushering Amirav to the door, I thought to myself that at least I was safe. Since no one on the Palestinian side knew about the initiative, I didn't have to worry about being jumped by irate nationalists at Birzeit accusing me of treason to the cause.

Word came from Arafat that he still wanted to see me in Geneva. We had never met, and as I already had the ticket, I thought I would go for the hell of it.

Arafat had known about me for some time now, both from Abu Jihad and from some of my outlandish public positions. He knew Father and

Mother, and during the last few days in Black September in 1970, when the Jordanian army launched its onslaught against him and his Fatah troops, he had hidden out at my aunt's house in Amman. (Later, the Jordanian army burned the house to the ground after they found it had been his hiding place.)

Our meeting in Geneva was formal but open. At his suite at the Intercontinental, into which I was escorted by his bodyguards, I mingled with some other guests. That night I was asked to join him for dinner at the home of the PLO representative, where many other guests were present. In retrospect, and having later gotten to know him better, I now believe that his decision not to meet with me in private was calculated: he wished me to be awed by the splendor of his entourage at this first encounter; and he probably wished to maintain a physical distance from me that would allow him later to deny being a party to any compromising deals.

My return from Europe went without a hitch. Back in Birzeit, the atmosphere was remarkably tranquil. This was one of the times when you get lulled into a false sense of security only to have an awful surprise sprung on you.

Faisal's lawyer, Jawad Boulos—a figure I'll return to at length—asked me to appear in court as a character witness for Faisal, who had to appear because the government wanted to renew his administrative order arrest but needed a judge's permission to do so. The government, explained Boulos, hadn't built a case as much as resorted to the hackneyed clichés that had worked so well in the past: that Faisal was a terrorist bent on the destruction of Israel. "If the court can hear what you have to say, they'll see how ludicrous these charges are." Boulos didn't have a clue what I would say—we hadn't told him about our meetings with Amirav—but Faisal had assured him that my testimony would be important and pertinent. This put me in a bind: Should I divulge in front of the court the secret I needed for the sake of life and limb to keep concealed? Faisal obviously wanted me to.

Upon arriving at the hearing, I recognized the Israeli "journalist" I had met while waiting outside the courtroom with Amirav. Nodding at them, I headed into the courtroom and gave my statement to a group of jurists and lawyers, hoping of course that it wouldn't leave the courtroom. "Faisal couldn't be bent on the destruction of Israel," I told them, "because he was involved in a groundbreaking initiative with none other than the Likud Party, an initiative he committed himself to despite great personal risk, and if successful it would have legitimized the existence of Israel in the Arab World."

That afternoon, radio reports carried more or less warped versions of what they called the "secret initiative." Amirav was mentioned by name. By the evening, it was the top news story on television, and the next morning the paper *Kol Ha²Ir* carried a full report.

The storm broke.

Shamir's political opponents went to work to scuttle direct talks with the PLO. Defense Minister Rabin ordered the bombardment of a Palestinian refugee camp on the West Bank.

Shamir at once denied all involvement. "Messrs. Husseini and Nusseibeh," he told the press, "who are known to be PLO men, exploited Amirav's naïveté, but this has nothing to do with the Likud, which is united in its negative attitude toward the PLO."

Interviewed on Israeli TV, Amirav tried to protect himself by claiming that his talks weren't aimed at the PLO. All he'd done, he claimed, was to start up talks with "friendly" non-PLO figures such as Sari Nusseibeh. But even that didn't help him. Viewed by many as a traitor to the cause, he was sacked from Likud.

The more Amirav sought to duck behind my name as a "friendly non-PLO" man, the worse things became for me among my own public. As before, the pro-Jordanian *Al-Nahar* spearheaded the media campaign against me. Their claim was that my talks with Likud had been aimed at implementing the old Likud scheme for limited autonomy. On the very next day, a Saturday, I made my way to Birzeit to teach my class. But upon entering the classroom, I didn't find any students there. Being constitutionally absentminded, I assumed I had mixed up the time, or that there was some big event on campus I had failed to take notice of. Shrugging my shoulders, I drove back to Jerusalem without giving it a second thought.

The next day the media was still preoccupied with the hubbub surrounding the "secret initiative." I assumed that things would blow over, as in the past. Most of the day I sat at home preparing for my Monday morning lecture at nine o'clock. The theme was to be John Locke, liberalism, and tolerance. Typically three hundred students would show up for such a lecture.

On Monday morning I arrived in the lecture hall, took my place at the podium, and immediately launched into my thoughts on Locke. As soon as I got into a groove, all the worries and excitement of the previous few months vanished. I was caught up in seventeenth-century England and the Glorious Revolution of 1688.

The lecture finished and most of the students filed out of the hall, while a few stayed behind to ask me some questions. A couple of colleagues in the department also lagged behind, and as I slowly moved toward the door surrounded by a small huddle of pupils, one female colleague informed me in a rather shaky voice that a pack of masked men with clubs were outside in the hallway stalking a "traitor." It was only when I reached the door that it occurred to me that *I* was the "traitor."

Five kaffiah-wearing attackers came right at me. As they attacked me with fists, clubs, a broken bottle, and penknives, I tore myself away from them and ran into an open elevator. A female student rushed in with me, taking some of the blows. Frantically pressing the buttons, she realized that the elevator wasn't working, and rushed out again. One of the attackers clubbed her as she ran away. Now, as I stood by myself with my back to the wall of the elevator, I felt at least protected from behind; they could only get at me from the front. I did my best to defend myself using arms and feet, but I knew it was like swimming against a strong current. If I stayed I'd quickly succumb to exhaustion, and the five assailants would finish me off. For some reason, the American saying "sticks and stones may break my bones" shot through my mind.

With a rush of adrenaline, I threw my whole body at the hooded thugs, caused a breach as in a rugby match, and dashed pell-mell through the hallway and down the staircase, with the attackers in hot pursuit. It was only upon reaching the ground floor, which was crowded with students, that they fled. By now blood was oozing from my forehead and wrists, and my heart was pounding loud enough to pop my eardrums.

The colleagues who had been kept away with knives ran up to me. One was the husband of the woman who had warned me in the lecture hall. He offered to drive me straight to hospital. A friend from my Café Troubadour days put my good arm—the other was broken—around his shoulder, and helped me to the parking lot.

Lucy had just finished teaching when it all began. She heard the hubbub and asked someone what was happening, and got a shrugged response, "Just a traitor." It was only later when my friend called her from the hospital that she realized what had happened.

In the hospital in Ramallah where I was first taken, the surgeon stitched up the gaping gash above my eyelid. My broken arm was set at the French Hospital in Jerusalem. I noticed that one of my most valuable possessions, the wristwatch I had taken off my father's wrist as we carried him into the hearse, was gone. Someone had pinched it after it fell off during the scuffle.

The public reaction was muted, to put it mildly. A few people called or showed up at the hospital, among them the stalwarts Samir and Hamzeh. The university administration came out with a halfhearted and very general statement denouncing political violence on campus. The union said nothing; only its Fatah faction, led by another stalwart, Sameer Shehadeh, came out against the attack. The Fatah student organization couldn't figure out what to do, so they put out two statements, one in my defense and the other hinting that I had had a good beating coming to me.

The clearest institutional support I got was from Abu Jihad. Raymondah Tawil—the former Ramallah salon hostess and future Arafat mother-in-law—rang me up to tell me that Abu Jihad was beside himself with fury. His gut instinct, she said, was to finger the Islamic faction. "Who do you think did it?" she wanted to know. I replied that I didn't have the foggiest idea. "It's just another riddle."

The following day Abu Jihad issued a forceful statement condemning the attack against me by letting it be known that he would "cut off anyone's hands" who dared lift a finger against me. (One of the attackers, I should add, later came around to my views and eventually married his daughter.)

Why a riddle? Initially everyone seemed convinced that either the Islamists, who had always had it in for me anyway, were behind it, or the extreme leftists in the Popular Front. The newspapers all said this, as did Abu Jihad. I knew this couldn't be true. Somewhere in the bowels of Fatah someone was playing a game.

That the game was serious was confirmed a few days later when a general Fatah leaflet distributed in Jerusalem attacked me. It would also have included Faisal in the philippic had it not been for the last-minute intervention of Jibril Rajoub, a Fatah leader I'll have a lot more to say about later.

Out of sheer self-preservation, I determined to get to the bottom of the story. I had shored up support locally and at PLO headquarters, and still I had been beaten. Part of the problem was the structure of Fatah. There was a "militant arm" and a "diplomatic" one, and the two often had nothing to do with each other. I obviously was considered part of the latter, and up to this point I had had few dealings with the activists, called Tanzim, operating on the street.

The longer I thought about it—and a broken arm and stitches can get the imagination going—the more I was convinced that someone on the *outside* must have given orders to the Tanzim to nail me. Absurdly, I even suspected Abu Jihad.

Samir and Hamzeh did some preliminary detective work on campus, and what they dug up only confirmed the message of the leaflets, namely that Fatah was divided. Half the student faction supported me and the peace strategy I represented, and the other half was implacably opposed.

A week after my thrashing, some friends from Peace Now invited me to speak at a Tel Aviv rally. Standing on the stage with my cast and bandages,

I read out a statement in Hebrew to thousands of Israeli peace advocates in the crowd. (Cousin Zaki had helped me write it.) The statement reiterated my commitment to negotiations and a peaceful solution to our conflict. "And they can't beat that out of me," I said to a roar of applause.

A few weeks later I flew to Paris with Lucy to recuperate. There I met Abu Tareq, a man with whom I would have regular contact during the intifada in the coming year. He had moved to Paris from Beirut during Israel's invasion to establish an international contact point for Abu Jihad, who had sent him there, fearing that the Israeli siege of Beirut might cut the PLO leadership off from all contact with the world.

It was in Paris that some of my suspicions about my attackers were confirmed. Abu Jihad obviously hadn't had a hand in it. Abu Tareq told me that his boss had set up a committee to investigate the beating, which they determined might have been an "internal" Fatah job.

Back in Jerusalem, I finally found out what happened. My friend Fahed Abu al-Haj tracked down the perpetrators, even naming them individually. All were students at Birzeit, and a couple I knew quite well. One, the biggest and most brutal of the five, a C student, was suspected of working for Jordanian intelligence. The others later realized their mistake and came to my office months later to apologize. Two even came over to my side politically.

The picture I formed of the plot goes something like this: Just as Rabin's security people were irate at our initiative with Likud, so was Jordan's security. In the background, of course, had been the Israeli-Jordanian rapprochement at the time, worked out in meetings between King Hussein and the Labor Party's Shimon Peres. And out of this common interest to derail us, the two organizations decided upon a division of labor. Rabin locked Faisal up, and I ended up with a broken arm.

Fatah had several offices in Amman charged with operating Tanzim cells in the West Bank. Communication took place by capsule. One day, the Tanzim contact for the Birzeit Fatah student movement received a capsule from his operator in Amman. Straight from the intestines of the smuggler, the message was unambiguous: Sari is a traitor and must be dealt with at once.

Chapter Eighteen

The Exorcism

IT AMAZES ME TO THINK that the best writers of spy novels and murder mysteries live tranquil lives on quiet well-lit streets, and that the sounds of bombs or the crackle of gunfire echo only in their imaginations; whereas the people who experience crime and killing rarely have the luxury of writing about it. At first I looked at my beating as meriting a mystery-packed novel I hadn't the time to write. Within a year it seemed a rather harmless episode at best deserving an extended footnote. The real drama, a three-year insurrection against Israeli rule known as the intifada, began after my arm had healed.

In December 1987, I stumbled across Father's account of the 1948 war. He never published it; my uncles had advised him against it because his description of Arab generals as "grinning apes" would only have brought trouble.

Most of the stories I already knew from family lore, though the conclusions Father drew hit me with special poignancy. With the Palestinian insurrection against Israeli rule at the front of my mind, I felt that Father's call for Arabs to do some national "spadework" was uncannily relevant.

The trouble with us Arabs is that we do not like spadework. Spades are not desert instruments. But we must, I think, realize that other people do not either and that, therefore, our plausible charm notwithstanding, they are not likely to work for us. Our great tradition is now threatened with extinction. The Palestine hoax is only a preamble. That it need not be, that we can still preserve our tradition, enrich it and by doing so make a contribution of value to the world, goes without saying, but we must accept the challenge, seek no shortcut, and get used to the idea of using a spade.

Father's archetype of the true Arab, and the model against which he measured himself, was doubly romantic and admirable: the true Arab for him was a being of such dignity that he disdained material wealth and physical comfort. Even life itself was of little value when measured against the higher call of honor. Father loved reciting the odes by ᶜAntara, the pre-Islamic warrior poet of the desert. ᶜAntara considered the highest reward of battle neither plunder nor the sweet taste of victory but rather the safeguarding of honor. In Father's estimation, it was here that Arab leaders, generals, and aristocrats had so woefully failed. The only ones who acted like true Arabs were those who knew something about working with spades: the fellahin, men and women who had toiled the earth for generations.

The great example of Palestinian political spadework started on December 9, 1987. A traffic accident may have sparked the intifada, but in retrospect the real cause was an intrinsically corrosive force eating away at Palestinian society. It was the degrading realization of being coopted by a system responsible for land confiscation, lawlessness, and mushrooming settlements. It was the feeling of being slowly choked of their breath. The contradiction of using Israeli paint to scribble out anti-occupation graffiti was becoming so insufferable as to make an explosion inevitable. The body, as it were, was finally joining the head.

For months, tensions had been building throughout the West Bank and Gaza; confrontations at Birzeit were becoming once again a daily affair. On December 4, soldiers storming the campus to end a nonviolent sit-down strike ended up tear-gassing the strikers and shooting two students to death. Many more were wounded. Troops later broke into a hospital and took away the wounded students.

The next day the UN General Assembly censured Israel for its "grave breaches" of the 1949 Geneva Convention Relative to the Protection of Civilian Persons in Time of War. The actions at the university were "war crimes and an affront to humanity." Benjamin "Bibi" Netanyahu, Israel's emissary to the UN, proclaimed to the world that Israel's was the most benign military administration in history, and that the incident at the university had been the fault of rioting students who had attacked Israeli soldiers with rocks and metal rods. No country on earth cherishes academic freedom more than Israel, Netanyahu noted. Freedom, however, was not a license to riot.

On December 7 something strange started happening. The epicenter of protest shifted from the university campus to the refugee camps. Students didn't play the leading role here, nor did the diplomats in East Jerusalem; ordinary people did. It began violently when day laborers from a Gaza refugee camp knifed an Israeli labor contractor to death. The killing was a sign of the combustible tension experienced by ordinary Palestinians, for the man they slew had given them employment, yet at the same time he symbolized the military power trampling on their rights.

Two days later an Israeli tank transport vehicle plowed into a minivan in Gaza, killing four Palestinian workers returning home from work in Israel. Rumors spread that the truck driver was a relative of the dead businessman and was seeking revenge.

Like lava bubbling and smoking for years until spitting out from a volcano, protests burst out helter-skelter throughout the territories. In Gaza City the masses poured out onto the wide boulevards that Ariel Sharon had bulldozed through the Gaza refugee camps back in 1972. From the ninth of December, violent protests spread out into every village and city in the territories.

The intifada took everyone by surprise. The PLO leadership, locally and abroad, were as dumbfounded as the omniscient Shin Bet. At first our "professional revolutionaries" didn't know whether it was a good or a bad thing that people were speaking up for themselves. At first Bashir Barghouti, local head of the Palestinian Communist Party, decided that the unruly street scenes didn't accord with his revolutionary handbook. It took some time for him to throw the weight of his party behind the rebellion. PLO leaders abroad hedged their bets by issuing a few statements in support of the "heroes and martyrs" in their fight against the "Zionist entity." In an ex post facto admission a month later, Arafat fudged the truth: "On the first day of the uprising, we decided that our brother demonstrators should not use firearms."[1]

Defense Minister Rabin was in the United States when the trouble started. Upon disembarking from the plane in Tel Aviv, he was bombarded with questions from dozens of reporters. Rumor had it that the defense minister was swaying back and forth under the effects of heavy drink, which may explain the unusual candor of his signature baritone response: "We will break their legs so they won't be able to walk and break their hands so they won't throw stones."[2]

Soldiers taking him at face value were later caught on film breaking the bones of sixteen-year-old stone throwers. This only fueled more demonstrations, strikes, and riots, to which the Israelis responded with more broken bones, thousands of canisters of tear gas, home demolitions, and shootings. In the first weeks, Israeli soldiers killed dozens of protesters; hundreds more protesters were wounded or arrested.

Nothing helped. If at the beginning of December 1988, Israel maintained its grip on the West Bank with seven hundred soldiers, Rabin's eight thousand troops now weren't nearly enough to pacify Gaza alone.

Like everyone else, I was stunned. Most of my life I had been reading about "peoples' uprisings"—Fanon's work is full of them—but it was only when I came across the barricades thrown up by local merchants, carpenters, and schoolkids in front of Mother's house that I experienced one for the first time. It was staggering to witness people in cities, villages, and refugee camps acting on their own and for themselves, as a people with a will, as a subject of history and not just an object of pity or contempt, or as charity cases to be cared for by the UN Relief and Works Agency (UNRWA) or controlled by the Israeli military adminis- tration, which always gave with one hand and took back tenfold with the other.

I got so caught up in the mood that I injudiciously told a reporter for the *International Herald Tribune*, "It's a kind of exorcism to throw a stone at Satan." A better way of phrasing this would have been that rocks thrown at tanks were helping to exorcise our demons of humilia- tion, inferiority, and self-contempt.

The routines of life changed overnight. Universities and schools were shut, roads blocked by roadblocks and tanks, shops shuttered. Wher- ever you looked there were violent clashes. The Israelis' first instinct was to identify Birzeit as the epicenter of the unrest. It had all been hatched in the classroom, they thought.

At Birzeit everyone was prepared for trouble: the soldiers showed up with their guns and riot gear, while we ordered ambulances, broke out the first aid kits, and prepared the press releases. The army declared the campus a closed military area and surrounded it with troops. The mili- tary commander delivered a list to Hanan Ashrawi, demanding that she deliver up students suspected of anti-Israeli behavior. She refused. The commander warned her that if she didn't comply, soldiers would have to storm the campus. Hanan cautioned them that this could lead to a mas- sacre. "This campus always gives us a lot of trouble," the officer told her. "[Students] invite trouble. They go out and demonstrate and disturb the peace. They force us to shoot them."[3] He threatened her again, and again she refused. The standoff ended peacefully just before midnight. All the students were loaded onto buses and dropped at their homes. The next day the military ringed the campus and announced that the university would be closed indefinitely. It wouldn't open again for more than four years. Shabibah, the Fatah youth movement, was outlawed, and soon afterward Marwan was expelled from the country.

In the first few weeks of the uprising, there was no central leadership, and no broad strategy. The marches and stone throwing were sponta- neous, and if there was a leadership at all it was as improvised as the ac- tions. More often than not, every demonstrator did what he thought best, and the more established leaders raced to catch up with him.

In Gaza, the Muslim Brotherhood movement (later to combine with another Islamic faction to form Hamas) issued its first intifada leaflet, which was little more than emotional rhetoric cheering on the unfolding reality on the street.

Local Fatah leaders were just as lost as the demonstrators. In Jerusalem, where the main leadership was now centered, two local PLO activists put out a leaflet that was just as rhetorical as that of Hamas. Anyway, the crushing force of the Israeli military response, and the arbitrary arrests that swept hundreds of activists into prison, put a quick end to the au- thors' careers. They were already in jail by the time their flyers hit the streets. But unknown even to them, that flyer was to become the first of the monthly serialized leaflets of the uprising.

Faisal was still in prison, but the informal group that met at the Orient House to discuss and decide on political issues was still going strong, and immediately after the insurrection began, we met. Among those present were Radwan Abu Ayyash, Ibrahim Karᵓaeen, Jamil Nasser, Ziad Abu Zayyad, and Hanna Siniora, all associated with the Fatah. Our group would later include figures, including Zahira Kamal and Samir Hleileh, representing other factions. Many of them later became minis- ters in the PA.

The waves of arrests and the ubiquitous security patrols on the streets of East Jerusalem made it risky for us to meet, and so to avoid arousing suspicion, we kept our discussions brief and intermittent.

The only reason we risked this at all was because the intifada, with its anarchic nature bordering on chaos, needed a clearly articulated political direction. As I was generally regarded as being closest to Faisal, and with a lot of practice in penning political statements, I got the job of collating the ideas that came up during the brainstorming and putting them into an organized literary form. As there were good strategic minds not included in our Orient House talks, I added suggestions by people such as my Ramallah friends Izzat Ghazzawi, Sameer Shehadeh, Fathiyya Nasru, and Samir Sbeihat. This latter group constituted an extended think tank, and many of their members would later be arrested or deported.

Our first attempt was to draft a public declaration. Ziad and I drafted the final document. Just by chance it had fourteen points, like Woodrow Wilson's famous statement on a "just and lasting peace." Our Fourteen Points ran the gamut of issues relevant to Palestinians under occupation. No grievance was left out. Israeli administration touched the lives of Palestinians from all walks of life, and thus our demands reflected the immediate concerns of farmers, workers, students, prisoners, landowners, and merchants.

Our plan was to present our list of demands during a press conference at the National Hotel in East Jerusalem. In ex post facto fashion, we would point to these fourteen points as the political objectives of what had been a spontaneous eruption.

To give our press conference more breadth, we decided to involve other PLO factions, and to have the conference led by an independent figure. Someone suggested Gabi Baramki, acting president of Birzeit.

I contacted the representatives of the PLO factions at Birzeit to solicit their endorsement of the statement, and to request representatives for the press conference. Given my relatively recent beating, the first response was less than enthusiastic. Some of the factions only grudgingly agreed to take part. The head of the executive committee of the union, a communist by the name of Tamer Issawi (and a critic of my various diplomatic escapades, in particular my meeting with Peres) told me he would attend only as a member of the audience. It took some convincing before Baramki agreed to chair the event.

The press conference took place on January 14, almost five weeks into the intifada. The Fourteen Points stated the obvious: that only by ending the occupation would the violence end. One point demanded direct negotiations between the PLO and Israel for the creation of an independent Palestinian state with East Jerusalem as its capital. Another called upon the Israeli army to withdraw from populated areas, while another insisted on free municipal elections, as well as the free election of members of the Palestine National Council in the Occupied Territories. Other points were far more practical. One pressed the occupation authorities to allow farmers to dig more wells for desperately needed water; another asked that Israel put the taxes deducted from Palestinian workers' paychecks into a central labor fund.

The Fourteen Points was far from a terrorist declaration of war. There was no call for arms, no denunciations of the "Zionist entity," and the document was predicated on the belief in a final peace with Israel and on the democratic empowerment of the local Palestinian leadership. Peace and democracy were at the document's core.

Given the thousands of people killed over the subsequent years of the conflict, Israel would have done well to take our demands seriously. Instead, Israeli policy makers tried to scuttle the conference by threatening to arrest those who attended. We held it anyway.

With the Fourteen Points, the intifada got a coherent political message outlining how the intifada could end forthwith. Israel's frenzied reaction to the conference ensured the intifada would continue, in the form of a major civil disobedience campaign. In the serialized monthly leaflets, it quickly got a communication system to spread this message throughout the territories.

My friend Sameer Shehadeh was in Amman visiting some relatives when the rebellion started. He stayed in Amman for a few weeks and assessed what was happening from the distance of this mountain capital. There he met often with Abu Jihad, and they both recognized that the intifada needed a strategy, and that the Fourteen Points was a good start. Abu Jihad charged Sameer with the task of contacting other faction representatives upon his return to the West Bank, to form what later came to be called either the Unified National Leadership of the Uprising or the Unified Command (UNC).

Sameer started by putting out a third intifada leaflet, the first one institutionally sanctioned by Abu Jihad and the Fatah leadership. Two factions agreed to sign off on it (the Communist Party still declined), and it was written in a format that remained constant over the next two years. Called Leaflet No. 3, it was also the first of the UNC's monthly leaflets.

To help in the brainstorming process of writing the leaflets, Sameer turned to his close friends at Birzeit, both in the union and the student movement. One was Abd el-Rahman Hamad, who kept Sameer abreast of what was happening on the ground in Gaza, and who also was a conduit for disseminating the flyers in Gaza. Fathiyyah Nasru, another of Sameer's contacts and a colleague of mine at Birzeit, was his contact person in the West Bank. And Izzat Ghazzawi was his link to me in Jerusalem.

Soon after Sameer's return from Amman, my conversations with Izzat began. With the Israeli security apparatus hauling in activists by the hundreds, it was important for us to take special precautions when we met to swap political ideas or conspired to come up with strategies. As in many police states, we mastered the art of dropping hints.

It wasn't exactly the cloak-and-dagger scene from a spy novel. Izzat and I had our meetings in Mother's living room. These chats were ostensibly between two innocent intellectuals. If someone had listened in with an electronic bug, he would have heard some interesting banter, but nothing unexpected, given the fact that everyone was speaking about politics at the time. We spoke in general terms and avoided catchphrases and particular references that might have given rise to suspicion. Izzat didn't state openly that my input was needed for the new leaflet, and I didn't dictate word for word how it should read. But Izzat and I knew each other well enough by now to be able to easily encrypt our conversations.

Almost immediately, with the wide circulation of Leaflet No. 3, the hitherto unplanned street actions in the territories fell in line with the political directions as articulated in the leaflet. It was like watching musicians take cues from a conductor.

For people at the grass roots, the monthly leaflet—serialized and appearing like clockwork on the ninth of each month—became the indispensable pointer for what to do next. At the end of each thirty-day cycle, street activists and ordinary people swept up in the uprising awaited the fresh issue with a new set of instructions from the mysterious creature called "The Unified Command." And because, without fail, the leaflets addressed concerns of Palestinians in the most far-flung villages, people came to believe they had a mysterious presence in their midst. The UNC, anonymous, surreptitious, on the run, and yet seemingly omniscient, got the reputation of being an unprecedented new Palestinian force. No wonder the Shin Bet regarded it as enemy number one.

With the UNC becoming the stuff of legend, speculation was rife as to who belonged to this mysterious leadership issuing these monthly missives. Journalists must have asked me a hundred times about the UNC. In response to my feigned bafflement—"When you find out, let me know"—Daoud Kuttab, the sharpest journalist in Palestine, offered the theory, based on "credible insider information," that the UNC was a special PLO task force that had recently infiltrated the borders and was now operating from the pit of a hidden cave in the West Bank, a variation on the old Sheikh Cassam myth. His alternative theory was that the UNC comprised Hebrew-speaking ex-prisoners disguised as Jews and meeting in the coffee shops of the hip Tel Aviv district of Shenkin.

Israeli media experts, pundits, and professors all joined in the guessing game. Listening to all the theories brought to mind how in *The Wizard of Oz* the booming voice of the little man behind the curtain gave the frightful impression of a powerful demigod pulling the levers. I suppose we got away with it for so long because the truth—that we were a handful of professors and intellectuals—was so unlikely.

Just as Sameer finished Leaflet No. 6, the Shin Bet managed to track him down through the printer who worked on the leaflets. Following his arrest, the Israelis arrested a runner with thirty-five thousand copies of the leaflet. They also hunted down a number of members of the Unified Command.

For 124 days, interrogators used on Sameer their most effective methods of black hoods, scalding and freezing water, and a tight cage, forcing him to stand for days in painful positions. They never got a revealing word out of him.

Having caught him and some of the leaders of the other factions in the Unified Command, Israel's top Shin Bet officers must have toasted their victory. They had the leadership of the intifada behind bars—or so they thought. Israeli newspaper headlines lauded the Shin Bet's brilliant success.

Almost instantly, Abu Jihad found someone to replace Sameer, and Abu Jihad and the other factions named new representatives to the UNC. To the chagrin of the Shin Bet, Leaflet No. 7 appeared on the ninth of the next month.

The Shin Bet experienced similar disappointments over and over. The noose of Israel's security would tighten, and there would be arrests. The Israeli media would be rife with speculation on the final denouement of the UNC and the hated leaflets, and hence of the uprising. Then, with bated breath, everyone would wait to see if the next leaflet would come out, which it always did. The professionals in the Shin Bet grew ever angrier and more humiliated.

My involvement in the leaflets deepened as soon as the Israeli government proved its unwillingness to come to terms with the intifada politically by completely disregarding the Fourteen Points. I believed it was imperative that the intifada be sustained, but how? Built in to the anarchic nature of the uprising was the danger that it would degenerate into mere violence, and would eventually die out without having achieved a thing. How could one keep it from self-destruction?

That the risk of this happening was real can be seen in the basic disagreement between two contradictory strategies within the notoriously squabbling Palestinian factions within the PLO. The UNC, because it included representatives from the various wings of various groups, was by nature ideologically unstable. Some wished to escalate the intifada into an "armed people's revolution" à la Algeria. With Abu Jihad as our patron, our think tank managed at first to push through our view that the intifada had to remain a nonviolent civilian uprising. Right from the start, Abu Jihad and many others among my colleagues in Fatah agreed with me that the intifada must culminate in peaceful negotiations with the Jewish state.

My goals were henceforth to keep the civilian uprising going while simultaneously keeping it in line with our stated nonviolent political objectives. The leaflets became the lifeblood of the intifada, because they balanced both.

The think tank met for a number of brainstorming sessions before we devised a basic strategy for the leaflets. What we came up with— later dubbed "the Jerusalem Document"—became Fatah's hallmark during the intifada. It outlined a campaign for civil disobedience.

The Jerusalem Document laid out a step-by-step strategy for severing the vast network of contact points between the occupier and the population under the occupation. To go back to my pre-intifada article, we sought to employ the "guillotine method" in resolving the contradiction between "freedom slogans" and "spray paint." We wanted to realign the body with the head—to dismantle the ties between occupier and occupied, which ranged from jobs, consumer goods, the payment of taxes, and the use of Israeli-issued cards and IDs to the inherently obsequious rite of seeking permits and licenses.

But before we broke out our guillotine, we had to call to life self-organized "service" structures, or community-based networks, which could provide security, emergency help, conflict-resolution mechanisms, food supplies, education, and all the other things the occupation had at least theoretically been responsible for. The logical end station of civil disobedience was to be the unilateral declaration of independence.

Once we finished writing up the plan, I sat down with Izzat Ghazzawi and some other Fatah people in Ramallah to get their opinions. Then a smuggler swallowed the capsule and made his way to Abu Jihad in Amman, who took it directly to Arafat. The timing was auspicious because at that very moment Arafat was huddled together with some other top PLO leaders discussing how to keep the intifada going.

"We have a plan." Abu Jihad beamed as he walked in the room and headed straight for Arafat, clutching the document in hand. All those in the room excitedly gave Abu Jihad the green light to send his agreement back to us, and we distributed the document in capsule form throughout Fatah's network in the territories.

Back in Jerusalem, I opened up an information bureau called Holy Land Press Service in my father's old law office on Salaheddin Street. My partner in this was Hamzeh Smadi, my editor at *Al-Mawqef*. On the surface, the bureau provided news of the intifada to Israeli and foreign correspondents and diplomats. Lucy helped me set up *The Monday Report*, an English-language weekly aimed primarily at the diplomatic community. It contained an analysis of developments from a Palestinian's perspective. *The Monday Report* brought news of events and local leaders in towns and villages, and provided translations of the leaflets. (Cousin Zaki did the Hebrew translations, and another cousin the English.)

Hamzeh established reliable contact points throughout the West Bank and Gaza. It was largely his doing that Father's old office became a central switchboard for all information pertaining to the intifada. Even the Shin Bet, with its army of collaborators and surveillance techniques, probably kept a less accurate tab on what was happening on the ground.

Holy Land Press Service was the perfect cover because, as far as the authorities were concerned, I was collating and distributing material, not producing it. On the surface, it was a fairly innocuous activity for a professor whose university had been shut down. Nor did they realize that my correspondents around the territories were activists who communicated with me and one another through our office.

In need of a secretary to manage the office, I asked Mother if she could recommend one of her students at the Young Women's Muslim Society. One morning a young girl named Hanan dropped by. A traditional Muslim, she had a dark and beautiful complexion and a sharp intelligence in her eyes. The school had done its work well: her English and Hebrew were good, and her secretarial skills excellent. Mother swore by her, so I hired her on the spot.

Hanan eventually became our partner in producing the leaflets. The danger of arrest had by this point become so acute that it was no longer possible to process a leaflet through normal channels. Hamzeh and I did

Arches of the Via Dolorosa, Old Jerusalem
(Photograph by Benedictus Stolz, rights held by Anthony David)

Father in sailor's clothes, at age five, with cousins from the Nusseibeh family

Father and Mother, as newlyweds, at Mother's country house

Father welcoming King Hussein as he
steps down from the airplane at
Jerusalem's airport, ca. 1964

Father (right), as Jordan's ambassador,
accompanied by Princess Margaret
and Lord Snowdon, at the court
of St. James, ca. 1965

Israel's Moshe Dayan (left) at
a debate in Jerusalem with
Father, organized by the
Hebrew University
in 1968

Me at age four, holding the hand of
my older brother, Zaki, and pouting

Standing with St. George's high school friends at graduation, certificate in one hand,
literature prize in the other

Leaning on red MGA with Lucy, somewhere in Europe, early 1970s

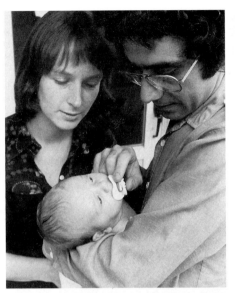

Lucy and me, looking at our firstborn, Jamal. Cambridge, Massachusetts, 1977

Early 1980s, holding Jamal during an outing with Birzeit University students

Me with the three boys,
hiking in the West Bank,
1985

At parents' garden, after
attack by students, 1986

Me (front left) on my way
to Aksa in my role as
PLO Jerusalem
representative

Me (front left) at a sit-in
protest at the Damascus
Gate during the siege on
Arafat's compound, 2003

My family with Yasir Arafat

Contemplating the future at a spot overlooking the Jordan valley and the Dead Sea, late 1990s

all the typing late at night, not wanting to get Hanan involved in something that could have her end up in prison. Then, one morning, I came into the office and noticed that she was already at her desk. She had a strangely affectionate glimmer in her eyes. A glance over at the fax machine explained the reason. The previous evening, having faxed a leaflet to news agencies as I sometimes did (my common cover story was that someone had picked the leaflet up in the street), I had forgotten to remove it from the machine, and that morning she found it, read it, and realized, as she probably had for a long time suspected, that there was more happening in the office than met the eye. I told her to forget what she had seen, but it was too late. She knew that I was implicated in the famous leaflets.

Like a good newspaper editor, I knew that the leaflets would maintain their effectiveness only if they were responsive to the constantly shifting challenges and concerns of activists throughout the territories. The inflow of accurate and detailed information was therefore necessary. What were average people thinking? Did they want to increase the strikes and protests? Were they suffering because of them? What did they want from the leadership?

I tried to glean what I could from the cabdrivers in my Old City haunts, and from my various grapevines. The constant inflow of information to the office, whether from the territories or from prisons (Hanan transcribed the materials smuggled out of prisons in capsules, typed them into the computer, printed out the text, erased it from the hard drive, and burned the original) helped to make sure that UNC's leaflets always "spoke to the street," and thus maintained their relevance.

To dig deeper I carried on conversations with activists, casual enough not to let on that I was coming up with new material for an upcoming leaflet. A man named Abed al-Haleem was one of my best sources, and to this day he's a friend and coworker who is more privy to subaltern information than most journalists. A tall, spindly man with a long and gentle face, Abed was the Fatah activist responsible for Abu Dis and the six villages around it, and would often stop by my house for a nocturnal conversation over coffee. We could speak only at night because the authorities were on his tail. For twenty-two months he furtively slept at his cousins' house or his brother's or a friend's. During the day he stayed indoors.

Abed didn't know what my role was in the writing of the leaflets. As far as he could tell, I was just a curious professor always ready for a twilight chat. Indirectly, I asked him about people's attitudes. Much of what he told me found its way into the leaflets. A few days after he unwittingly helped write one, his immediate contact from Jerusalem would pass him a copy at the appointed time. Abed would then arrange for local distribution of the leaflet. He got one copy, photocopied it ten thousand times, and passed bundles on to others, who took them by foot, car, bicycle, and mule to various villages and neighborhoods.

Another ally I had was Naser Al-Afandi. We met in Abu Dis, where his father ran a small shop and had a few sheep. Naser had already spent years in prison, and between 1980 and 1985 he had shared a cell with Jibril Rajoub. Among their techniques to squeeze information out of him, Naser's captors hung him from the ceiling in chains, like a butchered lamb.

Abu Jihad's exuberant announcement to Arafat "We have a plan" set us to work. Using leaflets as our means, we got the word out to the masses, and all but a handful of people regarded it as their duty to join the campaign. Employees working for the military administration—tax officers, police officers, zoning officers, teachers, and Israeli-appointed village and town officials—resigned from their posts. As the number of resignations increased, committees were established to fill the gap. Palestinians now had their own police officers, judges, and teachers. A wide-ranging economic boycott kept from local shelves Israeli products that could be produced locally. This turned the local manufacturers into our most enthusiastic loyalists. For obvious reasons, the most popular instruction we included in the leaflets was the tax boycott.

In the intifada leadership, a major concern was how to support people in the banned underground organizations, various unions, women's groups and sports clubs, and the families of detainees and the professionals who had quit their jobs with the occupation authority. If we really wanted people to cut off their ties to Israel, we needed large amounts of cash to be brought into the territories and distributed.

Money smuggling soon became another of my illicit activities. On Abu Jihad's instructions, I began to work closely with Akram Haniyyah, a Fatah veteran from the National Guidance Committee days who had been expelled by the Israelis just before the outbreak of the intifada and was now living in Tunis. The two of us worked out a system. It wasn't entirely safe, but it worked. My main contact person regarding money and the leaflets was Abu Tareq, a PLO man I'd met in Paris.

Our first transaction took place during a visit to a European capital. Akram introduced me to a man in a coffeehouse, who agreed to smuggle money on his business-class flight to Tel Aviv. We met later in an Israeli hotel lobby. Just as in a 007 adventure film, we had identical Samsonite briefcases. He sat down next to me in a lounge chair to read the paper, placing his briefcase next to mine. We made the switch, and I headed back with my first batch of cash.

I often did the distribution personally, driving my Opel with sacks of money from Abu Jihad, Israeli public enemy number one. Eventually, $150,000 a month was to pass through my hands. It was quite amazing to handle tens of thousands at a time when I had to hit Mother up for loose change for a haircut. While we were counting every shekel at home, Lucy found one of our sons playing with stacks of hundred-dollar bills in the bathroom.

Another of my illegal activities was to help people in the underground evade arrest. When a group of fifty men found themselves on the run, it was my job to find a place for them to sleep. On such short notice, the best I could do was the great outdoors, which made the owner of a local sporting goods shop happy, if astonished. I asked him if he had sleeping bags.

"Of course," he replied.

"Great. Give me fifty."

Chapter Nineteen

A Declaration of Independence

FOLLOWING MY NATURAL INCLINATION, I did my best to look and act like the good soldier Schweik, naïve and not entirely of this world. My day job as a coffee shop philosopher both was a pose and reality, a convenient cover and precisely where my heart was. With all the exuberance and excitement, I wanted to call people's attention to the humanism without which our rebellion was doomed to turn into just another Palestinian catastrophe—and farce.

In 1987 I was invited to the University of Pavia in northern Italy to deliver a lecture. At the entrance of the university I saw posters festooning trees and buildings proclaiming the merits of our cause. This brought back memories of 1967, when we were the pariahs of the world, and the only avid supporter we came across was an English Nazi. The intifada had turned us into the underdog du jour for the European left.

In Pavia, I chose to give my talk on the predicament of Palestinian prisoners, and my entrée into the subject was the notion of freedom, and how the will was inextricably linked with personal and national identity. I told my audience about my observations of students who had spent long hours in the interrogation cell, and how by refusing to confess, they came out of it with a new sense of self and, often for the first time in their lives, a genuine experience of freedom.

Freedom, I said, isn't some innate quality stamped on our foreheads like a product bar code; nor is it something external like a particular passport or the right amount of money in the bank. Freedom is an expression of the will, and the amount you have of it is in direct proportion to your mastery over fear and egotism. By exercising the will, the individual carves out a distinct identity. There was as much Avicenna as there was of my father in that lecture.

If identity is created and not passively inherited like blue eyes, it admits of degrees. Individuals can have strong identities or almost none. The same holds true for a nation. Like an individual, a nation has to forge its identity through constant acts of the will. As Palestinians, our internal sovereignty and identity consist precisely in freely exercising our will, in defiance of the power employed to crush it. Through an act of the will, our nation can neutralize our jailer's truncheon and his psychological weapons, and can transform the physical instruments of oppression into symbols of the interrogator's utter impotence.

> A nation can mysteriously develop a common sense of itself and a common sense of purpose . . . With this revolutionary consciousness, the national will becomes an instrument with which to achieve inner freedom, and with which to translate this into acts of objective struggle. A nation under occupation, just like a prisoner inside the cell, comes thus to be free through its acts or non-acts.

Lecturing on questions of identity while playing a part in a spy novel was more my style than being a nationalist leader stirring up crowds. But soon I was given no choice but to take a more public stance.

From the outset, Faisal and I established a good division of labor. He was the more public figure—he certainly behaved and dressed the part more. With his aristocratic demeanor and royal Husseini bloodline, he was ideally suited to drive home the message that Palestinians weren't shadowy revolutionaries but civilized people squirming out from underneath a heavy boot. He was the public face of what we called "our white and unarmed revolution." His Arab Studies Society at the Orient House became a diplomatic center for press conferences and meetings. For my part, I was always happy to play a secondary role in politics—that is, as long as I felt matters were going in the right direction.

But Faisal's very civility got him into trouble with the Israelis, who were eager to paint him with the terrorist brush. (One official lampooned him as "the executive producer of the PLO.") During the intifada he was constantly getting hauled back into prison: a month in, six months out; three months in, two out; and so on. In 1987, at the end of a "town arrest," the authorities put him in prison for three months, then released him and imprisoned him again for six months more.

The circumstances behind some of Faisal's arrests say something about both his role and what the Israelis found objectionable. On one occasion, people from Peace Now asked him to debate some Israelis at a public auditorium in West Jerusalem. He was ready to do it, and Peace Now launched a major PR campaign to promote the event. Hundreds of Israelis showed up to hear Faisal repeat word for word what we had agreed with Amirav: that both sides must recognize each other's right to national self-determination.

Two days later, the police arrested him again and sentenced him to six more months in prison. The impression the Israelis gave was that they arrested Faisal *because* of his position on nonviolence. (An instructive comparison to make is between Faisal and the Hamas leader Sheikh Yassin, who was left alone by authorities despite his 1988 Hamas charter, which sounds as if it came straight from the pages of *Der Stürmer*. Article 22 says about the Jews: "With their money they formed secret societies, such as Freemasons, Rotary Clubs, the Lions and others in different parts of the world for the purpose of sabotaging societies and achieving Zionist interests.")

When Faisal was in prison, I had to take charge of the diplomatic and media campaign needed to keep the intifada going. The Arab Studies Society at the Orient House became our operation room for preparing visits by foreign and diplomatic delegations: our talks with Václav Havel and Dennis Ross, the U.S. special envoy for the Middle East, took place there.

In my more clandestine work there were plenty of close calls. Once I was driving around the West Bank with a hundred thousand dollars stuffed into a canvas bag. Not many private cars were plying the roads in those days, and when I noticed another car on my heels, I grew nervous. I swung the wheel at the first turnoff and steered into the back streets of Ramallah. With a quick series of maneuvers, I managed to shake my pursuer. Just to make sure, I made a few more circuitous loops around town, before idling the car in front of the house of a colleague from Birzeit. I rushed in the front door carrying the canvas bag. The astonished professor of English let me stuff the bag under one of the tables. Rushing out, I said I'd be back to collect it soon. Later in the day I returned to fetch the money.

On a different occasion, it was late at night and I was just leaving the town of Kabatyah in the Jenin district when Israeli Special Forces suddenly leapt out from behind some trees and surrounded my car. I was ordered to turn off the lights. With blackened faces and drawn machine guns they motioned for me to get out of the car. Hands held high and doing my best to look harmless, I complied. One of the soldiers reached into my pocket and pulled out my ID. "Are you Sari Nusseibeh?" he asked, which was a silly question because he had my picture ID in his hand. My first thought was that they had finally nabbed me. Stuffed under the driver's seat were enough capsules with enough sensitive intifada information to fill a stomach. All they had to do was look. Luckily for me, the trap they had laid was for someone else, and the soldiers wanted to get back to their hiding place. "Get lost," said the soldier, handing me back my ID and waving me off.

My fast-thinking secretary averted another disaster. We were about to print out a draft for a leaflet when an army officer came into the office unannounced. Before he could see what was on the computer screen my secretary rushed up to him with a smile and offered him some chewing gum. While she got it out of her purse I managed to delete the document. She saved the day one other time when a different detective came into the office seconds after we had faxed a new leaflet. "What's this?" he asked, picking up the leaflet from the tray.

"Oh, it just arrived. Would you like a copy?"

I first laid eyes on the Shin Bet man personally assigned to my case while at a friend's house. Hamzeh, Sameer, and I went to visit a poet by the name of Mutawakkil Taha, who had just been released from prison. No sooner had we sat down than we heard a knock on the door. The poet got up to answer it, and found two soldiers at the door. They stepped in and looked around. "Did you see some kids come up this way?" the first soldier asked. Looking puzzled, Mutawakkil shook his head.

"Some kids threw stones at our patrol car, and we thought we saw them come upstairs." The apartment was on the second floor.

The soldier apologized and left. Our host was on his way back to join us wearing an amused smile and doing some theatrics with his arms (a pantomime of a kid throwing a rock) when the door suddenly flew open. In walked my Shin Bet man in civilian clothing, followed by soldiers and detectives.

We were all ordered to remain seated while the soldiers searched through the house. After the search, we were each asked to go into one of the rooms, one by one. There each of us was stripped naked and thoroughly searched—and I mean *thoroughly*. Troops ringed the building in case someone tried to crawl out a window.

The search lasted well over an hour, and yielded nothing. We all told my Shin Bet man—who identified himself as "Jacob"—the same story: we were just friends relaxing after a week of hard work. We weren't hatching any plots, and we certainly weren't writing clandestine leaflets.

As Jacob and his friends were strip-searching us, a hundred thousand copies of the leaflet were being printed only a few blocks away. Hamzeh, Sameer, and I had finished the leaflet that afternoon.

. . .

Less than eight months into the intifada, Israel hunted down the man more responsible than anyone for keeping the uprising surprisingly unsullied by terrorist outrages.

My admiration for Abu Jihad had grown steadily over the years. It spoke in his favor that he was free from the taint of corruption and thuggery infesting the ranks of other PLO apparatchiks. He was also capable of changing with the times. The man who was once considered the Che Guevara of the movement—he had been in charge of commando units—had realized after the PLO's expulsion from Lebanon that liberation would never come about through a military victory from beyond Israeli borders, but through a mass movement in the territories themselves. The effectiveness of his new belief was now being proven daily.

Terrorism, in other words, had nothing to do with the Israeli government's decision to eliminate him. On the contrary, what must have driven the military planners out of their wits was that the enemy's most potent weapon was not bombs or hate-filled bombast—easy things to counter—but assertive nonviolence and a well orchestrated "white and unarmed revolution." And having failed to snuff out the source of trouble in the territories, they decided to go after the "mastermind."

The assassination of Abu Jihad took place in the quiet suburban neighborhood of Tunis where he lived with his family and where the ex-guerrilla leader spent much of his free time gardening. It was late. Abu Jihad and Um Jihad, his wife, were in their apartment talking about the latest news: Anthony Quinn was considering playing the character of Yasir Arafat in a new movie. Happy at the latest sign of our cause going Hollywood, his wife went to bed.

Meanwhile, Ehud Barak was circling overhead in a Boeing 707, radioing instructions down to twenty commandos on the ground. Hearing a noise, Um Jihad got up to see what was happening. She saw her husband with his pistol in hand walking to the front door. She tried to follow him but he waved her away. Then she saw him: a blond man in his early twenties wearing a surgeon's mask. He looked like a young doctor prepping himself to take out someone's tonsils. Abu Jihad tried to get off a shot but the young man coolly and without a word emptied the clip from his machine gun into Abu Jihad. Two more commandos emptied theirs before they all left. Not a word was said. A buxom female commando videotaped the execution.

As chance would have it, I was in Milan making arrangements for the next financial smuggling operation when the killing occurred. Besides feeling the natural shock—but also incredulity at the stupidity of murdering a man who had opted for nonviolence—I knew we had been robbed of an irreplaceable source of strength. Of all Fatah leaders, Abu Jihad had developed the best sense of what was doable—and what wasn't. And since his moral authority in the West Bank was unquestioned among activists, he more than anyone else, Arafat included, had been in a position to steer the Palestinians toward compromise with the Israelis. Now they had shot him dead. Once again, the comparison with the Israelis' treatment of the Hamas leader, Yassin, was dizzying.

On the flight back to Tel Aviv, I felt sorrow I hadn't known since Father's death. Back in Jerusalem, a different emotion overtook me: fear. Fury at the killing had unleashed a massive wave of protests, and the violence Abu Jihad had tried so hard to contain now threatened to spill out from every pore of every Arab in the street.

What came to mind was the way Faisal had turned Father's funeral into a protest march past Ariel Sharon's home. There must be some way of spinning this dross into gold, I said to myself, of using these passions to further a strategy Abu Jihad would have endorsed. Instead of allowing his death to undermine what he had built, which was what the Israelis wanted, I sought a way of strengthening our "white revolution."

This time I worked alone, without the think tank. In my mother's living room, I jotted down ideas to take us to the final stage of our civil-disobedience campaign. I wasn't conscious of this at the time, but the experience of standing at Monticello years earlier had left a residual impression. I wrote a declaration of independence.

What came out of that evening alone with Mother came to be known as the Husseini Document. Weeks after I wrote it Faisal was released from prison. Eager to get his opinion, I gave him a copy, which he read and then put in the drawer of his desk for safekeeping. Within a few days he was back in jail, and the soldiers who raided his office found the document and assumed he had written it. Hence the name. By this point, however, the "Husseini Document" had already received a thumbs-up from leaders around the territories and inside the jails, and it landed on Arafat's desk.

The text set out to formalize our disassociation from Israel, and to institutionalize our evolving civilian rule. This could be done, I proposed, both through a unilateral declaration of independence and by the public establishment of a provisional government, with members appointed from within the territories and from the PLO leadership in exile. Once established, the provisional government would offer to negotiate with Israel for a two-state solution.

After the aforementioned office raid, the Israeli security people leaked the existence of a "seditious" document to the press. Ehud Yaari, the Arab expert on Israeli TV, broke the news. Innumerable screeds followed in the Israeli press.

Among Palestinians there were the usual detractors and critics. "It's just one more useless fantasy cooked up by Sari," some said.

The intifada of the late 1980s was very different from the armed fiasco that broke out in 2000. Our goal in the first intifada was peaceful negotiations leading to an amicable division of historic Palestine. We also knew that the only realistic hope of getting this was by convincing the Israeli public that it was in their self-interest to help us win our independence. Their government's policies were leading both peoples into a dark pit.

Indeed, while one sensed in the Israeli media a grudging admiration for the rebels of the intifada, the points we were scoring would mean nothing if we didn't get Israelis to understand our position intellectually. The real utility of children's rocks was to shatter myths and lies that had governed both peoples for half a century. Unrest had to be translated into practical political gains, and this could happen only by our appealing directly to the Israelis' self-interest as a nation.

For this reason we told the Israeli man on the street that we didn't seek to destroy the Jewish state but only wanted to establish ours alongside Israel. The leaflets were unambiguous: the Unified Command accepted UN Resolution 242 and as such the moral and political right of Israel to exist within the 1967 borders.

One leaflet stated:

> The intifada, the latest form of the Palestinian struggle, voices the Palestinian cry for peace . . . Our fight is not to cause pain to others but to deliver ourselves from pain. It is not to destroy another state, but to create our own. It is not to bring death to others, but to give life and hope to ourselves and to our children.

Fueling my optimism regarding the Israeli public was work with the Israelis, primarily the members of Peace Now. In December 1988, after the PLO echoed what we had been stating in the leaflets by agreeing to recognize Israel's right to exist, Peace Now organized a mass demonstration in Tel Aviv to pressure the government into establishing direct talks with the PLO. For me, the tens of thousands of Jews supporting our independence were like antibodies to the disease of their government's hard line. I put it like this in an article:

> I see the face of the *Zaddik*—the Jewish holy man. I see him, or her, as they refuse to serve in the occupied Palestinian state. I see them wearing black, on vigil every Saturday, defying the contempt of their fellow Jews. I see them in the Knesset pursuing, proving, and exposing Rabin's policies, even more assiduously and meticulously than the Palestinians themselves. I see them performing the miracle of crossing political barriers, as they make solidarity visits to the

villages and camps of our occupied Palestinian state, where children had been killed, where houses had been demolished, where trees had been uprooted, where mothers had been forced to miscarry, where curfews were imposed for days and weeks on end, where electricity and water supplies had been cut off for prolonged periods, where true terrorism reigned.

I kept the face of the *"Zaddik"* in my mind's eye as our work turned even riskier.

Chapter Twenty

Interrogation

W HEN I STOOD UP IN ITALY and talked about the metaphysics
of interrogation I wasn't yet clear just how much blood was
going to be spilled for an elusive "outer" freedom. While I was certain
that civil disobedience, not guns, would over time win our liberty and
the liberation of our land, I didn't know—and still don't—when it would
happen. Another thing I didn't know at the time of the lecture was that
I would soon be in an interrogation cell faced with the choice of fighting occupation or losing my family.

At the start of the intifada, everyone, from schoolchildren to grand-
mothers, was marching gladly into clouds of tear gas—a spirit of defiance
miraculously animating a million people. Like most Palestinians, I didn't
think twice about involving my family. Lucy, a Palestinian by choice,
was as committed as any native, maybe even more. Call it a conscious,
deliberate act of will to make the tragic fate of another people her own.
Even my son Jamal, not even a teenager, was furtively slipping out the back
door at dusk to practice his graffiti skills. From a distance I watched
proudly as he and the ragtag band from the local Fatah "cubs" hoisted
Palestinian flags and covered walls with anti-occupation slogans.

In 1990, two years into the insurrection, I was still so intoxicated by the purpose and meaning of winning our freedom that my brothers had to remind me of my fatherly duties. "What the hell are you doing?" my younger brother Hatem, speaking for the others, demanded of me at a family reunion in London. "You can wreck your own life with your wonderful revolution but you don't have the right to inflict this on your children." At first I didn't know what he was talking about. "What do you mean?" I rejoined.

"Education! Our father gave us the best education, and your children deserve the same."

At the time, the children were all attending a Jesuit-run school inside the New Gate. Jamal was just entering high school. It was a fine school, as Jesuit schools tend to be. Besides, I retorted, my sons were having experiences not to be had at any of the world's fancy prep schools. Hatem scoffed at me. "You may think your revolution is meaningful, but don't forget you've *been* to the best schools. You should give your children the same choice. Afterward they can decide how to use their education, just as you did." As always putting his money where his mouth is, my older brother, Zaki, offered to pay for a finishing year at Eton for my three sons after they completed the local high school.

Why not? I thought to myself. "Okay, you got it. One year at Eton."

What won me over wasn't so much Zaki's generosity as the unfolding of political events. I was getting nervous about what could happen to me, or to them. "Baba," said my youngest boy, Buraq, from the backseat of the car as I drove him to school one morning. (He couldn't have been more than seven at the time.) "I'd like to know something. Was there ever life before the intifada?" The question cut through my heart like a knife.

The assassination of Abu Jihad was still fresh in my mind. Wherever I looked I saw more activists, many of them close friends, being jailed or dumped over the border. In 1990, on Eid ul-Fitr, the Ramadan feast, soldiers in Gaza opened fire on demonstrators, killing three and wounding hundreds, thirty critically. Around the same time, a group of messianic Jews calling themselves Temple Mount Faithful, their brains addled by years of Greater Israel talk, planned to march up to the Noble Sanctuary and lay the cornerstone for the Third Temple. The minute word of their intentions leaked out, rioting at the Noble Sanctuary left 18 Palestinians killed and 150 wounded by police gunfire. Faisal's description is worth citing: "All around me, moans were filling the air; curses were rising up in the holy place. The smell of blood mixed with gas and gunpowder congesting noses and eyes. In the midst of this stifling atmosphere, gloomy with death and catastrophe, I began to prepare my plea and my prayer: . . . Oh God the spirit is full of fears . . . do not change them to hatred."

I was in Ramallah when I heard about the shooting. At the first hint of a potential confrontation, Jamal's school shut down and sent the kids home. But Jamal didn't go home; he made a beeline for the Noble Sanctuary and found himself in the midst of gunfire and rioting. A friend who accompanied him was shot in the leg. Jamal saw how the soldiers stationed on rooftops shot into the crowd. A helicopter overhead sprayed the protesters with machine gun fire.

Mother, Lucy, and I spent two frantic hours trying to find him. When he finally showed up, thankfully in one piece, he had some awful stories to tell, so many in fact that an American television producer for *60 Minutes* tracked him down for an interview. Mike Wallace did the segment, which included a videotape that a tourist took showing the soldiers, unprovoked, opening fire. Jamal similarly debunked the official Israeli account according to which Arabs had thrown stones at the Jewish worshippers, instigating the Israeli response. Speaking innocently and clearly in his perfect English, he put to shame Israel's ambassador to the UN, Bibi Netanyahu. Netanyahu, expert salesmen that he is (his former job was selling high-end furniture), couldn't compete with an honest boy speaking matter-of-factly about what had really happened.

One day I asked an activist friend, Salah, who'd joined us in the talks with Amirav, if he was worried about his own young children. He had just been released from administrative detention.

"What do you mean?"

"Well, don't you miss them when you get thrown into jail? Don't you ever ask yourself if it's worth it, I mean to be away from them?"

The smile Salah nearly permanently affixed to his face disappeared. He looked at me with uncharacteristic gravity. "It's all for our children," he exclaimed lowering his voice to a hush as if telling me a secret. "I go to jail so one day they don't have to."

Salah's answer summed up to me what we were all doing. We were all struggling to achieve for our children a future without roadblocks, tanks, tear gas, or administrative detention. A future not shadowed by a pervasive sense of our being wronged.

The noose was tightening, as the Shin Bet edged closer to figuring out the workings of the mysterious Unified Command. No matter how obfuscating or professorial my conversations (speaking about liberation strategies through a gloss on Kant was one of my favorite tactics), and however much I restricted my direct contact with Fatah activists, the continued arrests and interrogations of activists were cumulatively contracting my margin of maneuverability. Time was running out.

At one point, Jacob ordered *The Monday Report* shut. (Lucy's English-language paper was so popular it had subscribers not only from all the foreign delegations but also from the Israeli newspapers and agencies.) Sometime later, my friend Samir Sbeihat ended up exiled from the country. Another colleague working at the office was arrested. On yet another occasion, the Israelis managed to hunt down Fahed Abu al-Haj, my main contact with groups in Ramallah. Naser Al-Afandi was also arrested again—he had already spent years behind bars. This time (years before Abu Ghraib) the Israelis put a peaked black hood over his head and chained him in a painful squatting position for a month.

The longer the intifada lasted, and the more of its leaders disappeared into the prison camp or ended up on the other side of the border or dead, the less discipline the UNC was able to impose on the Palestinian people.

A rash of killings of "collaborators" broke out. The incoming reports from the various regions were alarming. At the beginning of the intifada, we in the leadership had announced an amnesty for all Palestinian collaborators. All they had to do was to admit to it publicly, in the main square of their local village or town, and ask for forgiveness from their fellow citizens.

I also began to see a new pattern. In one region after the next, provocateurs were returning with guns from safe houses within Israel to which they had fled, helped by the Israeli security services. Also, though Hamas had already begun turning against the occupation, fights were breaking out between Hamas and Fatah activists. Given close family relations among Palestinians, clashes between two people can easily morph into major conflagrations dividing up entire villages. Internecine strife erupted between various factions.

Similar reports began trickling out from the prisons, where bloody fights pitted Fatah against Hamas. Here, too, fratricide had a pattern. Usually an agent turned out to be the trigger. Violence radicalized the base, and made it more difficult to keep activists behind our "white revolution." The demands by the factions wishing to push the intifada toward violent confrontation increased, and more and more radical statements made the rounds.

It didn't take great strategic intelligence to figure out that a new Israeli offensive was afoot. Killing Abu Jihad, or arresting tens of thousands of people, hadn't worked. Their new secret war was to administer the blows from within. Playing the Islamic card was, as it remains, a choice strategy in dividing up Palestinian society into warring factions.

To scuttle Israel's tactics, I organized clandestine meetings in Jerusalem on Fatah's behalf, at the house of a devout Muslim and Fatah supporter who didn't want to see a civil war tear our people apart. Jamil Hamami, representing Hamas, agreed with me to bury whatever hatchets there were between our two movements, and to form a united front against the occupation. During our conversation we began drawing up the first joint Hamas-Fatah leaflet.

I tried to bring Hamas and Fatah together only because I knew that the Israelis were using Hamas to undermine the secular nationalists. Hamas continued its fight against us, but by this point it had grown strong enough to turn against the Israelis, too. Yassin's new mantra was for a holy war against Zionism *and* the PLO, leading to an Islamic state stretching from Tel Aviv to the Jordan River. In 1989, Hamas went on a killing spree against Israeli citizens. The Israeli government now banned the organization and arrested the sheikh after Yassin ordered his minions to kidnap and murder two Israeli soldiers.

My attempts to prevent the intifada from breaking down into a slugfest with the Israelis were only stopgap measures. Even a defensive stalemate with the occupation—with our throwing rocks, and their breaking bones and throwing us into jail—would spell defeat. Israel had far greater logistic depth of manpower and weaponry. We either continued on the offensive or we lost. And in my thinking, the best offensive weapon in our arsenal was our declaration of independence, the creation of a provisional government, and the invitation to Israel to negotiate on the basis of mutual recognition.

By way of my Paris contact, I knew just how alluring the Husseini Document was for the PLO. Now with Abu Jihad gone, what the men in Tunis liked best, unfortunately, was the declaration itself; they were less enthusiastic about the other component, the creation of a provisional government in the West Bank and Gaza.

The Husseini Document explicitly forecast the scenario of Israeli arrests that might follow. The Israeli government would never tolerate such a government, and any ministers we named to it would be arrested at once. "Let them lock us up!" I told people. "We'll just keep on appointing new ministers and civil servants to take our places. The more they take in, the more we'll hire. Each time they arrest the new appointed judge or minister of education or postman, the more the world will see the nature of the occupation. Their fight against our civil service will make a mockery of the occupation."

When Faisal finally came out of jail, I felt a deep sense of relief. Hours after his arrival in Jerusalem, I had a closed meeting with him in one of Jerusalem's hotels. "We need to lay down the preparatory building blocks for our provisional government," I told him. "I believe this should be your main mission."

Whatever I said wasn't very convincing. "I'm a bulldozer, not a builder," he said when I had gone through the scenario of the revolving door of appointed and arrested ministers. "My mission is to clear the grounds and defuse the mines. Those who follow me can build." He spoke like an Old Testament prophet; even so, he left me unconvinced.

The next time I brought up the provisional government was at a meeting of our think tank at my house in Abu Dis. Faisal was there. I had asked Radwan Abu Ayyash, a journalist, to prepare a paper on ways the various self-rule committees could be brought into centralized governmental departments. The paper he presented was precisely what I had had in mind: what he proposed, and what we discussed, was the structural foundation of a provisional government.

The provisional government never got off the ground, partly because in November 1989 Arafat announced that he was going to come out with a declaration of independence in Algeria—not at the Noble Sanctuary in Jerusalem as the Husseini Document had advised, and without the establishment of our own government. His declaration was written by the masterful Palestinian poet Mahmoud Darwish, and as such was stirring and finely crafted. From my perspective, it was also long on lofty words and short on practical suggestions to end the occupation.

Still, even without a government in place, the declaration was an important milestone, and like everyone else, I looked forward to its unveiling. On the day it was to be announced, a few friends and I went around to the mosques and churches in the Old City and asked the clerics to sound their bells and make their calls at the appointed hour. The plan I came up with was to read out the declaration to tens of thousands of people gathered at the Noble Sanctuary. I wanted a people under occupation, the people of the intifada, to congregate at the center of our universe, and to celebrate our independence.

On the day the declaration was read, Israel slapped a total curfew over the territories and East Jerusalem. It was the most draconian curfew in memory, and life for us came to a halt: no cars, no people on the streets; even the birds seemed to be gone. I should mention here that for my family, curfews were a blessing in disguise. Locked inside, I could finally spend long stretches of time with my sons.

Curfew or no, I was determined to get to the Noble Sanctuary. And so, defying the authorities and venturing out into the eerie silence of the city, I crossed two valleys on foot, before heading down the Mount of Olives and entering Jerusalem through the Lion's Gate, where Father was buried. Of the few people who had managed to get through, most were the mosque's clergy, who lived near the compound. Hanna Siniora and his wife, who is a Christian, were also there. Hanna, a staunchly secular man, looked out of place up on the ancient Temple Mount. He had probably never set foot there before, and certainly not in the company of religious clerics.

Together, we all walked into Al-Aqsa mosque. At the appointed hour, as the bells from the Holy Sepulcher swung, and calls wailed out from the minarets, we all solemnly read our declaration of independence:

Palestine, the land of the three monotheistic faiths, is where the Palestinian Arab people was born, on which it grew, developed and excelled. Thus the Palestinian Arab people ensured for itself an everlasting union between itself, its land, and its history.

Resolute throughout that history, the Palestinian Arab people forged its national identity . . . Nourished by an unfolding series of civilizations and cultures, inspired by a heritage rich in variety and kind, the Palestinian people added to its stature by consolidating a union between itself and its patrimonial Land. The call went out from Temple, Church, and Mosque that to praise the Creator, to celebrate compassion and peace was indeed the message of Palestine. And in generation after generation, the Palestinian Arab people gave of itself unsparingly in the valiant battle for liberation and homeland. For what has been the unbroken chain of our people's rebellions but the heroic embodiment of our will for national independence. And so the people was sustained in the struggle to stay and to prevail.

Over the coming weeks, I intensified my calls for negotiations. In the English edition of Fatah's *Al-Fajr*, I called openly upon the PLO to show leadership by giving people what they wanted: peace. I urged the PLO to declare a peace strategy. The title of the article was "The PLO Represents the People, Not Itself."

I also tried to get my message across to the Israeli public by repeating my argument that the two-state solution was in both peoples' self-interest, but I pointed out that it was an option that might slip from our hands. "The national psychological readiness for a two-state solution is not a permanent fixture of the Palestinian psychology. It is in the Palestinian heart now, but it can quickly fade if there is no response to this feeling of opening up. It's like a star or a comet that comes close by and then goes away. One has to catch it when it is close."[1] If they didn't watch it, I implied, reissuing my old argument, instead of a peaceful movement for independence Israelis might have an antiapartheid campaign on their hands.

My mood in those days can be felt in a missive I sent to Desmond Tutu on Christmas Day, 1989.

> *Your Excellency,*
>
> *On this universal day of peace, in this land of peace, a people yearning for peace welcomes you as a messenger of peace, as a symbol of the invincibility of mankind's moral strength. Whether in South Africa or Palestine, the powers of discrimination, injustice, and usurpation of rights are being challenged by nothing less than the power of the people's will and their desire for freedom and equality. Our joint struggle against the forces of racism and exclusivism is but one among countless battles waged throughout the history of mankind, and exemplified by the Prophet of Peace, whose birthday we celebrate today, in his struggle to advance the cause of humanity.*

The only official Israeli response I got for my public stance was greater diligence on the part of my private Shin Bet agent. Jacob and his colleagues were methodically filling out their flowchart to pinpoint my place in the leadership. Even without evidence, they began to attack me indirectly. Right from the beginning, their line of attack was calculated to produce fear. They probably did a psychological profile and determined that the best way to control me was to threaten what I loved most, which wasn't my reputation, career, or my own life and limb. It was my mother, my wife, and my kids.

One evening, as my family and I sat around at home watching TV, I heard a scuffling sound outside. Someone was moving around in the backyard, where our car was parked. At once I switched on the patio light and went outside. There I saw three overweight masked men around my battered Opel, one of them carrying a gasoline can and a rag, obviously about to torch the car. I shouted and ran at them, which was a foolish thing to do—I was wearing slippers and armed only with the television remote control—but it succeeded in chasing them away. They probably lumbered off because they thought I was a bodyguard.

Hearing my shouts, a few neighbors came over to help. As we walked around the house to inspect the property, one of my neighbors pointed out freshly painted graffiti on one of the walls. THE PROPHET OF BIRZEIT . . . went the unfinished message. It looked to me like the work of collaborators. The first sign of this was that they had been middle-aged and potbellied—hardly the picture of the young and agile activists Hamas normally fielded. Their plan was to torch the car and, with the graffiti, create the impression that I was being punished by Muslim factions for my heretical, anti-Islamic ideas. This would in turn show that my efforts at mediation between the factions had not only failed, but that I was one source of their mutual rancor.

My instinct was later confirmed. My friend Abd el-Halim made some inquiries. We discovered from the local gas station attendant, where the men had bought the gasoline, that they were known collaborators living in the area.

On another occasion, the Shin Bet used the "leaflet" trick. Israel's security sometimes issued leaflets of its own, under a concocted name of some hitherto-unheard-of Palestinian "faction." These had several uses, one of which was to sow confusion among the population or, better yet, spark brawls or infighting. The leaflet war was part of Israel's offensive to break the will of the insurrection from the inside.

One such leaflet—distributed to what seemed like every mailbox in the territories—denounced me as a "salon prince." The authors didn't have Machiavelli in mind; I was a "prince" because of my privileged family background and my "white hands," unsullied with the blood dripping from the hands of the true intifada activists. I was a guy who vacationed in the Swiss Alps while fellow Palestinians braved bullets. A man with no blood on his hands had no business in politics, and certainly shouldn't be talking about peace. (To get some captured UNC members to talk about my role in the uprising, the interrogator used my frequent trips to prove that their aristocratic friend was skiing off in the Alps while they were rotting in prison.)

When an Israeli journalist asked me how I felt about the scurrilous pamphlets, he must have anticipated my taking umbrage because what I said left him wagging his head in disbelief: "Why should it bother me to be described as having 'white hands'? Surely it's by a special grace of God that any of us can have truly white hands. I can only be grateful that my hands are white. And I only pray that they be whiter still, and I am grateful that my compatriots can see I'm blessed with this grace."

In 1989 the Shin Bet and Agent Jacob got lucky with the latest crop of arrests. One figure they captured was Fatah's most senior representative in the territories, a man I greatly admired. At the onset of the intifada, he had been immediately placed high on Israel's Most Wanted List, and went into hiding. Through the two years of unrest, he kept a low profile.

The two of us had occasional meetings, with Fahed Abu al-Haj acting as our go-between. Fahed arranged clandestine meetings between us in apartment basements, in the middle of fields—wherever we could talk. The main purpose of these risky tête-à-têtes was for me to fill him in on Fatah's strategy as expressed in its leaflets; he, in turn, passed information on to Fatah's organizational network. He then let me in on developments within the network. Another way we worked together was in financing the rebellion. He passed on the money I smuggled in from abroad to fugitives on the run.

As soon as I got word of his capture, I felt a sudden stab of pain. It was the pain of empathy, and of fear. I knew that the interrogators would pull out all the stops to get him to talk.

Several weeks later, I received a call summoning me to the prison in the Russian compound. Upon my arrival, Israeli army officers summarily marched me from the reception office, through an area covered with coils of rusting barbed wire, and into the prison. There they took me directly into an interrogation cell. They hadn't officially charged me with anything, so I knew my visit would be brief, unless I slipped up and voluntarily gave something away. But why had they taken me to a cell? They could have asked me their questions just as easily in any one of the offices or rooms in the Russian compound, outside the prison walls.

The officers in charge of the interrogation informed me without further ado—no introduction, no small talk, no pleasantries—that they had succeeded in squeezing serious information about me from a prisoner. They now had evidence that not only had I maintained contact with the head of Fatah in the territories, but also that I had sent him large sums of money.

I didn't fall for his trap. Instead of talking to my interrogator, I began inspecting my nails. If the interrogators really had forced out a confession, I thought to myself, my heart racing, they would be bringing charges against me, not bragging about their investigative successes. They obviously suspected that the prisoner and I had worked together; they just couldn't prove it. By sounding me out, they hoped to get a confession out of me so they could bring charges against both of us. I wasn't biting.

"Yes," I told them breezily, "I believe I've met this chap before." I added that beyond this casual meeting, I had no idea who he was or whether he had any connection to the intifada or to Fatah. As far as I knew, he had approached me because I was a public figure. That was the whole story. "A lot of people want to talk to me. Israelis, too. I'm a professor, you know. I'm a polite person and can't in all propriety say no. My work at Holy Land Press requires that I meet with political activists of all stripes and colors."

The interrogators stuck to their original story that they now had something on me. At this point I switched tactics. "Such a mean liar this coward has turned out to be," I said of the prisoner. "Why on earth would he wish to implicate me if not to hide his true contacts?"

For several hours we went back and forth: they insisting that they had a smoking gun, and I admitting to have met the prisoner but adamantly denying everything else. Eventually they realized that their trick wasn't working, and they released me.

More arrests followed. In one roundup the Israelis not only nabbed a number of members of the UNC but also Izzat Ghazzawi and Hamzeh Smadi, my co-worker at the Holy Land Press who helped me with the monthly leaflets.

All of the detainees were taken to a special prison facility in Petah Tikva. For weeks, I couldn't find out anything about them. Lawyers were usually able to glean bits of information about detainees' whereabouts, their charges, and how they were being treated. This time there was absolute dead silence.

Only when Hamzeh got out of prison two years later did I learn about the nightmarish interrogations. On the wall of one of the interrogation rooms was a chalkboard. Interrogators jotted down several names with lines connecting them. On the top of the chart was the name of my Paris contact Abu Tareq. Immediately under him came the name Sari. Under me were written several other names, including those of Hamzeh and his fellow prisoners. Between some names were solid lines, while between others were question marks. Those under interrogation were asked to fill in the gaps, and to provide the skeletal structure with content. How did all the lines tie up? In particular, could a formal link be established proving that Fatah's representative in the UNC was taking his direct instructions from me? Or could it simply be—this was what I had been telling the Israelis—that I had a lot of visitors, and if one of them turned out to be a member of the UNC, it had nothing to do with me?

By now, the experts in the Shin Bet were tired of feeling duped. Time after time they had rounded up UNC members thinking they'd decapitated the leadership, only to discover on the ninth of the next month that there was an invisible network operating in the shadows, keeping the whole thing running. Slowly, they were beginning to cast light on those shadows, and with such high-quality prisoners in their hands, they prepared the rack.

The interrogation methods were so extreme that four veteran prisoners who had endured hundreds of hours of interrogation in the past now cracked. One was my friend Fahed Abu al-Haj, who had worked with me at my newspaper. For twenty-five days the interrogators put him into a sealed room, chained him in a standing position to a bathroom door so he couldn't sleep, and only once a day they took off his shackles to allow him to eat and wash himself. Once, an interrogator hit him hard enough that he went temporarily blind.

They eventually got a signed confession out of him, with a fingerprint smeared on the page for additional proof of authenticity. "In the name of Allah the Merciful," began the confession, "I, Fahed Hussain Ahmad Abu al-Haj, testify to the following:

[. . .] Around the month of September 1988, Zuhair Qaisi told me that he was a member of the Unified Command for the intifada and asked me to be his messenger. He was wanted by the Israeli authorities. Zuhair asked me to deliver a small letter to Sari Nusseibeh. I told him I would . . . I did this, and Sari gave me approximately 4,000 Jordanian dinars [$12,000] to give to Zuhair. This I also did. I as well delivered several letters from Sari to Zuhair and from Zuhair to Sari.

Several times I delivered drafts of leaflets from Zuhair to the printer. Before December 6, 1988, I delivered letters between Zuhair and Abdul Fattah Shuhaded. Two weeks later Abdul Fattah came to me at Birzeit University and asked me to deliver a letter to Sari and to take money from Sari for the intifada. I gave the letter to Sari, and two days later he gave me 100,000 Jordanian dinars [$300,000]. I gave the money to Abdul Fattah. At the same time, Abdul Fattah gave me a letter to deliver to Sari. Sari gave me 80,000 dinars [$240,000] to give to Abdul."

A second prisoner's confession was even more damning:

I, the undersigned, testify to the following: I was released from prison on Aug. 18, 1988, and stayed for a month in my home in Al-Fara, a refugee camp, at which point I moved to my home in the village of Birzeit. Two weeks later Zuhair Qaisi visited me in my home on the occasion of my release from prison. We got into a casual conversation about life in prison. Then he visited me again and told me he was wanted by the authorities . . . He asked me to go to Hassan Abed Rabbo, who works at the Journalist's Union in Jerusalem, and to take him a draft of a leaflet. I think it was Leaflet No. 32.

During that period Zuhair came to me and told me that Sari Nusseibeh had money for intifada activities and he asked me to go to Sari's office in Jerusalem to pick up the money. The next day I went to Sari and told him that I was sent by Zuhair to take the money that he was holding. (I've known Sari since 1985, during my studies at Birzeit University, where I took his course on the subject of Palestine.)

Sari told me that the money hadn't yet arrived and that I should pass by again in two days. I returned two days later and discovered that the money had arrived. He gave me $80,000 in front of the American Colony Hotel . . . Two days later I received $50,000 from Sari from his car (a gray Opel Ascona) . . . Two days later I received another $50,000 from Sari's office.

A third confession, every word of which was of course true, like the others, filled in the few gaps that remained in the Shin Bet flowchart:

I testify in God's name: I was appointed by Abu Tareq from the Fatah organization in France to oversee suggestions for Leaflet Nos. 33–35. Abu Tareq appointed me to oversee the process of adding comments on the leaflets. He called Sari Nusseibeh concerning this

matter and informed him of my coming to him. There was constant
telephone communication between Abu Tareq, Sari, and me.

I met with Sari Nusseibeh and put suggestions for the leaflets so
it would be delivered to Hassan Abed Rabbo . . . The final say regarding suggested items of Leaflets Nos. 33–35 was Sari's, since he is
Fatah's top man in the Occupied Territories. This statement I willingly wrote by hand.

One reason a Manichean view of the Palestinian-Israeli conflict, with
one side all light, the other all darkness, is impossible to take is that just
when you are happily convinced of the total justice of your position and
conversely of the bestiality of your opponent's, your own side shoots itself in the foot, while the enemy actually does something right for a
change.

By the beginning of 1990, Israel was clearly gaining the upper hand.
Its attempt to crack the Unified Command and the intifada leadership, and to take down its leaders, was showing the first signs of real
promise. In the daily grind of a deepening stalemate, the enormous im-
balance of power began to show. The euphoric unity Palestinians felt
when the first rocks started flying was breaking down, and for very understandable reasons. The closures and strikes were making economic
conditions so dire that just to put food on the table workers were beginning to drift back to their jobs in Israel. The boycott spelled out by the
Jerusalem Document, and that was an integral part of the civil disobedience campaign, was running up against the hard reality of raw
survival.

There were grotesque scenes of activists trying forcibly to prevent
workers from earning their daily bread in Israel. The inevitable brawls this
caused further frayed the social fabric. Fatigue was beginning to set in.

From the outset, we had been the ones on the offensive, beginning
with the outburst of defiance, then the Fourteen Points, the Jerusalem
Document, and the declaration of independence. Now all that seemed
left of the creative energies of our people's revolution was disgust—

disgust at the occupation and, increasingly, disgust at ourselves for having to put our hands out again just to feed ourselves.

The roles were now reversed, and it was Israel's turn to make a move. Defense Minister Rabin had by now concluded that as a political offensive, the intifada could not be defeated by breaking our bones; it had to be countered by an Israeli diplomatic offensive.

Rabin was a practical man, constitutionally suspicious of ideologies and always more than willing to change course if circumstances demanded it. In his search for a diplomatic opening, he enlisted the expertise of Yaʾakov Peri, the head of the Shin Bet. Through his network, Peri was to make contact with local Palestinian leaders to run suggestions past them that would later appear in the "Shamir Plan."

Yaʾakov Peri visited Faisal in jail, where the discussions centered on the idea of holding elections in the Occupied Territories. He also contacted Hamas leaders, to see what their views on such a plan might be. (Sheikh Ahmad Yassin was released from jail soon afterward.)

In the meantime, the four UNC prisoners at Petah Tikva Prison suddenly found themselves on a different footing with their captors. Their food improved, the chains disappeared, and the guards, polite to the point of deferential, ushered them into a room in a different section of the prison, this one with a negotiation table instead of a rack. Now the interrogators wanted to talk politics. "What were the intifada leaders really after?" probed the Israelis on Peri's instruction. "Did they really want a negotiated peace, as the leaflets claimed?"

Negotiations ensued. Some of the issues raised seemed lifted straight from the Fourteen Points (e.g., withdrawal of the army from population centers), while others had come up in our talks with Amirav. As the two sides discussed topic after topic, the Israelis took notes. In the end, after five days of talks, the Shin Bet men had sketched out a page-and-a-half document outlining a possible approach to negotiating a solution to the Israeli-Palestinian conflict. A central component in the draft was the holding of elections. In this extraordinary meeting of minds between captors and captives only one point remained unresolved: the prisoners stated emphatically, with half-blind Fahed the most categorical of all, that their agreement would go nowhere without the endorsement of the PLO leadership in Tunis.

"We know that," the Israeli officers retorted. "But how do you suggest the PLO leadership get involved?"

"We'll have to consult our leaders before continuing," they told the negotiators. When asked which leaders they were talking about, the prisoners mentioned Faisal and me. "No problem!" the officers said. "If you want, we could even bring them here to visit you, and you could consult with them directly. Or just send a message and see what they say." The prisoners, understandably nervous and loath to bring us into a trap, asked to see Faisal's lawyer, Jawad Boulos.

As an Israeli Arab and the top lawyer for most of the leading Palestinian political prisoners, Jawad was a familiar figure among the Israeli security people. Gregarious, Hebrew speaking, and always immaculately dressed, Jawad was a man they liked and admired. Now they contacted him and invited him to meet the four inmates. It was during his talks with them that he learned both about their confessions and about the subsequent negotiations.

From the jail, Boulos returned to Jerusalem and headed directly to my home in Abu Dis. "Sari, I just met four guys who informed the Israelis that you were the one who's been writing the leaflets. In their confession they stated that you and Faisal are the leaders of the intifada." I was just catching my breath when he handed me the page-and-a-half document. He informed me that the Israelis wanted it to be passed on to Tunis, but the Palestinian prisoners had asked that I look it over first.

From my house Jawad headed directly to Faisal to tell him what had happened. Faisal's first reaction to the negotiations was incredulity. "These fools have to stop negotiating!"

For my part, I immediately faxed the document to Arafat, via Abu Tareq in Paris. By this point I had nothing to hide. The game was over; the Israelis knew my role, and I could stop pretending.

There was no reply from Arafat.

· · ·

Prime Minister Shamir disemboweled the Petah Tikva working paper. In its place he put the "Shamir Plan," as it was called, which went directly counter to a negotiated peace. It talked about elections, but only as a clever means to defuse the intifada. There was no clear indication what would happen after those elections. The plan was little more than a reissue of the old Israeli dream of taking all of our best land and leaving us to sweep our own streets and dig our own sewage lines. No hint of Israeli withdrawal, of giving us back our water and other resources, or of uprooting settlements or military bases. What was the upshot of it? The prerequisite for elections was the return to ordinary life, without protests and stone throwing and unrest, without an intifada. The only baffling thing about the "plan" was that Shamir and his party apparatchiks believed we would fall for it.

Oddly enough, when the Shamir Plan was announced, Sheikh Yassin made a statement to the effect that elections in the Occupied Territories would be a "welcome step." Even after branching off into terrorist outrages against Israelis, the sheikh was still playing the Village League politician, doubtlessly to further build his organization at the expense of moderates truly willing to compromise with Israel.

I was baffled, but also angered. Once again, a historic opportunity to arrive at true peace through a genuine negotiation effort was being squandered by a politician's small-minded machinations, and after all the blood spilled I wasn't going to sit passively and watch it happen. I worked away at my Holy Land Press office in Salaheddin Street, doing my best to expose the Shamir Plan as a sham. The statements I came up with alerted the international community and the Israeli public to the plan's real intentions. (After Shamir was voted out of office in 1992, he would reveal what he had been aiming for: "I would have carried out autonomy talks for ten years, and meanwhile we would have reached half a million people in Judea and Samaria."[2])

On one hot summer morning in June 1990, my Shin Bet man, Jacob, and his team showed up with soldiers at the Holy Land Press. It was early and I wasn't yet in the office. They proceeded to gather up all my files and computer discs and place them in boxes. "If we find anything," they warned my secretary, "we'll lock you into a hole and throw away the key."

She had phoned me the minute she saw Jacob's face at the front door, and I headed over without delay. The street outside the building was swarming with border police, the most trigger-happy in the force. Pushing past them, I ran upstairs. "And what do you think you're doing here?" I demanded the minute I entered the office. "This is an office. We earn our living here. This is the way we buy our bread."

"Go buy some cake instead," snapped one of the officers in a variation on Marie Antoinette.

They ordered us out of the office. Then they welded the metal doors shut and on the front of the building pasted a military order. The office was closed for two years by order of the government.

Soon afterward, stories began appearing in the Hebrew press about all the confessions Israel's security had from me. One headline described me as the "paymaster of the intifada," like the smart accountant who keeps Mafia bosses in business. Minister of Industry and Trade Ariel Sharon used the confessions as fodder for his lobbying campaign to get Faisal and me deposited over the border. This was something the chieftains of Gush Emunim had been saying for years. Only after exiling us, Sharon insisted to his colleagues in the cabinet, could the intifada be defeated. He even cited the American invasion of Panama as a useful precedent. In Reagan's America "a democracy has decided to defend itself because it perceives a threat to its citizens. It is high time for Israel to do the same against those who endanger Jewish life."

Sharon's solution got some traction. One day, as I drove through a West Jerusalem street, I saw a group of Israelis holding banners in front of the prime minister's house. Some of them were children, and one little girl carried the oversize placard: DEPORT SARI NUSSEIBEH. Tzahi Hanegbi, the former chain-swinging, Arab-beating student activist who also had belonged to Amirav's circle, publicly called for me to be put on trial.

The Petah Tikva prisoners headed back to their cells. In the bills of indictment brought against them (Bills 108/89 and 109/89, respectively) the government prosecutor got some things right, others wrong. He rightly fingered me as a conduit for money for financing the intifada and for being responsible for "drawing up reports and leaflets for the intifada." Where fact faded into fiction was the accusation that I supported calls to "throw firebombs" at Israelis and "fight with knives."[3]

Following the closure of the office, I reduced my illegal activities to the bare minimum. At first I shifted operations over to Mother's house. In any case, I had less to do because Faisal was out of jail and hence could reassume the leadership role that I had taken on in his absence.

I was relieved to step out of the public eye. From my point of view, the uprising had run into the sand. I still participated in some Palestinian-Israeli dialogue groups and diplomatic meetings, and once or twice I wrote a leaflet. But for me, the intifada's spirit was dead. The only thing it was now achieving was aimless pain and suffering.

By November my pursuers had had ample time to sift through all my files and computer discs. They ordered me back to the Russian compound for questioning. This time Jacob had three officers along with him in civilian clothing. All three spoke passable Arabic, and the most fluent one did the bulk of the talking. Pointing to a pile of papers he called "seditious material and literature," he asked me to identify it. "I'd rather not say anything without my lawyer," I replied. Feigning a yawn, I added though that the pile "seems in general" to belong to my office. They were "field documents" and I needed them for my work. I asked them to kindly return them at the first opportunity. "A man has to make a living."

For four hours they grilled me on the intifada, all the while informing me that in the eyes of the government I was already in "way over" my head. Without spelling it out, they insisted that I was acting in the "danger zone." As a hint of what could await me, they said they were now on the verge of issuing an order to expel my friend Samir Sbeihat, as they had already done to Marwan, Jibril Rajoub, Mohammed Dahlan, and Akram Haniyyah. They also had enough information on me to expel me, or put me behind bars for years.

I stuck to my stock narrative of being someone people like to talk to. "No, no, no. You've got it all wrong," I assured them with all the insincerity they deserved. "I'm not an organization person. I just know people. How was I supposed to know that these guys were involved in the intifada?" I knew they didn't believe me.

They spent hours running through a Chinese menu of all the things they suspected me of doing, or that various prisoners had accused me of. I continued to feign incredulity, all the while doing my best to conceal my trembling hands.

After a couple of hours, their tactics changed. In a mood of light jesting, as if in a show of having concluded the interrogation, they started telling jokes to one another. Their faces all grins, they beamed at one another and at me.

After cracking a few jokes, they turned to me laughingly and, as though having forgotten our earlier conversation, came out with several underhand questions. The inflection in their voices was now vulgar, like a conversation between street hoodlums.

"Your wife is English, isn't she? (*English* was repeated between them a number of times, each time with snickers.) "What's her name? It's Lucy, right? Luuucy." (More giggling.) "She drives around in a red Peugeot, doesn't she?" one crowed. "Yeah, with yellow plates," another chipped in. "Tell us." Jacob turned to me in a more serious tone: "Aren't you worried that some people might think she's an Israeli? Especially when she's driving to your home in Abu Dis, with those hairpin curves. Anything could happen. Your own intifada guys could easily mistake her for the enemy." ("Ha-ha-ha-ha!") "She could end up burning up inside her car from those Molotov cocktails your leaflets are so full of." One officer at this point wagged his head in mock commiseration with me. "*Poor Luuucy.*" A moment of silence followed.

The conversation started up from a different angle. "You have three children. Your eldest is . . . Jamal, right. Fair hair, isn't that right? Jamal, huh, doesn't this mean 'beauty' in Arabic?" Laughter. "And the other two . . . both go to the same school, don't they? The school's just inside the New Gate. Right? Difficult place to turn your car around."

The officer with the best Arabic described in photographic detail Lucy's routine of driving the kids to school through the New Gate and then picking them up later in the afternoon. He knew exactly the time she arrived. He added darkly, "Don't you know how dangerous that narrow street is? You know, people hang around, and sometimes the soldiers shoot. Imagine, a demonstration can suddenly flare up. Lucy has just driven in. She can't turn around. The kids are caught in between. Scary thought, don't you agree?"

"And what about that old mother of yours?" They pretended to be concerned about her well-being. "She lives in such a big house all alone, right? Aren't you afraid, in the midst of this intifada craziness, that something could happen to her? People can get so crazy, you know."

After five hours of this they sent me back home. It was in the middle of the night, and I began to tie up the logic of interrogation sessions one and two. Their message rang clearly: "We know how to deal with you. If you love your family, you'll pack up and leave the country."

A few days later I met with my Israeli lawyer, Mr. Arnold Spaer, the German Jew from Danzig who had studied with my father in the early 1940s. He told me he had been in touch with the public prosecutor, who said that the government had enough evidence to put me away for fifteen years. They gave me two options: either they would put me on trial or they'd wipe the slate clean if I agreed to go into voluntary exile for three years.

This forced me to take some of my own medicine. How could I cave in to threats when for years I had been singing the praises of rebels who had defied their interrogators, and at a much stiffer price than imprisonment or exile? I had no choice but to swallow my fears and go on.

I told my Mr. Spaer that I *wanted* a trial. I could use it as a platform to defend our rights for a nonviolent rebellion. He delivered to the authorities my response to their accusations, the gist of which was this: "In none of my opinions have I expressed an incitement to violence or the adoption of calls for the extermination of Israel. On the contrary, I have argued that we should adopt a nonviolent strategy, and that we should reach the point where we can negotiate a two-state solution with Israel."

The Israelis chose to do nothing. As it would turn out, they were waiting for a more propitious time. The crisis in the Gulf would give them the cover they needed.

Chapter Twenty-one

Ramle Prison

I come from there and I have memories.
Born as mortals are, I have a mother
And a house with many windows,
I have brothers, friends,
And a prison cell with one cold window.

—MAHMOUD DARWISH, "I COME FROM THERE"

I N AUGUST 1991, attention in the Middle East shifted away from the stones and tear gas of the Holy Land to the fertile crescent of Mesopotamia, the land of Gilgamesh, al-Ghazali, Sinbad, and now the killer Saddam Hussein.

Invoking past border disagreements with Kuwait, but with his greedy raptor's eyes on its oil wealth, Saddam Hussein began rattling his sabers. Emotions in the Arab world ran high. Then one day the dictator struck. Overnight, Iraqi troops ingested Kuwait.

I read about the invasion in the morning paper, sitting with Mother at her home. "How could such a thing happen?" I asked her incredulously and already heard in my mind what she was thinking: "Politicians!" My brother Zaki, with his uncanny knack of seeing things for what they were, free of blinkers and delusion, told me, "The countdown has begun. American troops will be in the Middle East before we know it."

For me it was appalling that a big powerful Arab state such as Iraq should pounce on its small neighbor. Here we were, year after year trying to expose all the evils of occupation by pointing to a people's natural right of self-determination, and all of a sudden the bully Saddam crushes a neighbor with his tanks and troops.

My mind was abuzz with ways our national leadership could express its outrage at this new occupation when Faisal came unannounced through the front door. (He felt as though he were a member of the family, which, given the way Mother always treated him, he was.) As usual when something big happened, we didn't need to say more than a few words. We instinctively understood each other.

"You heard?" he said.

"Yeah."

"We have to come up with a strong statement."

"Already on it," I assured him.

Within hours we put out a press release with a clear and forcible statement expressing condemnation by the people in the Occupied Territories of the new occupation, and demanding that the rights of the Kuwaiti people be respected.

Unfortunately, the PLO leaders abroad didn't take their cues from us. Some, such as Nabil Sha'th, a member of Fatah's Central Committee, and Abu Iyad, the strongman on the committee, shared our reaction. But Arafat was the head of the organization, and he thought he could use the invasion to score some points for the Palestinian cause. He threw his lot in with Saddam.

The intifada was over for me. My office had been welded shut, my cover blown, and the intifada had drifted away from its nonviolent moorings. No curtain fell, no ushers passed around a hat for all the victims. The cause died from exhaustion. A "whimper" sums it up better than a "bang." Or better yet, a series of whimpers, followed by Arafat's fatal embrace of Saddam. Images of Arafat kissing Saddam on the lips were an embarrassment for us, and a PR coup for the Israelis. With one embrace all our gains seemed to vanish.

Rabin's decision to negotiate with the Petah Tikva prisoners had been fueled in part by his appreciation that because of sheer demographics, Israel and the Palestinians had to work out some form of settlement. But these first tentative steps went nowhere. With the seesawing I've learned to expect from politics in our part of the world, Shamir now cobbled together a new Israeli government that excluded Labor and therefore Rabin. The government's new temporary solution to demographics, which they also knew better than Palestinians to be the hard kernel of the conflict, shifted away from a territorial swap to mass immigration from the Soviet Union.

Shamir, emboldened by the crisis in the Gulf, let it be known that a vague "autonomy" was the most the pernicious Palestinians could ever hope to get. This time he had much of the world's sympathy.

When interviewed by a reporter for *The New York Times*, I admitted that the struggle for the creation of an independent state had reached an impasse. I brought out my trump card by telling him that between the options of "autonomy" Shamir-style and living in a single state as a citizen with rights equal to those of Israeli Jews, "there is little question but that I would opt for equality."

No one was listening. In any case, world interest had shifted over to a major theater of potential battle; world players—the United States, the Europeans, the major Arab governments—were beginning to show up on the field. Our conflict was now a sideshow.

The intifada's ignominious demise gave me some much-needed time. Over the preceding years, circumstances had required of me to master a certain chameleon-like adaptability: as metaphysician, professor, union activist, rebel, press agent, dissembler. Now I was able to go back to something closer to my real self. I spent more time with my family, my much-diminished circle of student activists, and my cabdriver friends. I also had more time to think and write.

Merle Thorpe, the president of the Middle East Peace Institute, in Washington, D.C., came up with an idea. He wanted an Israeli and a Palestinian to put their heads together and come up with a joint picture of what a two-state solution might look like. The New York publisher Farrar, Straus and Giroux agreed to publish the resulting book.

Such a joint thought experiment had never been tried. On the Palestinian side, no one had ever gone far beyond thinking about a two-state solution theoretically, as if they were talking about a futuristic colony on Mars. Some Israelis had given thought to ways of putting flesh on the idea; one such scholar was the Israeli Canadian Mark Heller from the Jaffe Center of Tel Aviv University.

I immediately liked the idea. Maybe the time had come to dot some *i*'s and cross some *t*'s. I had already been involved in authoring working papers and leaflets calling for a Palestinian state; this project gave me a chance to draw up the blueprints.

Merle Thorpe brought Mark and me together, and we started work. The title Mark proposed, *No Trumpets, No Drums*, appealed to my distaste for nationalist histrionics. Hoping that the PLO leaders in Tunis would also begin giving thought to the practical elements of nation-building, I sent each chapter as we wrote it to my friend Akram Haniyyah, who had become a close adviser to Arafat.

For a time, the Gulf crisis looked like a game of tug of war between Western and Arab powers, with the United States issuing warnings and Saddam sticking to his guns. In the Arab world, this sort of brinksmanship shifted attention away from what Saddam was doing in Kuwait and toward his show of muscle, his brazen defiance of America. Knowing that this played well on the Arab street, Saddam went a step further and really got the crowds roaring by invoking the unsettled score with Israel, America's main ally in the region. Not only would he repel the Western invaders, he boasted, but he would also unleash his famous Scud missiles on Tel Aviv. Many people in the West scoffed. If Israel had made short shrift of the entire Arab world's armies in six days back in 1967, the American-led coalition would need less than six hours to finish off Saddam and his myth of Arab power.

On January 17, 1991, the telephone woke me in the middle of a dream. It was my exiled friend Jibril Rajoub calling from Tunis. "It started," he told me. American-led international forces had begun the attack against Iraq. On CNN that night I heard the euphoric Western media predicting a crushing victory within hours.

Saddam had asked for it, of this I had no doubt. And yet I didn't like the chauvinistic tones surrounding the lightning invasion and conquest. Was it necessary to portray the war as if the Israelis and the Americans were fighting the same foes? As if the war was not between the UN-sanctioned coalition and a dictator sitting in Baghdad but between "Western democracy" and "Arab tyranny"? And why present Saddam's pathetic fight as yet another case of crushed Arab pride? For all these reasons I published an article against any efforts to use the invasion to "humiliate the Arab world and rub the Arabs' nose in the dirt."

The next great Israeli PR opportunity came when Saddam began lobbing his Scuds at Israeli cities. For all too many in the Occupied Territories, the sight of rockets shrieking across the night sky on their way to Tel Aviv was a welcome change from television images of cruise and other "smart" missiles hitting Baghdad, or Israeli phantom jets zooming off to Lebanon. Journalists caught on film images of Palestinians dancing on their rooftops, cheering at the sight of the Scuds. As damage control, I explained the reaction to *The Guardian* in this way: "If Palestinians are happy when they see a missile going from east to west, it is because, figuratively speaking, they have seen missiles going from west to east for the last 40 years." I could have cited W. H. Auden instead: "I and the public know / What all schoolchildren learn, / Those to whom evil is done / Do evil in return."

Shamir made the most of it by inviting into his government the extreme right-wing Moledet Party, a group whose central platform called for the expulsion of all Arabs from Israel's ancestral "Judea and Samaria." It was as if in the United States the Republicans were to hand over a Cabinet post to the grand wizard of the KKK.

Moderate Palestinians once again came under pressure, this time because the Israeli foreign minister published a document warning his government that one consequence of Arafat's blunder was the strengthening of the internal Palestinian leadership "that will be less dependent on external PLO leadership and thus will take part in a diplomatic process." To show the world that there was "no one to talk to," Shamir promptly painted moderates with the same brush as Arafat. Hundreds were arrested. My friend from Abu Dis, the gentle-faced Abed al-Haleem, was given twenty-seven months.

As a consequence of the Iraqi invasion, the Israelis imposed a forty-five-day curfew on all Palestinian areas, including Abu Dis. My home was not too far from Jewish areas, and since the Scud rockets were notoriously inaccurate and could carry chemical weapons, we felt as threatened with a gas attack as Israelis in West Jerusalem did. We followed Israeli government directives to seal all windows and doors, and nervously kept the masks on hand for whenever the sirens sounded. We stocked up on lots of videos and food, and huddled together, hoping for the best.

With the curfew, we couldn't leave our house, except during the occasional break to get groceries. This reduced my family's human contact to one another, and sometimes to the bored soldiers patrolling the streets in front of our building. "Sari! Hey, Sari!" I recall the soldiers in a jeep calling up to me. "Come downstairs. We have some graffiti for you to clean up."

Our only other lifeline to the world was the radio, television, and most of all the telephone. At night, after a missile had flown over and the sirens had died down, all over the country everyone wanted to find out where it had landed and what damage it had done. Before Israeli TV could flash pictures of the site, people called to check on friends and loved ones. I always called Mother, relatives, friends, and acquaintances, in that order.

One night, after a missile had passed, I heard a knock on the door. It was my landlord, a simple man from Abu Dis who peddled poultry in the village. "Did you see it?" he asked as he walked in.

"See what?" I said, wondering about the source of his excitement.

"The Scud that just flew over?"

"See it? Are you crazy? I was hiding under the table with my family," I admitted.

His eyes grew perfectly round like those of a child watching a circus, or like mine must have looked when Father told me the story of the Night Journey. "From the middle of the dark evening sky it suddenly appeared. It approached with lightning speed. Then, just as it arrived over Jerusalem, it suddenly stopped."

"Stopped? In the middle of the sky?" I interrupted.

"Yes, just above the Al-Aqsa mosque. The rocket froze in place, made a salute, took a bow, and then zeroed back on its target and zoomed downward to the west. I saw it with my own eyes."

On another occasion, my poultry man insisted that I go out with him to the balcony. He wanted to show me something.

"Don't you want to see?" In the hushed voice of reverence he said that the face of Saddam Hussein was filling up the full moon. "Come out and see for yourself," he implored.

"No, I believe you," I answered, wanting to get back to a movie on TV.

During the day, the telephone was ringing off the hook. Journalists covering the Palestinian-Israeli scene were constantly hungry for news and analysis. I spent hour after hour talking to one journalist after the other, explaining why Palestinians felt as they did. I was also in constant touch with Jibril Rajoub in Tunis, who would later become a close friend and partner. Jibril wanted to be updated on what was happening and what the public mood was like.

I was also in constant dialogue with Israeli peace activists, who were worried about the negative image Palestinians were getting in the Israeli press. They wanted us to issue a joint statement clearly denouncing Saddam's Scud attacks and his rape of Kuwait. We decided to finalize the wording in person during the next lifting of the curfew.

At the appointed time, a group of Peace Now leaders arrived by car, led by Janet Aviad—a peace warrior if ever there was one. Before the war started, Janet, an American Israeli and someone who smoked nearly as much as I, delivered an illuminating lecture in which she diagnosed the "Israeli macho" mentality as the main culprit preventing peace between our peoples. It didn't take us long to agree on a text. As always, sensible people can easily arrive at a compromise once they are aware of the other's basic concerns. We jointly condemned the use of violence and upheld the universal principles of peoples having the right to be free. Iraq's occupation of Kuwait had to end, and Saddam had to withdraw forthwith. But we also insisted on the Palestinians' liberty from the occupation.

A few days later I was arrested. Lucy, who of the two of us is far better at putting two and two together, believes that it was my joint statement with Peace Now that led the Shin Bet to act (because the statement went counter to the image of people dancing on the rooftops at Scud attacks). The demonic image of the Palestinian had to be maintained, especially if by doing so it allowed Jacob and his friends in the Shin Bet to settle some old scores.

I had imagined it a thousand times. You're hunched over a secret manuscript when two policemen wearing helmets with sleek visors and black body armor crash their way through the front door and drag you out the back without saying a word, frog-marching you away. (Like Harry Tuttle in *Brazil*, a movie we watched over and over during the curfew.)

My arrest was far more mundane. On the night of January 29, 1991, Lucy, the kids, and I were watching *A Fish Called Wanda* on television when, all at once, a rumbling sound came from outside. I put my head out the window and saw jeeps and a large contingent of soldiers spreading out in all directions. Judging by the firepower, you'd have thought they had cornered Saddam himself. Maybe they were looking for a military cell, I thought to myself before returning to the movie.

Then came a knock on the door. Lucy opened it, and soldiers politely informed her that I was under arrest. "For what?" I called out, shoving the bowl of popcorn to the side and getting up from the sofa. The commanding officer, with a respectful tone, laconically informed me that he had his orders. He handed me a piece of paper signed by Defense Minister Moshe Arens stating that I was under "administrative detention" for six months, which meant I could be held for six months or longer without charges or a trial.

There were no helmets, no black body armor, no screams, no coercion, no *Brazil*; on the contrary, the officer stood there quietly with a slightly apologetic look while I put my things together. Lucy made sure I packed a warm pair of pajamas and my toiletries. Absal and Buraq moved around uncomfortably, unsure what to do. There was a glint of tears in their eyes. Jamal dashed into his room and quickly reappeared with a copy of *The Hitchhiker's Guide to the Galaxy*, volume one. (It was only when I started reading it in my cell that I appreciated his discriminating choice.) As I was being led away with my hands pinioned behind me, I turned to my sons and asked them to look at this as just another one of my trips abroad.

The drive to the Russian compound took twenty minutes. Upon our arrival, they unloaded me from the jeep and marched me in the front gate, booked me, took me into a wing for common criminals, and shut me up in one of the cells. But they left the door to my cell unlocked. Outside of it, the other prisoners, all Jewish, wandered around freely.

A strange possibility flashed through my mind: with Israeli hysteria at Palestinians mounting because of the Scuds, had the guards left the door unlocked so the other inmates could finish me off? From the looks of my fellow prisoners, I wouldn't have put it past them. They looked like assassins and drug addicts conjured up by some malevolent spirit to haunt the place. One man had a tattoo on his neck. Another was scar-faced.

This was just another case of my spotty prophetic powers. Soon after, as I sat on the edge of the bed wondering what this all meant, I heard roars of laughter reverberating from down the hall. "Sari," said the tattooed man in Hebrew. "Do you hear the radio? Listen, Bibi [Netanyahu] just said at the UN that you're the head of the spy ring for Hussein." I lost count of how many times Hamas people had called me a spy; this was the first time the Israeli government had—and in front of the entire United Nations!

More guffaws came from the next room. With contempt in his voice, the tattooed man continued jokingly, "Listen to what these crazy sons-of-bitches are saying about you."

For the rest of the evening I was their guest. "What can we do for you?" they kept asking, as they brought me tea, soap, and cookies. The scene brought to mind the characters in Fanon's *Wretched of the Earth*, who don't believe in the establishment because they know from experience how crooked it is. My feelings performed their usual somersaults. Who could have expected such decency inside an Israeli prison?

As the night hours passed into dawn, my mind spun in dizzying circles around my predicament. I couldn't figure out why they had arrested me. All I could come up with was that Shamir and his cronies in the security establishment believed that someone who still believes in peace should be put behind bars. Did they want to crush my morale? My sense of hope?

Melancholy and wistful, I soon turned spiritual. A short passage from the Koran popped into my head:

In the name of Allah, the Beneficent, the Merciful.

I swear, by the early light of dawn,
And by the darkness of night as it pervades.
Think not that Your Lord has forsaken you, nor has He withdrawn,
  for surely
what will come next is better than what has gone before. Soon your
  Lord shall
provide for you, and you will feel pleased.

Did He not find you an orphan and give you shelter?
And did He not find you lost and guide you?
And did He not find you in want and free you?
Therefore, as for the orphan, do not oppress (him).

And as for him who asks, do not chide (him),
And as for the favor of your Lord, do declare (it).

More surprises were in store.

The following day I was moved to a prison in Ramle, not far from Grandfather's tomb. It was there I learned the details of the charges against me. They had detained me, said the government press release, "for subversive activities of collecting security information for Iraqi intelligence." Government spokesmen announced that several members of an Iraqi spy ring had been caught, some of them Jerusalem residents. The implication was that I had been hauled in as part of a larger sweep. Roni Milo, the normally levelheaded minister of police, told *Ha'aretz* that I had "performed severe acts of treachery and collaboration with the enemy."[1]

The official order dictated that I be locked up for an initial period of six months, starting on January 31, 1991. It stated that I was "an enemy" and a danger to the "security of the state and the physical and spiritual well-being of its citizens." The "spiritual" part was what really puzzled me.

Right-wingers started howling for my immediate expulsion, and even some people on the left were giving the government the benefit of the doubt. My old Israeli comrade-in-arms Jossi Sarid, for whom I had resigned from the union at Birzeit, belonged to Israel's Foreign Relations Defense Committee. He said he had seen convincing evidence that I was a secret agent. Even my coauthor on *No Trumpets, No Drums*, Mark Heller, for whom Israeli security sources were infallible, fell for the spy story. It seemed that my friend the chicken peddler was not the only person suffering from war delirium.

Common criminals, philosophers, Middle East policy wonks, and fiction writers did a much better job of sniffing out governmental fabrications than left-wing politicians—at least in Israel—for the accusations against me brought derision and scorn from the people who maintained their common sense. Lucy was hard at work appealing to everyone for help. I communicated with the Israeli prosecutor's office through my lawyer, Mr. Spaer—we spoke by phone—that I had no doubt I was being held due to my stance on peace with Israel, conditioned upon the recognition of the rights of the Palestinian nation. My ability to communicate with the world was limited, but plenty of people on the outside spoke out.

Saeb Ereikat put out a statement on my behalf. "This [arrest] is a message to us Palestinian moderates," he said. "Israel's message is, 'You can forget about negotiations after the war because we are going to make sure there is no one to talk to.'"

A letter signed by Allen Ginsberg, Arthur Miller, Edward Said, and Susan Sontag and sent to *The New York Times* stated, "We are acutely dismayed by the continuing detention of the Palestinian intellectual and activist Sari Nusseibeh . . . We are concerned that the Israeli government is exploiting these difficult days of war against Iraq to crack down on precisely those figures whose moderation and opposition to violence will be essential to the conclusion of a just war and to secure peace between Israelis and Palestinians in the aftermath of this war." In the London *Times*, another letter was published carrying the names of public figures and philosophers from Oxford, including Isaiah Berlin, H.L.A. Hart, and Peter Strawson. Amnesty International identified me as a "Prisoner of Conscience." The U.S. State Department declared that I was someone "whom Israel should be talking to, not placing under arrest." My favorite lines came from a staff writer for the Tel Aviv daily *Haʾaretz*: "For me it was a deep shock that this fuzzy-headed professor from Birzeit was accused of being a spy. If it wasn't tragic, it would be comic!"[2]

After three days in Ramle, I was driven back to court in Jerusalem, where the arrest order was to be confirmed. A group of supporters was waiting at the back entrance of the court building. In addition to seeing Lucy and my children in the crowd, I also spotted my friends from Harvard, Guy and Sarah Stroumsa.

Inside the courthouse I was allowed to see Mr. Spaer for the first time. He looked deeply worried. Being a suspected rocket-spotter, guide, and spymaster for Saddam was altogether different from being a scribbler of leaflets. I felt that it was I who had to comfort him. "They have nothing on me," I said to him, assuring him that we had a good case. "I know exactly what they will bring up, and I can tell you what happened."

As quickly as I could, I filled Mr. Spaer in on one of the nocturnal telephone calls I had gotten from Jibril Rajoub in Tunis. After an exchange of pleasantries, I explained, Jibril passed the telephone to an acquaintance who wanted to say hello. He was the Iraqi ambassador in Tunis. It was the only contact I had with an Iraqi during the war, and it was a rather banal conversation. I spoke to him as I might have to a newspaperman. I certainly didn't direct rockets, or spot them. Taking cover with Lucy and the kids under the kitchen table, huddled with our gas masks, I didn't even dare look at them. "The Israelis just don't like my political views, and have turned me into an Iraqi spy in order to shut me up. I think we should challenge them in court," I forged on. "Their charges are baseless."

Mr. Spaer left me for a few minutes to consult with the public prosecutor. Very soon, he returned. "If we challenge the arraignment," he said matter-of-factly, "the prosecutor will bring up the old files, and press different charges related to your intifada activities. Given the confessions on you, he will ask for fifteen years. On the other hand, if we let matters be, he will drop the six-month detention period to three. Which will it be?"

It was a bitter choice, and I began to waver. Visions of that iconic shot of Mandela with his hands shackled together, waving defiantly to the cheering crowd, flashed through my mind.

But Mr. Spaer, a very practical man, talked some sense into me. "The public mood in Israel is absorbed by Iraq and the Scud attacks. Your plea on the witness stand for Palestinian freedom, and your talk about nonviolence, will be totally drowned out by the sound of exploding Scuds. Sari, take the three months." It was sensible advice.

And so the original administrative detention order was confirmed, only cut in half. The trip from Jerusalem back to Ramle prison gave me a taste of the personal journey I was about to begin.

Prisoners call the vehicle that shuttles them around from prison to prison the "postal truck," as if we were sacks of mail. In the truck I was joined by a group of teenagers; some weren't yet thirteen. They had been arrested for demonstrating, throwing stones, writing graffiti, or clambering up poles to hoist Palestinian flags on electric lines. It was amazing to see their morale. They all sat huddled together in the "postal truck" laughing, telling jokes, and singing nationalist jingles. When I asked them if they were afraid of prison they assured me it was like going to a summer camp. "We will stay together."

The truth is that I rather enjoyed my time behind bars. From the point I agreed to head up the Birzeit union till then, I had been active in politics, with hardly a moment to myself. Prison was a three-month vacation from accursed politics.

The prison was divided into two sections: one for inmates with blue cards, Arab residents of Jerusalem; and another for those with green cards, West Bank Arabs. (My friend Naser Al-Afandi from Abu Dis was in this section.) In our wing, there were five inmates from East Jerusalem, and twenty-four from Lebanon and Jordan—either Palestinians belonging to Fatah or Lebanese Shiites loyal to Hezbollah. The Jordanian and Lebanese inmates had mostly served their terms, and were waiting to be deported to their countries. Some of the Lebanese had been captured by the army as hostages to be used in prisoner exchanges. One prisoner from Jerusalem was an old friend of mine who in jail had swapped Marxism for Sufi mysticism.

At first I was in solitary confinement, a glorious state to be in. The long hours alone left me with my thoughts. My first night I listened to the whistling noises of the train in the distance traveling through Ramle on its way to Jerusalem. What a paradox, I reflected, that Grandfather died in Ramle; his daughter moved to Jerusalem; a war divided up Palestine with Ramle on one side; another war rejoined the parts; and now a grandson he never met sits in prison close to his tomb for trying to divide up Palestine again into two states.

The prison authorities soon assigned me to a cell with another prisoner. By the luck of the draw, the roommate was a Hamas man serving a long-term sentence.

As prison routines go, ours was tolerably humane. The cell itself was minuscule: a bit over ten feet long and five feet wide. At one end was a shower directly above what is variously referred to as a French or Turkish toilet, which is a hole in the ground. A single wall separated the toilet from the narrow gap leading to the locked metal door, with its small iron-barred window. If I wanted to stretch my legs, I began at the bunk bed, took two steps, veered to one side with the third, and took my last step to the door. Then I retraced the four steps backward. Back and forth I went, over and over until I worked up a sweat. I must have looked like a madman, or a fly bouncing against a closed window, over and over and over.

Once every twenty-four hours we got sixty minutes of exercise in the courtyard. For the first ten minutes we marched at high speed in twos or threes around the yard. This was inevitably followed by a game of soccer, normally Palestinians versus Lebanese. Being locked up in a cell for twenty-three hours a day, I longed for that daily forty-five minutes of soccer. It had taken me twenty-five years since dropping out of Rugby before I finally apprehended the natural affinity between thinking and kicking a ball around.

The three months in Ramle prison afforded me a bird's-eye view—or jailbird's—of the elaborate cultural and political life of prisoners, a subject that had intrigued me for years. I had the uncanny feeling of being at home, like the boys in the "postal truck" heading off to "summer camp." My fellow prisoners knew everything about my case—their extraordinary communication system was more detailed and accurate than any newspaper. They welcomed me as a member of their club, a mark of distinction far more valuable to me than my embossed Harvard diploma stashed somewhere in a box. Nearly every day I heard faceless shouts from behind the wire-mesh-covered windows overlooking the yard.

Prisoners on the other side of the windows recognized me and called out their greetings. I could make out only their fingertips sticking out through the wire mesh, but some shouted out their names and then added, "Remember me? I took your class on al-Farabi."

My first day in the courtyard, as I was wandering around enjoying the sun, one of the prisoners from Lebanon approached me and gripped my hand with warm strength. He was a Fatah guerrilla caught offshore by the Israeli marines on his way to carry out a raid inside Israel. Like everyone else, he had heard about my case. He was in charge of interrogating incoming inmates. One of his jobs was to find out if prisoners had confessed to anything during interrogations, and if so, if there was someone on the outside in danger of arrest; another task was to ferret out Shin Bet plants—"birds" in prison jargon. He had spent almost ten years in jail and was waiting for the Red Cross to return him to Lebanon. Because this could happen any day, he wanted to pass on to me as much insider information about my fellow prisoners as possible.

In the course of our loop around the yard, he mentioned in passing that one of the inmates he had come across over the past few years was the Arab whom the Israelis had arrested for the killing of the German backpacker in front of the Lemon Tree. But this Arab had confessed to Fatah people in prison that he was a "bird" planted by the Israeli security agency, and that he hadn't killed that German. That was just his cover story to be able to mingle with prisoners, and then to pass information on to the Israelis. "The man didn't do it," said the Fatah guerrilla. "The Israelis did." My mind raced back to the Arabic-speaking girlfriend who must have been working for the Shin Bet.

When not kicking around the soccer ball, I enjoyed chatting with the Shiite members of Hezbollah. They were all true believers deeply influenced by Iranian mullahs, of whose religious writings they had a small library. When I was tired of rereading *Hitchhiker's Guide*, I read some of their holy books, and engaged my pious colleagues in theological discussions. Of the various Muslim sects, Shiites are typically the most philosophically inclined. They respected my freethinking ways enough to offer me a gift. After hearing that Lucy's birthday was coming up, and knowing that she was English, two of the Hezbollah men carved out her name in Latin letters on a white domino piece, ornamented it with different colors, and then turned it into a pendant by nailing a hole in its top. They asked me to pass it on to her as a birthday present from them.

My Hamas cell mate and I had a room on the top floor, which meant that we were living in relative luxury because the rats were usually downstairs, near the kitchens. But they sometimes made their way up to us. On one occasion a rat managed to invade our cell through a hole, and bit my pious cell mate on the nose. We plugged up the hole at once. Combating the bountiful fleas and cockroaches was more of a challenge.

Food takes on nationalist importance in prison. Long years of struggle were needed to improve its quality; even so, Arab prisoners insisted on spicing up what they got with Palestinian flavor. During my stint in Ramle I learned a raft of recipes, such as how to turn juice into marmalade and milk into yogurt and even how to bake cakes. I felt like a child in chemistry class as I watched wide-eyed as my Hamas cell mate turned an empty Coke can into a stove. He spread out margarine on a thin sheet of toilet paper as if it were a piece of bread, then rolled the sheet up and stuffed it into the soda can. Leaving a wick on top, he lit it up with a matchstick. Now the contraption was ready to heat up whatever assortment of vegetables or tinned products or eggs the prison authorities provided us with.

Prison culture itself was bafflingly rich, and in unexpected ways. There was the Russian Jewish guard who befriended a prisoner who had studied in Moscow and therefore spoke Russian. The prisoner was serving a twenty-seven-year sentence. The homesick guard was even lonelier than the prisoner, and the two spoke for hours through metal bars in the neighboring cell.

Just as you would expect in a high-security prison, roll call took place three, four, or fives times a day. As the sound of the truncheon banged against the iron bars of one cell after another, we had to stand up to be counted. When the guards came to our area, we stood up straight, no one bent his head, no one deferred to them. What was as-

tonishing for me was that the officers and the prisoners showed no outward signs of disdain for one another.

I was full of ideas in prison, and with so much time on my hands—
and no telephone calls or disruptions, and with the comfort of knowing
I couldn't be thrown into prison because I was already there—I read
and wrote more than I had in a decade. Besides the books I had taken
with me the first night of my arrest, and the religious texts I borrowed
from the Hezbollah inmates, my reading list included *War and Peace*.
Jamal wanted me to read it. I had always admired Tolstoy's ruminations
on freedom and the will, and now with my outward freedom taken from
me, I reread the relevant passages with special relish. During a visit, Jamal also gave me volume two of *The Hitchhiker's Guide to the Galaxy*.
Mother, perhaps as a joke inspired by my birth in Damascus, sent me
her old battered copy of Dostoyevsky's *Crime and Punishment*.

The galley proofs for *No Trumpets, No Drums* were ready, and I read
through them sitting on my bunk, which was something my Hamas cell
mate found amusing. "They stick you in jail and you still want peace
with them?" My other, more academic, pursuit was to write a review for
the journal *History and Philosophy of Logic* on a book on al-Farabi by
Fritz Zimmerman, my German friend from the Warburg Institute. I
signed the review and gave "Ramle Prison" as my return address. (When
the review appeared, the editor had regrettably replaced "Ramle Prison"
with "Jerusalem.")

My thoughts also turned to religion and Islam, not because of a
blinding light but because of my roommate, who, like true believers
everywhere, was so convinced that the daily weather report could be
gleaned from his holy writ that he read it incessantly.

I had never shaken off my belief in Islam's basic humanism and its
essential harmony with rational thought. Thanks to Mother, God and I
had a long relationship behind us, interrupted by years of relative indifference and skepticism, He for me, I for Him. Now here we were again,
together in the same cell.

While an Israeli prison may not be the most obvious place to ponder the divine, over the three months, I read my cell mate's Koran over and over, not skipping around, but in one go, from cover to cover. Each time I finished I was left with the impression of an extremely rational text in which you are guided through a very elaborate and clever system. The whole business of divine rewards and punishments, which at face value seems like a gruesome mixture of terror and pleasure, in fact fits into a psychological regimen engineered to guide humans away from wrong-doing, and to encourage them to be good.

The other thing I noticed is something Islamic scholars have a way of glossing over, and for good reason, given its radical implications. Islam's message to Man is that he's on his own; he can no longer count on mir-acles or divine revelation or the deus ex machina. I gleaned this from the fact that Mohammed marked the end of the long period in mankind's infancy during which angels whispered in our ears as parents do to their children. After eons of messengers, oracles, and prophets, Man's age of intellectual puberty had come. The time had arrived for Man to throw off the training wheels and look to Reason for future deliverance.

One other message I got from my reading was one regarding human dignity. If an illiterate camel driver named Mohammed could close the final chapter of Revelation, then, according to Islam, one person wasn't inherently better than the next. All were equally capable of achieving true knowledge and living a good life.

Once a week Lucy and the children came to visit, and brought me books and news from the world outside. Making the arrangements for the visits was a bureaucratic headache of the first order. Lucy first had to get a permit to drive during curfew hours, and then another one to visit the jail. Once there, she and the children were frisked, searched, identified, and vetted, and suffered interminable delays until we got our fifteen minutes of talking and touching fingers through holes in a wire screen. By this point, prison officials knew about the capsule-in-the-mouth trick and didn't allow kissing.

For me, the week began and ended with these fifteen minutes. My family came and went, and I was led back to my cage to worry about them all alone in the house in Abu Dis, in the midst of curfews and political chaos. Jacob's dark intimations were more alive than ever in my imagination.

When I urged her to be careful, Lucy reassured me. With my arrest, she said, she suddenly felt more secure than ever. Our neighbors had become an extended family, and kept an eye on them. One night they even deposited two sacks of sugar and rice on our doorstep. "You have no reason to worry about us."

One day the communist serving the twenty-seven-year sentence gave me a book his brother, serving a sentence in another jail, had sent him to pass on to me. "To Sari, the humanistic nationalist," ran the dedication, "the steadfast olive tree, with my heartiest wishes, Mahmoud Safadi, Nafha Jail, 1991."

It was a journal, fifty blank pages bound with sturdy cardboard. Mahmoud had made it with the thought that I could write something for my family. On the cover he had pasted together a collage of an Arab peasant woman walking as though in the midst of a forest of barbed wire. Above the image, he had glued the word FREE in red, cut out from an English magazine. On the spine he added the phrase CHILDREN ARE THE ULTIMATE VICTIMS.

I ended up filling the book with a letter to my three sons. I write to them about my arrest and life in prison; about what I wish for them in life; and what I wish for our people. The book begins with a preface:

> Ramle Prison, January 29, 1991. I give this letter as a present to my children who will also be my friends in the future. This gift will not give you pleasure like other presents I've brought back from trips to London or Paris. However, it may last longer than those other gifts, and it may be more useful to you in the coming years, though I would not dare to make that judgment. It is a collection of thoughts to you and about you that have crossed my mind while away from you.

My first aim was to assure them that prison wasn't such a terrible place. I refer them to my cousin Salim, who served sixteen years of a life sentence for planting a bomb in 1969. "Give him a ring. He'll tell you what it's like."

The letter describes the lives and fates of my fellow prisoners, such as a Palestinian refugee from Lebanon who had served out his sentence and was now waiting in vain for a country to receive him. "He wants to go to Algiers, but he can't arrange it. He said to the representative of the Red Cross, 'Take me anywhere, Cuba or Tanzania, fly me out or by foot, or on a limping donkey, take me to Hell, just get me out of here.' 'Unfortunately, Hell does not have a government immigration office to look into your request,' replied the Red Cross worker."

I write about a pitched battle between a Fatah man and an aggressive rat, with the former, after a long touch-and-go fight, finally winning the day. Then come the cockroaches. "Today we're launching a campaign against cockroaches. Comrade Mohammed has promised to clean up the crumbs from his table . . .

"So you can see," I conclude after a few more stories like these, "things aren't so awful. Look at it as a place of rest and recuperation. Here I can lie down for hours, there are no telephone calls, no meetings, and the food comes to our room, like room service at a hotel."

I assure them that I also have access to newspapers, radio, and TV, luxuries available to me thanks to a generation of political struggle inside the prison system. "You might think that once someone ends up here the struggle is over. In fact, he continues his struggle, now for a bar of soap, now for a book, a visit, a cigarette, for decent food. Many men have died confronting the prison authorities . . . It seems to be our destiny as Palestinians to hop from one struggle to the next . . .

"Prison is not for us," begins another page of reflections, quoting a fellow prisoner. "It is for thieves and murderers and drug addicts and smugglers, just not for the honest student and the businessman, the father and mother whose only crime is to fight for their freedom.

"Why was I arrested?" I ask rhetorically.

Thousands, tens of thousands of Palestinians share my fate; over half a million since 1967. In my case, they couldn't pin anything on me earlier, so they used the Gulf War as a pretext . . . They've become so loony that someone in the Ministry of Defense has said I'm the brains behind a spy ring; Bibi Netanyahu is still telling the world that his government is investigating other members of the same ring. The truth is that I am for peace, but that the Israelis don't like my voice of moderation. I want a true, balanced peace that isn't capitulation and that preserves our dignity and serves the interests of the two sides, not just one at the expense of the other. This is what I've been writing, speaking, and living for.

The truth prevails . . . we will soon have victory, we will be free and our people will have their independence. If we today are paying the price for this it is so that you and your sons will not need to go through the same suffering, and that you will breathe freedom and advance the progress of mankind through your creativity.

I feel guilty that you don't have a normal life like everyone else. Perhaps the fact that your mother is English might make it more difficult for you by alienating you from your society. This is the reason why you must have a strong will. To search and find the solid rock within you. Once you find it, you will find yourself. This rock consists of being honest with yourself—and coming to terms with yourself. It is a matter of hanging on to what is right, and with sovereignty deciding your own thoughts and actions.

This was the rock that my father always talked about when I asked him about the source of his strength. He was one of the few people I've ever known who had this strength, as if he carried it around in his pocket. This is the rock of the self that you, perhaps even more than others, need to discover. Maybe the difficult conditions in which you find yourself may help you by making you stronger. I wish for all of you to be creative without any restrictions or fears—to determine your identities as you yourselves wish them to be determined.

Above all, I want you to know that I love you and your mother, and it is because of this love that I am now in prison.

Chapter Twenty-two

Madrid

T HE LETTER TO MY CHILDREN also recounts the sense of irony I felt when reading *War and Peace*. How can it be, I ask them, that Tolstoy has had a more lasting impact on culture than the great Napoleon, whose shadow falls on every battle scene in the book? In prison I thought a hundred times about leaving politics behind and devoting myself to philosophy and teaching, maybe even branching off into fiction writing. One of my literary ideas was to finish my fairy tale, another belletristic invention that came to mind was a Graham Greene–style detective story. The plot I sketched out centered on the backpacker shot to death on the Via Dolorosa in front of my home. I also pledged to spend more time with my children, perhaps even talk Lucy into having another child, this time, I hoped, a daughter.

Running away from politics has been an ingrained habit since youth, and I would have heeded the wise counsel of childhood if it hadn't been for the fickle Middle Eastern climate pulling me forcibly back into it.

The Gulf War ended in February 1991, while I was still in jail, and right away the American administration turned its attention to the Israeli-

Palestinian conflict. The Americans had a debt to pay to the Egyptians, the Saudis, and to the Arab world at large for having supported the war, and one way they paid it was by launching a Middle East peace initiative. Out of the blue George Bush, Sr., made a stunning policy statement: "A comprehensive peace must be grounded in . . . resolutions 242 and 338 and the principle of territory for peace." He went so far as to couple Israeli security to Palestinian political rights. And if that wasn't enough for Prime Minister Shamir, James Baker made it clear to the Senate Committee on Foreign Relations: "I don't think that there is any bigger obstacle to peace than the settlement activity." I was dancing in my tiny cage after hearing this.

On the surface, Shamir was distinctly unsettled. After a war that had promised him so much—the destruction of the mighty Iraqi army and, more important, the sidelining of Arafat on the outside, with us on the inside—President Bush and his secretary of state, James Baker, were coming at him with talk of "linkages," a "Middle East International Conference," and UN Resolution 242. Shamir took on a grim public pose. Certain Arab and Palestinian leaders came out in support of the new American policy, if only because it seemed to make the Israeli prime minister squirm.

Based on my earlier Likud contacts, my gut feeling was that Shamir *wanted* negotiations and was only pretending to kick and scream in order to improve his hand. But having to be dragged into something puts you in a better position than someone who shows up eagerly with his hands out, as if he'll take whatever he can get.

The experience with Amirav and the prisoners in the Petah Tikva prison taught me to see behind Likud's fiction of a life-or-death struggle against the "gang of PLO thugs." What was driving Israeli policy was an objective demographic interest in maintaining a Jewish state. Like any market haggler, Shamir wanted to get the best deal possible, and if we let him he'd walk away with the store, a radiant smile pasted on his face. But if we were smart, we could cut a good deal.

With this in mind, I cautioned Faisal against jumping too eagerly into negotiations. I was afraid that with Arafat desperate for diplomatic redemption after his disastrous dalliance with Saddam, he'd give too much away.

Faisal had asked a visiting Arab member of the Knesset to get my opinion on whether or not to meet with Baker during his upcoming visit. "Let's wait," was my message to Faisal. "We have an excellent negotiating position, and have to make the most of it." Israel had a keen self-interest in getting a peace process off the ground. Solving the conflict with us promised Israel a prize of incalculable political, economic, and security value: it guaranteed the demographic survival of the Jewish state and the normalization with the entire Arab world. One mustn't give all this away for cheap.

To drive the point home I asked Lucy to deliver some reflections to the London daily *The Independent*:

> Palestinians and Israelis today stand on the threshold of what may be a very promising future. But Israel cannot have its cake and eat it too. To expect that Israel can become a full and productive partner among the Middle Eastern states without either simultaneously or in advance accepting to resolve the Palestinian problem is to expect a miracle. The Palestinian problem, in turn, cannot be addressed except through the recognition of the Palestinian people's sovereign right to live in freedom, as masters of their destiny.

I hadn't yet finished my three-month sentence when Secretary of State James Baker held his first meeting with Palestinians. It took place at the American consulate in West Jerusalem. Faisal led a Palestinian team that included Hanan Ashrawi and Saeb Ereikat, a fellow academic best known at the time for his work as editor at *Al-Quds*. Saeb and I had a lot in common. His uncle had been a military attaché and government minister in the British Mandate and then the Jordanian administration. His father had run a big bus company, only to lose it in 1967. Like me, Saeb had gone off to Britain and to America to study, and we had both returned to teach around the same time. He had gotten into trouble with fanatics on both sides of the conflict. In 1982 he called for dialogue between Israelis and Palestinians, and was at once labeled a traitor. The following year the military government arrested him for "fomenting dissent" among Israelis by inviting some Israelis to meet with his students at his university in Nablus. Fostering sympathy between the two peoples was—and in certain Israeli circles still is—tantamount to a crime.

It was a stormy meeting at the American consulate. Baker didn't pull a magic wand out of his briefcase to end occupation with the same finesse and speed with which American troops had cleared the Iraqis out of Kuwait. He showed up speaking of a "staggered" approach. UN Resolution 242 was the general yardstick for a final peace deal, Baker said to Faisal, but for now the Palestinians had to make do with "autonomy."

After years of Israeli machinations and the various permutations of the term (the Village League's, to name one), *autonomy* had turned into a four-letter word in the Palestinian lexicon. It's hardly surprising that Faisal and his group of negotiators left the consulate grumbling.

The follow-up session two days later left everyone happy. Baker had had time to ruminate over the failure of the first meeting, and his advisers had probably given him a primer on Palestinian sensibilities. Whatever the reason, both sides felt that things were moving ahead.

Sitting on my cot for twenty-three hours a day, I found it hard to assess what was really going on. In terms of substance, were the Americans offering anything new? I began to suspect not, after Lucy came by for her weekly visit. She told me that Faisal had called her for linguistic help following his second meeting with Baker. "What is the difference," he wanted to know, "between *self-government* and *autonomy*?" As a born and bred Englishwoman with a fine appreciation for the nuances of words, and a classicist with mastery of Greek and Latin, Lucy assured him that the only difference between them lay in their linguistic origins: *autonomy* is Greek, *self-government* Latin. Otherwise, they mean the same thing: self-rule. The Americans were playing semantics.

At the beginning of April, I got out of prison, but before I could even unpack my bags, the Israeli security people called me to the Russian compound again. "Don't think that you're off the hook," they warned me darkly, with Jacob pointing his index finger at me. "You still have to consider the options of jail or exile." Meanwhile, a far-right faction of the Israeli coalition representing the settlers threatened to drag down the government if I weren't put on trial. Geula Cohen, the faction's leader, accused the government of turning a blind eye to the evildoers Faisal and me. By not putting us on trial, she concluded cogently, the government was already in effect negotiating with the PLO. (Geula Cohen is a former member of the Stern Gang and the mother of Tzahi Hanegbi, the thug who had once attacked Arab Hebrew University students with chains. Father had Cohen's autobiography around the house: *Woman of Violence: Memoirs of a Young Terrorist, 1943–1948.*)

But Faisal and I had nothing to worry about, at least not from the Israelis, because the entire political landscape was changing. Immediately out of prison, I rushed headlong back into politics.

I've always been aware of the dangers of hiding behind words, and Lucy's late-night chat with Faisal raised a red flag. More flags began to wave when some members of Faisal's delegation dropped by the house to talk. After the customary greetings—every released Palestinian is fêted—we got down to business. One of my guests excitedly reported that they had actually gotten Baker to change his original proposal, with the new one now promising "self-government" instead of "autonomy." Just as I had feared, the word *government* in *self-government* had created the impression that Baker was offering something new. This capacity for swallowing an illusion, or rather engaging in self-delusion, was to dog our diplomatic efforts for a long time to come. It still does.

The suspicion that we were being bamboozled deepened. A couple of days later I visited Faisal at his home. When I walked in the house, Faisal was pacing the room. His wife stood aloof in the background, and Hanan Ashrawi sat on the couch, with her legs crossed holding in her hands a draft of what came to be known as Baker's "Letter of Assurances." Faisal asked Hanan to give me the letter. I scanned it over and stated rather abruptly, "Oh, I see; what they're offering is autonomy." Hanan, uncrossing and crossing her legs again, was visibly irked.

"Why do you use the word *autonomy?*" She took a long drag from her cigarette.

"Because that's precisely what this letter boils down to," I told her, and handed it back to her. "Look, if we're smart, what do we have to lose? But at least we need to get things straight from the outset: this *is* autonomy."

The logic behind the upcoming Madrid Conference was that all sides in the conflict—Israel, Syria, Lebanon, Jordan, and us—would discuss their differences face to face and in a format jointly sponsored by the United States and the—gravely ill—Soviet Union. In effect, the Americans would run the show.

Leading up to the convening of the Madrid Conference, Baker and the Palestinian team held several more talks. Faisal, Hanan, and Saeb were the main Palestinian players. Through Akram Haniyyah they were in constant contact with Arafat. Having missed out on the first talks, I was a latecomer. I attended two talks in Jerusalem and a third in Washington, and that one only by chance. (I happened to be there promoting *No Trumpets, No Drums*.) In all three I detected the magical power of self-delusion furiously at work. In key areas, the Israelis got away with offering far less than during our talks with Amirav.

In Jerusalem, Shamir won one important concession after the next by giving the impression that he had agreed to the peace talks only under extreme compulsion. One red line he could not cross, he told the Americans with his legendary histrionics, was talking to anyone from the PLO. The official Israeli position insisted on bilateral talks with a Jordanian delegation that would include—but only as a sub-component—a Palestinian delegation. Naturally Shamir, the same man who had conspired to blow up the King David Hotel in 1946, used the "terrorism" canard to sell his clever negotiation tactic. Sidelining the PLO from the outset also pushed full Palestinian sovereignty, which was what the PLO symbolized, into the margins.

Shamir got his way—again despite the fact that he had shown that he was more than willing to talk to the PLO in 1987—because the Americans and the Palestinians thought he really meant what he said. Arafat and his people in Tunis, wanting legitimization for Palestinians from the Americans even at the price of PLO exclusion, went along.

By the time I sat in on my first meeting with Secretary Baker and his two senior advisers, Dennis Ross and Daniel Kurtzer, the idea of a joint Jordanian-Palestinian delegation had already been ironed out, and all that remained was to determine who would belong to it. When we showed up at the consulate, Baker expected Faisal to hand him a list of names. But there was some unfinished business to clear away first.

Baker's Letter of Assurance contained loopholes large enough for the Israelis to drive cement trucks through. Literally. The letter made no clear reference to the cessation of all settlement activity. Worst of all, East Jerusalem wasn't to be included in the autonomy plan.

It couldn't have been an accident that the Israelis wanted to bracket out the settlements and East Jerusalem. Of the two, the issue of East Jerusalem bothered me most. The fight over Jerusalem was existential, not because it is a magical city but because it was, and is, the center of our culture, national identity, and memory—things the Israelis had to extirpate if they were to have their way throughout what they called Judea and Samaria. As long as we held on to Jerusalem, I was certain we could resist them everywhere else.

I had known all along that the Israeli plan was to destroy East Jerusalem by ridding it of the people and institutions that had defined it for 1,300 years. From 100,000 settlers in 1989, the number now stood at 137,000. In a few cases, as with the Goldsmith's Souk, settlers had managed to move inside the walls of the Old City. Sharon, now the Israeli minister of housing, had set up a special committee to buy or otherwise acquire strategic properties in the Old City, and then transfer them to settlers. During the Greek Orthodox Easter in 1990, a group of 150 settlers took over St. John's Hospice in the Christian Quarter. (They claimed it had once belonged to a Jewish merchant driven out during the riots in 1929.) If such a steep rise in settler activity had occurred during a time of conflict, I asked myself, what would happen if we called a truce without getting the Israelis to agree to a halt in settlement construction?

In the course of our talks, Baker nearly floored me by his comments about settlements. The U.S. government would not stand for their continuing expansion, he informed us; in fact, President Bush was prepared to take a political risk by requesting Congress *not* to approve a pending ten-billion-dollar loan guarantee to Israel unless Israel pledged that *none* of the money would be used for settlement construction, and that no creative accounting would use the American money to free up funds elsewhere in the government budget for settlements. In the long history of American inaction against the single biggest obstacle to peace, this was a first.

Baker showed far less flexibility, however, with regard to Jerusalem.

The Letter of Assurance pledged that Arab Jerusalemites would be able to vote in the proposed Palestinian elections for the self-governing council. Because much of the Palestinian leadership resided in Jerusalem, we suggested slipping in the expression "and be elected." But the matter had already been settled in the back rooms, and Baker wouldn't budge. I finally proposed substituting the word *vote* with *participate*. With imaginative ambiguity, I reasoned, we might be able to achieve something down the road. Baker liked the idea. Turning to Kurtzer, he asked him to see if the Israelis could live with it. We parted on the understanding that during the next meeting Faisal would hand over the list of names for the joint Jordanian-Palestinian delegation.

That evening, we went to Hanan's house to discuss what to do next. I was confident, buoyed in part by Baker's earnestness and what he had said about settlements. The American engagement was serious, I told my colleagues, and it seemed to me that the thorny issues of settlements and Jerusalem had been settled. As it turned out, I was only half right.

Two days later we were back at the American consulate, this time the one in East Jerusalem. Faisal brought along various public figures, and before handing over the list of names to Baker, he read out a list of the sundry daily ordeals Palestinians faced: the checkpoints, the constant searches, the house demolitions, and so on. Faisal wanted American help in improving people's lives, and quickly. I kept silent, but the longer the conversation drifted away from elections in Jerusalem, the more nervous I got.

I finally passed Faisal a note to remind him to bring up the elections. He took the note, glanced down at it, and slipped it under the files he had on his lap, but he didn't bring up elections.

Molly Williamson, then the U.S. consul general in Jerusalem and a very sharp observer, saw me give the note to Faisal, and must have detected my agitation, because once the meeting ended, she pulled me aside.

"What's up?"

I trusted Molly, and told her precisely what I had written in the note. "But that's already been settled," she stated, rather startled. "I thought you knew." She explained what had happened. Kurtzer had indeed spoken to Shamir, who had put on another of his acts. "Out of the question!" he had snapped. I pictured his gnomelike face taking on a look of implacable resistance. He made it clear to the Americans that he and his government would never permit any ambiguity in the issue of elections. On his watch, no Arabs from East Jerusalem would be able to stand for a Palestinian election in the West Bank.

The answer had been relayed back to Hanan in Ramallah the previous evening. She had told Faisal, and Faisal had told the PLO leadership in Tunis. All agreed to go along with Shamir's condition. I felt a bout of nausea coming on.

Shamir chalked up another victory before the peace talks began. With the Letter of Assurance excluding Arab East Jerusalemites from standing for election, he demanded something that logically followed: that no East Jerusalemite be allowed to serve on the Palestinian negotiation team, just as he wouldn't tolerate any of the outside PLO leaders. When our side tried to fight this, Baker erupted with the charming but misplaced quip, "The souk never closes with you people!"[1]

PLO leaders acquiesced, but this time they huddled together in Tunis and thought up a clever way to maneuver around Shamir. The peace delegation would indeed include only the names of non-Jerusalemites from the West Bank and Gaza. The delegation was to be headed by Dr. Haidar Abdul Shafi, a decent and respected man of great integrity from Gaza who was also the head of the Red Crescent, the Arab Red Cross.

But behind the scenes a second group that the PLO leaders called a "team" came into existence that day. The ruse was that this "team," composed of the negotiators as well as of Jerusalemites, would be a higher-order entity of which the delegation was a subset. It would include Dr. Shafi, but also representatives of various factions in the territories, along with Faisal, Hanan Ashrawi, and me. Faisal, who answered directly to Arafat by way of Akram Haniyyah, was to head this team.

The peace conference was scheduled to open on October 30 in Madrid. In the days leading up to it, the Orient House was full of frenetic activity. There was the predictable rush of public figures trying to elbow their way into the delegation. A lawyer would show up and argue the merits of members of his profession being a part. In the national interest and for the good of all Palestinians, he would invite himself onto the team. Someone else would say that his geographic region wasn't properly represented. How could his local people support the negotiations if they didn't have their own representative—in other words, him?

Faisal did his best to control all the jockeying, and on the appointed day, two blue Pullman buses pulled up in front of the National Hotel to drive the delegates to Amman, from where they would fly to Madrid. The sendoff from the National Hotel was festive. Reporters surrounded the buses and delegates, while muscular Fatah activists filled the streets to keep the delegates safe. Molly Williamson turned up to forestall any last-minute crisis.

I waved goodbye to the delegates as they sped off down into the desert and back up to Amman. Faisal and Hanan were on the bus, leaving me as the only "team" member left in Jerusalem. I was about to head home when the Fatah activists who had been keeping an eye on the buses approached me and informed me that I needed "protection."

"Against what?" I probed.

"You're the only one left," they reasoned. "This makes you a prime target for rejectionists who might wish to cause harm to the negotiation team." I was like the voodoo doll Hamas could poke to torment the peacemakers in Madrid. Hamas had just formed Izzeddin al-Qassam Brigade, its military wing, named in honor of the 1930s cleric Sheikh Izzeddin Qassam.

I tried my best to dissuade my protectors from following me home, but to no avail. And so I went, trailed by ten brawny activists sworn to my protection. They got the message that I really didn't want body-guards only when Lucy reacted to them. "How do you expect us to live with all these people around?" She was adamant enough that by the next morning my bodyguards had gotten the hint and left.

Convened by Bush and Gorbachev, the Madrid Conference was her-alded by the media as a historic breakthrough—as it was. Given the fact that we'd been at war for forty years, sitting down face to face was a major accomplishment, even if that was the only thing that was accomplished.

It began on a sour note. Back in Israel, Shamir kept up his act by as-suring his constituents that he was playing games in Madrid. The man he designated as head of the Israeli delegation, a savvy lawyer by the name of Eliakim Rubinstein, made some opening remarks that strength-ened this impression. Rubinstein, a man with a high, raspy voice, fired his opening salvo by informing his Palestinian counterparts, "Palestine has been occupied territory ever since the Roman empire . . . We con-sider the Palestinians to be refugees who have stayed in our country since the time of the Jordanian occupation. We are ready to given them human rights, just not political rights."[2]

When Dr. Shafi's turn to speak came, I recall the sensation of hud-dling around the television set with some activists, curious how he would respond to Rubinstein's humbug. Denounced by the Israelis for decades as bloodthirsty killers, the Palestinian leadership was now in the world's spotlight. Would Dr. Shafi throw a tantrum? No. This gentle physician from Gaza addressed the world, the Israelis, and us with a self-respecting composure that not only put Rubinstein to shame but also touched the hearts of the average Palestinian: "Ladies and gentlemen," he began, and referred back to the glory days of Moorish Spain:

> We meet in Madrid, a city with the rich texture of history, to weave together the fabric that joins our past with the future, to reaffirm a wholeness of vision, which once brought about a rebirth of civilization and a world order based on harmony in diversity.
>
> Once again, Christian, Muslim, and Jew face the challenge of heralding a new era enshrined in global values of democracy, human rights, freedom, justice, and security. From Madrid we launch this quest for peace, a quest to place the sanctity of human life at the center of our world and to redirect our energies and resources from the pursuit of mutual destruction to the pursuit of joint prosperity, progress, and happiness.

We needed to touch all the Palestinian hearts we could. The day the conference opened brought new troubles with Hamas. To protest the talks with the Israelis, Hamas called for a three-day protest strike throughout the territories, to show that the Palestinian public were against negotiation. I was beginning to have second thoughts about having sent my protectors away.

I knew Fatah had to do something. What I came up with was an ad hoc pep rally in Ramallah. The idea was to show that the average Palestinian wanted peace, and hence supported our delegation in Madrid. We rented a hall, and I got Ahmad Hazza², a particularly popular Fatah activist who had just finished an eighteen-year prison sentence, to address the crowd. I, too, spoke out in support of the negotiations.

The hall was so packed that the raucous crowd flowed out into the open yard leading up to it. Activists hung Palestinian flags on every available spot. Songs were sung and spirits were high—so high, in fact, that on the spur of the moment, Ahmad and I decided to lead the tumultuous swarm on a peaceful march to the center of Ramallah. Hundreds of people carried Palestinian flags and olive branches as a statement of our support for peace.

As we came close to the main square in downtown Ramallah, armed Israeli soldiers, thinking we were up to no good, sped over in their jeeps to stop us. The olive branches we all carried, as in the closing scene of *Macbeth*, only made them more nervous. I was at the head of the demonstration, and as we got closer to the jeeps, and the possibility of a clash became real, a fellow demonstrator swiftly jerked me away from the showdown with the soldiers and whisked me into a side street. It was Hussein al-Sheikh, an eleven-year veteran of the Israeli prison camp. That day was the first time we met, and he later became one of my partners in turning our pro-peace rally in Ramallah into a nationwide campaign.

I got out of Ramallah without a scratch, and headed home with a hundred images and ideas jostling around in my mind. I thought about Dr. Shafi's shattering words in Madrid: "We seek neither an admission of guilt after the fact, nor vengeance for past iniquities, but rather an act of will that would make a just peace a reality." I thought about the strike called by Hamas; the immense crowd that had gathered to support the Madrid talks; the ex-prisoners now fighting for peace; and on top of everything, the ever-present danger of violent confrontation. All along the road back to Jerusalem I saw olive branches affixed to the doorways of the houses.

The rally in Ramallah put me in an unexpected leadership role. I'd always been averse to spotlights and especially to crowds, yet here I was standing in front of one. And my listeners weren't fellow academics and students, as at Birzeit, nor was I acting as Faisal's stand-in during the intifada. Instead, as our smartly dressed negotiators were talking to the Israelis and Americans, I was addressing average Palestinians. What's more, that night I began my work with what could be called the "unsung heroes" of the negotiations: the unlettered ex-prisoners and Fatah activists, people whom the Israelis liked to describe as "terrorists."

Without these street activists, the peace process would have died at birth.

It was obvious to me, as it was to others, that our negotiators needed more than one rousing mass meeting. To sell the idea of speaking to our enemies, and just as important to marginalize Hamas and other radical factions that likened negotiating with Israel to speaking with the devil, we needed an ongoing campaign. My main partner in this was Jibril Rajoub. We had a big job cut out for us. Father would have called it "spade work."

Jibril had spent a total of seventeen years in Israeli prisons, where he learned Hebrew well enough to translate into Arabic Menachem Begin's *The Revolt*, a book about Begin's underground war against the British. Never formally charged with a crime (they say he tossed a grenade at an army convoy), Jibril was released in the same prisoner exchange as my cousin Salim, who had planted a bomb after the 1967 war. The minute the intifada broke out, the Israelis picked Jibril up again, drove him to the border, and at gunpoint told him never to come back. During the Madrid talks he was still living in Tunis.

Jibril contacted me shortly after the Madrid Conference opened. I flew to London and met him at the Hilton. The venue could hardly have been more incongruous. Jibril looked as awkward in a suit as I did, and even more out of place in a five-star hotel lobby. Maybe this was the reason we felt such immediate affection for each other. People still poke fun at the fact that a vulgar-tongued muscle man—Jibril likes to curse—and a tweed-jacketed professor could get along so well. But he's one of the rare cases in which a crude tongue is in some mysterious way wired to a vigorously strategic mind. We almost always see eye to eye on political issues.

Sitting with Jibril in London brought back memories of hammering out ideas with my Birzeit students over hummus and cheap Omar cigarettes. Jibril and I spoke late into the night, as we did the next night and the one after that.

Thinking back on it now, I'm amazed at the cavalier ease—others would soon see in it as a conniving "will-to-power"—with which the two of us, sitting in a fancy hotel lobby, put down on paper a strategy to revolutionize the PLO "revolution." It was also a key to turning the meaningless autonomy that Israel and the Americans were offering us into something far closer to sovereign nationhood. We couldn't state any of this openly because Fatah was still very much an illegal organization, and under Israeli occupation, mere membership in it led to long jail sentences.

What Jibril and I came up with was the establishment of a country-wide structure of political committees in support of the peace process. Members of those committees would be primarily Fatah activists or supporters who, because they were at the grassroots level, could get the word out to the masses. Then came a coordinating body, which would organize these committees. We called it the Higher Political Committee. It would have fourteen members from the West Bank and Gaza. I would be the chairman, and Ahmad Hazza' the vice chair.

None of this would break any Israeli laws: the whole point was to support the peace talks, after all. That there was a secretive element to this can be inferred from the fact that we filled all the positions in the Higher Political Committee with ex-prisoners. The Higher Political Committee was the direct successor to the Unified Command of the intifada. Sameer Shehadeh, who had created the UNC with Abu Jihad, was the first name we thought of.

The Higher Political Committee was to be the public and legal cover for a clandestine body we called the Fatah Higher Committee. While the first would drum up public support for the Madrid talks, the second—with the same members switching caps—would transform Fatah, its power structure, its very nature, from a guerrilla movement into a democratic political party representing the interests of the people living under occupation. After liberation, the Fatah Higher Committee could become a party leadership capable of governing an independent state. In short, the plan was to shift control of the local Fatah groups from the likes of the brutish fellow with buffed wingtips I had met in Amman in the early 1980s, back to the grassroots leadership in the Occupied Territories.

Behind the plan was the fact that the old underground guerrilla movement was in need of a thorough overhaul. Under the old system, leaders living abroad controlled the Fatah movement in the territories. The branch offices were military cells or "Tanzim," run by eighteen desk officers sitting in Amman.

If you're running a partisan war, this may make a lot of sense; for a civil society, however, it's a formula for a Baathist-type dictatorship. The old system of underground cells, without institutional anchoring in the society they were supposed to liberate, could never run a free society. To create our own state we needed leaders born and bred under occupation who were personally rooted in the country. The old guard sitting in Tunis or Amman was more in touch with the local Mercedes dealership than with the needs and concerns of the people under occupation.

The Fatah Higher Committee would be the main power center for younger leaders such as Jibril, Marwan, Sameer, and Dahlan. Once peace was concluded, the old guard would have to acclimatize itself to an open-party structure, with internal bylaws addressing how to advance our people's social and economic concerns. Like it or not, the "liberators" would have to adjust to freedom.

The next element in the plan was to link up the Tanzim with this new leadership body. Just as the Higher Political Committee would be the legal face of the Fatah Higher Committee, the political committees drumming up grassroots support for Madrid would transform the Tanzim from secretive guerrilla cells into the grassroots leadership of a democratic political party. The Tanzim would be linked up regionally with one another so that regional representation could be established, with the Fatah Higher Committee running the affairs as a whole.

One effective way to do this was to change the way funds were distributed. In the old system, the PLO raised money from donors and then farmed it out through the eighteen offices in Amman; the directors took their cut, and then, if anything was left, it dribbled down to the cells. Our idea was for the money to be centrally managed by the Fatah Higher Committee, and then distributed to the local chapters. We wanted the new body to take control of these funds and distribute them in a transparent manner, in which the average man on the street would benefit. This also was the only effective way of combating Hamas, with its far-flung social network.

Jibril returned to Tunis to sell the idea to Arafat. Arafat supported it, over the objections of many of the people around him. Some vehemently opposed emasculating the Tanzim, these mighty centers of military prowess, by turning them into what they dismissively dubbed "peace leagues." Others didn't like the new way of doling out money. By redirecting all the funds flowing through this committee, functionaries sitting in offices outside Palestine could no longer subtract their "administration costs."

I returned to Jerusalem and began work. To create the committees, I drove around the West Bank and Gaza to meet with the Tanzim. The task was made considerably easier thanks to my earlier arrest by Jacob and the Shin Bet. On the Palestinian street, time in an Israeli prison was a prerequisite for respect. ("It is an unhappy country that needs heroes," writes Brecht.)

The man I found to head up the political committees for supporting negotiations project was Ziad Abu Zayyad, the editor of the *Al-Fajr*, and one of the first PLO members to call openly for a two-state solution. His belief in dialogue with the Israelis was strong enough that he had picked up Hebrew and even put out a newspaper in Hebrew called *Gesher*, or "Bridge."

Very quickly, a community of ex-prisoners countrywide and Fatah activists toiled day and night to ensure public support for our negotiation team and the peace process. We established a headquarters in Ramallah, where we often met. Hussein al-Sheikh, the man who pulled me away from the soldiers, ran the office.

Chapter Twenty-three

A Shadow Government

W ITH THE CONCLUSION of the first round of talks in Madrid, the Palestinian team headed off to Tunis to meet with Arafat and the PLO leadership. There they stayed long enough to make sure everyone knew that they were taking their cues from the PLO. From Tunis they flew to Amman, and after a brief stopover, they boarded the buses and headed back for Jerusalem.

Ahmad and I wanted to roll out the welcome wagon for them and commemorate the triumph of common sense over a generation of ideology. And what better way to do this, we thought, than to bring together all the committees we had created to support them! It was like a surprise party, because no one on the bus knew what we had been up to.

We sent one of our activists to meet the buses at the bridge and tell Faisal about the hard work we had done drumming up support for his efforts. When the buses pulled up to the National Theater in East Jerusalem, where we were gathered, Ziad Abu Zayyad acted as master of ceremonies.

The party atmosphere we had expected didn't quite materialize. I could already see through the tinted glass the worried looks on our negotiators' faces. They didn't know where all the celebrating people in the rowdy crowd had come from, and seeing that many of them were leading activists with strong street credentials, they feared our reception party was a coup d'état. Had they driven into a trap? Was Arafat behind it? *Was he trying to burn them?*

Suspicion turned in my direction. They had left me alone in Jerusalem, and a short while later they returned to find me leading a gang of ex-prisoners in what must have seemed to them a highly dubious grassroots project. Faisal was the most alarmed of all. Had his second in command suddenly developed independent ambitions? Was a Nusseibeh challenging a Husseini? From that moment on our relationship lost some of its trusting intimacy. It would never fully return.

My other role during the Madrid period tended to stoke suspicions. When the people in Tunis created the "team" to get around Shamir, they included three Jerusalemites: Faisal, Hanan Ashrawi, and me. Faisal became the head, and Hanan the official spokeswoman. In all fairness, they thought, scratching their heads, they had to come up with something for me. Someone suggested putting me in charge of the technical committees needed for the team. It sounded like a good solution, and everyone in the room agreed. The fact that there were no technical committees to manage didn't bother anyone.

I first found out about this when an ex-colleague from my union days, who had attended the meeting, gave me a call. He explained the difference between the official "delegation" and the "team." "You're a member of the team," he announced. "You've also been given the job to create technical committees."

"Great," I told him. "But what does this mean? What am I supposed to do?"

"I don't think anyone has a clue," my friend said chuckling. "Just do what you usually do. You always seem to manage."

All I had to go on were the words *technical committee*. I was glad the position didn't come with a job description. As someone with a fondness for blank slates, my imagination wandered for several minutes before leading me back to the nub of the problem I had sensed at the outset of the entire Madrid process: namely that the Israelis and Americans were intent on buying us off with a fraudulent "autonomy." Transforming Fatah into a real political party was one way to prevent "autonomy" from becoming just another name for Israeli domination, this time with PLO compliance. Could these nonexistent technical committees do the same? Under the nose of our Israeli occupiers—and PLO functionaries in Tunis—could they function as embryonic ministries of an independent state geographically anchored in East Jerusalem?

I was alone on the balcony. It was a warm evening, and in the distance the floodlights illuminating the Dome of the Rock had turned it into something otherworldly, a shimmering vision floating in midair. As often when pondering a riddle, I smoked one cigarette after the next, emptying out a packet of Camel Filters, my new brand, before some provisional answers began to crystallize. The negotiators, I reasoned, obviously needed information in order to negotiate. How could they talk about water without knowing where the aquifers were? The technical committees could be the brain of our emerging state by thinking through every issue, and presenting our negotiators with informed policy statements and advice, with data, position papers, and negotiation scenarios.

But these committees could go far beyond this. It came to me that they could become the shadow government I had pushed for when I penned the declaration of independence. With a bit of rumination it struck me that the technical committees were the linchpin of the peace process. I had found a solution to a problem pestering me since I first heard about the Madrid talks in prison.

As I had been preaching all along, the signs of sovereignty—a flag, handshakes, a national anthem, or the face of an Arab general on the currency—meant nothing without the meaty substance of independence. If our nation remained a ghostly entity with no institutions of its own, then Israeli recognition would be just as insubstantial. There wouldn't be anything for them to recognize. It would be an "autonomy" that would only immortalize their domination. Only after the infrastructure for a future Palestinian administration was in place would the political negotiations on borders, refugees, and so on lead to a meaningful agreement.

The question of national freedom was similar to that of identity: the interrogator offers freedom from pain at the price of inner servitude. By contrast, the prisoner does not receive true inner freedom from his master; he seizes it without asking permission. Palestinians needed to *seize* sovereignty.

I accepted the job and then set about creating a shadow government.

Though I had obviously never created a state from scratch, *No Trumpets, No Drums* had sharpened my mind on ways of doing so. I had also actually learned a thing or two during my brief stint working for an oil company in Abu Dhabi. The job had taught me a lot about compromises in negotiations. I also got a bird's-eye view of a country being built from the ground up. It was just starting while I was there, but in the years that followed, partly thanks to my brother Zaki, the sheikh's most trusted adviser, the country was becoming the Singapore of the Middle East.

My first move was to find people who could help. I started calling up some professional colleagues, academics, economists, lawyers, and political scientists, and asked them to come by Mother's house for a brainstorming session. Fahd, my contact man with the tanzim, showed up. Hassan Abu Libdeh was also there. Hassan had an uncanny knack for materializing ideas into detailed strategies, then executing them. Samir Hleileh, also a brilliant mind, showed up.

I explained to those gathered what the technical committees would do, their political importance, and the role I saw for them in a two-state solution. To get our enterprise off the ground, we needed to involve academics and professionals from all fields.

During the meeting my colleagues asked if I had any financial backing.

"None whatsoever."

"What about from the PLO?"

Not wanting to raise any false hopes, I leveled with them: "I wouldn't count on it."

What I admired about my friends—and it's a quality I've noticed recurrently over the years—was their willingness to commit themselves to what sane people would regard as hopelessly pie in the sky. They had faith in our ability as a group to defy the laws of gravity. "Well," said one of my colleagues after a moment of awkward silence, "we'll just have to scrounge around for resources, won't we?"

My friends and I worked hard over the following days and weeks to put together a skeleton for the structure we needed to carry out the work. Having identified the various sectors in need of committees-cum-ministries, we started headhunting for the right person who might act as coordinator. Sectors ran the gamut from security to electricity, tourism to education, economics to infrastructure. On paper, the emerging skeleton rapidly took the shape of a shadow government.

With what little money I could borrow from Mother, I rented a room in a building across from her house. I called in my secretary, Hanan, to run the office, and hired an ex-student who used to work with Faisal at the Arab Studies Society to help put together stationery with a letterhead and to scour the world for possible donors. Initially all we managed to get was printing equipment and a fax machine donated by the British consul general.

We soon moved the office over to the Orient House. But rather than occupy the room with the chandeliers—it was too public for our needs—I made my office out of two converted bathrooms that made my prison cell in Ramle look spacious. From this unlikely spot (the plugged pipe to the john was under my desk), my team and I set out to build our state.

For the first meeting of the coordinators, twenty-three people showed up at Mother's. With the heads of what we called the human resources and strategic planning units, there were twenty-five in all.

In the appointment letter I sent to our nominees, I outlined three main questions I wanted them to ponder as they formed their committee: In a perfect world, how should their particular sector of our society work? What's the Platonic ideal of, say, a finance department? The next question was meant to bring us all back to earth: How do things look now? What sort of human raw material are we working with? The last question bridged the first two: What are the steps needed for us to get to the first level from our present broken-down reality? By answering these questions, went the letter, we would be outlining a roadmap for our negotiation team. Negotiators would have an exact idea what to seek from the Israelis, and what to avoid.

The coordinators set to work, and the support they received from the Palestinian professional and business community can only be described as fervent. Hundreds of professionals volunteered their time in the various committees, which over time produced volume after volume of material. More important, they developed valuable networks and relationships for the future. (Many of the ministers in the ensuing Palestinian government were coordinators or members of the various committees in the shadow government.)

The main reason why hundreds of volunteers worked so tirelessly, and why I sat for two years without pay in a converted lavatory, was because we believed we were creating the state out of its institutions rather than the other way around.

The emotions in play then are not easy to put into words. *Euphoria* doesn't quite capture the mood I experienced each time I walked into the Orient House. Maybe you'd have to go back to Jefferson's America to find such spirited activity among would-be state-builders. Until then, our technocrats had never been able to meet without drawing Israeli soldiers. When Faisal tried to work scientifically on questions of population statistics at the Arab Studies Society, ham-fisted authorities put a stop to it. Now, in a different climate, a committee gathered empirical statistical scientific data on demographics and income. Capturing knowledge about our emerging nation was for us like wiping away decades of powerlessness by showing ourselves what we were made of—that we, like other peoples, could govern ourselves. We were not "hewers of wood and carriers of water." That was a message we were certain would seep out over time, from our studies and position papers and training courses, and enter into the psyches of both the Israeli and Palestinian population, and hence their leaders.

We didn't mind if our work was passed over by the press and politicians, or that the "man on the street" didn't know what we were up to. The main show was in far-off Washington; it was there where people expected a dramatic breakthrough. None of this perturbed us in the slightest.

A couple of brief examples of what came out of these committees show just how much flesh we were putting on "autonomy."

The Swedish government provided a grant to produce the first trial broadcast of an independent Palestinian television station. The economic committee, with its seventy-two members, worked with twenty-one experts from the World Bank to put together the first five-year plan for the Palestinian Territories in five volumes, called Investments in Peace.

An even better example of our entire state-building exercise was the work of the education committee. Fathiyyah Nasru, a professor at Birzeit who had been one of Sameer's first contacts at the start of the intifada, headed it up. Over months of work she and her 136 coworkers composed fourteen volumes covering every discipline in education. A separate booklet summarized the main strategies for our transformation of Palestinian elementary and secondary schools. (The fact that Fathiyyah's booklet quotes Noah Webster on American revolutionary education says something about the kind of changes we were aiming at.) The main goal was to uproot the old system of passive, rote learning, which dulls rather than sharpens the creative mind.

In a society in which tradition and religion can be used to cripple rather than release creative potential, the educational philosophy the committee came up with stressed the ways tradition must serve the present and the future, not enslave them. "As the learner acts upon *her* present condition she employs the heritage passed down by previous generations creatively and inseparably from her sense of future. Past, present and future are not seen in a sequential linear fashion . . . Here the human being—the learner—is bending tradition to address her own needs."

The pamphlet also contained a subtle warning, one might be tempted to call it a prophesy, to our future leaders: "Even if an authoritarian government were to exist, this government would not be recognized by the Palestinian people as a national government."

Madrid was just the icebreaker. The venue now shifted over to Washington, D.C., for the launching of a two-year process. In June 1992, the talks got a lift when Rabin defeated Shamir in the Israeli national elections. The Labor Party softened the Israeli position by permitting Faisal to head the Palestinian delegation. This brought direct negotiations between Israel and the PLO a major step closer.

The talks were divided into two parts. There were bilateral talks between Israel and the Palestinians, with the main issue being a five-year interim self-government arrangement followed by final status talks. The other talks were multilateral and covered issues such as water resources, the environment, and economic development.

Abu Ala—later the Palestinian prime minister—was in charge of the multilateral talks. An accountant by training and a member of the Fatah Central Committee, Abu Ala was a man with a practical bent of mind and a biting wit: a rare combination for a Middle Eastern politician. He drew heavily on our committees, and enlisted members of the committees on water, transport, settlements, refugees, and the environment to be delegates to the multilateral talks.

I made it a point to keep the technical committees separate from the political committees Jibril and I had set up. Indeed, I saw the enterprise as consisting of two separate parts. One part had to do with the building up of a government structure, the other of a party structure. Our future state would need both, though in different ways.

• • •

There was no one who had a better idea of what I was up to than Yasir Arafat. He had an actively mistrustful mind, anyway, and he was now becoming uncomfortable that I was acting on my own without asking his permission. Things came to a head with Arafat when he began to suspect I was forming my own private army behind his back.

Besides everything else we were doing in the technical committees, we had set up a security committee in anticipation of a future police force. Ex-guerrillas and prisoners needed professional training, so I raised some money to send them off to police academies in Cairo and Amman. Rumors about my hidden agenda for doing so reached Arafat from various sources. As I was to learn, while flying high over the Jordanian desert, my position was becoming tenuous, even dangerous.

I was on my way to a general leadership meeting in Tunis chaired by Arafat. In the plane sitting next to me was the head of the Communist Party, Suleiman Najjab, a very affectionate and gregarious man with a sense of humor surprising for a man who had had so many close encounters with death.

Suddenly, after telling me a joke, he took on a somber expression, leaned over to me as if he had something confidential to say, and whispered in my ear, "Arafat is very concerned about what you are doing, and people are filling his head with all sorts of nonsense. Apparently you decided on your own to send some people to do military training in Egypt and Jordan. He knows about it. And he has heard that you are trying to launch some private venture apart from the PLO. If you don't want everything to blow up in your face, you're going to have to convince him you're not trying to usurp him."

This was lethal business.

In Tunis I waited until the day's business was done before approaching the Old Man. I walked into his office as he sat scribbling on the countless papers always on his desk. I had heard, I began, that he suspected I was trying to do something on the sly. "Let me say that if you don't trust me, I'll quit. My job is hard enough as it is. I'm doing it because I believe it is in our national interest. I'll continue doing it only if I have your trust. If not, tell me now." I meant every word.

Arafat respected people who spoke frankly as much as he despised sycophants. The fact that I was being honest and direct made him push aside the mistrust others had been drilling into him. "No, no, don't worry," he muttered curtly. "Don't worry. I trust you. Keep up the good work." He returned to his stack of documents.

I didn't feel fully reassured until I got a call from him the following morning. "I want you to come to the airport. You are to accompany me on a state visit to Vienna. And get yourself a real suit."

Arafat made me sit next to him at the official table in the ornate Baroque palace where the meeting was held. Introducing me to his hosts, he said, "This is Sari Nusseibeh, the chairman of our technical and advisory committees to the negotiations. You know, these are essential for our peace efforts."

The technical committees spun off countless ideas, papers, books, and paved a career path for dozens of future civil servants. There was also a hidden link between our shadow government in the Orient House and a peace agreement with Israel. Whether by accident or by fate, a casual conversation at a conference on Middle East water was one of the forces that led to the Oslo Agreement.

The multilateral talks under Abu Ala's direction made great strides, as experts from both sides developed good professional relationships and thought of practical ways of solving problems.

The bilateral talks in Washington, by contrast, got no traction at all, nor could they have, given their parameters. By maintaining the public fiction that Israel would never sit down and talk with PLO "terrorists," Shamir had only added a layer of complication in the negotiations. Everyone knew that Arafat was the only one who could close a deal. Shamir's successor, Rabin, and Rabin's foreign minister, Shimon Peres, were also well aware that Faisal wasn't about to close a deal without Arafat's approval.

One day, I was sitting in my father's former law office (the metal doors were no longer welded shut) when Jad Ishaq, a founding member of the technical committees and the coordinator of the water group, dropped by to tell me about a "fantastic opportunity." The Swiss were organizing an international conference on water and had invited him to attend. The Israelis would also be there, which had led Bethlehem University, where Ishaq worked, to decline the invitation. Without hesitating, I told him he could bank on Fatah's support.

The fact that we and the Israelis would be participants in the conference aroused the predictable boycott instincts. A number of top PLO people made some blustering threats. But in the end they went along. Some of the most vociferous critics actually showed up for the conference.

Something portentous occurred in Switzerland. Yair Hirschfeld, an Israeli professor of Middle Eastern history, pulled me aside and said he wanted to talk. Hirschfeld, a Vienna-born intellectual, had in fact been involved in countless meetings with us during the intifada. With a razorlike mind not given to fantasy, he locked onto a problem, asked the right questions, and if he was satisfied with your logic, acted without hesitation.

Hirschfeld wanted my opinion on the glacial pace of the negotiations in Washington. I told him that the talks were fated to poke along, and in fact would go nowhere. Thinking about the Petah Tikva prisoner negotiations, I explained that only by directly involving the decision makers could a breakthrough be possible.

"Who do you think are the key people on the Palestinian side who need to be involved?" he wanted to know. There were three people, I replied: Arafat, Abu Mazen, and Faisal. I knew of course that Arafat relied on Abu Mazen in the dialogue with Israelis. Abu Mazen always represented a sane understanding of our conflict with Israel. He and Abu Ala worked closely on the multilateral issues. I added Faisal because I also wanted someone on the inside to be involved.

Little did I know that Hirschfeld was to continue his trip from Zurich to London to meet with Abu Ala in what later was described as the Oslo process.

Chapter Twenty-four

Oslo

I N THE SPRING OF 1992, Lucy gave birth to our daughter. She was delivered by the same old family friend who had helped with Absal's and Buraq's birth. I remember thinking, as she lay in the crib in the pediatric ward with her curious-looking eyes wide open and scanning the strange new world around her, that fate had given her a ravenous appetite for knowledge. We chose the name Nuzha for our new baby girl because it is Mother's name. In classical Arabic it is also resonant of the purity of the desert.

In the meantime, all our boys were now in high school at the Quaker-run American Friends School in Ramallah. The broad streets leading up to the school felt safer than the cramped lanes near the New Gate that Jacob and his Shin Bet friends had warned me of. In a year Jamal was to head off to Eton, safer still.

There were some new developments in the legal imbroglio over the Goldsmith's Souk. Cousin Zaki had managed to get the case before a judge. The proceedings were reminiscent of Kafka's *The Trial*, because justice was never a part of the equation. The judge was a family member of one of the settlers, and threw the case out on a technicality. The yeshiva students then picked up the pace of the takeover.

We all needed a break from Palestine. Sitting in prison, I had dreamt of going off somewhere with my family, writing a book or two, or just watching the birds, as I did as a boy with my pigeons. But then came Madrid, and month after month I worked to lay the groundwork for a future Palestinian democracy. I felt I had done my duty to my people, my own conscience, and the memory of my father. Now it was time for me to return to private life. My old hero al-Ghazali won his freedom by snubbing his nose at society's expectations and going on a Wanderjahr. My mode of escape was to be with my family. After all the years of overwork and putting them into the line of fire, I dearly wanted to devote myself to them.

"Out of sight, out of mind" went one of Father's hackneyed sayings, which I now began chanting to myself like a mantra. If only I could disappear from view the way as a child I fled my parents' salon! Sticking around in Jerusalem after the PLO establishes a government would only guarantee that I'd be willy-nilly drawn into its machinery. But if I were "out of sight" they'd find someone else, and I could return to Jerusalem after a year or so and glide smoothly back into private life.

I began scouting for opportunities abroad. The Woodrow Wilson Institute in Washington, D.C., offered me a fellowship starting in the fall. Jamal was going to Eton anyway at that time, and the idea of strolling with Lucy and my other children through a fall forest blazing with colors asserted itself with such force that I snapped up the opportunity without a second thought.

When I told my friends in the Fatah Higher Committee about my plans, no one could believe it. "Now?" they all exclaimed in unison. "*How could you leave now?*" I reminded them that from the start I had always said that I would leave politics the minute the conflict was over. They obviously thought I had been jesting. When I talk this way, most people just assume that, all my protestations to the contrary, politics runs thick in my veins. People in the technical committees were just as surprised.

The scoop in the Israeli media was that plans were in the works to prevent me from leaving, not by the Shin Bet but by Fatah. Newspapers reported that I was about to be kidnapped by Fatah activists and somehow taken to Arafat, who wouldn't hear of my leaving. The journalists may have made up the story, though there was a grain of truth to it. Arafat tried his best to persuade me to stay put. He sent a group of Fatah colleagues and friends to my house in Abu Dis, begging me not to leave the country. Arafat left me alone only when I told him Lucy needed an operation in America. It wasn't exactly a lie, but nor was it the truth.

Another reason I needed a break was because I had found myself rubbing my blue worry beads more than ever. Despite the ongoing negotiations between Israelis and Palestinians in Washington, I was getting nervous. "I think people who say they are not afraid probably don't think," I explained to an American reporter. "Thinking and fearing go together. The secret is not to stop fearing: it is to learn how to live with it." I added with a hint of stoic resignation, "If it happens that someone comes up to you one day and shoots you, that's it."

This may sound like overwrought angst at a time of blossoming peace, but, objectively, things were direr than ever. For the first time in history the Jews and Palestinian Arabs were sitting down face to face, and this was stirring all the demons of the past. Negotiations with the Israelis were a long, drawn-out process touching painful memories half a century old, mainly the expulsion of Palestinians from Israel. Disappointing people's expectation of finally getting perfect justice for this outrage can be dangerous business. Within Palestinian society, violence and criminality had also set down deep roots, the internal social resistance to them having been broken down. Added to this came the depredations of trigger-happy settlers, whose numbers continued to mount by the day.

The Fatah people were more worried about my safety than I was; in their estimation, since our farewell party sending off the two busloads of delegates, the risks had substantially increased, or so they feared. I was the cofounder of the Fatah Higher Committee, and a steady stream of Israelis was passing through my lavatory office. I was organizing rallies in support of peace in Gaza and the West Bank, and was constantly meeting with fellow activists to discuss the peace process. I had become a prominent target, and Fatah sent a couple of comrades to shadow me from a distance.

I only found out about this two weeks later when an exasperated friend and fellow member of the Fatah Higher Committee approached me. "What's up with you? We assigned a couple of guys to you, but you're impossible to follow. You're always going in and out of taxis and buses, into shops, and back into a crowded street. These poor fellows can't keep up with you." As in a slapstick movie, my well-developed self-preservation instinct had led me to shake off the very people trying to keep me out of harm's way.

What really spooked everyone, including me, was yet another deadly puzzle. In early 1992, three mysterious murders struck close to home. The first victim, a lawyer from Gaza, was a key player in the political committees. Thousands of people gripped with shock and anger showed up for his funeral. We marched all the way from his home in Gaza City to the graveyard outside of town. No one knew who had done the killing, or who had ordered it. A close friend of the slain man, a respected Fatah veteran, gave the eulogy. I remember his speech well. "I shall not rest," he pledged to the mourners, himself, and probably God, "until the murderers responsible for this heinous crime have been found and brought to justice."

Not only did the speaker fail to track down the killers, but they struck again. Within the space of two weeks, another murder was committed under similarly mysterious circumstances. The new victim was none other but the veteran Fatah man himself. His killing at least narrowed the field of possible killers. Hamas hadn't had a hand in it, if for no other reason than the second victim's son was a young and respected Hamas leader. So who was behind the assassinations?

In the West Bank, unknown assassins also gunned down the Birzeit archaeologist Professor Glock. Glock's family and most Palestinians were convinced that the Israelis were behind his killing. He had been working on a book documenting the four hundred villages cleansed of their inhabitants and then leveled by the Israelis in 1948. By tracing the origins of the Palestinian refugee problem, went their reasoning, Glock was coming up with evidence that would have greatly strengthened the Palestinian hand in talks related to the refugees and their property. And this was something the Israelis couldn't tolerate.

The Israelis claim that Arab hit men did it.

Two years later, an investigator commissioned by the Glock family to find out who was behind the professor's murder visited me in my office. He told me that in his inquiries he had discovered that police at Ben Gurion Airport, acting on a tip, had arrested an American Palestinian associated with Hamas. Interrogators found out that the man was linked to a terrorist cell run by Adel Awadallah, the notorious bomb maker and then Israel's Public Enemy Number One.

In the confession squeezed out by the interrogating officers, the man fingered Adel Awadallah as the one personally responsible for the murder of Professor Glock. There was more: The reason the private investigator came to my office was to deliver some unpleasant news. The man arrested at the airport told the police that Awadallah was under instructions to carry out another assassination, this time of the Palestinian people's Enemy Number One, me. My death sentence, which for some reason he hadn't yet carried out, was punishment for mobilizing the public for peace.

The Washington talks were becoming an industry. The sixth round gave way to the seventh, the seventh to the eighth. The ninth round rolled around at the end of April. After fifteen months, the wearying process had yet to produce much. To be sure, good ideas were being tossed around, and sitting across a table was a lot better than throwing rocks and shooting. The central figure on the American side was Dennis Ross, a tall, broad-shouldered man with a boyish demeanor and eyeglasses the size of saucers. Despite his obvious support for Israel, he was a man oozing with eager goodwill for Palestinians. It was he who interceded at my request with the Israeli authorities to allow for the free movement and travel of Fatah's negotiation supporters—all activists with previous records. He also gave the impression of a Boy Scout counselor with no experience of the snake charmers and flying knives of the Middle Eastern souk.

The best efforts of the Americans notwithstanding, a pattern developed between the opposing sides that made progress incremental at best, and mainly a routine of one step forward, two steps back. The Palestinian side stood firm on wishing to get two matters clearly settled: a viable five-year interim period of autonomy that would have all the trappings of independence immediately transferred to them, and a clearly defined basis for the final-status negotiations—talks that were to center on borders, Jerusalem, settlements, and refugees—which would guarantee a full Israeli withdrawal from the territories occupied in 1967.

The Israeli side tried to get away with the precise opposite. Their negotiators worked to whittle down the authority of the Palestinian autonomy as much as possible until it was a repackaged Village League, and to frame the final-status agreements in as vague terms as possible.

Then there was the brinksmanship du jour: one side or the other would come out with a threat, and the other would huddle together with the Americans to find a solution, which was never more than a stopgap until the next crisis, such as when Rabin expelled 415 Islamic activists to a frozen Lebanese field following a Hamas terrorist attack.

But just as the ninth round in Washington was getting off the ground, the forth round of secret talks was under way in Oslo.

Like everyone else who was not directly involved in the Oslo process, I didn't have a clue what was happening there. I didn't know that following the water conference in Switzerland, Hirschfeld had contacted both Abu Ala and Abu Mazen. Abu Ala then met Ron Pundak, a history research fellow, for a long weekend in Oslo, all organized by Terje Larsen, founder of the Norwegian Institute for Applied Science. Eventually, the two sides came up with a six-page Declaration of Principles.

The closest I got to finding any of this out was a fortuitous chat I had with Abu Ala, who could have told me everything but chose not to. He and his fellow negotiators left everyone in the dark, even President Clinton.

My chance meeting with Abu Ala took place in an airport VIP lounge—being a member of the "team" had bumped me up to business class—where I was awaiting a flight from Tunis to Paris. I saw him walk into the lounge in his typical unassuming style. He, too, he informed me, was catching the Paris flight, in order to meet one of his sons.

Happy to see each other, we launched into a long discussion about the Washington talks. While deep in conversation, the VIP officers came to take us to our flight. The security car dropped us at the bottom of the stairs, wished us well, then spun around and drove off.

The plane was empty. Assuming that the other passengers and crew would board soon, we carried on our conversation. An hour passed and still no one boarded. By now we sensed that something wasn't right. We stepped out onto the boarding platform and, not seeing a soul, started waving down a passing service vehicle. Finally, the security people who had dropped us off turned up again. They had mistakenly put us on a plane scheduled to leave for Istanbul. Our Paris flight had taken off long before.

For three hours, until the next Paris flight, and then on the plane, we talked about everything under the sun *except* Oslo. Abu Ala didn't mention a word about it, nor did he confess that he wasn't heading to Paris to meet his son but would be boarding another plane heading to Norway.

But even without insider information, I had a strong hunch that a peace agreement was around the corner. Being a member of the "team," director of the technical committees, and working closely with Abu Ala in the multilateral talks, I was in a good position to analyze the unfolding peace process. In Jerusalem, I was also privy to all sorts of unofficial contacts taking place between people involved in the process at one level or another. All evidence to the contrary—settlement construction was continuing at breakneck speed—my reading of the political map led me to believe that something was about to give. I just had no idea what.

I was so certain that there was serious progress being made toward an Israeli-Palestinian agreement that the day before meeting Abu Ala in the airport I predicted to Marwan over dinner in a restaurant that an agreement would be in the bag by the end of that summer.

This may have been less a matter of the "prophet of Birzeit" reading his tea leaves than wishful thinking, because the hint of such a dramatic development hit me like the promise of liberation, liberation from fear but also from politics and the stench of ambition among politicians. I didn't want to wake up one sunny day and find out I had done nothing with my life but politics.

News of Oslo broke in the summer of 1993, a few weeks before I left for America. I was in Gaza attending a conference when I first heard, and I was so jubilant that I contacted my colleagues at the Orient House and asked them to prepare for a victory celebration. Marwan was convinced I had been in on the secret negotiations. How else could I have known that a breakthrough was imminent?

I headed out from Gaza the next day and raced up the mountain toward Jerusalem to make it to the party on time. But just as I started plying my way up the last hill, my old beater died on me, something I'd grown wearily accustomed to. I still made it to the Orient House, just too late, and sweaty from standing on the side of the road flagging down a cab.

The outside courtyard was packed with revelers. Flags were everywhere, the loudspeaker was blaring, and faces beamed with joy. The minute I walked in, a few young activists rushed over and hoisted me up on their shoulders. For the next hour I stared down from my perch at the singing throng with their nationalist songs, hardly believing that we had really done it. Peace. Liberation. No more politics! America! *Monticello!*

None of us had yet read what the agreement was or knew any of its details. What we knew was what counted: a deal had been struck between the Israeli government and the PLO. Just as I had always predicted, reason had prevailed. This could only lead inexorably to an independent Palestinian state with East Jerusalem as its capital. How could it not? No one at the Orient House that evening had the slightest doubt that our work had paid off. We had finally achieved our objective of peace.

The later rancor, so bitterly poisonous, has to be seen in the light of this innocent joy. The suicide bombers plaguing Israeli cities, and Sharon's twenty-foot wall with watchtowers slicing through our Palestinian lands were still a decade away.

Everyone likes a good mystery story, and the Oslo Agreement had all the ingredients of a great yarn. There were the secret meetings in an icy, moonlit, far-off European city, where behind the backs of career politicians a couple of professors with their heads in the clouds, as people say, ended up making more progress than the negotiators had over a year and a half of official talks, with all the American pressure and cajoling and with all the Boy Scout skills of Dennis Ross. President Clinton gave the agreement his full backing, and the official signing ceremony was slated for September 13 on the White House lawn.

We called our agreement the Declaration of Principles. An acronym shortened it to DOP. Once disillusionment set in, wisecrackers had a field day: DOPED, DUPED, and so on. On the eve of its signature, a letter as a preamble was exchanged between the two sides. The PLO agreed unequivocally to recognize Israel's right to Israel, and in return Israel finally acknowledged the PLO as the legitimate political representative of the Palestinians. This implied that the Palestinians would get their own PLO-led government in Palestine.

The other points flowed from there. The two sides agreed on a timetable for creating a Palestinian Authority, first in embryo form in Gaza and Jericho and then eventually stretching throughout the West Bank. Simultaneously, the Israelis would withdraw their troops from major population centers. Elections would be held. The most contentious issues, such as Jerusalem, settlements, refugees, and borders, were kicked down the road, after some trust was established. These "permanent status" negotiations would begin after two years, with the whole thing wrapped up within five.

Peres, in a letter he gave to Arafat upon the signing of Oslo, promised that Palestinian institutions in Jerusalem would not only not suffer during the interim period but would be allowed to develop and expand.

In hindsight it is easy to trace all the failures of Oslo back to a badly worded clause or a fuzzy detail in DOP. In drafting the agreement, the Palestinians didn't have any international contract lawyers with them, a fatal mistake when dealing with Israelis.

What has proven most deleterious from the Palestinian point of view was that the major issues of borders, Jerusalem, and settlements were bracketed out as "final-status" issues to be hammered out within five years. By agreeing to DOP's amorphous parameters, Palestinians also relinquished the very concrete hope of ever getting back the lands lost in 1948. Only the 27 percent of historic Palestine conquered by Israel in 1967 was on the table, and there was no guarantee that Israel would even agree to hand all of it back. We had to make due with "autonomy" over a few slivers of land, and hope that "final-status negotiations" would give us the rest. Meanwhile, DOP put no cap on settlement construction or on the creation of new Jewish neighborhoods in Jerusalem. In other words, the Israelis pocketed their gains in 1948, while our part fell under the category of "disputed" territories to be divvied up between the two sides, one vastly superior in military and diplomatic muscle. It was like negotiating a prenuptial by intentionally bracketing out marital fidelity. In other words, DOP was a perfect formula for disaster.

But in August 1993 no one could have foretold how the agreement would play out, and there was an understandable sense of euphoria. Arafat couldn't have been happier. Just two years earlier he had been the world's number-two pariah, just after Saddam. All his funds had dried up and the red phone in his office barely rang. He was one of the world's last surviving old revolutionaries, and the most forlorn. Now he was basking in the limelight.

The average man on the street introduced elsewhere in this story was just as exhilarated as the revelers at the Orient House that evening. For him it meant that the long occupation was coming to an end. Arafat, a leader who in his mind embodied his own hopes, was being treated like a head of state, which meant that the state couldn't be far behind. No more harassment by soldiers, no more road blocks, no more random arrests, no more land confiscation, no more settlements, no more settlers with their Uzis playing feudal masters. There would be jobs and open schools and hope for his children to live as the Israeli children did: in a free world full of opportunities, respected by the world and looked upon as an equal, not a handout case, not a dog.

There was no lack of critics who didn't share the average man's innocent hope. The indefatigable Noam Chomsky tore DOP to shreds by predicting with unerring logic that, because there was no brake on settlements, Oslo meant the *end* of the two-state solution, the very thing the agreement was supposed to auger. The Palestinian negotiators at the bilateral talks in Washington felt betrayed because the deal had been done in secret and behind their backs. They had poured their lives into negotiations that they thought would lead to statehood, and a small knot of professors had beaten them to the goal. Saeb Ereikat put it this way: "We delegates were the appetizers. The PLO is the main course." Faisal and most of the delegation were out of the country when the news broke, so they weren't at the party. Faisal wouldn't have shown up anyway. As it was, he disappeared from public view for a few days just to absorb the shock.

Nearly to a man, the negotiators quickly put on a good face and lined up behind the Oslo Agreement. There were also Palestinians who remained critical even after the effect of the shock disappeared. Dr. Shafi refused to go to the signing at the White House because a termination of settlement construction wasn't part of the package. He shared Chomsky's suspicions. Abroad, the most prominent critic of Oslo was Palestine's academic pride and showpiece, Edward Said.

The most vociferous enemies of Oslo, such as Hamas and some splinter parties on the left, denounced the agreement with visceral pathos; they were against *any* agreement with Israel. At Birzeit, radical students on the left and Islamic right clashed with their peers from Fatah. "How could Chairman Arafat shake hands with Rabin, a man who shot us and imprisoned us!" The acrimonious debates ended in fistfights.

In Israel, Benjamin "Bibi" Netanyahu and Ariel Sharon led the chorus of dissenters, and the country was rocked by massive demonstrations. "We had Arafat by the throat," they were saying. "He was bankrupt, discredited, at the end of the rope, and instead of finishing him off, you, Rabin, saved him!" After the famous handshake on the White House lawn, the demonization of Arafat took on eschatological qualities. He was Ameloch, the enemy of Israel. I recall seeing the bumper stickers and road signs tied to trees and shrubs and hanging from cliffs, ISRAEL B'SACANAH!—ISRAEL'S IN DANGER!

I spent the last few weeks in Jerusalem preparing for my upcoming sabbatical, and for Jamal's trip to England. Just as I was getting ready to leave, Jibril was preparing to return from exile. Already in Tunis, my partner in the Fatah Higher Committee was drawing up blueprints for a security force in liberated Palestinians areas. He preferred being in charge of security because he realized that it was where the real power lay.

Arafat was making his own plans—high-flying designs for himself and the country he assumed he would soon lead. No longer a pariah, he relished the cameras and the black limousine that took him from the presidential guesthouse to the White House—and more than anything the prospects of vast streams of foreign aid. The international community, delighted that the once-intractable conflict would soon be solved, pledged billions to finance Arafat's future Palestinian Authority, PA for short.

There was just one hitch. The donors were more than willing to assist in the creation of a viable Palestinian government. What they weren't about to do was hand the money directly over to Arafat and his cronies in the PLO. They pushed for the establishment of an independent and efficient development organization modeled on the fund created to rebuild Lebanon after its civil war. The World Bank, in deference to the donors, drew up statutes for the establishment of the Palestinian Economic Council for Development and Reconstruction (PECDAR). The World Bank asked the venerable Palestinian economist Yousef el-Sayegh to be at the helm.

Arafat wasn't at all happy about this. Mistrustful as always, and inclined to interpret everything in terms of raw power, he suspected that PECDAR was really an insidious scheme to usurp him. A deeper reason for his instinctive reaction was patronage. If the money didn't flow into his coffers, he would lose his ability to buy off possible challengers. He would not be able to continue his tried-and-true "management" style.

I got a good taste of Arafat's style of governance during the Madrid period. I was often in Tunis attending meetings of the PLO leadership, which often resembled rowdy boxing matches with fans howling from the bleachers. Members of one extremist faction or the other would scream at members of Fatah, hurling abuse at the peace process and issuing threats.

Afterward, there would be the inevitable line of people waiting to see Arafat before returning to their respective countries. What surprised me was that many of the people standing in front of his office were the very blustering extremists who had declared themselves hell-bent on recovering every square inch of Greater Palestine, from Tel Aviv to Petah Tikva, and that even to contemplate a two-state solution was to sell one's soul to the devil. Now these same people stood patiently outside the chairman's door.

When I asked Jibril what these people wanted with Arafat, he didn't mince words. (He never does.) "You want to know what these scum want?" he said, full of scorn. "To put their paws out for money, that's what the bastards are after." Arafat juggled the forces aligned against him by paying them off. If he didn't supply them with money, he feared someone else would. But Arafat had absolute contempt for them, and made sure they felt his disrespect. Jibril shared his contempt: "The shoe of a prisoner from the Occupied Territories," he would say, "is worth more than the lot of these pretenders put together."

Now with PECDAR, and the international largesse under someone else's control, how was he to keep his enemies in line? And if someone else controlled the money, would he be able to control the politics, too? Maybe a new juggler would emerge.

After much haggling with the World Bank, Arafat managed to keep PECDAR close to his sphere of influence. Yousef el-Sayegh walked out of a meeting never to return when he found that PECDAR wasn't going to be completely independent of Arafat's interference.

Now with el-Sayegh out of the picture, Arafat needed someone he could trust to run PECDAR—but who would also be acceptable to the World Bank. He thought I fit the bill and asked me to fly to Tunis to discuss a matter of "great national importance."

As he and I paced up and down the length of his office, Arafat explained to me the whole story of PECDAR and his worries. "These economists are saying that an economy has to be independent of politics. But how can it be? Politicians are the ones who control the economy. And if the professional economists control the purse strings, they're just politicians in disguise." We continued pacing, and I let him ramble on. "But what exactly are they hiding, these economists?" he muttered as if talking to himself. "Who is behind them? *Who's pulling the strings?*"

Arafat finally sat at his desk and stated that he wanted to level with me. "I trust you, Sari." He explained that Abu Ala would be the director of PECDAR. But Ala was still in Tunis, and PECDAR had to be set up in the Occupied Territories. It still wasn't clear when the PLO leadership would be able to return to Palestine, so in the meantime, Arafat needed someone to manage the billions pledged by donors. I was to be his man. He told me that he had no one else he could absolutely trust in that position.

I wasn't about to get drawn into Arafat's government, not with a year of freedom in America on my mind. I politely apologized and said that I couldn't accept the honor. Lucy's upcoming operation required my fullest attention. In the end, we agreed that I would go with Lucy to the States, but would attend PECDAR's board meetings in Washington until I got back.

. . .

I was exhilarated to be in Washington. For a decade I had been looking over my shoulder, slipping in and out of taxis to get away from Jacob and his men, fearing for my family, and worrying about Palestinian extremists. In America, I put my worry beads away and enjoyed knowing that no one was lurking in the shadows. It was liberating to be an anonymous nobody. Just a face. A fellow at an institute. A customer at a restaurant with some money in the bank for the first time in years.

Instead of my father's old law office in teeming, exhaust-filled East Jerusalem, my office in the Smithsonian looked out on gardens. On lunch breaks I visited ancient dinosaurs and stared up at the Wright Brothers' airplane.

Monticello was only a day trip. Lucy and I took the kids there to retrace our steps twenty years earlier—and to reconnect with the history of American democracy. With Clinton in power, America felt even stronger, more vibrant, and more tolerant than in the early 1970s.

I also had time to think. I was watching American football on television when it occurred to me how much Palestinian politics resembled the gridiron. It's thankless work to be a linebacker, and the guy with the ball also gets the most bruises. Best of all is to be the coach, and if you can't have his job, the next best thing is to be a TV commentator.

I thought I had laid PECDAR to rest but Arafat didn't give up. Days after I'd settled into my new life in America, he called me. After some small talk, he said he needed me to attend a meeting of PECDAR's board in Tunis.

I bought a round-trip ticket and went to the meeting. Once in Tunis, however, Arafat's game became more and more obvious. The meeting ended, and I wanted to go home, but he insisted I join him and his delegation for an important gathering in Oslo.

With Arafat, I always did what I wanted without giving him the impression that I was siding against him. (As the Islamic sage al-Farabi taught, sometimes it's best to keep a leader in the dark about your true intentions.) In this case, weaseling out of the meeting in Oslo didn't seem like a good idea. I boarded the private jet with him, and off we went. It was only after we were airborne that I found out we would be staying at the royal palace and that the meeting was in fact a state dinner hosted by King Harald V.

That night at the royal dinner I was on my best behavior. I wore a suit and tie, I combed my hair as best I could, and my mismatched socks were at least the same color. During the meal I managed to keep all the peas on my fork as I puzzled over Arafat's strategy. His assumption, I concluded, was that I would be so sucked in by the splendor of royalty in a fairy-tale castle that I would take over PECDAR if only for the occasional perks.

It was during dessert that I decided that by going to Oslo I had done my duty. I was now at liberty to do what I wanted, which was to get out of town. Later, after I retired to my gilded room, I picked up the phone and worked out a route back to Washington via Stockholm. I then ordered a taxi to pick me up in front of the palace at 5:00 a.m. The next morning, as Arafat slept, I absconded.

I was back in Washington less than twenty-four hours when the inevitable phone call came. "You took off," said the chairman. And then, he tossed in something I didn't need to be reminded of: "You are not like your father. *He* would never have done that! *Never.*"

The next time I heard from Arafat, I was still in America, and it came as an indirect message from his wife, Suha. Arafat was in Tunis readying his return to Gaza and trying to cobble together his first government. Suha rang me to let me know that her husband dearly wanted me to be a part. It was tough going for him because a lot of people were balking at the whole deal, worried about how the Palestinian people were going to accept a government of such limited autonomy. Arafat's choice of messenger was significant. He may have thought that Suha, a person I got along with quite well, would do a better job at winning me over.

What I came up with was deferential but also noncommittal. If his offer, I asked her to pass on, was being made as a gesture of confidence in and appreciation for my past work, then she was to let him know that from the bottom of my heart I was grateful for his confidence in me—but I'd still prefer to stay put. If, on the other hand, he needed me because no one else was stepping forward, then he could count on me.

As it turned out, within days Arafat had more potential ministers than he could use. The date for his return to Gaza was set, and he entered "liberated" Palestine as a hero and liberator. I watched the ticker-tape and firing guns from my apartment in suburban Maryland.

Just as I had planned, I reduced my political activities to the bare minimum. I attended the odd meeting in Washington with PECDAR delegates whenever they came, but, otherwise, I relished the freedom from public responsibility. I pushed a baby carriage with wide-eyed Nuzha around the wonderful park that began at the end of the street where we lived. When it snowed, Absal and Buraq took turns taking Nuzha down the hillside on a sled. In Washington, walking toward the Smithsonian along Independence Park, I often stopped dead in my tracks and marveled at my sheer happiness at being in America and doing what I was doing. I felt the stirrings once again of *Thaumazein*, the sense of wonder at life itself. Who could ask for more?

To follow the news back home I read *The Washington Post*—and as rarely as I could. The biggest news was a mixture of ancient Greek tragedy and modern action movie. The Greek playwright couldn't have picked a better spot for it: on ancient, hallowed ground replete with mythic associations. Nor could a Hollywood director have selected better means: an Uzi in the hands of a Brooklyn-born pediatrician.

In February 1994, Baruch Goldstein, living in the settlement of Kiryat Arba, outside Hebron, emptied his government-issue machine gun into a crowd of worshippers, dispatching twenty-nine Muslims during Friday prayers in the Cave of the Patriarchs, a Hebron site holy to both Muslims and Jews. In the riots that ensued, nineteen more died and hundreds were wounded. It was the bloodiest single day since occupation began in 1967.

The main cleric at the mosque in Hebron lashed out at the Oslo Agreement. "Our brothers are being massacred and our leaders are either asleep or negotiating with the Israelis."[1] Pictures of Arafat were burned throughout the West Bank. The local Hebronites greeted Faisal with stones when he tried to go to the scene. And in what was an evil portent for the future, Rabin, who personally loathed the settlers, decided to punish their victims. He slapped a curfew on the entire city of Hebron. His motive was probably blameless; he wanted to prevent reprisals. But by protecting the settlers instead of the Palestinians, he only emboldened the sworn enemies of the Oslo process and of his own government.

To make matters worse, Rabin pandered to the settlers by pumping billions of shekels into settlement defense and infrastructure. In all fairness, there are always people to buy off in Israel's fragmented parliamentary democracy, yet by building more settlements, Rabin was feeding the problem he needed to contain. A basic flaw in the Oslo Agreement began to surface. Since DOP, already being lampooned as DUPED, placed no obligatory freeze on settlement activity, Rabin had no compelling reason to confront his fanatics; it was more expedient to confiscate Palestinian land in order to build a bypass road for them.

The ancient Middle Eastern Moloch was slowly rousing from its slumber. In the wake of the Goldstein massacre, an Islamic student drove a car packed with three hundred pounds of TNT into a bus in the Israeli city of Afula, killing eight and wounding over fifty.

I had been in America for six months—I was working on a book in Arabic on the concept of freedom, at the Woodrow Wilson Institute—when a delegation from Al-Quds University in Jerusalem passed through Washington. One member of the delegation was Imad, who represented the Fatah employees' union at the university. Before 1948, Imad's family was one of the largest landowners in Palestine. His grandfather was a prince who owned five thousand acres of orchard land north of what is now Tel Aviv. In 1948, the Israelis showed up and sent the prince and his family packing. The land turned into a closed military area, and the forty-room mansion became a munitions factory. In the intifada days, Imad used to drop by my house with his colleagues for advice, where he impressed me with his intelligence and wily political instincts. He kept up his contact with me when I was working at the Orient House on the technical committees.

The delegation was now trying its hand at fund-raising for the poverty-stricken "university." I place "university" in quotes because the school was in fact a disconnected confederation of four separate colleges—a jumble of buildings, and a student body swarming with Hamas support-ers. As for its "administration," it had a coordinating council drawn from the boards of the four colleges. The original head of the coordinat-ing body was the mufti of Jerusalem, my father's friend, and the one who married Lucy and me. After he died, my father's youngest brother, a businessman, replaced him. The school's first president had just been appointed. He was Faisal's cousin Hatem, who had until recently been living in exile in the United States.

That was the extent of my knowledge about Al-Quds when Imad and his friends showed up at my door. After chatting for half an hour, Imad told me about the sour mood back home, but that he hoped that some-thing could still be done, especially at the university. When I asked him what he was talking about, he looked to his colleagues, who all nodded at him. Imad told me evasively that big changes were afoot at the univer-sity. A couple of weeks earlier I had been to Monticello, and Jefferson's academical academy flashed through my mind. I had to laugh at myself for making such a far-fetched connection. Imad then explained that Hatem had been diagnosed with cancer and would not stay at the job more than a couple of months.

Chapter Twenty-five

The Disappearance

I RETURNED FROM WASHINGTON in the summer of 1994, not long after Arafat and Rabin signed the Gaza-Jericho Accord in Cairo, and he and his fellow exiles began moving into the Occupied Territories.

On the way back, Lucy, the kids, and I stopped off for a few days in Cyprus. I must have had a premonition of what I was going back to because, sitting in a rental car in front of a pharmacy waiting for Lucy, I thought up the plot to a spy novel. I'd always liked the genre: the flash of the stiletto by moonlight, the smudged lipstick on the cup, the dusting of fingerprints. Thinking up plots—rather than being a victim of one—is even better than worry beads for fending off fear.

A thought came to me. *What would happen if I just vanished into thin air?* I imaged kidnappers sneaking up behind the car, thrusting their guns through the open window, and leading me off. By the time Lucy returned from the shop she would find only a smoking cigarette in the ashtray.

Later in the hotel room I sketched out the elements of the story.

My working title was *The Disappearance*. My main character is Samir Kanaan, whose father is a Palestinian Muslim and his mother a Jew. Samir studied Semitic languages at the American University of Beirut, where the PLO recruited him to work for one of its security agencies. Just before the Israeli invasion of Lebanon, he is sent back to the Occupied Territories to set up a network of resistance cells. Years later, during the intifada, he is randomly arrested by the Israelis and put in jail where he spends several years. With the coming of Oslo, he is released from prison.

With so many years behind bars, all Samir wants to do is to continue his studies. No politics, no espionage, no cloak-and-dagger adventures, no skullduggery. It is at this point that Jibril approaches him and tells him about his suspicion that an unholy conspiracy has been cooked up by Palestinian radicals and rogue forces within the Israeli security apparatus to wreck the peace process by unleashing a series of suicide bomb attacks against Israeli civilians. Desperate to trip up these plans, Jibril turns to Samir as the only one he can trust. The two shared a prison cell years earlier, and Jibril knows that Samir, a scholar and intellectual, has no political ambitions. The two devise a plan to scuttle the plot. Before they could execute it, however, the Israelis kidnap Samir while sitting in a rental car in front of a drugstore on the island of Cyprus.

The unwritten novel comes to mind because "disappearance" is also an accurate description of my public life between 1994 and 2000. I wasn't kidnapped, though according to some of my old activist friends, I might just as well have been. Leaving the active political fray was for me like slipping away from my parents' salon during their heated debates over the Suez War or the Cuban missile crisis. As a child I went into my room to play with sticks, and now, in my midforties, I was doing what I had been dreaming about since my first trip to the Shenandoah Valley: creating a university.

When I first arrived back in Jerusalem I initially thought I would run a research organization out of my father's old office on Salaheddin Street.

But no sooner had I returned than Imad paid me another visit. Hatem, the president of Al-Quds, had in the meantime passed away, leaving the institution, such as it was, rudderless. Imad repeated all the arguments he had used in Washington to convince me to take up the post.

Many of my friends from earlier days managed to persuade the university's board to consider me for the job. My uncle was now head of the board, and when he brought it up for a vote, only two members, both pro-Hamas, voted against me. I was offered the job.

I knew that it would take a Herculean effort, along with a lot of luck, to turn the place around, and I also knew the Hamas students, at 90 percent of the student body, would resist me at every turn. On the plus side, I relished the challenge. Had it been a straightforward administrative job, I wouldn't have taken it. But it also afforded me the opportunity to participate in our state-building efforts without being involved in politics. Memories of wandering around Jefferson's academical village once again came to mind. Could academic reform be a form of political activism? It may sound superstitious, but the American nickel, with its image of Monticello, had over the years become for me a talisman I liked to keep around, sometimes in my desk drawer, sometimes in my pocket. I started rubbing it more than ever now.

Without mentioning Jefferson's name, I alluded to his legacy during a conversation with Faisal's lawyer Jawad Boulos. We were in my father's law office sipping Turkish coffee when I told him I had accepted the position of head of Al-Quds. Jawad nearly fell over from shock. "What do you think you are doing?" he shouted. "You could do anything you want. You could be a minister in the government, or go back to Birzeit as a scholar. Why on earth would you want a job in a worthless institution where you can't be either a statesman or a proper academic?" He was flabbergasted that I would waste my time with such small potatoes. Everyone on the payroll—professors, cleaning ladies—added up to fewer than 120 people. "And the students! Don't forget what sort of people you've got up there!"

The way I responded got a laugh out of him. I was dying to pull out the nickel from my pocket but didn't dare because it would have convinced Jawad that I had finally gone over the deep end. "You're wrong, Jawad," I said simply. "Just watch. I can be both a scholar and a states-man." I poured him more coffee. "Any objections?"

I meant it, for I took the post only after a careful weighing of com-parative advantages. I added up all the factors—the bungling PA, the student body, and Israel's aggressive expansionism—and concluded that I'd be far more useful trying to revive a dying institution than fight-ing a losing bureaucratic battle within the PA.

Then came the unstated political agenda behind my comment to Jawad, which was intimately related to my earlier strategy of forming a shadow government. To an astonishing degree, Al-Quds was a micro-cosm of the many ills besetting Palestinian society. It was poor, shoddily run, and seething with religious fanaticism. If an effective modern admin-istration could turn Al-Quds around, on a national level such an ad-ministration could also dramatically improve the lives of the Palestinian masses, and eventually usher in political liberty. Al-Quds was my labo-ratory for my thesis about identity, liberty, and the will. The flipside of forging an identity and seizing liberty was to fight the forces aligned against the will. I vowed to prevent the Arab civilization I was raised to love from being squeezed out of my native city by Israeli actions, and there was no better way of doing this than building a fine university on a hill overlooking Jerusalem.

By January 1995 I was installed at Al-Quds. "Have fun!" my mother told me with a wry grin when I started. At least Jacob and the Shin Bet would leave me alone—or so she hoped.

The dream of an Arab university in Jerusalem goes back to the high-water mark of Arab nationalism. In 1922 the World Conference of Muslims responded to the Jewish dream for a Hebrew University in Jerusalem by proposing to create a competing Arab university, an effort tripped up by the British Mandatory Authority. In 1995 the Hebrew University had more than 20,000 students and 1,200 tenured faculty, while the Arab university existed more in name than in reality.

By taking on this project I was following a family tradition started by my father. As Jordanian minister of education in the early fifties, he had managed to extract a governmental decision to establish such a university. King Hussein had other plans, and he shelved Father's idea in favor of setting up Jordan's first university in Amman. Father tried again after 1967. Palestinians thought about building a university in the city, and Father backed the plan in spite of annexation, or rather *because* of annexation. Arabs had to stand their ground. But his opinion lost out to the boycott-minded nationalists in the National Guidance Committee, who argued that the university would come under Israeli control.

When Al-Quds finally got off the ground, it did so more as a legal technicality than by design. In the late seventies, four separate colleges began to spread out slowly from East Jerusalem to Ramallah, each one with different boards, academic heads, budgets, and purposes. One college was a squabbling Islamic theological institute; another a women's college housed in a building in front of the Orient House. (It was originally established for the orphans of Dir Yassin in 1948.) A nursing college was established in Ramallah. The largest of the four colleges—and the seed for the institution I was to build—was the science and technology school set up in Abu Dis with the support of Kuwaitis atop one of Jerusalem's hills near the old village center, about a fifteen-minute stroll from our apartment.

The four colleges entered into a nominal alliance in the early eighties. Each had applied separately to the Arab Federation of Universities for accreditation but were asked to apply under a single name, as if a single institution. A nominal unity was thus forged. Over the next ten years a coordinating board chaired by the mufti of Jerusalem was established from the four colleges to create actual unity.

Efforts at unifying the four colleges ran into the typical Middle Eastern sands of inertia. The coordinating board, later headed by my uncle, deriving respective powers from the four colleges it represented, controlled the entire operation.

On my first day on the job I wandered around the Abu Dis campus and wondered if I knew what I was getting myself into. This plot of earth was no sylvan Virginia. In Jerusalem, geography plays havoc on weather patterns. By the time the winter clouds reach the campus they have already lost most of their moisture, hence the barrenness. From the crest of the hill, I looked out over the sprawling settlement of Maʾaleh Adumim. Directly to the east were the desiccated canyons, redoubts of ancient prophets, leading down to the Dead Sea. In front of me was the backside of the Mount of Olives, and the Dome of the Rock.

I toured a few scattered buildings in the slapdash concrete style of the 1960s and '70s. The only ornaments I saw were the Hamas placards festooned to the few trees that managed to cling to life on the denuded, rocky hill.

My first glimpse into the inner workings of the institution was just as disheartening. The office of president had no independent budget and little authority, and no clear mandate from the board, because the only vision shared by its members was that Al-Quds would somehow hobble along without embarrassing them too much. To make matters worse, at the same time I was appointed, functionaries in the Ministry of Higher Education were floating around plans to attach the four colleges to other institutions, and do away with a university in Jerusalem altogether— which would have been simple, since Al-Quds didn't even exist on paper. As I now discovered, the school was a legal phantom, registered neither in the PA nor in Israel, and with no operational governing laws or bylaws.

The biggest hurdle I faced was money. Al-Quds didn't have a penny in its coffers. Tuition fees covered less than 30 percent of its running costs, with external subsidies to make up for the deficit. Two of its colleges were deep in debt.

Another formidable obstacle was the visceral opposition I encountered from many of the people I now had to work with. As mentioned, two board members were Hamas sympathizers; others supported me with what can only be called extreme ambivalence. With all the controversies littering my past, they were ready to pull the plug at a moment's notice.

The university staff was far more solidly behind me. Most were aligned with Fatah. I also had a number of old friends on the faculty and involved with the union.

The student body was another story. To quote Kant, it was a crooked piece of timber that I now had to straighten out. These students embodied the radical ideological break between my generation and that of the students. Bearded fanatics, energized by the spirit of Hamas, allowed for no intellectual freedom, and those who tried to introduce some found themselves under constant harassment. People were terrified to speak their minds freely. It was a daunting prospect to reform an institution dominated by a political-religious movement systematically throwing shackles on the mind.

I traced the source of the disease to a tradition of learning that embodied everything wrong with Palestinian education. Some of these ills I'd seen for years at Birzeit, but never in such a concentrated fashion or without a strong counterforce.

The four colleges operated more like technical schools, without a humanities program and hence without the freedom of ideas that tend to break up ossified thinking. Rote learning was the norm at Al-Quds, a parrotlike repetition of facts closely aligned with social conformity. Students for the most part reproduced existing social norms, thus merely adding more conformists to a social system already resistant to change and criticism.

I spent the first three months studying the institution and preparing a plan for its development. Administrative changes, a solid team of supporters, and budgetary strategies were the necessary steps for turning the place around.

First and foremost, the loose federation of colleges had to give way to a strong single leadership with enough authority to streamline academic, administrative, and financial procedures; find new sources of funding; and introduce new programs. There had to be a single line of authority with a single strategy.

Working together with my team, we came up with an elegant plan to achieve our two goals. The university would never get out of its financial hole as long as tuition covered only 30 percent of the operating budget. On paper, our calculations predicted that we could derive more than 80 percent of our running costs from tuition and new research, thus decreasing our reliance on unstable external assistance. To increase our relative income from tuition required increasing the number of students, which in turn meant offering more programs, and this required more faculty and staff. The goal of building a real university went hand in glove with creating a budget to finance it. In what seemed to skeptics like a variation on the Ponzi scheme or Reaganomics, we wanted to grow our way out of a chronic deficit.

My uncle and his fellow board members were all scratching their heads when I tried to show them with graphs and numbers, extending several years into the future, how income and expenditure lines would eventually meet. They went along, I think, because it struck them as the work of a good-natured dreamer, a scheme by the local Don Quixote who should be humored but not taken too seriously.

This mild tolerance for my plan began to turn into growing hostility the minute I shifted from blueprint to action. All the board members could see once I set to work was a frighteningly escalating debt they felt they would personally have to answer for, whether financially or legally.

Faculty members also began having their doubts, and for perfectly understandable reasons. The hitch in my plan was the absence of any funds to cover the initial expenditures, especially in salaries. We had no other option but the hard one of tightening our belts. Salaried staff couldn't quite come to terms with a policy that cut into their monthly checks (at one point we were five months in arrears) at the same time that I was hiring new faculty and employees left and right. The graphs and charts I was always ready to break out at faculty and union meetings were cold comfort. When staff balked, as they often did, I reminded the members of my team that the mind cannot listen to reason when the stomach is hungry.

A balanced budget would mean nothing, however, without a vision of education. I vowed that under my watch, our primary and driving ambition would be to churn out critical minds. In one of the early policy statements my team and I put out, our task as we saw it was to promote logical humanistic thinking that enabled people to develop strategies to solve problems, both intellectual and political. It was to educate men *and women* for leadership, peace, and democratic values. This idea went back to my work at the union and the various committees: our liberation won't come through the barrels of Kalashnikovs or from waving flags. It'll have to come from ourselves. Nothing could be more inimical to the dictatorship of the dogmatists than this.

From my operation up on the dusty hill, I followed political developments down below. Between 1995 and 2000, I adopted the stance of an engaged—sometimes bemused but mostly anguished—spectator. If I was rubbing my American nickel in one hand, I had my worry beads in the other.

It was quite amazing to see how what once would have meant jail time—such as flying a flag or carrying a weapon, as Jibril and his people did—now became routine. There were flags galore, and suddenly plenty of guns. The PLO people who returned from exile included young leaders (the so-called "insiders") such as Marwan and Jibril, who had been tossed out a few years earlier, but mostly aging revolutionaries who hadn't seen the West Bank since 1967, some since 1948. These "outsiders" were a mixture of genuine idealists and revolutionaries, as well as a few malevolent thugs.

The regime they set up confirmed all the fears I had had before I left for Washington. Politically, the center of gravity shifted suddenly from the intifada activists on the "inside" to returning PLO functionaries, and geographically from East Jerusalem to Gaza and the West Bank, where the "outsiders" now lived. Needless to say, the bulk of the ministers were "outsiders," whereas their undersecretaries were, by and large, competent local people, many of whom had worked in the technical committees and hence had two years of preparatory work behind them. With elaborate studies and finely honed working papers in hand, they were ready to move quickly to build up competent ministries.

Unfortunately, they faced the reality of working with the returning apparatchiks. The new ministers, dazzled by the trappings of power—the cars, the adulation—had little inclination to study reports or listen to local underlings. Ignoring the multiple volumes already on their desks, our potentates preferred commissioning new reports, which is after all what ministers do. One favorite pastime of many ministers was to gather around Arafat's desk in Gaza, watching him conduct business and waiting to get their instructions directly from the Old Man. Some ministers, who behaved like demigods to the people under them, journeyed to Arafat to get his permission to hire an office secretary. No wonder that by far the most effective Palestinian institution was also the most independent: PECDAR, run by Abu Ala.

Rounding out the Palestinian political scene I so assiduously steered clear of, the Fatah Higher Committee, which with the coming of the PA was no longer a secret organization, became a magnet for aspiring politicians. Just as Jibril and I had planned, it represented the local Fatah power base, and as such, the man who emerged as its driving force, Marwan, was initially, after Arafat, the second most popular politician in the country; soon he'd be number one. The committee grew from fifteen members to more than seventy. Those who had helped found it, such as Jibril, Dahlan, and Sameer, belonged to it, as did representatives from the various regions. Even Central Committee members jockeyed to join.

Jibril and I continued to see eye to eye. (About Hamas and education, for instance, he said, "No one has a right to dictate their crazy vision to our children.") Back in Palestine, Jibril appointed himself head of West Bank security. No one offered him the job: not Arafat, the Americans, or the Israelis. He just thought up the idea and realized it. He sought and recruited only local Fatah people, mostly former colleagues from his prison camp days. Over time he built up a force of five thousand men in arms. Dahlan created a parallel force in Gaza.

Arafat went along but, never a man to put all his eggs in one basket, especially when it came to matters of physical power, he got American backing to set up other security forces, heavily composed of returning "outsiders."

Faisal wasn't part of the government because Jerusalem was bracketed out until final negotiations. He focused on Jerusalem. The Orient House, once the headquarters of the local national leadership, acted as an unofficial East Jerusalem municipality. And Faisal had his hands full countering an outbreak of home demolitions, land confiscations, and the nefarious policy of stripping people of their residence permits.

The most significant development I observed from my perch on the hill was the strangulation of Jerusalem. With our inexperienced administrators generally mismanaging the PA, our government was more or less incapable of figuring out and then countering the Israeli government's very determined, sober-minded plans. Chomsky had been right: the Oslo Agreement did not slow down the Israelis; if anything, it speeded them up. The thing that stood out most nakedly was the violence. Extremists on both sides, some using bombs and others Caterpillar tractors, soon undermined all the hopes raised by the Clinton-Arafat-Rabin handshake on the White House lawn.

The settlements that Oslo had failed to address were growing faster than ever. The slow takeover of the Goldsmith's Souk, to give an example close to home, continued apace. Meanwhile, Cousin Zaki riffled through crumbling four-hundred-year-old Ottoman records to prove our family's ownership. He came across so many documents on the history of Jews in Jerusalem that he decided to write a book on the subject. One of his findings came to him as a revelation. According to some of the Geniza records unearthed in an old Cairo synagogue, Jews had in fact welcomed Caliph Omar's entry into Jerusalem, because it brought an end to the centuries-old Byzantine ban on Jews entering the city.

Ironically, just as Cousin Zaki was breathing in centuries-old dust to reconstruct the surprisingly harmonic relationship between Muslims and Jews in Jerusalem, the battle for the city was really only beginning. As we had feared during the Madrid negotiations, the Israelis moved quickly to create facts on the ground, changing the geographical and demographic realities to fit the Israeli slogan of Jerusalem as their "eternal and undivided capital."

I got my first hint of this soon after I began my work at the university, when a friend (from my "troubadour" days) told me about an experience he likened to Gregor Samsa's in Kafka's *The Metamorphosis*. In Kafka's novella Gregor wakes up one morning to find that he has been transformed overnight into a cockroach. In the case of my friend, already a cockroach according to General Eitan's telling imagery, he woke up to find himself metamorphosed into an alien. My friend, like me from ancient Jerusalem stock, had lost his rights to live in his native city.

It was actually the second time he had undergone an involuntary change in his legal status. He had been given an Israeli residence permit when Israel annexed East Jerusalem in 1967. Like him and everyone else in East Jerusalem—my father, my mother, me—it was as if he had "moved" to the city and been granted, out of the munificence of the administration, a green card. Of course, he hadn't "moved" anywhere; it was Israel that had conquered his neighborhood. Regardless of how many strata of ancestors he had buried outside Suleiman the Magnificent's walls, his presence in Jerusalem was thus transformed, in the blink of an eye or one quick movement of a bureaucrat's pen, from a birthright anchored in tradition and common sense to a revocable privilege conferred upon a foreigner.

With the establishment of Arafat's PA and the territorial "autonomy" it brought, many Arabs who lived in East Jerusalem, but outside the municipal border as defined by the Israelis, were beginning to lose their residency rights. In my friend's case, before he went to bed, he was a resident in his native city; upon waking up, he discovered that he was a tourist and could be expelled at any time.

His fate, as well as the stories we were hearing from other people, got Lucy and me thinking. Now, just residing across the municipal border as defined by Israel could lose you your residence rights. In Abu Dis, only one wall of our home was within the Jerusalem municipal borders; the other three were in the West Bank. We slept in the West Bank and had breakfast in Jerusalem. Straddled as we were between the West Bank and Jerusalem, the Israelis could claim that we didn't actually live in Jerusalem. This was another of my paranoid "prophesies" that several years later proved deplorably prescient.

Lucy and I made the hard decision to move from our hillside view of the Dome of the Rock to the suburban neighborhood of Beit Hanina. What our new two-story house lacked in dramatic view it made up for in safety. The neighborhood was unambiguously within the Jerusalem municipal borders, which meant that the Israelis couldn't strip us of our citizen rights in Jerusalem.

The spread of settlements both precipitated and followed Palestinian terrorism. History began playing this lethal dialectical game before Rabin, Peres, and Arafat picked up their Nobel Peace Prize in December 1994. Peres was preaching his slogan of the "new Middle East" in October when Hamas blew up a Tel Aviv bus, killing twenty-two civilians. Rabin's response—roadblocks and closures—strangled the local Gaza economy. Living standards dropped by a quarter, and unemployment shot up to nearly 60 percent. As the economy began tanking, so, too, did support for Oslo. Hamas, whose terror had triggered the economic downward spiral in the first place, benefited because of the network of social services it ran. The PA's woefully ineffectual government had nothing comparable.

In January 1995, a month after the Nobel ceremony, Rabin promised Arafat to halt new settlements and to confiscate Arab land only for roads. Three days later came another terrorist attack, and Israel suspended negotiations. Three days after that—less than a week after Rabin made his promise to Arafat—the Israeli cabinet approved building an additional 2,200 housing units in the West Bank.

And so it went. That summer Hamas bombed two more Israeli buses, while the Rabin-Peres government adopted the "Greater Jerusalem" master plan, which included more construction on an outer ring of Israeli settlements extending deep into the West Bank.[1]

Rabin made additional plans (recently taken out of cold storage by Prime Minister Sharon) to immortalize the Israeli grip on the West Bank by unilaterally drawing a permanent border between Jerusalem and the West Bank. The plan called for thousands of homes and an industrial and commercial zone between Maʾaleh Adumim and the northern neighborhoods of Jerusalem. The idea behind linking up Maʾaleh Adumim with Jerusalem was to split the West Bank in two chunks and turn Arab neighborhoods and villages of Jerusalem into isolated islands.

I saw all this happen in Beit Hanina, our new neighborhood. Over the years since the Six-Day War, the Jerusalem municipality had confiscated much of the agricultural land in Beit Hanina using the customary white-collar chicanery of zoning it "open" land, thus preventing people from building on it or using it. Now the Israelis had declared the land "derelict and/or abandoned," and confiscated it using an old Ottoman-era law that deems such land property of the state. One morning on the way to work I saw earthmoving equipment, which would expand the Jewish settlement of Pisgat Zeʾev.

No one in Israel was listening to Palestinian protests because Hamas terror was creating a frenzied atmosphere in Israel that people likened to civil war. Tens of thousands of anti-Oslo protesters crowded the squares in Jerusalem. Neither Rabin's legacy as the "bone-breaker" nor the dizzying sums he spent on settlement "security" and expansion lessened their loathing for him and his peace plan. Palestinian terror and Israeli hostility to Oslo went hand in hand. The conspiracy at the heart of my spy thriller was looking terrifyingly on the mark. In one demonstration, headed by Sharon at Zion Square, in downtown West Jerusalem, protesters held up signs of Rabin dressed up as an SS officer. Sharon denounced the Oslo Agreement as an act of treason.

In October, one of Rabin's Jewish opponents murdered him. The setting was as well choreographed as the Hebron massacre: in front of more than a hundred thousand people at a peace rally in Tel Aviv. I recall watching the images on television. Rabin was onstage while the crowd sang a Hebrew peace song of searing beauty. Television images showed him at first mumbling the words awkwardly, then gradually more forcibly, until Rabin sang with a determined pitch. Yigal Amir, with his government-issue pistol, waited until he left the stage before gunning him down.

I was reminded of the reasons for my "disappearance" recently while reading *The Missing Peace*, Dennis Ross's eight-hundred-page history of the Oslo peace process. The book's broad sweep and the author's grasp of details make it a riveting read. Ross's painstaking account of the entire fiasco also left me so despondent at times that I needed a bottle of aspirin just to get through it. The 150 pages on the negotiations surrounding the Wye Agreement rekindled memories of the "Bibi" years and how his bulldozers were working away in the West Bank night and day. Just thinking about it can make a sane man desperate.

I had no role in any of the talks that preoccupied Ross and the two negotiation teams. President Clinton himself invested hundreds of hours of personal effort in trying to bring the Israelis and Palestinians together. And yet Ross's eyewitness account leaves the impression that the more effort the various protagonists invested, the worse the situation became.

After Shimon Peres became prime minister the suicide bombings started up again. With each new attack, Peres's efforts to cling to power faded. The famous "letter" he had given Arafat at the signing of Oslo, which promised that Palestinian institutions would be allowed to develop and expand, was now worth less than the ink it was written with. ("In the courtroom I can't cash in the letter on behalf of your university," my Israeli lawyer later told me when I referred to it in a legal battle to prevent the government from shutting down Al-Quds.) Peres picked up the pace of settlement construction.

· · ·

All this took place as Israeli flags were coming down from police stations and a few checkpoints. By December 1995, the Palestinian Authority had assumed control over the major towns in the West Bank. This set the stage for Palestinian legislative and presidential elections, which in theory were meant to increase people's involvement in governing their own lives. In fact, the precise opposite happened, for the minute that elections were over, people retreated to a pre-intifada passivity. Many questioned, and for good reason, whether they even had a government. It may have stroked the collective ego to think they did, but while the Palestinian flag was flying high, our land, resources, and basic liberties were being nibbled away. Under the surface, pressure was building, and judging by the chatter in the cafés and on the street, some kind of explosion seemed more and more imminent.

By the time Israeli elections rolled around in May 1996, Hamas had murdered enough Israeli civilians to sweep Bibi Netanyahu to power. Until Labor returned to power three years later, the two sides circled each other like wary combatants out to exploit every sign of weakness. Eventually the Israeli right found a way to embrace Oslo and the inevitable logic of a Palestinian state by redefining the kind of state it would be. It would have little territory, no control over its borders, no capital, or at least not one in Jerusalem, and no economic viability. According to one Likud politician, "Well, they want to call it a state? Fine, they can call it fried chicken if they want to."

This was the point in Ross's book that required the most aspirin, because I had to relive the death of Oslo and all the hopes it had raised. The grueling eight-day Wye negotiations are a good metaphor for this entire period. Sharon—the new minister of infrastructure and a man many Palestinians and Israelis saw as complicit in atrocities against civilians in his role as commander of the infamous Unit 101 in the 1950s, and later as defense minister—greeted his fellow Palestinian negotiators, many of whom had Ph.D.s, as "a gang of thugs." At Wye, Palestinians got some more land, an airport, and a harbor. In order to get the

Israelis to release more prisoners, the Americans gave them their tacit okay to build Har Homa (Jebal Abu Ghnaim in Arabic), a new settlement cutting Jerusalem off from Bethlehem. A few years later most of the released prisoners would either be killed or rearrested, while Har Homa was bustling with settlers.

In 1997 Ehud Olmert supported the American millionaire Irving Moskowitz who used money from a bingo parlor to build a Jewish neighborhood in Ras al-Amud, an Arab neighborhood east of the Old City. Meanwhile, Sharon told West Bank settlers, "Everyone living there should move, should run, should grab more hills, expand the territory. Everything that's grabbed will be in our hands, everything that we don't grab, will be in their hands."[2]

While settlers were flooding into the West Bank, a series of fortified roadblocks tightened the noose around Jerusalem by choking off access to Palestinians from the West Bank. Only those with hard-to-get special permits were allowed to pass the checkpoints. Needless to say, settlers zoomed past without question. Palestinians who had worked in Jerusalem found themselves jobless, and students, patients, and worshippers couldn't get to schools, hospitals, or religious sites.

The Israeli government, declaring at every opportunity that Arab East Jerusalem was theirs forever, used an effective mix of legal tricks and heavily armed troops from the border police to close down one Palestinian organization after the next. New regulations were introduced, or old ones suddenly enforced, to control the institutions they couldn't legally drive out. Under the canard of "security," now easier than ever for Israel to get away with thanks to Hamas, the tightening of the military state of siege on East Jerusalem dramatically throttled free movement between the southern and northern parts of the West Bank. Ami Ayalon, the new head of the Shin Bet and my future partner in peace, began to warn Israeli politicians of a cataclysmic explosion if settlement expansion was not stopped.

Chapter Twenty-six

Porcupines and Roosters

I HAD FEW DEALINGS with the Palestinian Authority in these years. There was the occasional meeting with Arafat, and we generally stayed on good terms. I could almost always count on his support for the university. When asked, he backed up a request to the Saudis to finance the building of a medical school, and one to the Japanese to equip it.

This doesn't mean that he had forgotten the way I had skipped out on him in Oslo, but we managed to strike an unspoken compromise: I avoided taking up a post in his government, while he informally kept me a part of it. At one point he made me a member of a creature he called his "Jerusalem ministerial committee." Like so many committees, we didn't go far beyond informal chats. To help Jibril out, I also agreed to head up the Preventive Security Academy in Jericho.

On another occasion, Arafat asked me to lead a delegation to the United States. He wanted us to drum up support from American Jews and to persuade them to pressure the American administration to release funds for the PLO. We met with Jewish leaders and the U.S. Council on Foreign Relations.

My only other major foray into PA politics came about for reasons related to our delegation's meager success: corruption. Arafat and his authority were barely limping along, though with the PLO in the saddle, Ramallah experienced a building boom. The city boasted new martini bars and a Mercedes dealership. The best legal expression of economic normalization between Palestinians and Israelis was a new casino not far from our police academy in Jericho. Until it was shot up by tank fire during the so-called "Al-Aqsa intifada," on a typical Sabbath the parking lot was packed with Israelis' cars. But the man on the street never drank martinis and never gambled. Living standards for him continued to plummet, and the civil service that on paper was supposed to improve the lot of the masses only made things worse. A study by the International Monetary Fund's Middle Eastern Department found that the unemployment rate among Palestinians in 1997 was 30 percent, double what it had been in 1993. Per capita income dropped by 20 percent.[1]

Just as serious for the man on the street was the reputation the PA was gaining as just another version of a sleazy Arab kleptocracy. Corruption charges were now cropping up with depressing regularity. After decades of preaching boycotts, many members of the PA were lining up to make deals with the Israelis and getting rich, while those who had earlier refused to cooperate with Israel out of principle and fidelity to the "cause" found themselves left out in the cold.

In 1996, I saw up close how corruption operated. I was on the board of trustees of the Vocational Training Institute, an organization set up to aid people injured during the intifada. We named the mufti of Jerusalem's cousin to be the director. When we later suspected him of pocketing sixty thousand dollars we confronted him, but he denied it and, what's more, refused to vacate his post. We were about to force him out when he went to the mufti, who defended his nephew to Arafat. Arafat, who took what the mufti told him at face value, wrote a letter to the director offering him protection. The first thing the director did was come to me with a triumphant grin and throw the letter in my face. I threw it back in his.

The corruption debate exploded into the open when the public comptroller, Arafat's cousin, published the first financial report on the operations of the Palestinian Authority. According to the report, someone in the PA was raking in money. The auditor determined that $326 million, or 43 percent of the entire Palestinian Authority budget, had been squandered through a blend of corruption and poor management. Another shocking fact was that only ten cents out of every dollar in the budget was going for education, health, and social welfare. Arafat's Office of the President got more, and the security services ate up over a third.

Far more worrying for Chairman Arafat than public opinion was the international outcry—because his PA was largely propped up by outside financial support and he feared the gravy train could end. The U.S. senator Phil Gramm asked Ambassador Martin Indyk about the report in the Senate Foreign Relations Committee. David Hirst, an intrepid correspondent for *The Guardian*, lashed out at Arafat for having "thrown up a ramshackle, nepotistic edifice of monopoly, racketeering and naked extortion, which merely enriches them as it further impoverishes the society at large."[2]

The report sparked an unruly debate in the Palestinian Legislative Council. Arafat, always on the lookout for conspiracies ranged against him, detected collusion between the United States and some people in the PA to oust him. In his instinctive zero-sum thinking, which allowed for no neutral power such as public opinion, popular umbrage at corruption had to have been incited by somebody.

On hand to broadcast this first explosion of democratic dissent within the PA, and on live TV no less, was Daoud Kuttab, the director of Al-Quds University's newly established television station. Kuttab, the journalist who had been convinced during the intifada that the people in the Unified Command were living in caves, came to me one day and laid out his vision for an independent station that would be neither a government propaganda tool nor a station putting out toothpaste commercials and dubbed American sitcoms. His idea was a national educational television network along the lines of PBS and CSPAN. Television, I thought, could be an "al-Farabi" moment—a way to influence politics indirectly. I agreed on the condition that the station diversify its offerings with children's programs, women affairs, and open debates on liberty and individual rights.

I pledged to Kuttab whatever university funds I could scrape together. We got George Soros's Open Society Foundation and the Ford Foundation to pitch in enough funding for a forty-watt transmitter. Naturally, we asked for and got from the Israeli and Palestinian authorities no licenses and no permission; and we invited no officials to cut ribbons. Abu Ala, who besides running PECDAR was chairman of the Legislative Council, gave us a tacit nod. In 1997 we just flipped a switch. The first test broadcast showed a goldfish swimming in a fishbowl to Beethoven's *Eroica*, which Beethoven dedicated to Napoleon before the emperor turned into a despot.

No one in the PA cared that we were operating without a license until Kuttab had the temerity to give the Palestinian masses a real-time glimpse into the unseemly details of PA governance. Since Kuttab had gotten Abu Ala's backing to broadcast the debate, Arafat at first suspected Abu Ala of having masterminded the entire corruption conspiracy.

Arafat got one of his security agencies to put an end to the broadcast. Like despotic governments worldwide, his people jammed the signals, and instead of a furious back-and-forth between legislators, all viewers got— I watched the debate from home—was a black rectangle. Kuttab responded defiantly by handing out cassettes to other stations so they could broadcast the debates.

When the jamming didn't work, Arafat gave the order to lock Kuttab up. With Jibril's help, I managed to persuade Arafat that Kuttab wasn't part of a plot but was carrying out important work for a democratic and open society. He was released after a week.

Following the Legislative Council debate, the council decided to set up a committee to investigate the findings of the comptroller and to come up with recommendations. Some other human rights organizations started their own investigations. Not to be outdone, Arafat established his own official investigative body, which was to report its findings only to him.

As a testament to his labyrinthine mind, Arafat asked Tayyib Abd al-Rahim, the head of his cabinet, to bring together five credible people to investigate the findings of the damning financial report. One was a Palestinian judge working in Dubai, another a member of the Executive Committee of the PLO, and three were local academics, including me. When we were first sworn in, Arafat put the entire PA at our disposal. We could call in anyone for questioning, from ministers to messenger boys. Tayyib then narrowed our mandate by putting the security agencies off limits. The first report hadn't touched on these areas, nor should we.

We swung into action. For three months we conducted hundreds of hours of interviews and meetings, mostly at Arafat's offices in Gaza. A secretary in Tayyib's office took down the minutes. But I kept my own notes. What we were digging up was so sensitive and bone-chilling I wanted to make sure I had my own records, if only to use as material for a future spy novel or murder mystery. In the end, all of us on the committee made copies of the final report for ourselves. We felt that the very least we could do was keep a record for history.

Gradually the general picture we came up with of mismanagement and corruption led us back to one of the places we weren't supposed to look: security. None of my previous dealings with the PA or even with the Israeli government could have prepared me for the levels of cynicism we uncovered. We discovered how power and greed had combined to undermine the world that most of us recognized as our own. The people guiltiest of corruption had no national loyalties, in fact no loyalties at all except to themselves. And they were willing to do anything and betray anyone to pile up riches.

The chairman personally came out clean. Arafat lived a monkish existence with few material needs. He never pocketed anything for himself and was personally far less corrupt than most autocrats, or CEOs for that matter.

His fault lay in his old habit of juggling people and cash, now paying someone off, now turning a blind eye to malfeasance. His management style, if you can call it that, had led to a total absence of organizational structures and budgetary plans, and of standardized rules governing the financial operations of various departments in the civil service. There was no streamlining of financial operations and no way to keep a tab on spending. Employees in the ministries were striking all sorts of deals, minor and major, on behalf of their ministries, with the inevitable bane of "personal commissions" taking priority over cost and efficiency.

The shady deals were so numerous that it would be impossible to catalog them here. A couple of examples will have to suffice. One instance of comparatively petty corruption was the informal car dealership that returnees from Tunis operated together with local cronies. The returnees exploited their tax-exempt status as government officials to import fleets of cars, and then made a killing by selling them at a steep discount.

A particularly appalling example related to the PA's monopoly over basic commodities such as gasoline. As we discovered, such goods were being brought into the Palestinian areas using Israeli ex-security officers as the middlemen. These officers were now on good terms with some of Arafat's closest aides: one Israeli was a man complicit in the execution of the two Palestinian hijackers of Bus 300 in 1984—a perverse twist if there ever was one on the theme of normalization between Palestinians and Israelis.[3] Together, they smuggled raw materials in and out of Palestinian areas, thus avoiding taxation on both ends. In the case of gasoline, Israeli tankers protected by Palestinian security men delivered gasoline to local stations, and because of the state monopoly, the owners had no choice but to pay steeply inflated prices.

Such racketeering forced the man on the street to pay higher prices, and it denied the government legitimate income. Security officials made millions, and their garish villas soon popped up next to squalid refugee camps. Meanwhile, fortunes were flowing into secret Arafat-controlled accounts.

As we gathered information piece by piece, we came to the conclusion, duly confirmed by Tayyib, that Arafat was aware of every case of corruption. He received and read every report and complaint that landed on his desk. Why, we asked, had he not put an end to it?

Arafat had an amazing faculty for picking out and remembering details. He could look at a disassembled puzzle and recall where each piece was on the table. What he lacked was the power to put the details together and see the pattern. In the case of corruption, he didn't see how the rot was undermining his ability to govern and to build up a state. Arafat couldn't make the link between his mismanagement and how a sense of despair was building among his people, despair at the hollow promises of liberation and of a better, more dignified life.

Our final three-hundred-page report emphasized the need to institute standard operating procedures and to require ministries to have in place organizational structures and plans. We gave ample examples of how the absence of these had led to waste, mismanagement, and the misappropriation of funds. The report suggested that the public prosecutor indict twenty top officials for embezzlement as a lesson to others.

The fact that only Arafat was to receive a copy of our report made many people nervous. As our work drew to a close and we were writing up our findings, committee members began to come under pressure. Two received threatening phone calls in the middle of the night. On the day we handed over the report, three committee members, al-Tayyib among them, sensibly made arrangements for extended vacations abroad.

The notoriously sloppy Arafat suddenly took on some features of a Prussian ruler: he expected our report on a certain day at noon, and not a minute later. After three months of hard work we finished the report with fifteen minutes to spare, or so we thought. Flipping through it for the last time, Tayyib spotted a major printing error. He threw his glasses to the table in utter despair. "We can't give it to the chairman like this," he groaned, on the verge of tears. Calmly, I took the report, made the necessary changes in the text, and handed it to the secretary, who quickly reprinted the page and collated the report once more. We were in the president's office at precisely noon, and handed over the report to a beaming Arafat.

Arafat took it, said thanks, have a good day, and did nothing. No one was brought to trial, and the chieftains continued in their ways.

Meanwhile, we were making progress at the university. I didn't think about it much at the time—working eighteen hours a day has a way of dominating the mind—but the university was shaping up as a model for turning a backward society around.

We set up our administrative office just up the block from Mother's house, in a British Mandate–era building in the lovely style of that age, next to the Rockefeller Museum of antiquities. From the top floor we had a panoramic view of the Mount of Olives and the walls of the Old City. In contrast with the lavatory at the Orient House, my office was roomy enough to accommodate a table for meetings.

Changes in the curriculum were slowly beginning to bear some fruit. In 1997, two years after taking over, wandering around campus I felt the stirrings of an intellectual community among students and teachers, as well as the budding signs of a new culture of freedom of thought.

All students, whether aspiring engineers or nurses, or thick-bearded theologians, were required to take classes designed to pry open their minds and erode religious and political prejudice. One class was on human civilization. Another required course was simply called "On Thinking." The inspiration was the Greek spirit of inquiry, the spirit that had animated the best of early Islamic thought—its openness to all that is human, and cold hostility against blinkered fanaticism. If I could have chiseled onto stone a motto for the class, it would have been: if people use their minds and wills they can accomplish whatever they choose, including political liberty.

To combat the evils of rote learning, we introduced a seminar approach to teaching that fostered dialogue, open debate, and respect for opposing opinions. Students were taught the skills of finding, preparing, and defending ideas. There was also a social dimension, as much of this was done as teamwork. The image of the lone scholar laboring away was not what I had in mind. The idea was to promote logical, systematic, strategic thinking in a social, collaborative framework.

New departments began springing up. The nursing school morphed into a medical school. For years people at the established universities such as Birzeit had been planning to set up a medical school. They're not cheap to build and, as already mentioned, thanks to Arafat's help we got Saudi and Japanese money to built and equip one. A business school was soon up and running, and a law school, too. In 1998 we created the Center for the Advancement of Peace and Democracy, named after Issam Sartawi, who was assassinated in a Lisbon hotel lobby in 1983 by Palestinian militants opposed to his willingness to engage in dialogue with the Israelis. That we managed to open this center without a student uprising was a sign that we were heading in the right direction.

From the moment I took over the university, I was determined to create a department of the humanities. Initially classes were held in cramped quarters in the engineering building. We eventually found a new home for the faculty after I drove past a large, derelict structure in my neighborhood of Beit Hanina. It was on a plot of land that had long ago been donated by the people of the village for educational purposes. I got out of my car and, looking through a broken window, thought it would be ideal for our humanities program. I asked around and discovered that for years it had been used for Muslim religious education, only to be abandoned after infighting between various factions. The last straw came when students beat up the dean.

We took it over—without asking anyone—renovated it with some money from PECDAR, hung up a sign, and opened it up for classes. It happened so quickly that no one stopped us.

My eye next turned to the Old City. Partly inspired by painful memories of the Lemon Tree Café, partly by the political urgency to resist Israeli efforts to extinguish our cultural life within the walls of the city, I began to wander the streets looking for a building to house a new institute. As I envisioned it, the Institute for Jerusalem Studies, as we eventually called it, would counter the parochial ethnic prejudices at work distorting Arab Jerusalem's heritage of cultural tolerance through what I called in an article the "selfish contention between two ethno-centric tribes."[4]

I wanted a place where scholars, writers, filmmakers, archaeologists, and historians from all around the world could study the civilizations that were piled up layer upon layer under their feet. Foreign scholars, even Israelis, could help Palestinians tell the pluralistic history of Palestine and its civilizations, its peoples and its archaeology, as well as gain a better appreciation of the Abrahamic religion, the source of Judaism, Christianity, and Islam. The mission statement we later designed is as follows:

> Because of Jerusalem's unique constitution as a mosaic crossroad of different nations, cultures, and religions, special emphasis is laid on introducing students especially, but the university community as a whole, to the multicultured heritage of human civilization . . . The student is thus encouraged to develop a worldly outlook, an appreciation of and tolerance for the other, and a humanist moral code.

I found the perfect location down the street from the old Lemon Tree. It was another badly dilapidated compound at the entrance to the Souk el-Qattanin (Cotton Merchants' Market), this one dating back to the Mamluk period. Sultan Saif ed-Din Tankaz ordered it built after his visit in 1327. Symbolically you couldn't conjure up a better place to study Jerusalem's multilayered heritage, with the compound sitting as it does between the Noble Sanctuary, the Western Wall, and the Via Dolorosa. Just by standing in the medieval bathhouse built into the compound, or in one of the small cells on the roof used by visiting Muslim writers over the ages, you feel the sheer accumulation and diversity of humanity over millennia.

At the time, I was also making plans for another center that at first glance runs directly counter to the pluralistic humanism of the Jerusalem project. Fahed Abu al-Haj, my friend who had had information

410 *Once Upon a Country*

410 *Once Upon a Country*

410 *Once Upon a Country*

about my intifada activities tortured out of him, and who then was one of the four negotiators at Petah Tikva prison, was busy establishing a center to commemorate and document the development of the Palestinian prisoner movement. The idea was to bring together in one spot the prisoners' art, handiwork, stories, letters, and manuscripts.

The plan began over a plate of hummus in Ramallah. Every day after dropping off my sons at the Quaker Friends School, Fahed and I used to meet at my favorite restaurant. One morning he began talking about the prospects for peace, and how very soon we would be neighbors and partners with the Israelis, and the hundred-year conflict would be stuff for history books. "What will happen to the heritage of the prisoners?" he asked me. "All this history will be lost if we don't do something." One fear was that ambitious young historians and researchers at the Hebrew University would gather together all the artifacts and write the history for us.

Together we came up with a plan to document the prisoners' movement by gathering together poems, letters, memoirs, and leaflets. I gave Fahed a computer and a room to work in. He started with notes he had written in prison and smuggled out in small capsules. My secretary typed them up and edited them. I wrote an introduction, and we published it under the title *Behind Iron Bars.*

Now I decided to integrate the project into the university, and make Fahed its director. The first thought was to name the center after Nelson Mandela. In the end we commemorated the memory of Abu Jihad, the PLO leader assassinated by Israeli commandos in 1988, by calling it the Abu-Jihad Center for Political Prisoners' Affairs.

On the face of it, it sounds like a stretch to liken a prison document center named after Abu Jihad to peaceful efforts at dialogue with the Israelis. But in my mind they are two sides of the same coin. The prisoner movement was one of our greatest national success stories. Prison was a forge that proved that nonviolence could defeat the interrogator, humanize an inherently unjust penal system, and instruct prisoners in the art of sovereignty. And Fahed was the model director. In and out of Israeli chains since the age of sixteen, he had become a thinking man who believed in peace and coexistence with Israel.

We at Al-Quds launched a number of joint Palestinian-Israeli projects aimed at fostering academic and scientific cooperation. Just as my father took me by the hand in 1967 and signed me up for an archaeological dig, I felt that science was an important point of contact between our two societies. Real lasting peace is made between peoples, not governments. For our students, working with Israeli scientists constituted an open meeting of equals, regardless of how wide the gaps were in resources or training. The bravery of the prisoner facing down the interrogator was matched by the bravery of the student and researcher defying the Palestinian culture of boycotts, but also his own inner fears and insecurities, or his antipathies and stereotypes.

An open attitude toward cooperation with Israel turned Al-Quds University into the leading research university in Palestine. In the early years the Belgian government financed the most successful project we had, which ran for three years and targeted the areas of agriculture, environment, and public health.

More projects were to follow. Kuttab's television station, which evolved into the Al-Quds Institute for Modern Media, got funding to produce a Palestinian-Israeli version of *Sesame Street*. The hope was to inculcate children on both sides with mutual respect and tolerance. Our Big Bird was Kareem, a proud but amiable rooster; the Israelis' was Kipi, a porcupine. The subjects dealt with by our rooster-porcupine team ranged from the physical and sexual abuse of children, to the environment, women's rights, public health, and family planning. Lucy collaborated with us, producing an accompanying magazine.

When I took over the university, a lot of people told me I was asking for trouble, and sure enough trouble came by the bucketload. What kept the university from sinking in those first turbulent years was faith in a vision and strategy shared by a handful of loyal colleagues willing to put in long hours.

By 1998 the university was up to five thousand students, with the percentage of Hamas students down precipitously from 90 to 50 percent. We were hardly rolling in funds, but at least salaries were being paid on time, and we were growing. As we grew, so did the opposition. One day, worn out by fights on various fronts, my staff and I withdrew to my office. I could see the exhaustion on their faces. I told them to go out and see the movie *The Matrix*. Life is really all a game, I mused, and it's up to our creative imaginations to set the borders between imagination and reality. What people think about us, and we about them, depends on us. No matter how many powerful enemies we have, they can't break our will.

Some of the problems were perfectly understandable. A close friend of mine who ran the Israeli Studies program couldn't stop complaining about his students. "They can't even write a proper paper, let alone do research." I had to pick up his spirits with the Arabic equivalent of "Rome was not built in a day."

A far bigger problem was Hamas. With their numbers and influence waning, they were putting up a fight. In fall semester 1998 they threw a fit when I tried to show the incoming class *Destiny*, a film by the Egyptian filmmaker Youssef Chahine. The film is about the Iberian Muslim philosopher and Cordoba judge Averroes, who has always been for me the embodiment of the spirit of free intellectual inquiry and rationalism. Chahine made the film to coincide with Averroes's millennial anniversary, and as a warning against the dangers of Muslim fundamentalism. The Hamas students on campus naturally didn't want to see it, or allow others to. At the last minute, the dean of students canceled the showing to avoid a riot.

But the conflict didn't end there. At one point I kicked out the leader of the Hamas student group because of a rock-throwing incident on campus. I got rid of a few more ringleaders after a brawl with some Fatah students. The dispute began after the Fatah students organized a folk dance in which women participated. For the Hamas students, mixed dancing was such a grievous contravention of Islamic law that they hung posters calling the women whores. This was too much for the Fatah activists, and they began tearing down the posters. The Hamas students attacked the Fatah students, who struck back.

I was in my office when I got an urgent call. A fight had broken out between Fatah and Hamas students. It was alarming news because a feud between the factions could have gone anywhere: shooting, vandalizing buildings, mayhem. A violent clash on campus would have attracted Israeli soldiers, whose presence would have inevitably brought flying rocks. The entire chain of events—violence, soldiers, rocks, rubber bullets—was so predictable that I stepped in at once to prevent the escalation. The last thing I wanted was to give the authorities an excuse to shut down the university.

I asked the people involved to come into my office. They had hardly sat down when the recriminations started. For the next ten hours I had to listen to pointless caviling, with neither side willing to apologize or back down. The Hamas students continued to insist upon their rights to enforce the morality of the Ayatollah Khomeini, and their Fatah opponents stood by their moral right to stop them, and to swing back if hit.

Eventually I'd had enough. By the next morning, I threatened, either the students must resolve their dispute and apologize or I would suspend them. Morning came and they were all as unyielding as before. I suspended all the Hamas people. Adel, the Fatah leader who had defended the women on campus, got off with a warning. Later I hired him to come to work with me.

The bigger threat than even Hamas came from the PA's Ministry of Higher Education, and from Israel. By the time Al-Quds began to grow, Hanan Ashrawi had already quit her post as minister out of disappointment with the PA. The new minister was Munthir Salah, a man I got to know when he was the president of An-Najah National University in Nablus. I was also well acquainted with his main adviser, Gabi Baramki, the ex-provost of Birzeit.

From their first day on the job, Munthir and Gabi gave the impression of men not quite content with their limited power. One of their main tasks was to manage the universities, but all but two universities ran independently of the ministry. With Al-Quds, which was not only independent of their ministry but geographically outside of the PA jurisdiction, Munthir and Gabi looked for ways of exerting control. They and some other people in the ministry were increasingly aware that an institution they had no control over was rapidly changing in unexpected and, for them, uncontrollable ways. Student numbers were booming, research grants were flowing in, new buildings were going up, and an all-too-close relationship with Israelis was being forged. Munthir and Gabi began to think of ways to take over Al-Quds.

The first attacks were all verbal, and easy to fend off. Critics inside the ministry accused me of being an "expansionist," using the same Arabic terms we use to discuss Israeli settlements. In a commencement address, I referred to the charge. "Some critics in the Ministry of Education accuse us of being expansionists. They seem to be a bit mixed up." I paused for a moment the way a standup comedian does when telling a joke. "They think we are an Israeli settlement." Laughter erupted. Taking on a sober tone, I continued: "But it is our duty as a national institution in Jerusalem to grow; and it is their duty to support this growth rather than criticizing it or standing in its way."

Munthir and Gabi soon went well beyond words. The battleground they chose was the medical school. They and others weren't happy that we had succeeded in leapfrogging over other universities such as Birzeit in establishing it. Munthir's plan was to wrest it from Al-Quds and place it under his authority. The way he went about it nearly worked: he talked Arafat into signing one of his "presidential decrees" stating that forthwith the medical school would be under the jurisdiction of the Ministry of Education.

Munthir and Gabi had probably been cooking up the deal on the sly for months. I only learned about it in the newspaper the following day. It was quite surprising, to put it mildly, to discover that I had lost one of the university's main assets. A day later we in the administration got a fax from the ministry with a copy of the decree, demanding immediate compliance.

Munthir and Gabi must have thought that with a presidential decree the matter was settled and we'd send over the keys to the front door. What they failed to factor in was that I had some experience with presidential decrees, and knew how to navigate around them. I dictated the following fax to the ministry: "We do not recognize the legality or validity of the reasons cited for the issuance of the decree, and we will present our argumentation to the president himself."

I took the best tack I knew with Arafat. I sent him a file bulging with documents along with a note explaining why his decree was founded on misleading information. Apart from anything else, I explained, his decree amounted to the confiscation of private property. I was sure, I added in the note, that the most honored chairman had no intention of seizing properties from a nonprofit charitable organization.

I knew in advance that upon receiving my ten-pound file that Arafat would practice his old art of avoiding a decision. And just as predicted, he shelved the decree and set up a committee, which turned competition over the medical school into yet another mind-numbing process that thankfully went nowhere—and the commission quickly fizzled out.

The minute word came down that the chairman had appointed a committee, Munthir and Gabi knew they had lost. Down but not out, they mustered their forces and tried a much more ambitious strategy. The best way to get the medical school was to take over the entire university. The new plan, concocted with the then head of the teacher's union at Al-Quds, was to depose my board of trustees, my administration, and me.

Munthir took his case to a meeting of the full cabinet headed by Arafat. To his colleagues and the chairman he outlined all the university's financial difficulties, and how they were a product of my "expansionism" and poor management. Munthir's performance must have been stellar, because he succeeded in extracting from the cabinet a decision to replace the entire top administration of the university and to appoint a new board of trustees.

Their trick was to present Arafat with a list of the new board members, which they did. The only name they didn't provide was that of my replacement as the president of the university. Their thinking was that they would find a new president once Arafat agreed to the list. But when Arafat signed the minister's paper endorsing the change of the board of trustees, he made one correction. In the blank spot next to "university president" he slyly added my name. The message was clear: you can get rid of the board, just not Sari.

I knew nothing about this meeting, and once again it was in the morning newspaper squeezed between the top news of the day that I discovered that I had lost my board. Our reaction was prompt. The next day, in a front-page advertisement in the local paper, the university declared that it was still being run by the same board, and that the Palestinian Authority had no right or jurisdiction to institute changes in an independent organization.

At the same time, I fired off a complaint to the cabinet, questioning the minister's motives, information, and methods, and demanding a full hearing in my presence. How could the cabinet take a decision based on one-sided information? I explained in the letter that the minister and the head of the union, in drawing up their report about the university, hadn't even bothered to interview any of the university's administrative staff for another opinion.

The members of the cabinet, tearing a page from their boss's book, avoided open conflict. They shelved their earlier decision and decided to "look into" the matter again. Once again, Munthir's stratagem designed to depose me foundered on the built-in inertia of PA decision making.

As long as Al-Quds seemed little more than a blot of ink on paper, the Israelis left it alone. As soon as they saw the fastest-growing Arab institution left within their "Eternal Capital," our legal problems multiplied.

A couple of minor encounters took place in 1998. In our renovation of the compound near the Souk el-Qattanin, workers digging in one of the rooms discovered a secret passageway into an ancient tunnel underneath the Old City. Days later, a platoon of Israeli soldiers showed up and threatened to confiscate the building if we didn't seal the entryway into the tunnel.

The other conflict occurred during our graduation ceremony in a building near the Orient House. For students living outside the municipal borders of Jerusalem, it was illegal to attend the event without special permits from the military authorities, permits so impossible to obtain that no one even bothered trying. Unlike today, enforcement of the absurd policy was still lax, so we went ahead with the ceremony.

By the time it was over, police were surrounding the building and asking everyone leaving the ceremony to show their IDs. They stopped only when I approached the commander of the police unit. "Hi, Dr. Sari," he said as if we were the closest of friends. Putting his hand out for me to shake it, he asked if I remembered him.

"I've met a lot of police officers," I mumbled awkwardly, not knowing what else to say.

He continued beaming. "You have to remember. I was the one who arrested you in Abu Dis during the Gulf War." He must have been the one with an awkward and slightly embarrassed expression on his face.

"Oh yes, but you were wearing a different uniform."

After a few minutes of friendly banter he withdrew his unit. "Really good to see you, Sari!" were his last words, as he waved at us from his retreating jeep.

A more serious encounter with Israeli bureaucracy occurred when several graduates from our School of Social Work, who were already employed by Israeli institutions, including the Jerusalem municipality, were suddenly informed that their degrees would no longer be recognized because Al-Quds didn't have proper Israeli accreditation. Thus began a series of court cases in defense of our graduates.

Soon, we found ourselves taken to court by a right-wing society calling itself "Betzedek" or "in righteousness." (The name comes from the

Biblical verse, "Lead me, O Lord, in your righteousness because of my enemies; make your way straight before me.")

Betzedek went to the Supreme Court requesting that we be shut down for two reasons: first, that we were an institution belonging to the Palestinian Authority in contravention of the Oslo Agreement (the PA was not allowed to operate within East Jerusalem), and next that we were operating within Israel without accreditation from the appropriate Israeli authorities. Betzedek also requested that the Israeli government, in the person of its prime minister, be censored for allowing us to operate illegally.

Thus began a long battle for survival. The first charge was easy to dispense with. Al-Quds was a nongovernmental, nonprofit institution, and as such we did not belong to the PA. Operating in Jerusalem, therefore, did not contradict the Oslo Agreement. The head of the Israeli Internal Security Ministry said as much in a report he filed with the Supreme Court.

The issue of Israeli accreditation was a far bigger threat. We were in fact operating with no licenses or accreditation, and in a normal society it would have been perfectly justified to shut us down. But nothing in East Jerusalem was normal. Our initial hope was that the Oslo process would lead to a final-status agreement, liberating our section of the city from occupation and eliminating any need for Israeli permission or accreditation. But with the Oslo process inching along at a snail's pace, we had to respond to the legal challenge.

The problem was that applying for Israeli accreditation implied accepting Israeli legal jurisprudence over East Jerusalem. The Palestinian minister for higher education unfurled his "nationalism" by warning Arafat that I was about to accede to the "Israelization" of the university. Others added their voices to the hysteria.

I was clearly in a bind. Weighing a court order to shut us down on the one hand with the nationalist passions on the other, I sought out Mr. Spaer's legal advice. What we came up with was a diversionary tactic to win some time. I instructed Mr. Spaer to tell the court that our lack of accreditation wasn't our fault at all. The Israeli authorities had never made the legal provisions for granting accreditation to an Arab degree-granting institution. For more than fifty years, Israel had never contemplated building, supporting, or even acknowledging an Arab university catering to its Arab population.

Betzedek had expected me to sing along with the chorus led by the PA minister of education and his colleagues, who rejected Israeli accreditation on principle. This would have left the Supreme Court no choice but to order our institution closed. Having called their bluff, however, we put the Israeli Council for Higher Education in a bind. Should it offer us legal status in Israel's Eternal Capital? The Supreme Court ordered it to. But should it comply? Suddenly it was the Israeli government, and not Al-Quds, on the dock.

Thus began a tortured legal procedure that has yet to end. The Israeli Council for Higher Education first tried to throw it back on us by saying it had never received an application. We should apply in accordance with the regulations. Mr. Spaer replied that his client would be happy to fill out an application, if one existed. The only application and accompanying regulations were in Hebrew, argued Mr. Spaer, and since his client was an Arabic speaker, the Israeli ministry had the legal duty to provide these materials in Arabic, it being one of the official languages of the State of Israel.

It took the educational authority more than six months to produce the regulations in Arabic. More tortuous procedures followed, reflecting I think the hesitation of many within the Israeli bureaucracy to register an Arab university in a city they were doing everything in their power, including every piece of legal chicanery in the book, to purge of Arab influence.

Chapter Twenty-seven

Holy of Holies

A POPULAR ARAB CHILDREN'S STORY I heard in grade school was about a hunter slitting the throat of a bird on a bitterly cold and rainy day. A child, seeing the hunter bent over the dead animal and mistaking raindrops on the man's face for tears, turns to his mother and says, "Look, Mother, that poor man is crying over the bird." "Don't pay attention to his tears," replies the mother. "Look what he's doing with his hands."

Many Palestinians must have had this story in the back of their minds as they observed Israeli negotiators going to and fro out of hotel lobbies and a dozen different international venues talking nonstop about peace, while Israeli settlements were expanding with accelerated speed. Particularly in East Jerusalem, the frenzied growth conveyed one message: Israel would never give our city back to us. For me, driving past the ever-growing Jewish neighborhood of Pisgat Ze'ev every morning was like entering into the official Israeli political mind. Plans conceived many years earlier were materializing into roads, sewage lines, telephone cables, water pipes, tennis courts, and red-tiled villas. There was for me no better contrast than that between the relentless Israeli expansion and the

PA's hapless bungling. By 1999 many people, myself included, had already delivered a eulogy on Oslo.

We Palestinians felt swindled. Compared with the euphoria generated by the intifada, people's experience of the Oslo years was one humiliating retreat after the next. Arafat's approval ratings hit rock bottom.

The PA's weakness can be traced back to all the familiar homegrown problems of corruption, bad management, and so on. The majority of Palestinians felt that our leadership, from the chairman on down to members of the cabinet and Legislative Council, were inebriated with the symbols of power. People suspected that too many of their "liberators" were more interested in enriching themselves than in solving the nation's pressing problems.

The biggest problem of all was still the occupation. If anything, since the PA's arrival there had been a massive tightening of the Israeli grip on our land and our lives. The man on the street had lost confidence in a government he held responsible for engaging in a negotiation process that had brought no benefit, that, on the contrary, had given cover for the Israelis to act unilaterally. Dennis Ross's account captures well the futile back-and-forth between the PA and the Israelis over every issue imaginable, while Israel went full steam ahead with its settlement activity. As in the story of the bird, Israeli leaders' tearful declarations about peace didn't tally with what they were doing with their bulldozers. I saw only the inexorable march of facts on the ground, as if it were all a big hoax and we were the fools.

A word should be added here about settlement activity. By focusing on the details—a demolition order here, a new bypass road there, a thousand new housing units on a hillside—it's easy to lose sight of the systematic nature of the expansion. Years that were supposed to build trust between the feuding parties saw a doubling of the settlement population, from one hundred thousand to two hundred thousand: hardly what we had in mind when we danced on the streets after Oslo. That settlers got away scot-free with murder and other depredations quite literally added insult to injury.

Another source of discontentment, to put it mildly, was the cordon of roadblocks and checkpoints that prevented people from traveling easily between regions controlled by the PA. These "liberated" areas became, as Palestinians said, a series of big prisons.

People who believed in peace shouted out their hosannas when Ehud Barak and the Labor Party won the Israeli general election in 1999. Barak was widely praised as a man with an ingenious grasp of complex operations. He had studied mathematics, had been a chief person in the daring rescue operation at the Entebbe airport in Uganda, had been a brilliant military chief of staff, and, to top it all off, was a pianist whose hobby was assembling and disassembling clocks. As one would expect, Arabs recalled some of his other exploits, such as his role in the assassination of Abu Jihad or the time he dressed up as a woman and shot his way into a PLO cell in Beirut ("Operation Springtime of Youth"). Yet no one doubted he was a big improvement over Bibi Netanyahu, and his victory at the polls promised to bring the moderates back into the government.

Among Palestinians, disappointment was immediate. To begin with, the coalition Barak put together included Orthodox religious parties and the ex-refusenik Natan Sharansky. Both would prove unreliable bedfellows, to say the least, in questions of peace with the Palestinians. Once installed as prime minister in July 1999, Barak turned away from the Palestinian problem and tried to reach a deal with the Syrians. When he talked about the peace process with us at all, he made it clear, first with hints and eventually with a full throat, that he was no fan of the underlying theory in the Oslo process that small trust-building measures were necessary before the two sides tackled the more contentious issues.

Arafat tried to get Barak's attention with some hollow threats. I recall one meeting I attended. By this point Arafat always assumed that Israelis were listening in on every word. Addressing his invisible interlocutor on the other end of the microphone he was sure was hidden in a potted plant or a piece of furniture, he declared with as much dramatic force as he could muster that the situation was becoming intolerable and might well "explode" if negotiations didn't lead to a breakthrough. He picked up the phone and called the head of the Ministry of Food Supplies to instruct him to make sure the silos were filled with flour because of the "impending" political crisis. For all of us who heard such talk, it was obvious he was blowing smoke to get the Israelis to pick up the pace of negotiations.

Barak came out with his own threats, which at least to the Americans sounded far more persuasive. He announced to the Americans and Palestinians that there were to be no more partial steps or trust-building moves. Even the agreements made by the previous Likud government he suspended. He wanted to go directly to the end game, a final comprehensive settlement. Once his strategy with the Syrians had failed, he returned to the Palestinian issue, and came up with the idea of a dramatic summit with President Clinton, and warned that without it, his government wouldn't survive. It was a high-stakes game, an all-or-nothing approach: either total agreement or apocalypse. You'd think a clock-maker would be used to fidgeting with something until it was fixed. But his approach to the peace process was either the clock worked to the second, or it was pitched onto the rubbish heap.

Clinton went along, and offered Camp David as a venue.

Arafat's response was that the two sides weren't ready. The back-channel contacts with the Israelis didn't yet promise a successful summit. Ever cautious, ever afraid of traps—he was a man who had escaped from a hundred of them over his lifetime—he tried to weasel his way out of it. But Clinton cornered him, and in the end Arafat had no choice but to attend against his better judgment.

For once, I agreed with Arafat. The two sides were already making public declarations that were totally irreconcilable with each other. Given these positions, I couldn't see how an agreement could be reached.

An idea Mark Heller, my coauthor on *No Trumpets, No Drums*, floated in an article in *The Jerusalem Post* made a lot more sense to me at the time than a summit fated to failure. By prior agreement of the two sides, Palestinians could declare a state with their ideal borders, and Israel could simultaneously recognize an independent Palestinian state in the borders Israel deemed best. The two sides could then enter into negotiations to bridge the difference between the two borders. That way, at least, we could keep the "peace process" alive.

I still managed to maintain my distance from politics. Indirectly, I was of course aware of the general mood. On campus, students were grumbling about the "peace process," and talk of another intifada made the rounds.

I was still attending meetings of the "Jerusalem Ministerial Committee" Arafat had talked me into joining, which often began with Faisal giving a grim report on the rapid takeover of East Jerusalem, such as the outer ring of fortified settlements being connected to Jerusalem through a series of bypass roads. As I've experienced often over the years, chatting seemed to be the preferred compensation for seriously addressing the mounting difficulties faced by the inhabitants of East Jerusalem.

The more I heard, the darker my pessimism grew. That the left-wing Labor Party was continuing to carry out the right-wing Likud's policies only confirmed the impression that nothing substantial was being achieved at the negotiating table. I agreed with the general feeling on the street that our leadership was simply deluding itself, and us, by pretending that this whole process was leading to the end of occupation. In March 2000, I attended a UN-sponsored meeting on Palestinian rights held in Hanoi, where I gloomily predicted that the chances for a separate and viable Palestinian state were quickly disappearing from sight.

Soon after I returned, in May 2000, there was fresh confirmation of this melancholy hunch: the city of Jerusalem granted approval to a group funded by Irving Moskowitz, the American bingo king, to build a two-hundred-unit Jewish settlement in Abu Dis, not far from our cam-

pus. Barak was also employing high-tech means to rid Jerusalem of unwanted Arabs. Now we had to show a government-issued magnetic ID
card before passing one of the nine checkpoints set up during the Gulf
War on the eastern roads leading into Jerusalem. This was designed to
prevent Arabs without the necessary documents from slipping back into
their ancestral city.

When the Camp David Summit opened in July 2000, my pessimism
wasn't shared by most of the friends and colleagues who dropped by my
office. Faisal and Marwan were upbeat. Jibril and Sameer in particular
were fully convinced that a deal was within reach. They were in close
contact with various Israeli politicians and security experts, who had
probably assured them that some sort of deal was in the bag.

The iconic television image of Barak pushing Arafat through a door-
way at Camp David speaks volumes. In the words of Susan Sontag in
The New York Review of Books, the chairman felt he was being "dragged
to the verdant hills of Maryland."

During the two-week summit, I often drove down to the quiet desert
town of Jericho for a long walk and a swim. My main source of news on
the summit's progress was Jibril, who was also in Jericho and was confident that Arafat could be brought around to some reasonable compromise. At night the two of us took long walks through the open country
outside town. Occasionally he got a call on his cell phone directly from
a negotiator, who would give him a live report.

For much of the time, Arafat and Barak had surprisingly little to
do. Only toward the end did Barak finally cut to the chase. He offered
hitherto-unheard-of Israeli concessions on land and Jerusalem in exchange for a legally binding "end of the conflict" agreement, according
to which there would be no mass repatriation of refugees to Israel. Israel
would keep its 1948 booty, and the Palestinians would get their state.

Both sides still quarrel over how much land the Israelis offered at
Camp David, because nothing was put down on paper, and all these discussions were considered "non-papers."

Barak—in Hebrew, the name means "lightning," but to Arab ears it recalls the name of Mohammed's magical steed—brought up the "Holy of Holies" by demanding partial sovereignty over the Noble Sanctuary, or Temple Mount. At one point he said that Jews should be allowed to pray on the Muslim part of the site. Saeb recounts that it was this issue, more than anything else, that made Arafat's blood boil. "Arafat literally began to tremble," Saeb said.

Clinton spent hours trying to find a formula both leaders could live with, finally suggesting to split the sovereignty: the Arabs would have it on top, where the mosques were, and the Jews would have it below, where supposedly the Holy of Holies was buried.

My Likud negotiating partner back in 1987, Moshe Amirav—who chided Barak for needlessly opening up this can of worms—writes that Arafat was boiling mad. "He really went nuts. He started to yell at Clinton, and asked him if he would ever agree for someone else to be sovereign over territory beneath the streets of Washington."[1] Trembling all over, Arafat refused to recognize that the Jews had any historical connection to the Noble Sanctuary.

The negotiators packed their bags and returned to the Middle East, but not before President Clinton did what he had promised not to: he pinned the blame squarely on the chairman.

The Arabs, after hearing accounts of the Israeli positions and postures, lost all faith in the negotiating process. Back in Palestine, Arafat stoked this with more myth-mongering. He used a verse from the Koran to prove a crazy theory that Solomon's Temple had really been in Yemen. At some point during the forty years in the desert, the People of Israel took a wrong turn and ended up far, far from Jerusalem. "Do you know the story of the Queen of Sheba sending a bird to Solomon that arrived the same day. How could a bird fly there so fast? Because the temple was in nearby Yemen!" When I heard this I feared that the chairman was losing his grip on reality.

The Israelis, after hearing about Barak's readiness to make concessions on Jerusalem and Arafat's total rejection of Israeli offers, lost all faith in the Palestinians. Few people seriously doubted Barak's line that Arafat had shown his "true face" and was no partner in peace.

The two sides, a whisker away from a historic agreement, now found themselves in a crisis. I heard from some of the people who had fervently believed in Oslo: "This means war."

Chapter Twenty-eight

The Possessed

It was a day of the unexpected; a day of the denouement of
many plots and the beginning of many future intrigues; a
day of sudden explanations and thickening mysteries.

—DOSTOYEVSKY, *THE POSSESSED*

OSTOYEVSKY, MY NAMESAKE for a few brief snowy days in
Damascus, directed his novel *The Possessed* against the so-called
"nihilists," those who wanted to destroy the old social order, lock,
stock, and barrel. "We shall proclaim destruction," one character ex-
claims, "because—because . . . the idea is so attractive for some reason!" The novel often came to mind after Ariel Sharon's jaunt up to the
Noble Sanctuary/Temple Mount in September 2000 set off a pandemic
of killing that stripped away both peoples' basic sense of decency. It was
as if everyone had lost their minds: Palestinians, the Israelis, the international press, everyone.

There had always been an unwritten set of rules that regulated the
Palestinian-Israeli conflict, and which prevented it from degenerating
into unbridled killing. Religious sites were rarely attacked, assassinations were kept to a minimum, and civilians were seldom targeted. Now
all bets were off. I saw it up close on campus—the enflamed students,
returning from the funerals of friends shot down in cold blood, waving
water pistols and cardboard AK-47s and demanding a tooth for a tooth.
The Islamists celebrated suicide bombers as heroes; once the number of

Palestinian victims rose into the dozens, then the hundreds, even Fatah people were doing so. It was as if, like a repressed memory, the respective political legacies of the Stern Gang and militant Sheikh Qassam had won out at last. For the Palestinians at least, the "second intifada" was a catastrophic slapdash brawl without leadership, strategy, or ideas; it was a ruinous and sanguinary fit of madness.

In dark times the wisest course of action is surely to tend to your own garden. But this was a luxury I didn't have, and my five-year break from politics came to an end at the very moment any sensible person would have disappeared for good. It wasn't nobility that threw me back into the fray, or a love for action, or even a princely sense of responsibility. I had no choice. The cycle of bloodletting, like the ancient sacrificial cult of Moloch, forced me back into the public eye, for if the so-called "intellectual" of a society refuses to oppose misguided public opinion, either because he fears for his life or hopes for personal gain or popularity, then that "intellectual" has lost his role in society, and his society will end up as lost as he is. Based on what I was seeing, intellectuals playing to the crowds in front of Aljazeera's cameras were more ruinous than the obsequious court philosophers who once kneeled low to kiss the ring of a king.

Once I took to the stage and started spouting my views—that Palestinians and Israelis share common interests in a two-state solution and as such are more allies than enemies—the predictable death threats, variations on old themes, began arriving back in the mail. Jacob stopped pestering me, though his successor, my personal Inspector Javert, began tracking my every move. But here I'm getting ahead of myself.

Dennis Ross opens his book at Camp David in the summer of 2000. In his mise-en-scène, President Clinton sits pleading with Chairman Arafat, who willfully rejects the best offer he could ever hope to get. Ross's account lends weight to the stock Israeli line that Arafat responded to Prime Minister Barak's generosity by unleashing a murderous new intifada.

But for all his failings—and he clearly blew it by not closing some sort of deal at Camp David—Arafat was neither sufficiently in control nor sufficiently villainous to devise such a conspiracy. Ross's view purposefully simplifies and obfuscates the various forces that conspired to trigger the so-called "second intifada."

Everyone shares some blame in the summit's failure. Barak can be faulted for bullying, with his either/or approach, and for trying to deal in nonnegotiable myth. Arafat's chronic indecision and never-ending suspicion prevented him from coming up with a reasonable counteroffer. After all the years of fighting, he had a chance to get most of what we needed; the rest he could have achieved by building a modern state under the rule of law. But he didn't do it.

In one respect, Arafat and Barak were equally at fault for allowing their frustration and anger to spill out for the entire world to see. Camps formed around the competing narratives of what went wrong. Clinton has to accept some responsibility for coming down so hard on the chairman.

With the peace process in crisis, and in an atmosphere of mounting pessimism, I did what little I could to bring people back to their senses. Asked by a German magazine about the Jewish claim to the Temple Mount, I shot down Arafat's "Yemen" theory by making it perfectly clear that Jewish roots in Jerusalem were existential and umbilical, as testified by the greatest Islamic tale of all, the Night Journey. Once word of the interview reached the mufti of Jerusalem, he spewed out his bile at me in the local press. His dislike of me was slowly turning into intense loathing.

In other interviews, I disagreed that the summit had ended in calamity. Since I hadn't expected too much in the first place, I didn't interpret its breakup in end-of-the-world terms. In fact, I thought it was extraordinary how far direct talks had drawn the two sides together. There was no reason, I averred to people who wanted to know what I thought, that the two sides couldn't get back to the negotiating table. In discussing the summit, I told Lee Hockstader of *The Washington Post*, "Maybe we weren't exactly seeing eye to eye, but we were roaming around in the same thicket of woods together." All that was needed was calm, reasoned deliberation, and a dispassionate reflection on our own self-interests. The tempest would pass, I had no doubt, and the two sides would return to negotiations.

To bolster my case that our two peoples, and the Americans, were joined by common interests, I pointed to a flourishing cooperation between Al-Quds University and Bar-Illan University, where Rabin's assassin had studied and which had the reputation as the most right-wing campus in the country. Crisis or no crisis, Al-Quds had also opened an American Studies Center with the financial backing of the U.S. embassy.

Indeed, at first there was no shooting, and the Middle East didn't grind to a halt. There was still security cooperation between Jibril's forces and the Israelis. Business was blossoming, the casino parking lot was always full, tourists continued to stream into the country, and corrupt officials of the two security services were happily making money hand over fist. Arafat was even in good spirits, having shown the Arab world and his own people that he wouldn't kowtow to the Americans and Israelis. His popularity ratings shot up. At our new American Studies program I had the pleasure of watching our students struggle through *The Federalist Papers*.

Sure enough, it seemed as if Camp David was going into extra innings, when the two sides began to regroup for new negotiations. Saeb Erekat and Barak's negotiator, the lawyer Gilʾad Sher, held more than thirty meetings trying to bridge the gaps. Some of my despondent friends, such as Marwan and Jibril, were beginning to regain some optimism.

Enter Sharon. One of Father's favorite English adages, "Fools rush in where angels fear to tread," applies here, because a four-year slugfest that has caused torrents of blood—as well as ink and videotape—began with Sharon's visit to the Noble Sanctuary on September 28, 2001, triggering what the euphoric crowds and journalists dubiously dubbed the "second intifada," which it was only in the sense that sequels are often bad copies of the original.

Barak was in political trouble, as the concessions his political opponents accused him of contemplating lost him a parliamentary majority.

Natan Sharansky, refusenik turned hardline expansionist, bolted from the coalition. Elections were imminent, and Barak's new foe was the formidable Sharon. Sharon was out of the country drumming up support when he announced that he would visit the Temple Mount. Barak had wrecked Camp David by bringing up the Holy of Holies, so this was exactly where his nemesis chose to go.

Sharon has always been a wily and often reckless visionary, with a record of deceiving prime ministers and defying the world in order to execute a plan. When I saw him on television strutting like a flatulent Rambo up on the Noble Sanctuary, I knew we were in trouble. The visit was transparently designed as a trap, but for whom?

The easy answer was first Barak, then us. Sharon plainly wanted to push the prime minister into a tight corner. If he blocked the visit, Sharon would hurl three thousand years of Jewish history at him. It would be obvious, the argument would go, that Barak intended on giving up sovereignty over the site to the Palestinians. Conversely, if Barak allowed the visit, the ensuing stone throwing and rioting that was guaranteed to break out would show the world the "true face" of Palestinian terror. The peace process would be over and Arab violence would be the cause. Either way, Barak would lose the election, and Sharon, his successor, wouldn't have to go back to the negotiating table, which he knew would require him to pull out of the territories.

Jibril also smelled a rat, and promised the Israeli foreign minister, Shlomo Ben-Ami, a leftist, that there would be quiet so long as Sharon didn't enter the mosques. Faisal, wanting to avoid trouble, ordered all the schools to remain open. He didn't want hundreds of inflamed youths throwing rocks at soldiers. Even Fatah's most militant factions weren't prepared for a confrontation. The Tanzim stayed home.

Not all Palestinian leaders were so prudent; some, their rational faculties already weakened by the general mood, tried to whip up the mass's emotions. Marwan, Hanan Ashrawi, and Mustafa Barghouti (a physician who had been a delegate to the Madrid conference and was heavily involved in the technical committees) appeared on local TV stations pleading with viewers to prevent the visit by rushing up to the Noble

Sanctuary. The sanctity of the holy place was about to be desecrated, they declared, and could be defended only by the people themselves.

The visit went as planned. On a Thursday morning, Sharon lumbered up with 1,500 heavily armed and bellicose border police, and marched directly up to the Al-Aqsa mosque. Standing before the site of Mohammed's miraculous ascension, Sharon declared Israeli sovereignty over the Temple Mount. "I come here with a message of peace," he said, surrounded by his small army. "I believe that we can live together with the Palestinians,"[1] under his terms, to be sure.

Only a relative handful of Palestinians heeded the call to prevent Sharon's visit. Faisal and a score of Muslim dignitaries were on hand to show their decorous objections. And the entire event probably would have ended with Sharon's symbolic speech and Faisal's symbolic opposition had it not been for something no one could have predicted.

At the top of the stairs leading to the *haram* a skirmish broke out between the police and the dignitaries. The television images beamed by satellite to hundreds of millions of Arabs around the world showed Faisal getting pushed around, which was nothing new. But this time the highest-ranking sheikh in Al-Aqsa also got roughed up. As chance would have it, his turban, a symbol of his exalted spiritual status, got knocked off his head and tumbled into the dust. Viewers saw the highest Muslim cleric of this highly charged Muslim site standing bareheaded. He might as well have been naked. Shame and outrage can be intimately coupled in the Middle Eastern psyche.

All through that day newscasters and reporters on Arab satellite stations relentlessly hammered up this affront to Islam. Arab Jerusalemites, probably feeling guilty for not having shown up in the first place to protect the dignity of their holy site, seethed with anger. They weren't about to miss the Friday prayer on the Noble Sanctuary. Then they would show their mettle to Israeli soldiers. It was going to be a mythic showdown.

The atmosphere in Jerusalem's Old City that Friday morning was electrified. Armed and nervous border police marched into the Old City by the hundreds, while hundreds of thousands of Muslims poured through the gates from neighborhoods and villages. The Tanzim, slough-ing off their role of "peace leagues," crowded onto the plaza.

The minute the Friday prayers were over, gangs of teenagers rushed out of Al-Aqsa mosque toward the Western Wall, hurling rocks down on the soldiers. The border police stormed into the compound from all sides, and their pincerlike attack spread panic among the sea of wor-shippers leaving the mosque. The soldiers, taking aim at the youths, fired with live ammunition. Within minutes, eight protesters were shot dead, and scores of others had fallen to the ground, wounded. The "Al-Aqsa intifada" had begun.

Cascading events, one feeding off the next, engulfed the Occupied Territories in violence. The Israeli military's response was brutal. Nine hundred thousand bullets were fired in the opening days of the fighting, with the overwhelming majority of casualties being Palestinian. Trouble even spread into Israel proper. In some of the worst rioting among Is-raeli Arabs, thirteen unarmed civilians were shot.

A macabre cycle set in. Every funeral led to new clashes with soldiers, resulting in more deaths, more funerals, more clashes, more shooting—and on it went. Leaders marched with angry demonstrators to army roadblocks, checkpoints, bases, and settlements. Inevitably, the chil-dren rushing ahead of the crowd and throwing rocks took the first bul-lets. Within three weeks, more than fifty children were dead. Parents, leaders, and the man on the street grew increasingly antagonistic toward the PA and its armed security forces for not using their guns to protect their children.

If the Israelis had wanted to draw the Palestinian security forces into the fighting they couldn't have picked a better way to do it. Unable to withstand the mounting pressure, one after another, members of the PA security forces shot back. Even Jibril couldn't stop them—and had it been possible, he would have. He was dead set against the intifada. Soon armed Palestinian activists started targeting soldiers, settlers, and any-thing "Jewish" that moved.

Arab satellite stations were guaranteed to be on hand to broadcast the latest scene of bloodshed and demagoguery. With a mounting sense of alarm and distaste, I watched as television newscasters and journalists were swept up with activists and street actors, victims, and violent thugs in a death dance. Spurred on by what they saw every day on television, hundreds of thousands of protesters took to the streets in various Arab capitals.

Palestinians and Israelis soon had their icons to prop up the barbaric image each had of the other. We got ours when a French cameraman captured on film the shooting death of Mohammed al-Durrah. In a matter of minutes the boy, who had been huddled behind his helpless father for protection, was slumped over dead. Viewers watched the father leaning over the body of his son in anguish, while the soldiers continued to shoot, as if one dead Palestinian boy wasn't enough. The searing images were aired, day after day. The Palestinians called the boy a *shaheed*, a "martyr."

A short time later—on October 12—it was the Palestinians' turn to prove their savagery. Two Israelis took a wrong turn into Ramallah on their way to an army base and were dragged from their cars, taken to a local police station, and lynched by a wild mob that dipped their hands in the blood of the victims as if in some frenzied pagan dance. This time it was the Italians who brought the repugnant scene to the world's television screens.

There is a way," writes the Viennese playwright Franz Grillparzer, "from humanity through nationality to bestiality." I felt I had to do something.

Twenty years earlier, I had entered into public life after a delegation of fellow professors showed up at my office at Birzeit. My recent "disappearance" from politics had taken me back to my basic nature, which was to be an observer and educator, not an activist. However hesitantly, I was now heading back into the fray, this time without a leadership structure to fit into.

Needless to say, delegations of professors were not knocking on doors looking for new recruits for one faction or the other. In trying to find a political foothold, I felt like a character in a Beckett play, looking for something that didn't exist. There was no leadership. The "street" had taken charge.

I didn't venture far from Jerusalem and my office during those days. Two decades of occupation in the West Bank and East Jerusalem had transformed the political geography to the point of obliteration. Checkpoints and roadblocks made travel nearly impossible. The degree of violence was vastly greater than in 1980, as were the chances of getting hit by a stray bullet, or a perfectly aimed one.

I continued running the university as best I could and spent a lot of time brooding over a new puzzle: How could one explain such madness breaking out just as peace was within reach? I knew that a mass psychosis had overtaken Palestinians when my dean of the graduate program, otherwise a perfectly rational woman, was as swallowed up by the war euphoria as any fourteen-year-old on the street. What had triggered this insanity? Was it just Sharon's visit? Was it Islamic militant groups fanning anger into a new Lebanon? Or was it years of frustration at Arafat and the PA? Was Robert Fisk of *The Independent* right in tracing it back to an entire society being "pressure-cooked to the point of explosion"?[2] Was it the pace of settlement construction that had picked up under Barak? (The Labor government had earmarked three hundred million dollars for it in the 2001 budget.)

It was clear to me that the increasing spiral of violence served no one's real interests. Naturally, those on both sides who believed in brute force thought they were making headway in the maddening bloodbath, but the nagging question on my mind was, What's going to happen after the terrorist bombings and assassinations stop?

In looking for answers, I watched a lot of television, including our university station, which was an indispensable window into the craziness that was unfolding like a bad B movie.

To figure out what the man on the street was thinking, I returned to one of my favorite haunts in the Old City, a hummus restaurant just around the corner from the Cotton Merchants' Market, where renovations of the Khan Tankiz were still under way for our Center for Jerusalem Studies. The opinion on the street was that we were justified in fighting back, even if nothing good was likely to come of it. People cheered on the violence knowing that the Israelis would dish it back at us tenfold. This was one of the occasions when Dostoyevsky's *The Possessed* came to mind.

Jibril and I spoke often, sometimes daily. As always, our assessments were identical. Jibril knew how catastrophic the violence was, and did what little he could to put an end to the rioting—until the Israeli military began employing Phantom jets and Apache helicopters. Bombing raids carried out in Ramallah and Gaza inexplicably targeted Jibril's security buildings, which only crippled his ability to rein in Palestinian violence. *Intentionally?*

For me what was most extraordinary was that there was no one to talk to among our leadership, which made a complete mockery of the Israeli presumption that a small cabal of evil conspirators was behind the violence. I tried to contact some top leaders, but they were nowhere to be found. It wasn't as if they had gone into hiding, as revolutionaries often do. Most were probably in bed with a bottle of antidepressants.

Indeed, the only similarity I saw between the intifada of the late eighties and its ostensible redux was that at the start of both, Arafat and his top people were caught by surprise. The chairman—for the Israelis, the evil mastermind responsible for the mess—panicked. At first he and his aids thought the fighting was directed more against them than the Israelis. They were so scared that they ducked out of public view for two months. The rogue's gallery of corrupt officials who had invested heavily in the Jericho casino or car dealerships now feared they would lose their millions. They, too, took cover.

It was a double disappearance because even our leaders' images vanished from the television screens. Whereas previously all you saw on television were Arafat, Abu Mazen, and Saeb Erekat, now other faces crowded the screen: Marwan, Mustafa Barghouti, and others who euphorically predicted justice for the Palestinians and an end to a peace process that had only brought more domination and more misery. Mustafa Barghouti, with an eye on political power, promised that the "Al-Aqsa intifada" would sweep away our old negotiation team and its terms of reference. "Real" negotiators and "genuine" terms were on their way.

Nonstop television interviews with both established and new "leaders," "analysts," and "spokesmen" provided more details than I could stomach. The more I listened, the more the talk reminded me of the hallucinatory rhetoric I once heard sitting in the Egyptian Information Office cafeteria on the eve of the Six-Day War. Our demagogues were telling Palestinians that they had drawn Israel into a final, existential battle.

At this point, some hitherto-unfamiliar faces made a cameo appearance. Armed militants from the younger generation with roots in the refugee camps appeared from nowhere, telling the nation that an armed struggle was needed to replace the Oslo-style peace process. Their repertoire of "strategies" included whipping up a million Israeli Arabs against their Jewish countrymen. Their fight was not for a democratic state alongside Israel; with the example of Hezbollah having wormed its way into their imagination, their fight was for Islam. The pacifistic Islamic students I had taught in the early eighties were now a very distant memory. Their Islam was just as armed as the Israeli border police, and even more trigger happy.

A group of such leaders from various factions formed themselves into "a unified command" or leadership of the Al-Aqsa intifada, ruinously believing that demagoguery and leaflets alone could bring back the glory of the intifada of ten years earlier. The more extremism they spouted, the more popularity they enjoyed, and with popularity came a leading role on the reality show taped live by Aljazeera, which in turn became a production center for a fresh crop of "martyrs" and "heroes."

Marwan was the one leader I did manage to track down. He was a man I had always admired, a scrappy fighter with a keen mind. But in those days he had lost it. In the most shortsighted and morally questionable act of his life, he reached for a gun.

Emboldened by the specter of Arab crowds marching from Cairo to Algiers and Baghdad, Marwan began talking about an "intercontinental intifada." He, who weeks before had been convinced that final peace was within our grasp, quickly reverted to underground guerilla leader, plotting attacks. He came out in public support of a military crusade aimed at the "forces of occupation," by which he meant soldiers and settlers.[3]

He was uneasy that his former teacher wasn't among those converted to the bellicose spirit he was busy projecting. He had been keeping up with my views through the news and our mutual friends. One day he wanted to talk. He must have felt he could win me over if we sat down face to face.

We met for lunch in a restaurant in Ramallah. I came with Imad, and accompanying Marwan was a friend from the Fatah Higher Committee days.

"What, for God's sake, is going on?" I asked him a few moments after we sat down. "Where do you think all this lunacy is taking us?"

Marwan laid out his thinking. He began by assuring me that he hadn't lost his political bearings. A peaceful two-state solution was still very much his political vision, "now more than ever." What came next sounded dangerously reminiscent of the old Israeli mantra: "Palestinians understand only the language of force." (In Hegel's dialectic, slaves end up adopting the thinking of the master.) In his reading of the Israeli political map, he explained, Israel wasn't yet ready to make the requisite compromises for a just two-state compromise. The Israeli political elite had to be shocked out of its political complacency through pain. Blood had to be drawn.

"But this 'intifada' of yours has absolutely no political message." My gaze locked onto him. "If your intention is to make Israelis recognize your genuine commitment to peace, this is certainly not what is coming across. All that's coming across is the cry for blood."

"When the right time comes, this message will come out loud and clear. But things aren't yet ripe."[4] I only watched him without replying. I signaled for the check, pulled out some shekels, and paid.

"You're not convinced," Marwan said as we stood up to leave. I didn't know what to tell him. "It'll turn out alright, you'll see," he assured me. Marwan is now serving a life sentence in an Israeli prison.

. . .

In early 2001 the only meaningful role I thought I could play was precisely the opposite of my clandestine activities during the first intifada.
I took to the public stage. I wrote articles, gave lectures, and did what I
could to preach some reason. There was still a glimmer of hope, I thought.
Clinton was still in office, Barak's government had fallen, but he, too,
was still in office until elections in May.

At the end of January 2001, with Clinton about to leave office, Barak
and Arafat made one last-ditch attempt at peace. Israeli and Palestinian
teams went to Taba to try to work out an agreement. The negotiation teams
couldn't have been better. On the Israeli side sat Yossi Belin, Yossi Sarid,
and others with similar political leanings; and on our side were Abu Ala,
Nabil Sha'ath, Saeb, and Mohammed Dahlan, the head of security in Gaza.
As individuals, the Israeli and Palestinian negotiators brought with
them a great store of energy, goodwill, and creative ideas. They closed important gaps, and this time neither Yahweh nor Allah were spoilers.

The problem was the changed political map back home. Taba came too
late. Arafat was ambivalent because he calculated that it made no tactical
sense to conclude an agreement with an Israeli government headed for defeat. Barak vacillated because he wasn't sure an agreement would win him
the upcoming elections. And it probably wouldn't have given the justified
anger in the Israeli street. For Israelis, it was hard to contemplate peace
when gunmen in Tulkarem had taken two owners of a sushi bar in the hip
Shenkin district of Tel Aviv, led them out to a field, and executed them.
The two had come to the West Bank to buy flowerpots for their restaurant.

Smirking like a satyr, Sharon prepared for elections whose results
everyone knew in advance. "The idea of making peace with the Palestinians is absurd,"[5] he stated on the campaign stump. The Israeli public
supported him to the same degree that they vilified Arafat as the evil
spook behind the uprising. It was the stock opinion that the PA's illegal
stockpiling of weapons, far in excess of objective needs, was evidence
that the Palestinians weren't serious about a conclusive peace deal.

Palestinians practiced their own myth-making after Sharon handily routed Barak in February. Putting on a brave face, our spokesmen pretended to believe that it was better to have an overtly belligerent hawk than an equally belligerent ex-commando camouflaged as a dove. The Palestinians were once again falling into that perennial trap Father knew so well: they thought somehow that the "world" would step in like a deus ex machina and set things right. And a Sharon-led government would only speed up the process: with more disaster and more blood, the international hand of Justice was bound to intervene. Except it never has and never will.

The final force that drew me back into politics was an intensifying vacuum that destroyed some of the few vestiges of sane Palestinian leadership. At the end of May, the Israelis tried to assassinate Jibril. *The Christian Science Monitor* got it right with its report:

> To some Israelis, a burly Palestinian police commander named Jibril Rajoub represents their best hope for a peaceful future. Long committed to peace negotiations, he has worked for years to prevent militant Palestinians from attacking Israel. Late Sunday afternoon, Israeli forces fired shells at his house from a tank and a helicopter. If Mr. Rajoub hadn't been walking between rooms to get better reception on his cellphone, he later said, he might have been killed.
>
> Coming on top of other actions that Israeli leaders have come publicly to regret, Palestinians are wondering what is going on. Either the most sophisticated military in the Middle East is mistakenly striking at the very Palestinian leaders who have eschewed violence and maintained a willingness to negotiate with Israel—or there is no mistake at all.[6]

Wisely, Jibril began to lay low.

Ten days later, on May 31, moderates lost their leader. I was in my office at the university when Abdel Kader el-Husseini, Faisal's son, phoned me at my office with the news of his father's death in Kuwait.

During the previous months, Faisal had been a ubiquitous presence bravely defending his city, his patrimony, though he never veered away from nonviolence. He was a master tightrope walker who knew how to point his finger at an oppressor without it being wrapped around a trigger.

Faisal had been on one of his regular fund-raising tours on behalf of a desperate population in East Jerusalem. He had retired early that evening to his hotel bedroom to rest. Two hours later his bodyguard checked in on him and found him dead. He left Jerusalem a seemingly healthy man. Palestinian rumormongers whispered that Israel had had someone slip something into his coffee.

News of Faisal's death hit me much like the death of my own father. I sat in my office for a few minutes in stunned silence, doing my best to contain the tears. I thought back on the years in which our bond was like one between father and son. Since the Madrid talks, tensions and misunderstandings had grown up between us, and it took Marwan's best efforts to patch things up. Shaking my head in disbelief, I recalled how Marwan, Faisal, and I had met nearly every evening at Mother's house for a month until the air was cleared. "Faisal's gone," I repeated over and over, feeling orphaned. Even with the complications that had crept into our relationship, he was a man I had deeply loved.

At the Orient House the dignitaries were already gathering. The major sheikhs and the mufti joined with the business elite and the Christian bishops to pay their respects, but equally to demonstrate their place in the social pecking order. When I arrived, officials at the Orient House saw me in the crowd and waved me to the front. Shaking my head, I made my way to the back, where the taxi drivers were congregated. There I sat on a tree stump, my face buried in my hands, and wept. At the most hopeful moment in the modern history of our people, the first intifada, the two of us had stood together; and now, with all our efforts in tatters, Faisal was gone. Was this the way Father felt when Faisal's father, Abdel Kader, was killed? Anguish, but also fear, clawed away at me. *What do we do now?*

On the following day I joined the crowds at the Muqata in Ramallah, waiting for the corpse to arrive in a special helicopter. I saw Marwan, who came to me and asked me to give Faisal's eulogy on behalf of Fatah.

Arrangements were made to bury him next to his father, at Al-Aqsa. Israeli authorities, in a rare moment of compassion, promised not to block the funeral procession to Jerusalem. Everyone wishing to walk in the procession from Ramallah could reach Al-Aqsa.

I mingled with the crowds as the slow procession began. What came to mind was Father's account of how he had walked in Abdel Kader's funeral, the day following the battle at al-Castal. All along the route crowds joined in. Women wailed at the doorsteps of their homes as the corpse passed. Palestinian flags were hoisted everywhere. Entering East Jerusalem without army roadblocks felt as if Faisal's death had liberated the city. In a way, I reflected sadly, it took death for Faisal's dream to come true, if only briefly on the day of his burial.

After he was laid to rest in the Al-Aqsa grounds, I gave the eulogy. Faisal was not just one man, I declared before the crowd. Jerusalem, its walls, which Faisal loved, and every stone and alley he walked and touched resonate with his memory. And everyone he ran out to help in the middle of the night and whose lives he touched—all will continue to bear testimony of him through their compassion, integrity, and dedication to restore life and honor to our besieged people and our beloved city.

Forty days later, at the Orient House, I gave a more prepared speech, though this time a hundred heavily armed soldiers patrolling the streets outside tried to prevent dignitaries and guests from attending. I got into the Orient House only by crawling over a back wall. In the speech I recalled my first encounter with Faisal, as he was taking a beating from Israeli soldiers on the day the Al-Aqsa was torched by the Australian religious nut. I also recounted how in 1967 Arafat had waded across the Jordan River, and while trying to build up a local military cadre, he often hid out in Faisal's house. Through the window I could see soldiers, heavily armed and speaking into crackling walkie-talkies. A helicopter, invisible but loud enough to waken the dead, hovered overhead.

Chapter Twenty-nine

Allies

ARAFAT WASTED NO TIME in sending out feelers to see if he could recruit me to take over Faisal's job as the PLO man in Jerusalem and the head of the Orient House, the de facto Palestinian center of government in East Jerusalem. Perhaps Arafat felt he needed somebody from a Jerusalem dynasty to meet visiting dignitaries, and from time to time to shake a fist at the Israelis. What was about to ensue was the story of PECDAR all over again. This time around, however, I got outfoxed.

I had always been in awe of Faisal's indefatigable energies at countering Israeli attempts to take over East Jerusalem. At the same time I dreaded the prospect of such a thankless task of stamping out the flames in one corner as the entire field was ablaze. What could one person do to help a city beleaguered by a powerful occupier willing to spend billions to take it over, while Palestinians, backed in theory by the entire Arab and Muslim worlds, were laying out pennies to preserve the city's Arab identity? The PA had flouted the Oslo Agreement in the number of guns it had bought, but it strangely went along with Oslo when it came to Jerusalem. Villages in the West Bank got more of its investment and attention than East Jerusalem, the heart and soul of Palestinian identity.

It wasn't just the certainty that being Arafat's man in Jerusalem would be a losing proposition that put me off, or my conviction that the only hope for the city was a political deal with the Israelis, nor was it just that the bloodbath was making a bad situation impossibly worse. Another reason I had no interest in the job was because I couldn't picture myself in a suit and tie welcoming diplomats and playing the role of Jerusalem aristocrat at the Orient House. That was my father and Faisal. I still felt more comfortable with the taxi drivers than with bishops and sheikhs.

I employed all my prevaricating skills. One way to deflect the pressure on me was to circulate a working paper suggesting that public leaders in East Jerusalem form an informal congress of representatives from the various sectors—religious, educational, business, and professional. Collectively, this body would appoint a secretariat to run the affairs of the Orient House. The idea floated around for a couple of months before petering out. Arafat didn't push it, no doubt because such a body could have developed too independently for his liking.

Another tack was something I was busy doing anyway: to speak out against the fantasies of an entire society, which is never an easy proposition, and in our society was potentially deadly. I decided to put my thoughts together in a short newspaper article. What I was aiming at was a variation on what Edward Said, borrowing from the Quakers, called, "speaking truth to power," though, unlike Said, the power in question wasn't our leadership, which was well aware of what I thought. The power in need of addressing was the man on the street, both the Arab and the Jew. With all the havoc and devastation, Manichean dualities of "us" and "them," Arab and Jewish, Palestinian and Israeli, had ceased being useful. Both societies were sinking together. Either we team up as allies to end the mad tango, or we all lose. Simple.

"What Next?" appeared simultaneously in Arabic and Hebrew newspapers in September 2001. Its message was straightforward: the minute we returned our pistols to their holsters, we'd have to sit down again and talk. And once we did, the taboos we'd been avoiding—Jerusalem, settlements, and refugees—would be on the table. But before tackling these seemingly insurmountable obstacles, it was imperative to remind people of the basic interests both sides shared. The average Israeli sought security and a Jewish state, and the average Palestinian sought freedom from occupation. There was an astoundingly simple formula for both sides to secure their basic interests: two states more or less divided along the 1967 border.

Israelis needed to know that for them to keep their Jewish state required a free Palestinian state along the 1967 borders, with East Jerusalem as its capital. Palestinians needed to know that to get their state required acknowledging the moral right of Israel to exist as a Jewish state. There could be no blanket right of return into Israel for the refugees:

> We have two rights. We have the right of return, in my opinion. But we also have the right to live in freedom and independence. And very often in life one has to forgo the implementation of one right in order to implement other rights.

If both sides failed in this out of expediency or weakness, we'd find ourselves one day in a hybrid state that fulfilled neither the Israeli quest for a Jewish state, nor the national Palestinian quest for an Arab state.

What Next?" took aim at nationalistic delusions. At first the article seemed drowned out by the din of war cries. Those who agreed with me, and some did, didn't say so too loudly; prudence required their keeping their distance and remaining silent. My detractors fired off articles, claiming, quite rightly, that I was disconnected from the public mood. Continuing with the violence, for them the true path to salvation, was for me a collective suicide mission.

I quipped to Lucy at the time that I felt like someone seeing a tourist bus heading for an abyss. He stands on the side of the road waving frantically at the speeding bus to warn it to stop, but the vacationers caught in the merriment of the trip—singing songs, eating their lunch, looking out at the passing landscape and at the crazy gesticulations of the pedestrian outside the window—ignore him.

The one person whose opinion of "What Next?" I still didn't know was Arafat. When I finally found out what he thought of it, the crafty chairman simultaneously patted me on the back and then strong-armed me into accepting Faisal's old post.

For five months I had been studiously avoiding the Old Man and his headquarters, out of fear of being pressured into taking up the PLO Jerusalem post. Soon after "What Next?" appeared, I finally visited him to ask for help in paying salaries at the university. I thought it was safe to show my face because so much time had gone by, and in any case my heretical views disqualified me as Arafat's "man" in Jerusalem.

Walking into Arafat's office I found him in his familiar pose, hunched over papers at his desk. Akram Haniyyah, his adviser, was sitting across from him. The second I saw Akram's grinning face I should have waved hello to both men, turned on my heel, and walked straight out. Akram always has something brewing inside his head. I should have been on my guard.

I sat down and fidgeted a bit in my chair because of the awkward silence in the office. Without uttering a word, Akram jotted down some notes on a scrap of paper and handed the paper over to Arafat, who read it and finally lifted his head to look at me. Still in total silence, he passed the scrap of paper to me. On it was written that Faisal's job was still vacant. I was sure they had practiced the routine before I arrived.

"Well?" Arafat finally said, leaning back in his chair. Taking off his oversize glasses, he looked straight at me. "Well?"

I hadn't expected the topic to come up, so I stuttered out a response. "Well, you see . . ." I explained some of the details of my plan to set up a collective of leaders, and told him the reasons why I thought no single person could fill Faisal's shoes. "It's like this . . ." But Arafat wasn't listening. "As I see it . . ." He looked impatient. I cleared my throat.

"Someone must represent the chairman before the diplomatic missions in Jerusalem," Akram cut in. I sat there, rubbing my blue worry beads.

"Hear that?" Arafat said, staring at me with big watery eyes. "Sari, you can be my point man. This is *very* important to me." From this I knew that he had approved of "What Next?"

The stall tactic I used only sealed my fate. "Everyone already knows I represent you. That's how diplomats and others view me anyway."

"If that's true, what's wrong with making it official?" Arafat gently insisted, implying that if I still refused there must be some other reason.

I had no fallback strategy. Over the years I had always tried to walk the fine line of maintaining my freedom from Arafat's officialdom without arousing his mistrust, altogether a bad idea. I had managed this friendly balance by never telling him no clearly to his face. There had always been a way to weasel my way out, such as skipping out from the royal palace in Oslo.

Seeing that I was a defeated man, Akram took a soft-sell approach. "Listen, Sari, you go to those diplomatic cocktail parties in Jerusalem anyway. What we're asking for is what you're already doing. It'll just be official, that's all. This'll be a piece of cake for you." Akram is a wily politician.

"Well," I began with a smile of defeat, "if that's how you want it . . ."

"We'll consider it a done deal," Akram said, finishing my sentence for me.

"Great," Arafat chimed in, and at once agreed to provide emergency assistance to pay my employees' salaries at the university.

The next morning, headlines in Arabic and Hebrew papers announced the appointment. The articles went into amazing detail, each with a slightly different version to suit their readers' particular slant. The Israeli left was eager to ham up the appointment of an Oxford man to counter something the Israeli president Moshe Katzav had told a group of bar mitzvah boys in May after two Israeli boys were found stoned and stabbed to death in a cave near a West Bank settlement: that we Palestinians "don't belong to our continent, to our world, but actually belong to a different galaxy." I was Exhibit A that this may not necessarily be true.

Taking over the PLO Jerusalem job brought back old memories of Father as governor of the city, or of my lavatory office and the stir and exhilaration of the technical and political committees at the Orient House. But Sharon, not Rabin, was prime minister now, and we were not in a peace process but a war. By the time I took up the post, the Orient House was off limits. In August 2001, the Israelis had made sweeping closures of Palestinian national institutions including the Orient House. They padlocked the gate and forbade entry. I set up an office on the second floor of the Imperial Hotel just inside Jaffa Gate. The shabby but charming hotel, redolent of Ottoman days, was a cheap favorite for backpackers.

On October 15, just three days into the job, I decided to present to the public, in as clear and as forceful terms as I could muster, what I considered my top priority. There were a dozen home demolitions I could have protested, or settlement expansions that were proceeding apace from a dozen different directions. I could have pointed fingers at the post-9/11 President Bush, who had bigger things on his mind than us, while his allies, the American Christian fundamentalists, were trooping through settlements by the thousands, Bibles in hand, to show their support for the Israeli takeover. But I knew, especially after the terrorist attacks in New York and Washington, D.C., that a different approach was needed to counter an Israeli strategy several layers deep. (One day I figured out, for instance, that the takeover of the Goldsmith's Souk was part of a plan to link up the Jewish Quarter with isolated Jewish settlements by way of our property.) Reconstituting the Camp David alliance, namely with the United States working with both sides to force a deal, was the only hope of saving Jerusalem. And the only way to get back to the table was for the Palestinian leadership to declare forcibly its rejection of violence and its desire to live in peace side by side with the Jewish state.

To get this message out, I joined a panel with the Palestinian political scientist and pollster Khalil Shikaki at the Hebrew University.

On the way to the meeting venue, I ran into the mayor of Jerusalem's adviser on Arab affairs, Shalom Goldstein, along with my old family friend Nabil Jaʾbari, son of the famous Sheikh Jaʾbari of Hebron.

Nearing the lecture hall, I was astonished to see a massive crowd near the entrance. My first thought was that a local rock band was playing or maybe a movie was being shown in an adjoining hall. "Perhaps we should stand in line and see what's going on," I said, nudging Shalom.

"Sari, I think they're here for you," he said, chuckling.

"Maybe they want to see what someone from a different galaxy looks like," I suggested, putting my arm around Shalom's shoulder.

Sure enough, the hall was packed. Khalil took the floor first. Using data he had been working on for a decade, he showed how public support for Hamas and violence were inversely proportional to progress in the peace process. The figures from opinion polls and graphs spoke for themselves. The more hope there was, the less violence. Palestinians weren't genetically crazy or suicidal. Their increasing extremism was a function of despair.

Now it was my turn. I didn't have any graphs or numbers, no empirical case studies to prove anything. First I stated something no one in the audience needed reminding of: that the Palestinian uprising was hopelessly mired in bloodshed. Next I came out with an idea supported by common sense, and it was a measure of the mood that summer that my piece of common sense was the most startling announcement my audience could have imagined—because in our era of suicide bombings it had become unthinkable: "Israelis and Palestinians," I told them, "are not enemies at all." A disbelieving hush spread over my listeners. "If anything, we are strategic allies."

The only sound I heard from the audience was coughing and some sniffles. Israelis may think that America is their real ally, I continued, and Palestinians think that Arabs or Muslims are theirs; in truth, the only two parties who are objectively allied with each other are the Israelis and Palestinians, because, like it or not, we have a shared future. Our mutual interest that the future be better than the present creates an objective alliance between us.

I went on to show that violence and force were self-defeating. "Israel cannot break the Palestinian will to be free by force, just as Palestinians cannot use force to push Israel back behind the '67 borders. Not only is the use of force inhumane, it is also politically useless. Only reason, as a guideline for negotiations, can dictate the terms of a deal that serves the interests of both peoples.

"Our shared future has to provide Israel with a secure guarantee for its existence as a Jewish state, but it also has to provide Palestinians with a secure guarantee for their freedom and independence in their own state."

What I had written in "What Next?" underlay my lecture. Negotiations could lead to frustration and extremism unless they isolated and addressed the source of our respective national diseases. Palestinians must give up the dream of return, Israelis the idea of settling Greater Israel, and both sides the prospect for unilateral sovereignty over all of Jerusalem.

My role as Arafat's Jerusalem man guaranteed that talk of Palestinians and Israelis actually being allies generated outrage back in my side of the city. But one thing I said to the students at the Hebrew University that didn't draw much attention at the time went back to my reading of Avicenna:

Long ago, the prophets that wandered this land taught humanity a belief in God and in life after death. Today, we sadly have to make do without such miraculous messengers sent by God. We're still in need of a miracle, and it's up to us to perform it. Just as our forefathers were won over to the belief in life after death, we must develop faith in life after the bloody conflict, after the horror. Our peoples together can bring about such life. They can perform the miracle.

Many Israelis responded to my line about our being allies as merely the private sentiment of a moonstruck dreamer like the errant knight of La Mancha. As I would soon learn, there were people in the Shin Bet and the government who deciphered my peaceful words as perfidious coded messages preaching a murderous incitement. Such talk was, according to their convoluted logic, a very clever way of undermining the Jewish state. It was a dirty PLO trick to dupe the credulous Israelis into thinking we extraterrestrials were humans after all.

Palestinians at least knew I was speaking openly, and as I had anticipated, my talk aroused shock and disbelief. "What sort of sophistry is this? How could our enemies be our allies? How can we have common interests with snipers shooting down children in the morning and hanging out in Tel Aviv bars in the evening?"

No sooner did my words hit the press than irate fellow Palestinians began demanding I be relieved of my new position. I had made plenty of unpopular comments before, but as I was now Faisal's successor, those words carried more weight. Threats and warnings came in from all sides. An organization of Palestinians living in the diaspora began circulating a petition to get me fired. "We urge you to write immediately to PLO Chairman Yasir Arafat," went the group's chain letter, "to demand that Dr. Sari Nusseibeh be dismissed forthwith from his appointment as political representative in East Jerusalem." "Watch out!" others warned me. "Don't cross the chairman's red lines. Remember what happened to Faisal!" Others cautioned me about "the Palestinian street"—assassination in short. Mother let me know in her wise but weary voice that I was wasting my time. "It's all for nothing. It's all lost. The Israelis will never agree to a thing." She was also afraid I'd become a target for fanatics.

My reply to all my nervous friends and family was that I was not a threat to anyone, because I had no personal political ambitions. "I'm not a political leader," I explained to an interviewer for an Israeli newspaper. "I am here only because I have to be."

To the fellow academics trying to get me fired, I sent my own reply:

Dear Sirs,

I read your appeal to ask Chairman Arafat to dismiss me from my new post. I would like you to add my name to the list of those signing

the appeal since, amongst other reasons, this assignment seems to un-
dermine my ability to express myself freely.

I spent the next two months sorting through files and materials on the administration of East Jerusalem. It was like digging into a bankrupt company. There was no master plan for running the city, and no budget. Arafat's habit of doling out money according to whim rather than policy bred corruption. To an Israeli interviewer I explained how people were "living in substandard conditions, leading miserable, depressing lives. People barely have enough to eat. They can hardly remember what it means to lead a normal life." Thirty-five years of occupation had destroyed a common sense of citizenship. People had become passive and myopically focused on their private concerns. I wanted to snap them out of their collective torpor through a "new dream of a different life. It is our task to implant that dream in the minds of people and to bring about its realization."[1]

The first thing I did was to ask my university team for help in putting together a comprehensive financial plan for East Jerusalem. Within weeks the budget was on Arafat's desk. Just as I had feared would happen, the request was archived.

The second thing I did was establish a local political committee made up of important civic and religious figures, businessmen, politicians, and some of the remaining patricians in the city. The working assumption behind the scheme was that by banding together we could achieve more, and resist Israeli colonization more effectively, than in our otherwise anarchistic ways. After two months of work and meetings, I gave up, and for two reasons: Arafat wasn't keen to see it succeed, and Israeli authorities had stepped in to outlaw it.

The most productive use of my time in the post wasn't with the PLO but with Peace Now, which had become nearly as marginalized in Israeli society as the peace camp had in my own. We were all scattered individuals whistling in the wind.

Some of the leaders of Peace Now and I met on various occasions and at various venues—my office, restaurants, hotel lobbies, and so on—to hammer out a short statement we called the Time for Peace document, which outlined a common vision. Violence of course had to stop, and talks had to resume on the basis of three principles: two states along the 1967 lines, Jerusalem as a shared capital, and a just and practical solution to the refugee problem. We added the word *just* in order to get Palestinians to support the initiative.

Our plan was to mobilize public support for an end to the conflict. We wanted to launch the campaign with a signature ceremony in which public figures from both sides would sign off on the Time for Peace document. Following the ceremony—went the plan—we would stage a series of joint peaceful protests to get the word out to both populations that there was still hope, still a solution, still a chance for a miracle. I was in touch with Antonio Bassolino, the governor of the region around Naples, who promised international backing for the launch. He promised to be at the Imperial Hotel for the signing ceremony on December 28, 2001.

On that day the hotel was bursting with people and activity. A peaceful march organized by Peace Now and Women in Black (a brave Israeli antiwar group) brought a large group of Israelis together with Palestinians and foreign supporters. The march snaked its way through Jerusalem, and ended at the entrance to the hotel inside Jaffa Gate. Attending our signing ceremony were Knesset members from the Labor and Meretz parties, along with Peace Now activists. Hundreds of Palestinian activists and public leaders attended. Close to three thousand people added their signatures to a book attached to the Time for Peace document.

Our spirits were high. So were our hopes. Governor Bassolino, Jossi Sarid, Yossi Belin, and Lucy and I walked out onto the balcony overlooking the square where the peace marchers were assembled, and released a flock of white doves into the sky above the marchers.

The following day we began a public campaign. We set up our headquarters in the Imperial Hotel, and with support from the European

Union, we began planning for a series of major events. One was the Human Chain initiative, slated to take place the next June. Our plan was to bring out hundreds of thousands of Israelis and Palestinians to form a human link all the way from the northern tip of the West Bank to the southern tip of Gaza. We wanted to demarcate our future border physically.

It was at this point that my Inspector Javert began to watch my every move.

Chapter Thirty

Checkmate

I N MY LECTURE at the Hebrew University I returned to a theme I had explored in my dissertation on Avicenna: miracles. How is it possible, I asked, that an act of the will can turn one thing into its opposite? Standing on the stage before a crowd of Israeli students and faculty, I said we needed to develop the miraculous knack of turning hatred into understanding.

Their response taught me that we didn't have to wait for an act of divine intervention, however appreciated it would have been. The empathy those in the audience showed, their *lack* of public hostility, revived in me the belief I had the first time I set eyes on the badly dressed Israelis cutting in line at Ben Gurion Airport in 1967: that some mysterious bond connects our two peoples. We *are* allies.

My talk at the university was also a good reminder of how insanely duplicitous Middle Eastern politics can be. Things are never what they seem to be. How do you make sense of Barak, a thoroughly secular man, torpedoing the Camp David talks over the Holy of Holies; or Marwan, in tears after the summit failed, planning ambushes months later; or

Sharon and his ilk telling the world that they were strategic partners in President Bush's war on terror while they were attacking Palestinian moderates, destroying the PA's ability to govern, and leaving the field wide open to Hamas? In my case, just as I was sticking my neck out farther than ever, my Inspector Javert and the Israeli right labeled me the smiling face of Palestinian terror, indeed the "most dangerous Palestinian alive."

Israelis went back to the old strategy of hitting the moderates while leaving the fanatics alone. They did this *not* because our feuding tribes were so far from peace, but because peace was so near, like a ripe plum ready for the picking. Polls on both sides showed that the desire for peace was far stronger than the thirst for blood. This scared Sharon as much as it did Sheikh Yassin. If the Israeli and Palestinian people were allies in peace, some of our leaders were allies in stoking the conflict.

In 2001 we needed all the miracles we could get, but they were in short supply. Classes at Al-Quds were often cancelled because of the fighting. The closures made movement from the West Bank to Jerusalem impossible, forcing us to move the humanities program from Beit Hanina to a high school in the West Bank.

The campaign to get me ousted from the Jerusalem job picked up steam. It was easy to ignore—because I, too, wanted Arafat to get rid of me. I already had my hands full keeping the university hotheads from drawing the Israeli soldiers into a pitched battle on campus.

My first attempt to resign as Arafat's Jerusalem man took place a couple of months after I assumed the post. The strategies, initiatives, and proposed reforms in Jerusalem city management were totally ignored. I felt that a PLO presence in Jerusalem was simply a fig leaf placed over a systematic Israeli colonization we were powerless to stop. (A daily reminder of this was a new highway, appropriately named after Menachem Begin, which cut my neighborhood of Beit Hanina in half, and connected the booming settlements of Neve Yaʾakov, Ramot, and Pisgat

Ze³ev with West Jerusalem.) Feeling that my own family's 1,300 years of history was on the line, I kept pounding away on the idea of returning to Camp David–style talks, and fast. Only in serious final status negotiations could we prevent Jerusalem from becoming totally lost to us.

With calls to get rid of me growing louder by the hour, I finally wrote up a letter of resignation and went to see Arafat. The letter stated that though I valued serving in the PLO, I cherished my freedom to speak my mind even more. If the chairman didn't like what I was doing, I would gladly spare him the trouble of firing me. I'd quit.

I handed him the resignation.

"What's this?" He quickly read it and handed it back to me.

"As you can see, it's undated." I motioned to the top corner of the page and put it on his desk. "You can fill in any date you want. Whenever you need to, just date and sign it, and fax it to my office."

As was his custom, he took off his glasses and rubbed his eyes, which looked bloodshot from too little sleep, too many worries. "But why are you doing this? Is anyone putting pressure on you?"

"No. I actually thought you might be under pressure on my account."

"Bullshit" is a good translation of what he snapped out. The chairman handed me back the paper. "You think I'd bow to pressure to stop you from speaking your own mind?"

This was another example of Arafat playing the trapeze act, carefully balancing himself between moderates and militants, unwilling and perhaps unable to come down firmly on either side.

In January 2002, the day we launched the People's Peace Campaign with fanfare at the Imperial Hotel inside Jaffa Gate, the Israelis intercepted a four-thousand-ton ship loaded with Iranian-made Katyusha rockets, mortars, mines, and advanced explosives plying its way around the Arabian Peninsula en route to Gaza. It was perfect propaganda for the Israeli right. For just as the PLO man in Jerusalem was holding hands with Israelis, other PLO types were arming themselves to the teeth.

A mass demonstration we planned with Peace Now on the spot in Tel Aviv where Rabin had been gunned down foundered on terror. The crowd of thirty thousand we had expected never materialized because an hour before the demonstration there was another terrorist bombing. The Israelis understandably preferred to sit home and follow the grisly news reports.

The Human Chain project we organized with Peace Now also failed, in spite of months of hard work. To strangle our efforts at forming a human chain along the length of the Green Line, the Israeli authorities simply tightened the screws, closing off some areas, imposing curfews in others, and turning back international supporters at Ben Gurion Airport.

All the while, violence on the Palestinian street was getting out of hand. Whatever the cause or causes, the bloodletting exposed a basic difference between our feuding tribes. On the whole, the Palestinian reaction to Israeli heavy-handedness was haphazard, emotional, and driven by blind rage. The so-called "uprising" continued as it had begun: a long series of improvised blunders. As soon as it was hijacked by infantile militarism, 99 percent of the Palestinian population was defenseless against the draconian Israeli counteroffensive. Israel's response was very determined and cold-blooded, and whether intentional or not, it was perfectly suited to destroying our governmental ability to calm people down.

When Arafat finally called for a stop to the violence (it took a lot of prodding), we seemed at last to have turned a corner. Enter Sharon again. Just as word of the cease-fire came, the Israeli prime minister ordered the assassination in broad daylight of a highly revered and popular militant activist in Tulkarem. The order was carried out, and Palestinian violence flared up again in response. And so it was, each time there seemed to be a lull, Sharon stoked the fires like a witch her brew.

Then of course there was the attitude among a frighteningly high number of Palestinians: "The Israelis have their Phantoms; we have our moving bombs." At first suicide bombings were almost entirely the work of Hamas or Islamic Jihad, and those groups' popularity soared.

"There are a hundred thousand Palestinians willing to become kamikazes," Abu Ala told Joshua Hammer of *Newsweek*, reflecting on the public mood. Not to be outdone by Hamas, some people in Fatah decided that to compete with Hamas they might have to adopt its methods. The grim mood among Palestinians guaranteed a steady supply of willing suicide bombers.

Humiliation has always been Israel's most powerful weapon against us. From the Palestinian perspective, this can either lead to a stronger will and greater sense of autonomy, or destroy a person's self-worth, tilling the soil for the nihilism of terrorists.

When a suicide bomber struck in 1996, there had been near-universal condemnation and abhorrence, because people still held out hope in the peace process. Now, five years later, it had become the order of the day, with hardly a peep of protest. When I condemned the insanity of these suicide bombers, few dared join me.

One day Lucy rushed to bring Nuzha home from school. A suicide bomber, passing in front of the school on his way to his target, feared a nearby policeman was on to him, and detonated his explosive belt. His severed head flew into the schoolyard where the children were playing.

Jibril loathed the attacks as much as I. "I spent 18 years in Israeli jail for fighting the Israeli occupation," he told one reporter, "but never would I have aimed purposefully an attack against civilians . . . Resistance against the occupation is one thing, and using pernicious means to kill people just because they are people is something else."

Jibril's staff at what was left of his Preventive Security Academy interrogated a number of people who had tried unsuccessfully to become human bombs. The staff determined that 80 percent were motivated not by religion à la Al Qaeda but by anger, depression, and a thirst for revenge.

One woman was a thirty-five-year-old mother of five. She was arrested by one of Jibril's men after she asked someone to give her a bomb. In the interrogation, she cited shame as her motivation. Soldiers had tried to strip her naked at a checkpoint and danced around with her as if she were an inflatable sex toy, and in front of a long line of cars and buses full of fellow Arabs. She preferred death, she explained, over having to face her own people after this, especially if she could take a few Israelis with her.

Another was a twenty-four-year-old woman studying media and communications. She wasn't religious and evidently harbored no hopes of Paradise as payback. She volunteered as a human kamikaze because Israeli soldiers had forced her at gunpoint to kiss a group of Arab men stopped at a checkpoint.

Judging by the polls and anecdotal evidence on the streets and in the cafés, as 2002 began, a bizarre schizophrenia was at work among people. People wanted peace, but then there were the appalling scenes of the masses celebrating violence as if in some primal ritual, which didn't break my belief in the basic decency of the Palestinian and Israeli peoples. They were just being temporarily misled by ideologues and fanatics, and I had no doubt that with a bit of time and some exposure to common sense, they would shake free of the political madness that had enveloped them.

"The killing of civilians in any form," I insisted to an Israeli journalist, "reflects a serious psychological state that needs attention and treatment." Employing a metaphor Muslims could relate to, I told audiences that the best kind of jihad in Islam was that of self-control, or the control of one's passions and rage. And to a rather astonished David Remnick for an article in *The New Yorker*, I switched metaphors again: "The Palestinians have to resurrect the spirit of Christ to absorb the sense of pain and insult they feel and control it, and not let it determine the way they act toward Israel. They have to realize that an act of violence does not serve their interest."

The image of Christ wasn't all that far-fetched, as Mother would soon prove. One day, while reading about two extraordinary philosophers with Jewish Viennese backgrounds, I ran across passages about the anti-Semitic scourge of the 1930s. As I read on, I felt the men's suffocating sense of doom and terror due to their problems with citizenship, residency papers, travel documents, venial bureaucracies, the threat of property confiscation, and other humiliations. All at once I was reminded of my own home and my own people's fate since 1947.

I'd always been quite aware of the hard facts concerning European anti-Semitism and how it had led to the barbarism of the Holocaust. But suddenly facts were coupled with emotions. The tale of these two Viennese philosophers gave me an empathic insight into their fate.

That night, during a visit with Mother, I posed a question. Just suppose, I began, that in the early years of the century an elderly and learned Jewish gentleman from Europe had come to your father to consult with him on an urgent matter. And suppose this gentleman told Grandfather that a looming human catastrophe of unimaginable proportions was about to befall the Jews of Europe. And suppose this gentleman added that as an Abrahamic cousin with historic ties to Palestine, he would like to prevent the genocide to come by seeking permission for his people to return to the shared homeland, to provide them with safety and refuge. What do you think Grandfather would have said? I asked her.

Her answer surprised me. I was prepared for a long conversation full of conditions and clauses and caveats, but instead she replied straightaway with a wave of her hand, "What do you think? How could anyone have refused?" It was amazing for me how easily compassion sliced through fifty years of pain.

I quickly thought up another story to illustrate what historically in fact happened. I imagined a frightened Jewish refugee fleeing Europe and parachuting into the Ramle area in search of safety. Gun in hand, as he floats down to earth he suddenly spots my grandfather in Arab headdress standing in the middle of a field gripping a shovel, looking terrified himself. My grandfather, shocked by the sudden appearance of a gun-toting flying man heading down straight toward him, prepares to fend the man off with his shovel. Running scared from the hell of the concentration camps and the gas chambers, the terrorized European logically starts firing at the Arab with the raised shovel.

And so the two strangers are each driven by fear and terror, totally unaware of the condition of the other. The Jew seeks space to continue living, while the Arab defends his space to the death.

· · ·

The one good thing that came out of my stint as Arafat's Jerusalem man was the trouble I managed to stir up. This earned me plenty of criticism and threats, but at least people were talking—a major leap forward in a time of bullets and bombs.

My position on the right of return kindled a nationwide debate. If it was salutary to get people examining words they'd been chanting for half a century, it wasn't always safe. Following an acrimonious verbal tussle with the mufti of Jerusalem, I finally agreed to take on two body-guards. I still have them.

I got a taste of what the public thought of my views after Jawad Boulos, now the lawyer for the university, invited me to speak to a high school in his village in the Galilee. What was supposed to be a fund-raiser turned into a public trial. "Who put you in charge of annulling the right of return?" one man demanded. Another accused me of talk-ing as though I weren't part of the leadership but someone "observing events from the side and making proposals." And a young boy chipped in: "At a time like this, when Israelis are bleeding the Palestinian people white, we need unity and not views that divide and weaken."

I was sitting on the stage flanked on one side by the head of the vil-lage local council and on the other by Jawad. As the criticism mounted, I quietly scribbled down some notes. A newspaper editor lashed out at me for my position on violence. "How can you compare the violence of the Israeli occupation against the Palestinian people with the intifada that was a response to that?"

After taking a few more shots from the floor, I stood up to respond. I was actually pleasantly surprised with the climate in the hall. My critics spoke in maturely democratic fashion: open, direct, and without threats or ad hominems. The young boy's comments especially had astonished me. I thanked them all from the bottom of my heart, reminding them that

I am really not an expert on these matters—certainly no more than you—and it's possible that I have been wrong right down the line.

I've never claimed to have some privileged access to the truth. But I want to say what I think openly and to the end. If I try to cheat myself, I won't be able to sleep at night. I must be honest with myself, but also with you, and whoever else asks me for my opinion. So, please accept my words as just one man's honest opinion.[1]

The most emotional meeting I had took me into one of the grimmest, most dust-bitten and gun-infested refugee camps in the archipelago: the Deheisheh camp, south of Bethlehem. The meeting place was full of militants from Deheisheh and three other camps in the area. As I was driving there, the voice of reason counseled me to turn around and go home. My heart was banging in my chest, for I had my doubts that I would return home safe and sound. I had decided to go to the camp after leaflets circulating around it accused me of betraying their right to their former homes and lands. A Fatah leader wrote that I had no right to hand over what didn't belong to me to someone who didn't deserve it. However foolhardy it may have been, I felt that my position on the right of return affected these people far more than anyone else, and they had a right to hear it from me directly, and to respond.

Not only did I survive the evening without a scratch, but I even came out with a fresh dose of faith in the integrity of my people. The heated debate, devoid of diplomatic protocol and niceties, went on for three hours. People stated exactly what was on their minds, and what came out was surprisingly civilized. At the end, many approached me and said that while they didn't like what they had heard—in fact, they disagreed with it totally—they nonetheless respected me for saying it. At least I was speaking openly about existential matters that they knew other PLO leaders were discussing behind closed doors, just not in the open—and especially not in a camp where outraged citizens could string them up. "We respect you for your courage and honesty," they told me. We all had tears in our eyes.

Far less pleasant, though not nearly as potentially perilous and entirely without tears, was a quarrel that broke out between Abu Mazen and me in Arafat's Muqata compound in Ramallah.

The meeting was billed as just another discussion of various topics related to the PA. Once Arafat read out the agenda for the meeting, Abu Mazen raised his hand. He wished to add another item: my pronouncements on the refugee question. Arafat jotted the item down.

When we reached that item on the agenda, Abu Mazen began to speak in a low and calm voice. On the whole, I quite admire Abu Mazen for his realism and political courage. Born in the Galilee but expelled with his family in 1948, he grew up in Damascus. He was one of the founders of Fatah and one of the first PLO people to have dialogue with Israelis. He is a decent man free of the opportunism tainting so many of his colleagues. He is repelled by demagoguery or grandstanding. He also knows the Israelis far better than some of his colleagues do, having written his dissertation at the Moscow Oriental College on the history of Zionism.

In a brief statement, Abu Mazen set forth his objections to my public position on the right of return. It wasn't, he said, turning to me and staring me in the eyes, that he was an extremist or a demagogue. "You know how pragmatic I am." But this particular matter was related to the process of negotiations. "You just don't declare your fallback position free of charge." For him, giving up on the right of return was a question of tactics. He knew that the specter of millions of Arabs swarming back over the Green Line terrified Israelis. This turned the issue into our trump card. In the Machiavellian logic of modern politics—a game the Israelis played with great flair—how could we afford to give up our strongest hand with nothing in return? Abu Mazen was our chief negotiator at the time. By taking away this negotiating chip, he felt I was torpedoing his strategy.

There was complete silence in the room, and all eyes were on the two of us.

My initial response was as calm as his. I told him that I disagreed with his negotiation strategy. In the past, it might have worked, but not now. It was an open secret to our Israeli interlocutors that we weren't going to insist on the wholesale return of refugees. The only people who *weren't* privy to this secret were our refugees and the Israeli people. The people in the camps, I continued, had a right to know what our position was, and that our national interest required that they accept less than full historical justice. The Israeli people also needed to know that we were not planning to swamp their country with refugees. If they knew this, it would strengthen our hand in negotiation, and put the Sharon government on the defensive.

In essence, I was saying that the right of return had ceased being a trump card, and the time for a step-by-step negotiating procedure should be replaced by "a package deal" approach. It was already clear to Israelis in power what we would be willing to give up under certain conditions. Sharon, the Shin Bet, the army, and other top policy makers all knew what our position was. So why pretend? And by telling the Israelis that we would insist on this right, we would be doing Sharon's work for him. He didn't want Israelis to trust us. And if we kept repeating our old slogans, they wouldn't. Why should they?

Abu Mazen didn't like what he was hearing. He raised the pitch of his voice, and I raised mine. "You have to level with us," I demanded. "What is it you want, a state or the right of return?"

Now he began to lose his self-composure. "Why do you say that? What do you mean by 'either/or'?"

"Because that's what it boils down to. Either you want an independent state or a policy aimed at returning all the refugees to Israel. You can't have it both ways."

At this stage Abu Mazen resorted to his seniority. "You must stop making those declarations. That's an order."

"I don't take orders from you," I snapped back, surprising even myself. "I take them from Yasir Arafat. If he wants me to stop, he can tell me. *I'll let the chairman decide what I should do.*"

No one in the room made a peep.

I turned and looked at Arafat, who had been watching the two of us like a Ping-Pong match. Softly and kindly, like a gentle grandfather, he began to speak. "Sari, we have to have sympathy for the feelings of Palestinian refugees in Lebanon and Chile." That was all he said. It sounded gnomic, and at first no one seemed to know what he was saying. On hard issues we often joked that he had a *La a²am* policy, in Arabic a combination of "yes" and "no." Pure ambiguity was his gift.

After the meeting, the consensus was that Arafat had backed my position, but at the price of Abu Mazen's estrangement from me.

It was a strangely topsy-turvy time. I was coming out with treasonous statements in newspaper articles, television interviews, and public addresses; people had been murdered for far less. I told people in gun-ridden refugee camps that they had to give up their dream of historical justice, not an easy thing to do among people who still keep the keys to front doors of homes that were dynamited half a century ago. Arafat's backing was equivocal at best, and there was no guarantee he wouldn't turn on me without warning.

With all the trouble I was getting from my own people, out of whatever calculation, the Israeli government chose to begin its own campaign against me. I didn't know it at the time, but a security expert employed by the police was carefully watching my every step. The file he had on me was getting fatter by the day.

The Israeli harassment had started already at the end of 2001, when Public Security Minister Uzi Landau labeled me "the pretty face of terrorism." My statements against suicide bombers, he averred, were nothing more than a conniving "trick" to seduce Israelis into complacence.[2]

In December, the Israeli government went beyond verbal assault. Like his namesake the famed submachine gun, the Israeli minister of public security began to take aim.

Yossi Belin invited me to a Labor Party discussion group in Tel Aviv. The reception reminded me of the reception at the Hebrew University: awaiting me was a throng of well-wishers eager to listen to my point of view. In the words of one journalist, "The local and foreign media pounced" on me "as though I had been sent by Arafat to do nothing less than co-sign a Palestinian-Israeli peace agreement with Belin."[3]

A couple of days later, Minister Landau made his first move. I planned a reception for foreign diplomats at the Imperial Hotel to celebrate the Eid ul-Fitr holiday marking the end of Ramadan. The idea was to invite dignitaries for a glass of orange juice and some cookies.

Landau's diktat forbidding the event came an hour before the reception was to begin. I was shaving when the telephone rang. Jawad Boulos was on the other line. "Listen, Sari. The Israeli police are waiting for you at the front of the hotel. They've declared the reception an illegal security threat." I finished shaving, put my toothbrush in my bag just in case I would end up spending the night in jail, and drove my car to Jaffa Gate.

But instead of pasting a note on the front door of the hotel, I waited until the guests had arrived to explain in person that the event could not continue. Landau considered this brazen defiance of his order, and had me and five of my co-workers hauled in. Police surrounded us and marched us off to the Russian compound. Back in jail, I found fond memories flooding back of my arrest during the Gulf War and the motley inmates at the same jail jeering at the absurd radio reports of my being an Iraqi agent. This time there was no such solidarity with the prisoners, though the police, not knowing what to do with us, supplied us with cigarettes as they listened to a soccer game on the radio. We were released two hours later.

Landau explained his actions as necessary to save the soul of the Jewish state. Such a reception would have, "heaven forbid, contributed to the loss of sovereignty in Jerusalem." Sharon backed him up. "This government has made a clear decision not to permit the PA to operate in Jerusalem, the capital of Israel," he told the Likud Knesset faction. "We were also criticized when we closed Orient House, but this is the policy and this is what it will have to be."

Yossi Sarid published an Op-Ed in *Ha'aretz* accusing Sharon of being "petrified" of me, because I "symbolize a more sober-minded, thoughtful approach that is also nonviolent."

What the government was up to seemed obvious. They wanted to provoke an anti-Israeli diatribe—and if they were really lucky, I'd come out with an anti-Semitic slur. With this in mind I had my office put out a press release: "It's too bad that instead of sending representatives with holiday greetings, the government chose to use an iron fist." When I was

interviewed in an Israeli paper, I tried my best to play up the difference between a quite traditional gathering for cookies and the Israeli bludgeon:

"Professor Nusseibeh, what did you feel on December 17, when the
police banned your event at the Imperial Hotel in East Jerusalem
and detained you for questioning?"

"I was mainly surprised. When the telephone call came, I was
standing in front of the mirror in my bathroom, shaving. I didn't exactly understand what the story was. I didn't imagine there could be
a problem with an event to mark Eid ul-Fitr."

"What was this, on your part—naïveté or feigned naïveté?"

"Naïveté, I suppose. I hope. I am a naïve person. Most of my
friends say that about me."

"You weren't angry?"

"No. I was very surprised, maybe a little amused."

"Amused?"

"Definitely."

The New Year 2002 ushered in new attacks. A scholar at the Hebrew
University published an article with the title "Sari Nusseibeh—Arafat's
Mouth, but Saddam's Eyes and Ears."[4] When I told fellow Palestinians,
"We are at a crossroads today, and in my opinion, we must take what we
can get," a member of Israel's cabinet called me a "Trojan Horse" invei-
gling my way through smooth talk into the credulous soft minds of
Israeli leftists, whose critical senses were damaged by having too much
conscience. My moderation was engineered to "infiltrate into the heart
of Israel's capital."[5] *The Jerusalem Post* managed to locate deviousness
in a petition I circulated calling for a stop to the suicide bombers:

Nusseibeh echoes the official PA condemnations of every attack.
There is never a moral judgment made, only a cost-benefit analysis.
That killing Jews is acceptable is quite simply taken for granted.
Once we understand that this is the situation in Palestinian society,
we reconcile ourselves with the fact that we are not in a struggle

against a political movement for national sovereignty. We are being victimized by a genocidal campaign for our violent elimination supported by the overwhelming majority of Palestinians.

I was getting used to being cast as a character worse than the Hamas leader Sheikh Yassin. Some of the attacks were amusing. The pro-Israel *National Review* labeled Father an "Arab nationalist ideologue" and claimed that Mother had carried on a passionate love affair with Evelyn Barker, the "British general responsible for the war against the Zionist underground." Both Mother and I fell over laughing.

My daughter Nuzha's favorite example of character assassination came from a Web site (militantislammonitor.org) that described me in appearance as "Harry Potter as a grandfather" and in behavior more like the evil Lord Voldemort bent on seizing control of the magical world through the practice of the black arts. With my magic wand, I had turned Al-Quds University into a "well-known center of terror activity."

An unusual visitor came to my office one day. Ami Ayalon was a former commander in chief of the Israeli navy and until recently the head of the feared Shin Bet. I knew of him primarily through public statements he made as the Shin Bet chief warning of an explosion; and then once the explosion had occurred, of how the Palestinians still desired peace but wouldn't buckle to military might. In the December 2001 issue of *Le Monde Diplomatique* he had been dismissive of the Camp David legend that "Israelis had been generous and [the Palestinians] refused," and of the even bigger fable that the so-called second intifada had been planned.[6] He knew that it had been a spontaneous revolt fed by hopelessness. "We [Israelis] say the Palestinians behave like 'madmen,' but it is not madness but a bottomless despair." I admired him for his directness and mental precision.

We had met once several months earlier in London, when he showed up with a well-known Likud member to a meeting at the London School of Economics. At that meeting Ami asked me if Palestinians were prepared to respond positively to an initiative.

"Sure. Why not?"

This time Ami wore the expression of a man with serious business on his mind. His smoothly shaved pate seemed to glow as if behind it was a brain spinning like a rotor. I asked him to take a seat. "What can I do for you?" This was the only thing I could think of to say to the former master of the Shin Bet.

Wasting no time, he explained to me that after our chat in London he wrote up a proposal. He'd already discussed it with several Palestinians, who liked it, but everyone told him that for it to go farther, I was the one he needed to contact.

Amazingly, as he would later explain, during his tenure in the navy he didn't have the foggiest notion what was driving the Arab-Israeli conflict. No matter how many meetings he sat through with the general staff, he still didn't know a thing. "It's not that I'm dumb," he said in an interview, "it's something that you also find in other senior officers. When you're in the military, you're familiar only with the military angle."

It was only when he became head of the Shin Bet that this began to change. Ami made his way to the top of Israeli intelligence because of his keen intellect and his willingness to learn, even at the expense of cherished legends. He did what any good administrator does: he spent much of his time snooping around, educating himself, reading intelligence reports from interrogations, but also acquainting himself with our history, culture, and literature. He read poets like Mahmoud Darwish, the man who wrote our declaration of independence. Over time he formed a mental picture that sounded like a gloss on my message to the students at The Hebrew University: Palestinians and Israelis actually mirror one another. By a large majority both peoples want a peaceful solution and are willing to make big compromises to get it.

Ami came to the additional conclusion that Sharon's tactics of bulldozing orchards and homes, seizing territory, and caging Palestinians into South African–style Bantustans—disconnected territories surrounded by fortified Israeli towns and military areas—would create a festering sore that would only encourage more fanaticism. Something had to be done.

He came up with a plan but was uncertain if he could find prominent Palestinians to support it publicly. In his experience, Arabs would talk to an Israeli, agree with him, smoke a water pipe with him, call him a friend, and invite him over for dinner, they would just never put their name on a joint Israeli-Palestinian document. They wouldn't come out in the open and say what they were perfectly willing to repeat over and over in private.

Sitting in my office, Ami narrated how, following our conversation in London, he had approached various Palestinian political figures. They all liked his plan and assured him that in the future they would be willing to back it. They just couldn't be the first. If he wanted to push ahead, they told him, talk to Sari. "They thought you might be crazy enough to do it."

"Do what?" I asked.

Ami placed a single sheet of paper on my desk. I saw he was missing half a finger, the result of a childhood accident. He asked me to read it.

"I don't want to read it. I want to hear it from you." It was important for me to watch him as he presented his ideas. If he had given me the impression of being just another game-playing political huckster, I would have responded with manipulation of my own, and the conversation would have ended there. But unlike most politicians on both sides of the conflict, he spoke viscerally and honestly.

As taut as a spring, Ami snapped out the principles at the heart of the paper. His thinking went like this: with a piecemeal approach, the conflict would never get solved. As quickly as possible we must put all the most contentious issues on the table up front, and leave the details for a later stage. Ami's approach was the exact opposite of Oslo.

The positions he outlined were very close to those arrived at by the two negotiation teams at Taba: two states along the 1967 border; no mass return of refugees; a demilitarized Palestinian state; and Jerusalem as the capital of two peoples. What I found far more intriguing—these positions were commonplace by this point—was the plan's more sub-versive aspect. "The only way to force the leaders to finally sign a deal," he said glancing up from the page, "is by first winning over both peoples." His was a bottom-up, grassroots approach. For once, the people should tell their leaders what to do. Ami threw out a million as a good figure. "Yes, I think a million signatures should do the trick."

I liked it. There was elegance in a million people forcing politicians to finally admit things they already knew but had been too afraid or too dishonest to say publicly. It's like telling a con man you're on to him so there's no point in carrying on with the charade. Ami also struck me as an ideal partner. His keen mathematical and strategic mind was en-tirely free of sentimentality. I admired his wound-up, frenetic energy and boundless assertiveness and determination. He clearly was not a person dogged by the cosmic doubts I'd wrangled with since childhood. His background in the navy and the Shin Bet also allowed him to cut through the propaganda of the right and the fool's paradise of the left in order to address the basic interests of both peoples. With his security credentials, I thought there might be a chance to reach the mainstream Israeli public, maybe even Likud supporters.

"Fine, I agree." We shook hands.

"Don't you want to read the paper first?"

"In due time."

I'd first met my new Inspector Javert a couple of years earlier, in what I thought at the time was pure coincidence, during a demonstration in the Old City against Jewish extremists stealing Arab property. All the Pales-tinian bigwigs were there. As usual, I trailed behind the procession chain-smoking and pondering some unanswerable riddle. At one point I asked a slightly bearded man walking next to me for a light. I assumed he was just another demonstrator. He gave me a light, and then took the opportunity to strike up a conversation with me in Arabic shot through with Hebrew inflections. Introducing himself as Rubin Barkov, he handed me his card. We shook hands.

I'd heard the name before: he worked for the police as a security adviser, a specialist on the Arabs. "I know Faisal very well," he told me. "We're close friends." He told me that Faisal's picture was hanging on the wall of his office. Barkov said all this with friendly exuberance. "If you ever have any problems, I can help you. I've got connections."

I put the card in my blazer pocket and forgot all about it. Now, in March 2002, Jawad Boulos told me Barkov had asked him to arrange a meeting. He wanted to get to know me better.

I received Barkov with all the hospitality I could muster. My hospitality lasted long enough for him to take a seat and open his mouth. He began issuing threats about the university, which was, according to him, entirely illegal and should be shut down. His tone was pompous, not that of a guest but that of a threatening occupier. Rubin had a triumphant smirk on his face.

"You're the most dangerous Palestinian we have," he stated, as if he were a zookeeper speaking about his animals. "You're a wolf in sheep's clothing." He told me to watch out, as my political activities at the Imperial Hotel and the university might lead to "undesirable consequences."

I could have taken his rudeness if it had been in an interrogation room at the Russian compound, but not in my own office. "I am a man being attacked by my own people," I snapped, "and now you say I am worse than bus bombers who kill children." I told him he could do whatever he wanted, even tear down the Noble Sanctuary if he liked, but I refused to put up with his offensiveness here. "Get the hell out of my office!" I pointed to the door. Visibly shaken, Barkov scuttled out.

My lawyer, Jawad Boulos, who was there watching the scene, ran after him. "You must be mad!" he said in the stairwell. "How can you accuse Dr. Nusseibeh of being a wolf?"

"You know how much I like Sari personally," Rubin went on, full of emotion, "but I know what I know. Sari is the most dangerous Palestinian enemy we have."

Jawad assured him I was a man of peace.

"No, no, no. He can't fool me. I *know* him."

Jawad ended their brief conversation with a hypothesis that still rings true today: "You're afraid of Sari and people like him because you don't like seeing moderates bravely speaking out against the right of return and violence. You'd rather deal with Arafat or Sheikh Yassin because they give you the excuse to do whatever you want."

At about this time *Jane's Foreign Report* published details on the army's plans to retake the West Bank and smash the PA. The Israeli attack would be launched immediately after a major suicide bomb blast. "The 'revenge' factor is crucial. It would motivate Israeli soldiers to demolish the Palestinians . . . It would also enable Israeli ambassadors and other officials to claim in talks with foreigners that the military action was a justified retaliation."[7]

The various verbal and police attacks on me, especially Inspector Javert's, got me thinking about Sharon's strategy. He knew how to elicit the kind of reaction from us that would then be a justification for going one step further. Each terrorist attack allowed the Israelis to expand their grip on the Occupied Territories by building more settlements. In the wake of one attack, Housing Minister Natan Sharansky—a man of sterling inconsistency who writes in his bestselling book on democracy, "Rights are secured by dissent and the free participation of the governed"— issued tenders for seven hundred new housing units in the West Bank. A few months later, following the bombing of a pizzeria in Jerusalem, Sharon and his security chieftains shuttered up several more Palestinian administration offices in and around Jerusalem.

In my calculation, Sharon's plan sought to render impossible another Camp David by destroying the PA, and then to implement a Sharonian settlement, which was to give the Palestinians scattered bits of territory in the West Bank and Gaza, all under hermetic security scrutiny by Israel. In Jerusalem, Israel would employ its vast military superiority to cement its rule over hundreds of thousands of unwilling civilians. All Sharon needed was for a few more Palestinian kamikazes to blow themselves up, thus allowing him to place the blame for his actions squarely on us. If an animal bites, you have to put it on a chain.

I went to Arafat's Muqata compound in Ramallah to warn him of the coming apocalypse. He didn't dispatch the bombers any more than he personally pocketed bribes. But he didn't do all he could to root out the problem, because he didn't recognize the evil the bombers were causing. It is a certain kind of craziness not to recognize a pattern, especially a debilitating one like repeatedly shooting yourself in your own foot.

The Muqata had a phantasmagorical quality to it that day. It was business as usual, and no one seemed aware of the abyss we straddled. In one office after the next Arafat's top aides were still vying for positions and new cars; and while the Israelis were finishing off the final preparations for reconquest, Arafat and his aides continued in their delusion that they were the masters of their own fate.

I managed to get a private meeting with the chairman. He was unfocused, his lips quivered, he seemed confused. The last time Sharon and Arafat went at it during the siege of Beirut, he was younger, more confident, a real leader. Now, he was uncertain of himself. For the first time in my life, I pitied him.

I tried to get my point across by using an example. "Do you play chess?" I asked him. He looked at me quizzically without answering. "Well," I barreled on, "I think the game Sharon is playing is like chess."

"How so?" asked Arafat, his large lips white and bloodless.

"In chess, as you know," I said, explaining the obvious, "a clever opponent will seduce you into thinking a certain move is safe and can help you win, when in fact it's a trap. What you don't realize is that your opponent is thinking ahead several steps with a much bigger target in mind." He remained silent. His gaze drilled into me. "Chairman Arafat," I went on, "the Israelis are out for checkmate."

"What is this?" he wanted to know. "What do you mean? *Who's being put into checkmate?*"

"You, of course!" I replied. "*You are!*"

Now his lower lip protruded out like that of a pouting child. He didn't say a word. Arafat couldn't shake off the old logic of anticolonial wars: of him, embodying the Palestinian cause, against the oppressor. It went against the grain for him to give up violence unequivocally and publicly as a strategic option.

Two weeks later the Israeli army attacked Arafat's headquarters, cutting him off from the rest of the world.

Chapter Thirty-one

The Iron Fist

The Bible says, "I have set before you life and death;
therefore, choose life." The time has arrived for everyone
in this conflict to choose peace, and hope, and life.
—PRESIDENT GEORGE W. BUSH ON JUNE 24, 2002

I HADN'T VISITED THE GRAVE SITE in a couple of years, so one day
I took a walk to a park in West Jerusalem. My destination was an old
Muslim cemetery squeezed between Wolfson Park and Jerusalem's premier bar scene. I could hear the sounds of raucous young crowds when
I found my way to a mausoleum housing an ancestor from the four-
teenth century. The thick-walled tomb was padlocked, but through small
grilled windows a generation of bar-goers had filled it with beer bottles,
half-eaten candy bars, condom wrappers, cigarette butts, and other debris. There was no name on the tomb, no sign of my family's long heritage in Jerusalem. Two years before, I had tried to affix a small plaque
to the mausoleum, identifying its inhabitant. The next day the Jerusalem
municipality took it down. I hadn't had a license. The melancholy sight
of a forgotten grave got me thinking about three generations of Nusseibehs:
this fourteenth-century ancestor, Father, and me. Curious thoughts about
time and change came to mind. Here I was, standing next to a family
monument while watching overhead the Apache helicopters and F16s
screaming off to West Bank cities in Israel's first full-scale invasion of
Palestinian territories since the Six-Day War.

The invasion had begun. The trigger referred to in *Jane's Report* came to be known as the Park Hotel Passover Massacre, a Hamas suicide bombing in March 2002 that killed 30 hotel guests and wounded 140 during the Passover meal. It was a ghastly crime no government could have ignored. Sharon surely had to do something. But he and his Israeli planners weren't interested in punishing the guilty; their massive retribution wasn't even directed against Hamas in Gaza. The blind Sheikh Yassin continued his daily rounds without a care in the world. Sharon's invasion, following the plan *Jane's Report* had talked about, was a studied and logical hammer blow designed to destroy the remnants of the Palestinian Authority in the West Bank.

The incursion, dubbed the Iron Fist, began with the bombardment of Arafat's Muqata compound, leaving Arafat and his aides without food or utilities. On Abu Dhabi television Arafat, the shivering old revolutionary with Parkinson's, asserted his defiance amid the rubble. "God is great," he muttered. "Don't you know me by now? I am a martyr in the making." He said three times, "May Allah honor me with martyrdom."

In cities all over the West Bank, tanks and armored carriers spread out while snipers took positions on rooftops. The high civilian toll was driven higher due to assaults on ambulances and doctors trying to get to the wounded. The Israelis shot up the pacifist Quaker high school where I had sent my sons. It joined a list of ninety other schools shelled by the Israeli military.

For me, the clearest signal that the Palestinians were at their wits' end was the way the invasion intensified the cult of the suicide bomber. Palestinian public opinion was whipped into a hysterical adulation of violence as if it were the sacred ground of being. A militia leader in Bethlehem spoke of "resistance in Israel's cities and mayhem from the Galilee to Cairo."[1] It was worse among the youth, for whom the *shahid batal*, the "martyr hero," became a kind of pop star. As a leader of the PFLP told an American journalist, "Thousands of young men and women are ready to be blown up. This is a new phenomenon. You have no idea how big it is."[2] All over, children were being taught to handle guns and jump through hoops of fire. So-called "collaborators" were strung up by hysterical mobs.

The incursion destroyed whatever was left of the PA's administrative ability to govern. The Israeli political scientist Baruch Kimmerling coined the term *politicide* to describe his government's plan. In the *New Left Review*, Kimmerling defines *politicide* as a "process whose ultimate aim is to destroy a certain people's prospects—indeed, their very will—for legitimate self-determination and sovereignty over land they consider their homeland."[3] How else do you make sense of soldiers ransacking the PA's Bureau of Statistics, or the Israeli police shutting down the Arab Chamber of Commerce offices? Troops also ransacked the Palestinian Ministry of Education, destroying computers and confiscating records.

Whatever remained of Jibril's security apparatus couldn't have put up a fight even if he had given the order, which he didn't. This didn't prevent Arafat from portraying Jibril—who had been warning Arafat against terrorism since the second intifada began—as a failure. In a tête-à-tête, hot-tempered Arafat pointed a gun at him and relieved him of his duties.

The Guardian ran a story: "Israeli intelligence officials began hunting members of Mr. Arafat's administration, including Sari Nusseibeh." A dragnet swept hundreds of activists into Israeli prisons. My old friend Sameer's youngest son was sentenced to three years in prison for a trifle. (Another son was already serving life for murdering a settler.) Marwan was cornered in Ramallah. He was lucky to have escaped the Israeli assassination teams combing the territories. "I am not a terrorist," he said after his arrest, his fists shackled together, "but neither am I a pacifist. I am simply a regular guy from the Palestinian street advocating only what every other oppressed person has advocated—the right to help myself in the absence of help from anywhere else."[4]

The "checkmate" worked as planned, and the West Bank degenerated into warlordism. In many towns, vigilantes and hooligans took over, and boys with peach fuzz for whiskers lugged around machine guns. This made the job of Israeli propagandists easy. Which democratic, freedom-loving country could be expected to sit down and talk peace with such people?

Driving to Beit Hanina from my office in Jerusalem I often saw smoke coming up from Ramallah, as if from a monumental funeral pyre. My two edgy bodyguards would turn their eyes to the skies to look out for an Israeli hit squad flying low in an Apache helicopter. In the darkness we knew that all we would see would be a flash of light before the explosion.

I was at the Ambassador Hotel with the Italian ambassador watching the Israeli bulldozers raze large parts of the Muqata on television when a call came from someone inside Arafat's office. We discussed trying to get some sort of international protection for those holed up in the compound, when the person on the line passed the phone over to the chairman. I promised Arafat I would do what I could to help.

"Are they going to kill Arafat?" asked one of my university staff members with me at the Ambassador. He was the Fatah student who had argued with the Hamas followers in my office for ten hours.

"I doubt it." I knew they wouldn't. Sharon needed Arafat to accompany his jingle "There is no one to talk to."

As the PLO man in Jerusalem, I was on my own. It was of course absurd to expect a budget or any kind of help from a leadership caged in a bombed-out office complex in Ramallah. My role was reduced to making sure the Red Cross was responding to the various emergency calls for aid coming from different parts of the West Bank and Gaza, along with going to the occasional meeting with the diplomatic corps and doing the odd interview and public appearance.

I did what I could, and this was largely symbolic. With tanks surrounding the Muqata, I organized a peaceful daily vigil, the way South African protesters had while Mandela was in prison. Our daily protests consisted of a motley group of us trooping over to the Damascus Gate, sitting on the steps, and holding a couple of olive branches and some candles.

Expert at the siege posture, the chairman managed to get even people sick of his rule to line up behind him. "Arafat may be a catastrophic leader," the saying went, "but we'll stick by him as long as Sharon is strangling him." The man on the street was a different matter. Arafat's fate aroused little more than indifferent shrugs. Shopkeepers and taxi drivers, my usual sources for getting at the pulse of the street, had to be cajoled into joining me in the vigils.

Whenever I could, I brought guests and friends to a vigil, if only to keep my staff and me company. One day a journalist for *Business Week* showed up at the university office, and I talked him into coming along. In his article he called me a "lonely Cassandra" with a "Kennedy-like coif" warning fellow Palestinians clearly with little effect that the "dirty war they are waging against Israelis would lead to disaster, not the end of occupation: "To set a nonviolent example, Nusseibeh leads the mildest of demonstrations each afternoon at the Damascus Gate, the medieval entrance to Jerusalem's old city. 'We have, how do you say it, been shooting ourselves in the foot,' he tells me."[5]

The most affected institute at Al-Quds University was Kuttab's Center for Modern Media, in Ramallah. Control over the media being a prime target, when the army invaded Ramallah the soldiers headed straight for the radio and television stations. Some took along their insalubrious home entertainment. The soldiers, once they took over, arrested the staff and broadcast porno.

Al-Quds's educational television station had a couple of days' reprieve because our media building was on the outskirts of town. During the invasion we supplemented our normal programming with a documentary we produced with UNICEF to help parents and children deal with the trauma of violence. We also broadcast medical service information, addresses and telephone numbers of hospitals and ambulance services, and films on first aid.

The tanks finally rolled up in the middle of cartoon hour. Soldiers broke into the offices and led the staff at gunpoint into the basement, where they were held for several hours. In the meantime, the entire building was occupied. The media center was turned into an improvised prison for people arrested in town.

At first the soldiers slipped in porn to replace the cartoons. Officers put a quick stop to this, instructing the soldiers to pitch all the transmission equipment, television cameras, and the entire video archives out the fourth-floor window. Our press release described the way a Hamas bombing had ended up destroying an institution producing an Israeli-Palestinian *Sesame Street*:

> Al-Quds University Educational Television . . . has also been completely damaged. After airing pornographic material on the children's program, the Israeli army destroyed the facility, smashing broadcast equipment with sledgehammers and throwing computers and other studio facilities out of windows.

For some reason I've always operated best when people are terrified and normal life threatens to spin off into chaos. Perhaps I got this talent from Father, who was always ready to put his best foot—which was of course his only foot—forward. He never gave up, even after losing most of his country. Because of his strength of will, he was always prepared to see a situation objectively for what it was, and then make the most of it. Nor did he ever shy away from painful self-scrutiny, the sine qua non for self-emancipation. This was his formula for discovering strength where others see only humiliation and defeat.

For a lecture I gave during the worst of the fighting I came up with a childlike parable to illustrate the curious strength of the weak: Suppose two people suddenly find themselves in a brawl. Neither is sure how it started, but each suspects the other of having maliciously provoked it. One manages to throw the other to the ground, and at once sits on top of him, holding him down by the arms. The one underneath kicks back, biting where he can, and whenever he manages to get one of his hands loose, he claws at his foe with all his might.

It seems like a stalemate. The one on top is afraid, yes, afraid, of loosening his grip or letting go of the man underneath him. The one wriggling underneath cannot for the life of him allow this bully to have the slightest chance of rest. Clearly, a gentlemanly exchange of ideas is out of the question.

A third man comes along, pleading with the man on top to let go and the man underneath to lie quiet. Each of them now is in a quandary. The man underneath is afraid that if he were to lie quiet then the man on top would not have any incentive to let go, while the man on top is worried that if he were to let go then the man underneath would quickly move to strangle him. Existentially locked into stalemate, each begins to suspect that the other is looking for salvation through his total elimination.

I made this scenario even worse by imagining that the two men are not on solid ground but in a pool of quicksand, and that with each blow or bite or bash on the head they sink deeper into the mud. Theirs is no zero-sum game: it is a lose-lose situation.

The reason I came up with the yarn was to show the respective strengths of the two fighters. In terms of raw physical power, the one on top obviously has the leg up. But psychologically it is actually more difficult for him to let go than for the man underneath to lie quiet. Paradoxically, being on top he has more to lose by deciding to act differently. He has a lesser margin of choice, or less power.

The man underneath, on the other hand, has less to lose, and less to fear by restraining his opposition. He has, therefore, more power, for he can afford to change his act. If he were to let go, the man on top might lose his advantage altogether. By stopping his physical resistance, the man underneath can always revert to wriggling and biting. He has no advantage to lose.

The upshot is that the man underneath holds the key to unlocking the puzzle, even without the intervention of a third man. Of course, it is not enough for him to stop wriggling. He has to consciously reach out to the other man's mind. He can't defeat him, but with some intelligence he may be able to win him over.

• • •

When I think back on it now, I see that this parable may have been indirectly inspired by something the Israeli philosopher and theologian David Harman once told me:

> Remember, Israel wasn't created by people who came out of Princeton or Yale and 300 years of American experience; it was created by people who came out of Eastern European and Islamic ghettos, by people with deep bruises on their psyches. The national psyche of the Jewish soul can't be healed by a Jewish psychiatrist; it needs a Palestinian analyst. So help me heal my traumas.

It was admittedly an unlikely time to harbor any such hopes of winning over the man on top, who weighed in at over three hundred pounds and was named Sharon. The West Bank was under Israeli boots, my bodyguards were still nervously looking up at the sky, and my university's media center—in my estimation the strongest voice in the Arab world for peaceful coexistence and partnership with Israelis—had been wrecked, *Sesame Street* interrupted by smut. And yet it was in the midst of the incursion that Ami and I were discussing ways of launching our peace project.

A big reason for my auspicious mood came from a very unlikely source: President George W. Bush, among Palestinians a close second to Sharon in their pantheon of political villains. He was a man who had given the green light for the invasion and had sat on his hands while the Israelis laid siege to the Church of the Nativity. A stone statue of the Virgin was destroyed in the shooting. The Crimean War had been sparked by far less. Yet Bush Junior was also a man who had delivered an unprecedented message of hope.

In June 2002, Bush gave a policy speech in the White House Rose Garden with Condoleezza Rice, Colin Powell, and Donald Rumsfeld at his side. A group of Americans came to my office afterward, including an officer from the American consulate. I knew that my guests had been appalled by the speech, either by the way they now squirmed in their chairs or by their apologies afterward. The Palestinian reaction was even more scathing. The speech was one-sided, everyone said. Bush had endorsed the Israeli canard that there was no partner for peace, and had tacitly given another nod to his Middle Eastern clients to continue their aggression.

To my guests' astonishment, I was enthusiastic about Bush's speech, because I essentially agreed with him. "For too long," the president said, "the citizens of the Middle East have lived in the midst of death and fear. The hatred of a few holds the hopes of many hostage." Who could argue with this? And who could dispute the fact that "the forces of extremism and terror are attempting to kill progress and peace by killing the innocent. And this casts a dark shadow over an entire region. For the sake of all humanity, things must change in the Middle East."

Bravo! What I liked most was the way Bush related the Israelis' basic interests to ours. He laid out the Camp David trade-off of Israeli security for a Palestinian state. But this was no "non-paper." It was official American policy announced in the Rose Garden.

> It is untenable for Israeli citizens to live in terror. It is untenable for Palestinians to live in squalor and occupation. And the current situation offers no prospect that life will improve. Israeli citizens will continue to be victimized by terrorists, and so Israel will continue to defend herself . . . My vision is two states, living side by side in peace and security . . . The Israeli occupation that began in 1967 will be ended through a settlement negotiated between the parties, based on U.N. Resolutions 242 and 338, with Israeli withdrawal to secure and recognized borders.

A very fine point was introduced in these lines, never before a part of U.S. policy. The terror and absence of security Israel had to contend itself with were directly tied to occupation, and ending the one was inextricably joined to ending the other. Until then Israel's "security" had been a good in and of itself, entirely divorced from the Palestinian problem.

In addition, I heard a language never before used in American diplomacy. The president made it clear that the *whole* situation that arose as a consequence of the Six-Day War must come to an end. Another strong point was his call on the Palestinian people "to elect new leaders, leaders not compromised by terror. I call upon them to build a practicing democracy based on tolerance and liberty." Stop the shooting, end the corruption, and build a democratic state. Again, who in his right mind could disagree?

I felt the speech actually put us in a stronger position than the Israelis, much like the parable of the two wrestlers. Invasion or no invasion, we had to put our own house in order. It didn't help to blame Israel for our incompetence in areas where we had full control, such as the courts, planning, and education in the West Bank. We had failed, and the time had come to say so openly.

More important, by freeing us from the illusion that we had a military option, the Iron Fist multiplied the potency of our real strength, which is an existential swap with the Israelis. If we would stop squirming and biting, and extend our hands to the bully pounding on us from above, we could exercise the freedom of our will.

The time had come to spin some gold out of dross. I was having frequent meetings with Ami Ayalon. Once I went to his house in a moshav called Kerem Maharal not far from Mount Carmel. His house reminded me of the bizarre—and for me risky—business we were launching. Before 1948 the town was the village of Ijzim. Its entire population of three thousand was exiled and ended up in refugee camps near Jenin. Part of Ami's house was built by one of those Arab families.

I rarely allowed my political associations with Israelis to be complicated by a personal friendship. This was not hard to do with Ami. He was as businesslike as a Swiss engineer building a bridge, and the absence of feigned intimacy made our jobs easier. We were dealing with common interests, not with sentiment. As Ami explained it to an interviewer, "From the outset I wasn't looking for new friends. Anyhow, it takes me a long time to connect to people." Referring to the stub on one of his hands he added, "I can count my close friends on four and a half fingers."

Months had passed since our first talk in my office. I had since gone over his paper, introducing a couple of changes after talking matters over with some friends. Lucy, cognizant of the emotional component of the refugee dimension, suggested a few changes in that clause. I phoned Ami with Lucy's comments. He agreed with the changes.

We were finally ready to sign a joint document. We decided the formal launch would be in Athens, in the presence of Bill Clinton. For the time being, we met at the Christmas Hotel in East Jerusalem to initialize it.

We called our document the Destination Map, because we wanted it to complement Bush's Road Map. A map does you no good if you don't know where you want to go. Our paper laid out the destination. No sugarcoating, no *La a²am*, and no legal hairsplitting or word parsing, but straight, the way a good surgeon lops off a cancerous growth, the cancer in our case being years of lies and half-truths. In a conflict that has generated millions of pages of studies and countless "non-papers" and "talking points," we kept our solution to a page.

- There will be two states for two nations.
- The permanent borders will be drawn on the basis of June 4, 1967, with the possibility of exchanging tracts of land, on a one-to-one basis.
- Jerusalem will be the capital of both states (the Arab neighborhoods under Palestinian sovereignty and the Jewish neighborhoods under Israeli sovereignty).
- Arab refugees will be able to return only to Palestinian territory and Jews only to Israeli territory.
- In cognizance of the suffering of Palestinian refugees, an international fund will be established with the participation of Israel for compensating and rehabilitating Palestinian refugees.

- The Palestinian state will be demilitarized.
- Both sides will renounce all claims after a political agreement is signed.

We skirted the sovereignty issue on the Noble Sanctuary/Temple Mount area by stressing that its significance rests in its holiness rather than in some nationalistic and bourgeois slogan of "ownership." By designating each side as "guardian" we underlined the site's divine status, a status that defies claims of human control. The arrangement we envisioned was that Palestine "will be designated Guardian of the Noble Sanctuary for the benefit of Muslims. Israel will be the Guardian of the Western Wall for the benefit of the Jewish people."

The personal attacks, which had died down slightly during the invasion, revved up again after the signing ceremony. My two bodyguards were constant reminders of how unpopular my opinions were. Mother thought I had finally lost my mind. "The Israelis aren't serious," she reasoned, "so why risk getting sliced up by extremists?"

Many people blasted me for appearing on the same stage with the man who had "attacked us, tortured us, and assassinated our leaders," as they referred to Ami.

"You don't make peace with peaceniks," I told them.

"But he symbolizes the system," they countered.

"That's exactly the point. Ami is the embodiment of the enemy. But he's an enemy we can work with because he knows what's best for Israel, which happens to be in our own self-interest. Our mutual interest is our bond. Not love."

Israeli right-wingers came out with the same hobgoblins I'd heard for years. The most charitable claim was that I was an intellectual living in ether. Israeli army radio quoted environment minister Tzahi Hanegbi, who had wanted me put on trial during the intifada, dubbing me an "esoteric character" with no following among the Arabs. Mostly, I appeared as a tweed-wearing, professorial villain. The title of one article in the country's largest mass circulation daily was "Dr. Sari Nusseibeh: Be Wary of Deadly Coral Snakes Posing as Harmless Skipjack Snakes."[6]

In June, Ami and I went to a Greek island to cut the ribbon on the peace movement. We were with former President Clinton in the shadow of the Acropolis. Meanwhile, back at home, Barkov's dossier was on Uzi Landau's desk, and the minister now felt he had proof that I was using the university as a "long arm of the Palestinian Authority." Landau, a gaunt, spindly man who looked more like a retired high school science teacher than a political demagogue, explained to the press, "Here in the heart of Jerusalem there is a governmental, civilian branch of the Palestinian Authority aiming to undermine our sovereignty in Jerusalem. Let Nusseibeh's gentleness deceive no one." To those who called me a moderate, he countered, "Compared to Arafat, he is a moderate exactly like Arafat is moderate compared to Sheikh Yassin." In other words, we were all the same.

Minister Landau sent the Shin Bet, accompanied by sixty members of the notoriously aggressive border police, to my Al-Quds administration building, across the street from the Rockefeller Museum. The main Shin Bet man approached my office manager, Dimitri, and pointed an Uzi at his head. The safety latch was up. "Dimitri, I suggest you show us some ID," said the Shin Bet man in Arabic. He identified himself as Captain James, an unusually non-Israeli name. In Dimitri's account, Captain James was short, thin, and badly dressed in green jeans and a plaid shirt. Like Landau, he didn't look the role: more of a computer geek than a secret service agent.

"If you know my name already, why do you need my ID?" Dimitri wanted to know in a disarming tone, or so he told me.

"Just give me the goddamned ID, Dimitri!" the captain snapped.

"One more question," continued Dimitri, handing over his ID. "Where do you shop for your clothes?"

Captain James looked puzzled and asked why he wanted to know. "Green jeans and that plaid shirt! What a combination! I'll have to make sure never to go there."

"Smart ass," the captain muttered under his breath in flawless American English.

Russian-speaking men took the hard drives from the computers and put all my papers into boxes—entire filing cabinets containing student and personnel records and research—for transport back to headquarters, but not before sealing off the offices, changing the locks, and installing heavy steel shutters to prevent anyone from sneaking back in. The building was declared a closed military zone, with nobody allowed in or out. Five of my employees were taken in for questioning. All the other university employees were turned out of the building at gunpoint.

It was certainly an annoyance to have an entire administrative apparatus shut down, and its lifeblood—databases, files, and correspondence— confiscated. But in a sense, the timing couldn't have been better. The entire logic of my work with Ami was that intelligent nonviolence was more effective than weapons. Now I had a chance to prove it.

Even without their offices, my team had years of contacts with Israelis, Americans, and Europeans. They went to work calling journalists, embassy employees, public figures, lawyers, and politicians. Appeals went out for public support from Israelis as well as from leaders around the world, including the White House.

Already on the first day of the closure a few dozen Israeli peace activists held a vigil outside the school's offices. Yossi Sarid, the head of the leftist faction of the Knesset, lashed out at the government: "This is the stupidity of our government. The government of Israel is talking quite often about the need to find moderate Palestinian leaders instead of Yasir Arafat, and then they do their utmost to insult them, to embarrass them, to weaken them."[7]

The government could easily swat away domestic critics, just not the American ones. *The Boston Globe* pointed to the closing of my offices as the final "proof that Israel's Prime Minister Ariel Sharon's real intentions are not just the suppression of terrorism but the relentless termination of Palestinian national aspirations."[8] *The New York Times*'s Anthony Lewis wrote more or less the same:

[Nusseibeh] is the perfect example of the new kind of leadership, peaceful and pragmatic, that Prime Minister Ariel Sharon of Israel and President Bush have said the Palestinians must have before there can be political negotiations on an end to the conflict. Why target him?

The answer is that important elements in the Israeli government do not want a real two-state solution and do not want political negotiations with a reformed Palestinian leadership. They prefer the present situation: the West Bank occupied or tightly controlled by Israel, with an increasing number of Jewish settlers. The last thing they want is a respected Palestinian interlocutor.[9]

Minister Landau hit back by releasing two documents his men fished out from my papers. One showed correspondence from Jibril requesting that we conduct some training courses at the university, primarily in law, for some of the people in his security force. Another letter was a general memo sent to Palestinian universities discussing the possibility of sending students to a summer course at Tehran University. All the letters were strictly related to the university, including letters sent out to all Arab leaders however unsavory their regimes—one letter was addressed to Saddam Hussein—asking for financial assistance.

On receiving news of the police raid in my office I left Ami in Greece and hurried back to Jerusalem. When, upon my return, journalists asked if the raid had been designed to discredit the agreement Ami and I had signed in Athens, I replied frankly, "In this part of the world nothing happens by coincidence."

Through Jawad Boulos I inquired into the legal basis for the closure, and contested it. It took a few days, including consultations with Landau's admirably reasonable legal adviser, to figure out that Landau's main claim was that my office belonged to the Palestinian Authority. I told the legal adviser it didn't. It was that simple.

"Would you be prepared to sign a document saying so? And also, that it will not be used as a PA office?" she asked.

"With pleasure." I assured her that my office had nothing to do with the PA, nor would it in the future. It was a university office and would remain so.

Both she and Jawad Boulos reacted with surprise to my attitude. Perhaps they thought I would squabble over symbols, or dig in my heels out of misplaced loyalty to Arafat. What they didn't realize was that even if the PA had asked me to run operations out of the office, I would have refused, preferring to maintain the independence of the university.

I signed the pledge, and within ten days of the closure Landau had no legal recourse but to reopen the school. Putting a good face on it, he said he was "ecstatic" that a senior Palestinian figure had recognized Israeli sovereignty over East Jerusalem, which of course I hadn't.

Weeks went by and the authorities still hadn't returned the papers from my office. They needed time to sift through every page. They must have thought they'd find the blueprints to the Al-Aqsa intifada or plans for a guerrilla campaign.

Now I got a telephone call from Rubin Barkov, my Inspector Javert. He wanted to know if we could meet for coffee. We fixed a time.

We were chatting for a few minutes when he started poking fun at Yossi Belin and other Israeli left-wing leaders, calling them "pussies" and "friars," Hebrew slang for naïve suckers. "They don't really get you Arabs, I mean the Arab mentality."

I let him ramble on like this for an hour. His soliloquy ranged from leftist "pussies" to his conversations with Sheikh Yassin. He bragged about his own knowledge of Islam, early Arabic poetry, and of course the "Arab mind." (I'm certain he cribbed much of what he said from Raphael Patai.) On he went, until enough time had passed that I thought it appropriate to change the subject. I asked him about the materials and computers confiscated from my office. "Are you guys finished reading through everything? I really need that stuff back."

Barkov's expression changed. Now in a serious tone, he repeated his bon mot from our previous conversation: that I was the "most danger-ous Palestinian enemy" out there. He leaned back in his chair and gave me a knowing look, as if I were trapped and the game were over. "I have been developing a picture of you," he explained with flaring nostrils and his index finger lightly tapping the table. With the confident movement of someone holding all the cards, he suddenly brought out a few pieces of paper he had in his pocket. "We found this in your computer."

After the closure of my offices at Al-Quds, he and his men systemati-cally sifted through my papers. Like someone scouring for a verse in the holy writ to prove a hunch, they looked and looked until they located what they considered to be irrefutable evidence that I was a dangerous man.

Out of hundreds of thousands of pages, they dredged up a letter asking Saddam Hussein for contributions to the university. I suppose because in Barkov's eyes I had once upon a time been an Iraqi agent directing Scud attacks, this constituted solid evidence. Barkov and his people also dis-covered on a hard disc demo video clips. One was an animated thirty-second spot of a girl being gunned down by a soldier; someone else is throwing a Molotov cocktail. Another cartoon showed a map of the region bisected by a line of Arabs and Jews holding hands, while an animated hand grenade erupts in the distance.

Looking at it, I recognized it as printout of a proposed advertise-ment a PR company in Ramallah had done for me at the time of the Human Chain event with Peace Now, and which I had viewed on my computer but then rejected.

"So what?" I really didn't know why he was showing them to me.

"*So what?* These drawings depict a child, rising up from a pool of blood, throwing stones and what looks like a Molotov cocktail at Israeli soldiers. Now I know that your civilian disobedience is a cover for vio-lent rebellion." He thought I intended to morph the Human Chain into an uprising. (The word *chain* was, according to his X-ray vision, a secret code word for armed revolt.) Rubin said this with a confident smile, as if the jig was up.

I was getting angry. "Did I ever use these things?" I asked sharply. "Did we put them on television? No!"

He waved his hand with aplomb as if to say it didn't matter.

"Just think about what you're saying. A company did the animation for me. I saw it, and decided not to use it precisely because of what you're saying. It doesn't fit with my philosophy."

He didn't like my answer. The gist of his message was that I might be able to fool credulous Israeli "pussies" and "friars," but he knew my secret agenda. Putting all his experience and professional training to work, he determined that something very dangerous was afoot, and it was his professional and patriotic duty to nip it in the bud. I might be more intelligent than the leftists I'd been seducing with my words of peace, but I wasn't smarter than he. Not by a long shot. And it was his job to protect Israelis from my wily intelligence.

I listened to his presentation with growing amazement at a man who suddenly seemed more like Inspector Clouseau than Javert. I asked him by what logic could anyone conclude that PR material I had rejected be evidence against me. "I know you didn't publicize this," he said with a conspiratorial smirk, "but you brought together all your friends to your office and showed it to them to get them behind you."

I felt angry but also strangely sympathetic, as if I was dealing with a man rapidly losing his marbles. As such, I probably should have pitied him—because all his prodigious efforts had led him nowhere. Like his boss, Uzi Landau, he was fully convinced of my true nature, but the raids on my office had turned up only unused cartoons from the overheated imagination of a twenty-year-old graphic designer in Ramallah.

"Sari, you can't fool me." This time his voice took on an aggressive, threatening pitch.

I'd had enough.

"My friend," I said softly, standing up from the chair and preparing to leave, "I think you've been working too hard. Maybe what you really need is a holiday. Obviously you're under too much stress."

As I turned on my heel and headed out the door I heard him say, "Sari, I *know* you."

A year or so later Barkov called in one of my close associates from the Jerusalem Fatah organization. Upon entering Barkov's office, my friend couldn't help but notice a big file on the desk with "Sari Nusseibeh" written in fat letters on the outside. Rubin told my friend that if he couldn't get me put away for the rest of my life in an Israeli prison, he was going to publish a book on me based on all the "dirt" he had ferreted out. "Your Dr. Nusseibeh is the single most dangerous enemy of Israel."

Afterward my friend came directly to my office to recount what he had seen and heard. "The guy's really nuts," he said between guffaws.

Chapter Thirty-two

"The Tigers"

We must accept the challenge, seek no shortcut,
and get used to the idea of using a spade.

—FATHER

B Y THE END OF 2002 my brief tenure as the PLO's man in Jerusalem was nearing its end. The first clear hint came when Arafat told an interviewer on Lebanese television that he had created another one of his "Jerusalem Committees" and appointed one of the leaders of a PLO faction to head it up. He was obviously trying to fend off critics who had accused me of stepping out of line. I took the chance to make myself scarce and began missing more meetings than I attended.

I was finally convinced I was wasting my time just before the Israeli general election in January 2003. Sharon's National Unity government was falling apart, with Labor preparing to pull out in preparation for new elections. Efraim Sneh, a Labor Party boss I'd known for years, asked to meet me at the American Colony Hotel. He brought with him a draft proposal for what he called the Labor Party's "peace platform," reduced to a few salient points on a single sheet of paper. He said the Labor Party chairman, Ben-Eliezer, would be presenting it to the Egyptians within days. Labor was seeking prior endorsement of their plan from the Egyptians, and, more important, from Arafat. After pulling out of Sharon's government, he explained, they wanted to use the platform along with the Egyptian and PLO endorsement as a return ticket to power.

The platform seemed like just one more vague formula for peace that had never gotten us anywhere. But Sneh was sincere, and I promised to talk it over with Arafat.

I made my way to the Muqata in Ramallah. After maneuvering around heaps of rubble and tanks, like something out of World War II Berlin, I went up to Arafat's office. There I explained to the chairman that rumors about a Labor pullout were serious, and that it was in our national interest to help Labor win the next election. Arafat, with a look of ambivalence on his face, took the proposal and told an aide to pass it on to his minister for liaison affairs. What I got out of the brief encounter was that he didn't want me in the picture. Neither Sneh nor anyone else in the Labor Party heard a word from him.

A few weeks later, Sneh came calling again. This time he wanted me to know that his party planned to announce its pullout from the coalition within the next two weeks. Not having heard a positive word about the "peace platform" from the Palestinians or Egyptians, he asked me if I thought my paper with Ami would get a response out of Arafat. "Do you have a copy?" he asked, as he pulled one out from his briefcase. Looking over it, he told me in a hushed voice, "We're ready to push for your program within our party. But for us to get any traction with Israeli voters we'll need your help." He wanted Arafat's explicit endorsement of the Destination Map, and thought that with it, Labor could show the Israeli public that there was a partner on the other side, and that only Labor could strike a final peace deal.

Back I went to the Muqata. This time Arafat was even more visibly mistrustful. "Why are they doing this?" he asked bitterly when I told him about my meeting with Sneh. He thought it was a trick, as if the Israelis were trying to get around him by making me the interlocutor and not him. "Labor needs us," I tried to explain.

"Us who? Who do they mean by 'us'? Who is 'us'? Which 'us' is us? How many 'us's are there anyway? *I'm 'us'!*"

It was obvious that to get a positive reaction from Arafat, Sneh would have to come calling personally. At any rate, the Old Man didn't want me to be the middleman. Once again, Sneh and his friends in the party never heard from Arafat.

My last official trip to the Muqata was for a cabinet meeting. Labor had pulled out, and the Israeli elections were around the corner. After Arafat read out the meeting's agenda, I asked that Israeli elections be placed as an additional item. Arafat murmured out an agreement.

When the discussion on the Israeli elections came, Saeb Erekat opened things up by emphatically warning our leadership not to do anything that would boost the extremist groups in Israel. By the time my turn came to speak, all eyes in the room were riveted on me. I repeated all the reasons that had made the so-called intifada so ruinous, and how the longer it lasted the less likelihood there would be a viable Palestinian state. "It is not the Labor Party's future that hangs in the balance; it's ours." An argument I returned to half a dozen times was that the Israeli elections should really be seen as our elections. As our main negotiating partner for a future Palestinian state was going to be the Israeli government, it was in our interest that Israelis elect a government that believed in a two-state solution. This they would do only if they felt they had a reliable Palestinian partner, and as such we had to declare clearly our desire for a genuine and conclusive peace. The upshot was that it was in our national interest to endorse a clear and unambiguous framework for a political settlement based on the Destination Map.

There was dead silence. I sensed that most of the people in the room agreed with me, but no one made a sound of support. In matters of high politics, they were to a man slavishly dependent on Arafat, and since he didn't want to lift a finger to help Labor, they weren't about to.

A week later, I repeated all my arguments in a front-page article in *Al-Quds*. But it was a losing battle. Labor's candidate was Avram Mitzna, a dovish ex-general and mayor of Haifa. Mitzna and his party did their best to win the Israeli public over to its peace stance; they even came out with the election slogan "Avram Mitzna is committed to the solution proposed by Ami Ayalon." But the public wasn't buying. Sharon trounced Labor, and not long after that I quit my post as Jerusalem man.

Quitting didn't affect my relationship with Arafat in the slightest. He was known to rant and curse and throw things at ministers. Once, he slapped someone across the face during a meeting. In Jibril's case, he waved a pistol. I never experienced any of this, and up until his death he continued to treat me with respect, as I did him.

Lack of respect wasn't the problem. He simply wasn't listening to me, or to anyone else, as far as I could tell. Trapped in his ruins, he was becoming increasingly fearful of possible challengers. At some point he may have gotten the impression—dead wrong, to be sure—that I had higher political ambitions. Word may have leaked out that someone at *The Jerusalem Post* was speculating on the "post-Arafat era." "Who wouldn't want a Harvard- and Oxford-educated president of the PA?" The writer, using an animal metaphor, then questioned whether a professor could ever become the leader of the Palestinian "pack."[1]

For most of my friends, a prime example of this lack of appetite for political office was the project with Ami. Ami called his organization the People's Voice. Mine was HASHD, an Arabic acronym for the People's Campaign for Peace and Democracy. What both of us aimed for was "people power," a hackneyed phrase perhaps, but one that captured well the logic behind our movements. We knew that leaders were well aware of the contours of an eventual solution. They just didn't act on what they knew *because no one was forcing them to.* As long as their populations were responding to the bugle sounds of armed conflict, they could avoid engaging in the far more difficult task of hammering out the details of a negotiated peace. Therefore Ami and I decided to appeal directly to the grass roots. Speaking at a Tel Aviv news conference, we said that our aim was to send a million signatures to the decision makers as a fait accompli, a deal signed between the two nations. My old friend Danny Rubinstein at *Haʾaretz* called our scheme "Bypassing the political establishments to peace."

Of the two, Ami's organization got off to a much faster start. On his board sat some of Israel's financial and social elite. A high-tech billionaire who pledged to devote some of his money and most of his time to the effort introduced Ami to other potential donors. Ami's inner circle also included a former national chief of police and a top official in the Mossad. Ami and his team quickly set up a Web site and started a big advertising campaign. The People's Voice had its headquarters in a wealthy Tel Aviv neighborhood near the stock exchange.

Things were not so easy in occupied, bombed-out, and lawless Palestine. "As compared to the financiers, managers and advertising experts who are working with Ami Ayalon," wrote an Israeli journalist, we gave the impression of trying to "navigate around a blocked dirt road in the territories with a beat-up old car."[2]

Indeed. Money was tight—there was a lot more of it when I was smuggling bags of it in fifteen years earlier. A Jewish philanthropist, a friend of my brother's in England, gave us some initial funding. I put out some feelers to European and American funds and got some interest, just no hard cash.

With so little money in the coffers I couldn't afford an ad agency, so my own staff at Al-Quds University did most of the work, helped out by volunteers from women's organizations.

We first wanted to kick off the campaign with great fanfare in Ramallah. Invitations went out, and even Arafat pledged to send a representative. But late in the evening before the planned launch, a rumor reached me that armed gangs under the command of some members of the Fatah Central Committee were prowling the streets waiting to break up our meeting.

I made some phone calls, and the unanimous feeling was that I should delay the launch. It would be an embarrassment to kick off a peace campaign with a riot. An old friend who had worked with Arafat for years suggested I give the chairman a call and tell him about the rumor. If Arafat pretended he hadn't heard anything—which he certainly had—I should take that as a sign there was definitely going to be trouble, in which case it would be wiser to wait. It was sound if convoluted reasoning. Sure enough, Arafat played dumb, and I canceled the event.

We launched in early June with full-page advertisements in several newspapers listing the names of two hundred grassroots supporters. Predictably, vituperative comments made the rounds. A couple dozen signatories, upon receiving threats, asked to have their names scratched from the list. But we went on advertising for three consecutive days, and by the end of the third day we had gained another two thousand names. Thereafter, we started advertising once a week, each time announcing in bold print the rapidly growing number of signatures.

In Jerusalem, we invited hundreds of civic leaders to a Ramadan fast-breaking meal. HASHD wasn't mentioned by name as sponsoring the event, though everyone knew what we were up to. The invitation said, "Let's hope that our dream of establishing an independent state with Jerusalem as the capital will come true, under the leadership of our brother and symbol, Yasir Arafat." Five hundred people turned up.

The campaign gained momentum on both sides. The more Palestinians signed off on our vision of peace, the easier it was for Ami to win over supporters. Suddenly the number one million didn't seem quite so quixotic after all.

Getting people on board in peaceful East Jerusalem was comparatively easy, and largely symbolic. Success or failure depended on making inroads where most Palestinians lived—Jenin, Nablus, Hebron, Gaza, and the camps. The telephone and the Internet were useless there. Someone had to canvass from door to door, asking people to do something unfamiliar to them. Palestinians were used to seeing decision makers, pen in hand, signing accords in Washington or Cairo. No one had ever placed a pen in their hands. To make matters worse, we were asking people to do something that flew in the face of the public mood. One taboo is a hard thing to touch; we were going after several at once: the cult of violence, the myth of the martyr, and the delusions of actually "punishing" the Israelis. To top it off, the clause on the right of return asked people to give up their most cherished illusion at a time when illusions thrived most fiercely: war.

Beyond these more psychological hurdles came the practical problem of just getting around. Army checkpoints had turned the territories into an unpredictable maze. You would drive until a tank or a bulldozer forced you to take a different route. Getting from point A to point B became an entire alphabet of detours and dead ends before reaching your destination, if you ever did.

During the initial stage, even someone with a Jerusalem ID could move around the territories only with hard-to-get permits issued by the military. Sometimes I had to go around on improvised trails carved out of fields. Sitting at an equally improvised roadblock and feeling my anger surge, I constantly had to remind myself how much worse the people had it who got around illegally by foot or donkey at the risk of being picked off by a sniper.

I knew from the start that the people who could help win support countrywide wouldn't be academics or urban professionals. They had to be activists themselves. I therefore sought out local Fatah leaders I knew, some from the first intifada. Already at the first signing event with Ami at the Imperial Hotel, I had brought aboard activists from Ramallah, Bethlehem, and Hebron.

I also went to some of my oldest contacts in the West Bank to figure out the best way to create a grassroots base for HASHD. One of my first stops was at Sameer's house in Ramallah. With two of his sons in an Israeli prison, Sameer listened and nodded his approval as I explained to him the logic behind the Destination Map. He liked the idea, but he warned me that the opposition was going to be ferocious, and if I didn't want trouble I would have to get the major Fatah activists on my side. A word from them could open up all the doors I needed.

One day a visitor came to my office at the university in Abu Dis. It was Issa Abu Iram, a well-known activist from the Hebron area. He wished to participate in the initiative, he told me, and said he could help build support for it. The unexpected offer felt like a gift from heaven. His street credentials, I reasoned, could help win us access to militants. I had known Abu Iram for years. During the first intifada he was close to Abu Jihad, and he had belonged to the Fatah Higher Committee until he was arrested and spent nine years in prison for wounding a settler in a gun battle. In 1992, with Oslo, he was released and got a job with

Jibril in Preventive Security. (He did most of the interrogations of would-be suicide bombers.) I knew his stance on the current fighting: he agreed with Jibril that it was Sharon's trap to drive the Palestinians deeper into violence.

"We're going to do this thing together," he announced without hesitation after I explained some details about the Destination Map.

His suggestions were simple. "For both of us to avoid getting gunned down" we needed to find our leaders from among the "tigers," the street designation for someone who had served time in an Israeli prison or had been hunted down and forced to slip into hiding. Time in prison or on the run would give them credibility in the rough-and-tumble neighborhoods and camps, and allow them to stand up and defend their position on nationalist ground, without being intimidated by a leaflet accusing them of treason, collaboration, or spying. Nearly all of the leaders we eventually recruited were tigers, and most had sat for years in Israeli prisons.

My friend Fahed, the head of the university's Abu-Jihad Center for Political Prisoners' Affairs, took charge in the Ramallah district. My pick to head up the office in Tulkarem was an activist who had spent eleven years in prison for killing a collaborator. Our man in Hebron, a Fatah leader from a refugee camp, had sat in prison for a decade before going to work with Jibril. The director in Nablus was once Abu Jihad's assistant. Another—who happened to be one of my bodyguards—had been in and out of jail during the first intifada because of his expertise at making Molotov cocktails.

The most tumultuous place in the West Bank was Jenin, the hotbed of Al-Aqsa intifada radicalism. Nowhere had the fighting been fiercer, or more futile. The tiger we eventually recruited for Jenin was named Mohammed, the head of legal affairs at the university there. In the first intifada, at the age of sixteen, he was shot in the thigh during a demonstration. He did his best to flee, but with part of his leg gone he didn't get very far. The Israelis locked him up. At the start of the second intifada he was finishing up his law degree and wasn't involved in the fighting. This didn't prevent his arrest, as the Shin Bet assumed he was a ringleader. The interrogator worked using the familiar formula of chains, a warlock's peaked hood, sleep deprivation, and rapid-fire questions.

With such talent on board, HASHD quickly emerged as one of the most organized groups in the territories, perhaps second only to Hamas—which admittedly doesn't say much, given the general collapse of civil society. We had a network of offices, by now adequate funding, and regular communication and meetings.

A high point for me was a training workshop in Ramallah for activists. If someone could have made me out through the dense cigarette smoke in the room, and watched me with my threadbare English tweed blazer discussing strategy with my tigers (Mohammed and dozens of others showed up from Jenin), he would have thought I was Mack the Knife building my own private army. In fact, during the training seminar I was making Immanuel Kant comprehensible to ex–street fighters.

As if to students in a classroom, what I hammered into them over and over was they mustn't lose their humanity. I phrased it in terms they could appreciate, but the gist of it was that you could condemn dehumanization only if you hadn't allowed yourself to be dehumanized. Resistance to occupation is justifiable only insofar as it does not undermine or blemish the principle from which it received its justification in the first place, namely, the safekeeping of human dignity. It was straight Kant, but it was also my father.

Putting moral theory into practice—never very easy—is a daunting task in a war zone. The first ads we put out may have stirred up opposition among some politicians, but the man on the street had more existential concerns. Danny Rubinstein, hoping for a journalistic scoop, wandered around for a few days after the ads appeared and described the anticlimax.

The owner of a shop that sells books and newspapers on Salaheddin Street in East Jerusalem says people buying *Al-Quds* last week barely noticed the ads, which appeared in the upper corners of the front

page. But they carefully examined the photographs from the curfews, the destruction and the dead, which took up much of the front
pages. He said that when Palestinians see and read about Israeli soldiers reoccupying the Palestinian cities, it's nearly impossible to persuade anyone that they are partners for negotiations and peace in
Israel.

Far more formidable obstacles lay in store for us. In Jenin trouble
started the minute Mohammed opened the HASHD office. Mohammed
looks the role of a street fighter, and with his slight limp, no one can question his devotion to Palestinian liberty. Or at least we thought so until
thugs broke into the office. The leader of the gang, a youngster from
a camp, came in waving a pistol randomly at our co-workers. "Who's
Mohammed?" he demanded. Mohammed stepped up to him and asked
him what he wanted. Pointing his gun at Mohammed's chest, he told him
to close the office. "You are not allowed to operate here." Mohammed
promptly called the West Bank head of the Al-Aqsa Martyrs Brigade,
hardly a fan of HASHD, and told him what was happening. He then
passed the phone to the teenage gunman, who took up the receiver and,
as soon as he realized who was on the other end, went pale. The leader
of the Martyrs Brigade told the gunman never to step foot in our office
again—or else.

On another occasion, I went to An-Najah National University in
Nablus to drum up local support. My bodyguard got a call warning us
against coming. En route, someone from the Israeli civil administration,
acting on a tip from his collaborators who warned of terrible trouble,
phoned my office back in Jerusalem with more or less the same message.

Upon arrival it was clear that the students from Hamas and the
PFLP didn't want me to have a public forum. The president of the university, who had invited me, was worried that things could get out of
hand. I didn't want to stir up unnecessary trouble for him. "Okay," I
told him, "so they don't want to listen to me. I don't want to impinge on
their right to protest." I agreed to cancel the public address and hold the
meeting in the president's office—only I made sure that the local tele-

vision station was there. The result was a blessing in disguise. Instead of trying to shout down five hundred angry students, I calmly delivered my message to the television cameras, and the entire meeting was beamed into every home in the region.

Israelis also threw up various obstacles, and the timing of their actions was as counterintuitive as ever. A year earlier, authorities had closed down the university offices shortly after I made a public appeal for the cessation of suicide bombings—an appeal that earned me threatening leaflets, letters, and telephone calls from fellow Arabs who saw suicide bombings as "heroic acts" perpetrated by saintly martyrs. Now, a year later, with HASHD getting off the ground, the military police arrested one of our militants turned peace activists at a checkpoint while on his way to a peace meeting in Ramallah. On a different occasion Shin Bet agents brought in some of our workers in Jenin for interrogation, and then tried to enlist them as collaborators. "Look," they reasoned, "you are already collaborating. You are working for Nusseibeh, right? Well, he's working with Ami, and Ami was once the head of the Shin Bet. Get it? Your boss works for us."

Israel Radio broadcast the official findings of a special committee of experts hired by Uzi's successor as minister of public security, Tzahi Hanegbi, which described me as a dangerous dissimulator working for the destruction of Israel. An Israeli journalist commented that it was "no problem" to find senior figures in the defense establishment who believed that "those like Nusseibeh are the most dangerous types of all," more threatening to Israeli security than Hamas. Rubin Barkov continued seeing in me a Trojan horse or a wolf in sheep's clothing.

In all fairness to Rubin, Uzi Landau, and now Minister Tzahi Hanegbi, behind my philosophical pose did lurk a political option that profoundly threatened their version of the Jewish state, for turning the armed intifada into a nonviolent crusade of civil disobedience would place them in precisely the sort of battle they knew they could never win.

In Rubin's case, like many undergraduates in a logic course, he conflated tactic for strategy. Organizing thousands of people to form a symbolic border, as we and Peace Now had tried to do with the Human Chain, could *also* have shown the Israelis the numbers we could muster if we decided to pursue a one-state rather than a two-state solution. An inseparable part of my strategy with Ami went back to my words from 1987: "Annex us!" Either give us our state or give us the vote. One or the other.

The entire logic of our joint project was to force the hands of politicians. The reasoning went something like this: if they could get away with it and it didn't endanger the demographics of the Jewish state, the Israelis would take as much of our land as they could, because they thought they had a historical right to it. With almost mathematical predictability, Palestinian leaders let them off the hook by harping on absolute justice and their own historical rights. But our respective absolute rights—the historical right of the Jews to their ancestral homeland, and the Palestinian rights to the country robbed from them—were fundamentally in conflict, and were in fact mutually exclusive. Even worse, the more historical justice each side demanded, the less their real national interests got served. Justice and interests fell into conflict.

One tack Ami and I chose made Rubin Barkov and his colleagues understandably nervous. The best way to convince the masses of an equitable two-state solution was to demonstrate how the status quo threatened their basic interests. And the best way of doing that was to play the demographic card.

My message was this: if negotiations were not held soon, the Palestinian national project would have to enter a new era of struggle, this time to achieve a binational state in historic Palestine, in which Jews and Palestinians had equal rights and responsibilities, which meant the end of the Zionist dream of establishing a national home for the Jewish people in the land of Palestine.

From an Israeli point of view, failing to reach a solution gradually placed Israel in danger. Sooner or later, Israel would find itself turning into a racist state unable to bring security or peace to its citizens, like the

apartheid regime that existed in South Africa. Such an outcome represented a strategic problem for Israel and required a preemptive measure
to prevent it. Thus, strategically, Israel was in need of a solution.

Ami and I returned to this theme over and over to convince Israelis
that full withdrawal from the territories was far more consistent with
their own interests than Sharon's dream of breaking up the West Bank
into South African–style Bantustans. To one interviewer, Ami warned
that within a decade Israelis were "heading toward a situation in which
Israel will not be a democracy and home to the Jewish people," because
Palestinians will outnumber Israeli Jews between the Mediterranean
and the Jordan River. I chimed in. "This may be the last opportunity to
reach an agreement. Soon territorial solutions like a Palestinian state
will no longer be on the agenda. The only alternative is then demographic, based on the struggle to attain equal rights between Arabs and
Jews within a single state."[3]

Chapter Thirty-three

The Perfect Crime

Do we not all have one father?
Has not one God created us?
Why do we deal treacherously each against his brother
so as to profane the covenant of our fathers?
—MALACHI 2 : 10–11, GRAFFITI ON THE WALL IN ABU DIS

IN A GOOD MURDER MYSTERY the perfect crime is when the villain gets off scot-free. Better still, it is when he turns justice on its head by getting the dead man fingered for his own murder. The victim was either suicidal or had it coming to him. I write this because, starting in 2004, I was witness to the perfect political crime, choking an ancient civilization of its last bit of air.

In December 2003 we looked back on a year of hard work and great strides for HASHD. Despite the terrorist bombs exploding all around us, hundreds of thousands of average Palestinians and Israelis were signing off on a historic compromise, because they realized that their interests coincided. No matter how ghastly the violence, an irrepressible desire for normalcy was forging a broad coalition between our peoples. By standing back and looking at demographics, average people realized that our two peoples were heading either toward a one-state solution or toward two independent states divided more or less along the 1967 border, with Jerusalem under shared sovereignty. Opinion polls showed that big majorities on both sides preferred the latter. According to one, if the Palestinian leadership were to embrace such a two-state solution, Israelis by a lopsided margin (70 percent versus 16 percent) wanted their government to enter into serious negotiations to conclude a deal.[1]

Sharon, seeing the trend better than most, decided to erect a wall between our peoples. Iron, concrete, and guns were his response to the natural instinct among average people to bury the hatchet and solve our conflict through dialogue and compromise.

Sharon's twenty-foot-high structure was the perfect crime, and not only because it carved up the West Bank and hermetically cut off East Jerusalem from the villages and cities that for millennia had been its natural hinterland. What really placed Sharon's masonry job into this literary genre was that few people suspected that the prime minister's real motive was not to stop terrorism. Cassam rockets can easily fly over a twenty-foot barrier. His real foe was human dialogue and the desire for normalcy.

The wall is the perfect crime because it creates the violence it was ostensibly built to prevent. It's like sticking someone in a cage and then when he starts screaming, as any normal person would, using his violent temper as justification for putting him in the cage in the first place.

Public opinion is a fickle thing. When Ami and I started our project, we had thirty people in the Imperial Hotel lobby: thirty is a far cry from a million. A recurring remark many Israelis made quite reasonably to Ami was that our agreement meant nothing. "Yes, yes, Sari's a nice enough fellow. If only there were a million like him over there! But, alas, we have to deal with the Palestinian rabble. We are not making peace with *him* but with *them*." Ami and his team managed to get a flood of signatures, 250,000 in all. Likud voters signed their names with the same avidity as Labor. On the Palestinian side, HASHD likewise scored more successes than anyone could have predicted. At first people told me that the only signature would be my own. We now had more than 160,000 people signed up, often at the risk of becoming social pariahs among family or friends. Signs of the inroads we'd made: In the Arroub refugee camp, near Hebron, 1,100 of 9,000 residents joined HASHD. In Jenin, we had 3,000 supporters and 70 leaders. Fahed and his team of thirty collected tens of thousands of signatures in Gaza, the hotbed of Palestinian extremism.

HASHD has set up a solid leadership. Working closely with a peace organization that Lucy runs, we've sent our "tigers" to a two-week training course in the fields of peace, democracy, equality, domestic relations, and nonviolence education; and they have taken part in a "Smarter Without Violence" summer camp near Hebron. The three-week camp for nine- to fourteen-year-olds teaches democracy and nonviolence through art, sports, and so on. The camp director, Jamil Rushdie, a member of our leadership group, is a nine-year veteran of the Israeli prison system.

Furthermore, we've made inroads into local politics. In an election for the council of labor unions in the southern West Bank, nearly half the people elected were HASHD members. Camp director Rushdie was the head of the council.

Our message of nonviolence was getting through. In 2004 we put out another ad denouncing violence. This time around, people were lining up to sign. The head of Fatah in Gaza contributed his name, as did the governor of Nablus, whose two sons were killed by the Israelis.

Even Arafat eventually came around. From the beginning, I sensed he would settle for the Destination Map if he could get a symbolic number of refugees to return. As proof of my hunch, while Sharon contemptuously dismissed us—the Interior Ministry consistently refused granting visas to our foreign volunteers—Arafat agreed to bankroll us to the tune of ten thousand dollars a month, a substantial sum for his bankrupt Authority.

The project was also garnering international attention. At the end of 2003, Ami and I took the show on the road, starting with Deputy U.S. Secretary of Defense Paul Wolfowitz. An intellectual who had once studied with Leo Strauss at the University of Chicago, Wolfowitz's hawkish views on the Middle East are legendary. Intellectuals on the left like to cast him as the dark prince of a warmongering president.

We had met a couple of years earlier, through a mutual friend, who also helped set up our meeting at the Pentagon. I went into Wolfowitz's office hopeful, despite everything I had heard about the man. Perhaps it was wishful thinking, but I assumed that a pupil of Leo Strauss, the great commentator on al-Farabi, couldn't be as bad as his reputation. Indeed, the legendary hawk turned out to be an immensely affable, charming, and intellectually pliable man eager to hear about our project.

Weeks later, Wolfowitz gave a speech at Georgetown University School of Foreign Service in which he pushed President Bush's vision of two states. To his audience he claimed that thousands of Israelis and Palestinians supported the president's vision. "How do I know this?" he asked rhetorically. "Well, right now there is a significant grassroots movement . . . in support of principles that look very much like the road map favoring a two-state solution." He mentioned our meeting and summarized our strategy of "mobilizing majorities on both sides who crave peace so that the extremists who oppose [peace] can be isolated."

Ami and I met next with Elliot Abrams in his National Security Council office next door to the White House. Like Wolfowitz, Abrams has a reputation as a neocon ideologue with a hard-line pro-Israel stance. In his role as the "White House special assistant to the president and senior director on the National Security Council for Near East and North African Affairs," it was he who was tilting Bush and his team heavily in favor of the Sharon position. Even his personal life seemed a formidable hurdle to surmount: by marriage he's related to *Commentary Magazine*'s Norman Podhoretz. Ami didn't think we had a chance with him. We went anyway.

Abrams began our meeting with a predictable recap of all the obstacles to peace in the Middle East: that Arafat couldn't be trusted and needed to be ousted; that Israel had a right to deal forcefully with terrorism and shouldn't consider any concessions until the Palestinians forswore violence; that the Road Map couldn't be implemented until every terrorist had been locked up; and so on. He also threw in a few lines about Palestinian corruption. Precisely what we had expected.

Not wanting to get embroiled in an argument, we agreed with him. "Fine, fine, fine," we said perfunctorily, "now let's get down to business." We gave him our stock speech: that the administration's Road Map wouldn't work unless two pages got attached to it. These pages, we noted, were in sync with President Bush's vision.

As we explained, the president's Road Map, while noble in inspiration, didn't describe with sufficient clarity where we were heading. It was silent on the borders of the two states and what would happen to the Jewish settlements and the refugees. Our plan gave the map a destination. Just as important, it created the necessary mass support for it by placing, as it were, the people in the driver's seat, thus diminishing the role of extremists on both sides whose agendas and concerns were entirely different from those of the ordinary human beings.

This last point caught Abrams's attention, and the mood in the office changed. He perked up and asked to see our paper. He read it, raised an index finger, and leveled with us. "Look," he explained, "what is sacrosanct for us is not the Road Map, it is the vision behind it. That is what we are committed to."

In other visits with officials, we got a similar response. Through his spokesman, Colin Powell read out a statement: "The secretary once again expressed his welcome of the efforts that are undertaken by people [such as us] to try to encourage . . . a vision of peace." Warren Christopher, Robert McNamara, and five former U.S. Cabinet members issued an open letter backing the Destination Map. They, too, came up with a statement of support:

> We believe that the best way to move forward is to address at the
> outset, not at the end of an incremental process, all the basic princi-
> ples of a fair and lasting solution. Postponing the final outcome
> makes any progress hostage to extremists on both sides.

In Israel, the Destination Map won a beauty contest of sorts. We were invited to present the plan at the 2004 Herzliya Conference, an annual gathering of the Israeli and Jewish world's financial, political, and academic elite. The conference, which tends to be on the conservative side of the political divide in Israel, has evolved into a forum for introducing new thinking on strategic issues facing Israel. The prime minister typically delivers his yearly message to the nation, an Israeli version of the State of the Union address.

At the conference, we presented our ideas in a panel discussion on various strategies to end the conflict. Besides ours, Yossi Belin and Yasser Abed Rabbo discussed their Geneva Accord, and Avigdor Lieberman, an ex-Russian nightclub bouncer and founder of the right-wing Israel Beiteinu Party, talked about his.

The Geneva Accord was in substance similar to the Destination Map, the main difference being our focus on bypassing the political establishment by going directly to the grass roots. Lieberman's solution was a different matter altogether, which was what you'd expect from a man who while minister of transport in Sharon's first government suggested drowning all the Palestinian prisoners in the Dead Sea. Lieberman proposed to the people at the conference that Israel annex all the empty land in the West Bank while amputating outlying areas of East Jerusalem heavily populated by Arabs along with the Wadi ᶜAra area alongside the Green Line, with its three hundred thousand Arab residents. Arabs remaining in Israel who refused to take a loyalty oath to the "Jewish-Zionist country" would be expelled. Nightclub bouncers tend to like simple solutions.

At the end of the session, the organizers put the three plans to a vote. Ours got the most thumbs-ups: 65 percent, against Belin's 25 percent and Lieberman's 10 percent.

I had never imagined that I would get such a powerful confirmation of my hunch about Palestinians and Israelis being allies. At a time of horror, bombing, demagoguery, and fire-breathing clerics, even this conservative audience opted for reason over rhetoric.

But it was hard to savor the victory because we were just the warm-up act for Sharon, who spoke later in the afternoon about his "disengagement plan" from Gaza. The organizers of the conference didn't put his presentation up to a vote, though they should have. It was as much an end-game plan as ours, and given the audience, it would have won hands down. Maybe Yossi Belin, Yasser Abed Rabbo, and Ami and I got the red carpet treatment from the Israeli elite only because the real game in town was Sharon's plan, not ours.

At the conference, Sharon, a master tactician, turned a fire hose on his opponents by transmogrifying himself into a leader of the realistic moderates. Strategically, his move was on a par with his counterattack during the 1973 war, when he crossed the Suez and trapped the Egyptian Third Army.

By the time the prime minister took to the stage, he had come to the conclusion that his old autonomy schemes were unworkable. It was pointless to try to crush Palestinian nationalism or to prevent a Palestinian state by peppering the territories with Jewish settlements. Years of endless conflict, combined with the future demographic threat posed by millions of disgruntled Palestinians, had convinced him of this.

So, without a tear shed, he threw the dream of Greater Israel in the dustbin; he decided to yank settlers out of Gaza, and announced a unilateralism aimed at preserving a strong Jewish majority within Israel, while locking up strategic assets in the West Bank and East Jerusalem— settlements, lots of empty real estate, and water resources—behind a wall. What sounded to most ears like a bolt out of the blue was in fact a repackaged version of plans Sharon had been mulling over for at least a decade. You could say that the concrete mixers followed the direction of the prime minister's ravenous appetite.

It was a clever stratagem that directly, one might say intentionally, threatened the Destination Map. Sharon even confessed to Ami that a major factor behind "disengagement" was our grassroots initiative. Sharon's "settler evacuations," Ami commented to *The Jerusalem Post*, were designed specifically to "*prevent* coexistence campaigns."[2] (Sharon's chief adviser Dov Weisglass put it this way: disengagement "supplies the amount of formaldehyde that is necessary so there will not be a political process with the Palestinians.")

Sharon's plan did this through a very different approach to the national interests dealt with in the Destination Map. Whereas we sought to create dialogue between the two nations, Sharon's unilateralism immortalized mistrust and suspicion, and so guaranteed the low level of violence needed to preclude negotiations. By clearing out settlers from Gaza—a classic red herring—he could divert international attention while he cut the West Bank to pieces.

The "Palestinian State" left by his surgical operations would be so dysfunctional and violent that it would guarantee the need for a security wall, and would, even more important, put off negotiations more or less forever. The predictable clashes between Hamas and Fatah, not to mention the occasional Cassam rocket fired over the wall, would prove to the world what sort of unruly neighbors the democratic Israelis had to live around. Meanwhile, more Palestinian land in the West Bank would be massively populated with Israelis. The key to this plan, of course, was that there be no dialogue, no trust, and no negotiations between the two sides. *In a word, that there be no significant grassroots movement for co-existence.*

Naturally, none of this was spelled out in Sharon's lecture. Poking around the lobby afterward, lost in thought and trying to make sense of the prime minister's speech, I found some materials from the two previous Herzliya conferences. I took the reading material home, and the more I investigated, the clearer the picture became. The good thing about Sharon was that at least he was very systematic, determined, and straightforward. He told you what he wanted and then did it.

His shift in strategy had begun back at the 2002 Herzliya Conference. The conference devoted a key session to the demographic conundrums facing Israel, a theme that had always belonged to the Arab-Israeli conflict. From the early days of Zionist colonization, Jewish leaders were well aware that they were a small minority in a "vast Arab sea," as they liked to call us. (I should add here that the idea of a wall goes all the way back to the spiritual founder of the Likud Party, Zev Jabotinsky, a man we've seen before in this story. Jabotinsky brought up the idea in his 1923 article "The Iron Wall: We and the Arabs.") The star of the conference was Professor Arnon Sofer, an unassuming geographer at

Haifa University who had made a reputation for himself as a prophet of the Arab demographic time bomb. In his address, he raised the hobgoblin of populations and land. How could the Israeli state keep much of the land in the West Bank, deny all rights to the people living there, and yet continue calling itself a democracy?

The professor set forth his thesis that Israel needed to draw borders at once; otherwise it would be inundated by Arabs. An ideal map, he explained to the Israeli elite, would split up the West Bank into three isolated cantons thickly populated with Arabs: one from Jenin to Ramallah, another from Bethlehem to Hebron, and the last encircling the city of Jericho. Professor Sofer suggested that electric fences surround all three, preventing unwanted Arabs from spilling out into all the lands Israel would keep for itself, which amounted to over half of the West Bank.

Sharon approached the professor after his lecture, shook his hand, and kindled what would become a very successful partnership.

Sharon presented a broad outline of his disengagement plan a year later at the 2003 Herzliya gathering. By this time the notion of a God-given historical deed to "Judea and Samaria" had become such a fringe argument of the messianic loonies that Sharon chose not to use it. His only argument was security. If the Palestinians failed to stop terror, he warned, "Israel will initiate the unilateral security step of disengagement from the Palestinians . . . Israel will greatly accelerate the construction of the security fence. Today we can already see it taking shape."

The idea of a security wall had begun when Labor was a part of the government, and was seen, at least by Labor, as a stopgap measure to defend a society besieged by suicide bombers. Sharon's innovation was to apply the fence to Professor Sofer's map. The wall was a logical extension of the settlements, of the checkpoint system introduced during the Gulf War, and of much of the infrastructure built over the years, such as highways and water pumping stations. It was also the embodiment of Israel's "eternal" claim to all of Jerusalem.

If the vision was inspired by demographics and the desire to draw boundaries most favorable to Israel, the justification he gave was security. (The East German communists similarly dubbed the Berlin Wall the "anti-fascist protection barrier.") The longer the armed conflict lasted, the more Palestinian territory he could colonize. Terrorism allowed Sharon to genuflect before Bush's Road Map, even as it protected him from its consequences.

Sharon could comfortably count on Arafat providing the necessary cover for what has turned into Israel's biggest land grab since 1948. The old revolutionary, harmlessly holed up in a half-bombed compound mumbling to himself, was the ideal straw man. Pilloried by the Israeli and U.S. administrations as the fountainhead of terror, he was to blame for all the Palestinians' woes. It was because of him that the Israelis were being forced to build their Security Fence.

The wall around Jerusalem was given the name the "Jerusalem Security Envelope," and the governmental body charged with building it was named the "Seam Zone Administration."

The wall went up with lightning speed. It now towers two feet from our old house in Abu Dis. Instead of glorious views of the Dome of the Rock, the balcony now faces a twenty-foot-high concrete slab. Just as we had suspected after our return from Washington in 1995, had we stayed in the house, we most likely would have lost our residency rights in Jerusalem. To visit Mother would have required a lethally hazardous scaling of the wall or special permission from a bureaucracy institutionally disinclined to issue it.

Soon enough I began to feel the pinch of Sharon's version of the "two-state" solution. At the university, the wall did more than just block the view. An interviewer for *The New Statesman* captured what was happening on campus, and inside my head, when he wrote, "Nusseibeh harbors no illusions. We have been talking at Al-Quds, the Arab university in Jerusalem where the Israeli 'security fence' cuts right through the campus, cutting hundreds of Palestinians off from their only source of higher education."

The main university campus straddles the imaginary municipal line dividing Jerusalem from the West Bank. One morning some people from the Seam Zone Administration showed up with rolls of blueprints under their arms. Behind them was Israeli army machinery. The plan was for the wall to ribbon its way down the middle of the university, leaving a third of the campus on the Israeli side, while all the buildings were to be severed from Jerusalem. Students living on the Israeli side, a third of the entire student body, would have to pass through Israeli gates in the fence, which from our experience of the checkpoints would more often than not be closed.

The planners in the Seam Zone Administration must have expected the same protests they had invited all over the West Bank. Typically, the Israelis showed up to do another section, and bands of Arabs started throwing rocks to defend their fields against expropriation. The rock throwers made easy targets for rubber bullets, and their violence reinforced the wall's raison d'être.

We surprised them. Or perhaps a fairer way of putting it is that the planners made a major blunder we then exploited to the hilt. The wall's original trajectory wasn't through a parking lot or an empty field, real estate with no emotional value, but through the university's soccer field, basketball courts, and land slated for a new sports complex and botanical garden. Exquisite PR.

I huddled together with advisers from Al-Quds and HASHD—who were in fact the same people—to think up a way to fight the wall. The plan we came up with was ideally sculpted to engage the dialogue Sharon was so eager to circumvent. What he thought would stop Israelis and Palestinians from talking ended up promoting intense engagement, and in ways not seen since he ambled his way up to the Noble Sanctuary. We turned the soccer field into a laboratory of nonviolent protest that taught students how to beat the Israelis with ideas and persuasion rather than rocks or Molotov cocktails. The protest lasted for thirty-four days, and we won.

The precondition for success was clarity. We set forth defined, limited objectives, and steered away from general criticisms of the wall as such. We didn't deny the government's need to defend its citizens against suicide bombers; we affirmed it. "Okay, if you want separation until there's peace, be our guest. Make your wall a hundred miles high, if you want," was the line we took. "Just build it along the 1967 border, not in the middle of Jerusalem, *and not through our soccer field."*

The grotesqueness of this twenty-foot barrier made keeping a lid on violence, an absolute prerequisite to fighting it, an arduous task. The situation was so tense that I feared that any organized protest, however carefully planned, would only degenerate into mayhem. To make matters worse, many students pointed to the wall as proof that dialogue with the Israelis didn't work. "You tell us about bridges and they come back with walls," the critics shouted, holding up their plastic water pistols to signify their proposed solution to the problem.

I managed to calm the students only by explaining how violence only helped Sharon. If rocks got thrown, students would be killed. The next day at their funerals we'd add a few more noble martyrs to our growing list, but the university would probably be ordered shut down, and no one would be left to stop the bulldozers.

My logic was supplemented by the strong-armed persuasion exercised by Naser Al-Afandi, the head of campus security and maintenance. A Fatah leader, ex-prisoner, and HASHD activist, Naser had worked for Jibril until the incursion, at which point the Israelis forbade him to leave Abu Dis. With an eye on the Israeli assassination teams, he prudently obeyed. Naser kept protests peaceful by importing three hundred Fatah people, all HASHD "tigers." Every day at the protest field they sang their songs and danced traditional jigs from seven in the morning till midnight. And it worked, though once a few students wearing masks started throwing rocks and petrol bombs at an Israeli bulldozer near the sports ground. Troops guarding the site fired warning shots to disperse them. No one was hurt.

Another thing we did every day to keep tensions down was to have the soccer team dress up and practice on the field. The first time we did it soldiers standing off to the side went from being nervous recruits with their fingers on the trigger to passionate partisans of one team or the other. The tension was gone, and the soldiers walked away smiling. For over a month the soccer teams played match after match. Every night we staged a party, and young people from Abu Dis and nearby villages came to socialize on the field. The concerts, food, bonfires, and a festive atmosphere were a throwback to the spirit of 1968.

Our "protest camp" was a large tent, under which we held meetings and examinations. It doubled as an information center for the international and Israeli media. With PowerPoint presentations, slide shows, and printed materials, we explained how detrimental the wall's course would be for the university.

The journalists who streamed into Abu Dis to cover the protest gave us overwhelmingly positive coverage. An article in *The Guardian* featured a soccer player named Samer: "'There are no more playgrounds in this part of our country, nothing left to play on,' says Samer, 25, who is studying for a masters in sports science at Al-Quds. 'And this is a place for people to meet as well. So we hope every day that our match won't be the last game here.'"

I put out a press release in Arabic, Hebrew, and English titled "Does the Wall Also Need to Cut Our Campus into Two?"

> The University, home to almost 6000 students, has been for the past few years in the forefront of the campaign to encourage Israeli-Palestinian academic cooperation. The University campus has for the most part during the past three years of bloody violence and confrontation been fairly quiet, with students intent whenever allowed to reach the campus on pursuing their research and studies.
>
> The ravaging of the campus grounds, and the erection of a high cement wall in its midst blocking the natural view across the valley, cannot but be an indelible statement of enmity, aggression, and political as well as human failure. This negative statement, written in concrete blocks in the face of university students, stands in direct opposition to the positive educational values we try to propagate at the University, such as the necessity of breaking down the barriers of enmity, and the building of bridges of understanding in order to enhance the prospects for peace.

On the same day I put out the press release—it was September 3—we invited various consuls general and diplomatic representatives to our protest camp. Among others, the American political consul showed up accompanied by representatives of Ambassador John Wolf, U.S. coordinator for implementation of Bush's Road Map. Italian consul general Gianni Ghisi, whose country presided over the European Union, spoke on behalf of the visiting diplomats. "Al-Quds University is a partner with us; any damage to its interests is considered damage to our interests. We will work together with Al-Quds University to get through this period." The consul general called on Israeli universities to show their support for Al-Quds University, adding, "Not only is Al-Quds University an intellectual laboratory, it is a laboratory of nonviolence and passive resistance."

It took thirty-four days of protest, but finally I got a phone call from the office of the Israeli army chief of staff. The message was that the Israeli government had agreed to move the wall away from our fields. The shift in their plans came about because our protests had reached the ear of U.S. national security adviser Condoleezza Rice, who subsequently raised the issue with Israeli officials in Washington.

Saving the soccer field was important for Al-Quds University, but it did nothing to stop the relentless building of the wall. The major settlements fell into Sharon's concrete lasso, but so did the key water sources and much of the best land. All over the West Bank, thousands of acres were being expropriated; villagers were separated from agricultural fields on which their livelihoods depended; hundreds of buildings and tens of thousands of fruit and olive trees had to make way for this jagged concrete barrier. In some areas, the wall penetrated deep into the West Bank, cutting villages off from one another, creating isolated enclaves, and destroying any hope of a contiguous Palestinian state.

If you set a thief loose in a department store for a night he'll go for the highest-quality stuff. Sharon's wall took in the biggest prize of all:

East Jerusalem, where vast tracts of land came under Israeli control. With one hatchet blow, thousands of years of sacred geography changed. The wall cut off Lazarus's town of Ayzariyah, close to Abu Dis, from the other Christian sites in Jerusalem. For a pilgrim to go from the Church of the Holy Sepulcher to the Church of the Nativity in Bethlehem suddenly required a long wait before a scene reminiscent of the Berlin Wall—the same concrete, rolls of razor wire, watchtowers, and edgy soldiers clutching weapons. Two million Muslim worshippers in the West Bank were unable to pray at the Dome of the Rock, a source of our collective identity as a people.

With one victory in our pockets, the time had come to expand HASHD's operations beyond collecting signatures. The only way to stop Sharon and his wall was by reviving the political process, and the only way to do this was to counteract Sharon's attempt to eliminate all dialogue and talk of coexistence through a hermetic separation. This in turn required convincing Israelis that it was in their interest to return to the negotiating table. We had to show them that Sharon's policy of caging Palestinians in enclaves would eventually lead to a South African situation (in an act of thoughtless indiscretion Sharon even called the enclaves Bantustans).

The central flaw in his admittedly clever scheme is that Palestinians will never stop fighting it, and by means both foul and fair. One day the Israelis may realize that the reason for the never-ending turmoil disrupting their lives has nothing to do with our opposition to the Jewish state but is rooted in the more mundane fact that human beings are not constituted to accept injustice. But by that time it is quite possible that the reality on the ground will make impossible a solution based on partition between the two sides. And so, out of the ruins of the Greater Israel ideology may well emerge extremist solutions such as Lieberman's "ethnic cleansing," a procedure that, if implemented, will make the conflict even more vicious, and impossible to solve peacefully. Meanwhile, those who will pay the price in terms of continued pain and suffering will be ordinary Israelis and Palestinians who seek to live normal lives within their respective societies.

Our new approach was either dialogue leading to a two-state solution, or a nonviolent campaign demanding full citizenship in Israel. If Israel continued its occupation, we would respond with an antiapartheid-style campaign of "one man, one vote" in a unified Arab-Israeli state. At HASHD, we began calling the Security Fence the "Apartheid Wall."

Ami issued an identical statement: "Unfortunately, the fence that Israel is building will make many people stop believing in peace. If Israel creates a situation similar to that seen in apartheid-era South Africa, there will be neither a Palestinian state nor a safe home for the Jewish people. Although Israel does have the right to defend itself, the way in which it is building the Wall will harm the prospects for a favorable future."

HASHD took on the wall in a variety of ways. In support of the Palestinian delegation, we sent representatives to the International Court of Justice in The Hague that was hearing the case entitled "The Legal Consequences of the Construction of a wall in the Occupied Palestinian Territories." We also redoubled our efforts to push for nonviolence within Palestinian society. With the slogan "Build Bridges of Understanding Not Walls of Separation," we made the point that the adoption of the Destination Map peace initiative would eliminate the pretense for the construction of the Security Fence and provide security and prosperity for both Palestinians and Israelis. Perhaps the most significant evolution of HASHD took place in July 2004, when we staged Palestine's first national demonstration modeled after Peace Now. Like a Peace Now gathering, we brought in people from all over the country.

We decided to stage the rally in the Qalqilya District, where the wall was having particularly painful consequences for the villagers in the area. In the village of Jayyus, for instance, the wall pared off nearly 70 percent of the villagers' lands, uprooted more than four thousand trees, and cut off six underground water reservoirs. The wall had destroyed the livelihoods of more than half the inhabitants of the village.

The military did its best to stop us. It declared Qalqilya a closed military zone, and soldiers set up eight checkpoints on roads leading to the area. At least fifteen buses and a large number of cars, all carrying protestors, were turned back. But hundreds of ever-resourceful Palestinian bus and taxi drivers managed to navigate their way through. The 1,500 Arabs who showed up made our protest the largest demonstration in Qalqilya since the collapse of the peace process. There were workers, farmers, shopkeepers, engineers, students, clerks, and a rowdy contingent of Fatah youth from Jerusalem. "This isn't your run-of-the-mill academics and types that I'm usually associated with in the Israeli press," I told an Israeli reporter for *The Jerusalem Report*.

Demonstrators wearing T-shirts reading SMARTER WITHOUT VIOLENCE held signs calling for a peace agreement based on the Destination Map's two-state solution, a halt to violence on both sides, and a call to build bridges of peace instead of walls of separation and expansion. Graffiti sprayed on the walls—over previous layers of paint put there by Hamas and the Martyrs Brigade—championed dialogue over confrontation. As a symbol of cooperation, some of the youth flew kites that penetrated deep into Israeli airspace.

Ami, the mayor of the nearby Israeli town of Kfar Saba, and four hundred supporters were on the other side of the wall, standing on a former rubbish dump. When our two sides spoke to each other we used megaphones and telephones, and Ami released a massive helium balloon bearing the message THERE IS SOMEONE TO SPEAK WITH.

Balloons did not stop the wall any more than our soccer games at Al-Quds did. Inexorably, like a scene in H. G. Wells's *The War of the Worlds*, a fleet of bulldozers, cement trucks, and cranes has changed the geography of the Holy Land more in two years than all the conquerors and their greedy violence had since my family arrived in Jerusalem 1,300 years ago. For Palestinians, Sharon's actions in Jerusalem can best be compared with Robespierre's beheading of King Louis XVI, or Lenin's order to gun down the Romanovs. We Palestinians have never had a king or a royal family around which to form a national identity; Jerusalem has been the cultural, religious, and geographic center of our identity; now, for most Palestinians living in the West Bank and Gaza, to visit Jerusalem would require a magic steed like Mohammed's. Any other method, such as climbing over the wall, would invite a hail of bullets.

The Seam Zone Administration has seen to it that not an inch of the eighty miles of wall comprising the Jerusalem Security Envelope comes anywhere close to the pre-1967 dividing line. The wall meanders in and out of Arab neighborhoods, at points thrusting miles into the West Bank. While most Palestinians find themselves on the wrong side of the wall, Sharon and his planners have included distant Jewish settlements such as Maʾaleh Adumim and Gush Etzion inside the Envelope.

The dispossession of Jerusalem continues in other ways, such as the shady sale of the Imperial Hotel to a settler group seeking to "liberate the lands of Jerusalem," as the Israeli newspaper *Maʾariv* phrased it. The place in which the Human Chain and HASHD campaigns began may now become one of the largest settlements inside the Old City.

A Night Journey

May we, beleaguered by negation and despair,
show an affirming flame.

—W. H. AUDEN

AT HARVARD, I HAD LONG DEBATES with my daughter, Nuzha, about the characters in my fairy tale. She had generally good things to say about Louise and the flying donkey. Her favorite was the noble knight standing guard, asleep, with ramrod posture before the Holy Sepulcher. Less convincing, she told me, with her precocious tone of authority, was Mr. Seems. "Where does he fit in?" she demanded. "Who is he?" I tried to explain that the impossibility of coming up with a straight answer to her query went to the heart of his character. "I could only tell you precisely who he is if he is who he seems to be, which he isn't nor can he be." I'd lost her.

Though I have supreme admiration and trust in Nuzha's discriminating literary tastes, I stubbornly held my ground: Mr. Seems really needs to stay in the story, I explained. I felt I had to keep him in because, for me, there is a dimension of mystery to the conflict in the Middle East that cannot be easily overcome. In a city as ancient and hallowed as Jerusalem, things are often not what they seem to be. More often than not, newspaper headlines and history books miss the essential, because at the heart of our conflict lies something difficult to put your finger on.

As I know from experience, what everyone expects to be momentous historic breakthroughs—secret talks or daring diplomatic moves—often lead to yet another dead end.

Since returning to Jerusalem after my year at the Radcliffe Institute— I got back in July 2005—one political earthquake after the next has rumbled through the Holy Land. Some things naturally haven't changed: the weather, the relentlessly expanding settlements in the West Bank, and Russian-born eighteen-year-olds barking out orders to old women at checkpoints. But Prime Minister Sharon's decision to clear out a few thousand Jewish settlers from Gaza, hailed as a world-historical event on par with General De Gaulle's decision to leave Algeria, was no doubt a revolution in terms of Israeli politics. None of the previous Israeli leaders, not even peace-making Rabin and Peres, had ever dared clear out a single settlement, and here was Sharon, father of the settlement movement, evacuating the entire Gaza Strip.

But for all its precedent-setting bravery, Sharon's unilateralism has only made things worse. The comatose prime minister was not conscious to experience it, but Hamas's blowout victory in the Palestinian parliamentary elections was one intended or unintended consequence of his actions. As a kind of distorted mirror image, his unilateralism gave impetus to a political movement dead set against dialogue. My old friend Jibril Rajoub, who has never wavered an inch from his belief in a negotiated two-state solution with Israel, ran for a seat in the new parliament and lost to a long-bearded Hamas man who believes that Jews are infidels.

Such a colossal victory by an organization that denies the moral legitimacy of Israel, that calls for the ultimate destruction of the Jewish state, and that refuses to renounce violence as a means toward accomplishing this goal, was disastrous for HASHD and other organizations set up to promote coexistence. Hamas and the wall are two sides of the same coin. Both slam the door shut on dialogue.

The electoral triumph of dogmatism and militancy left a lot of people scratching their heads. In Israel those on the right were euphoric: it was the final proof they needed that the Palestinian people were incapable of peace. Only cement, checkpoints, drone spy planes, and the occasionally "targeted killing" could keep us in line.

I had some hard questions to ask myself. Was the symbolic formula I had thought up while reading *A Tale of Love and Darkness* in the plane after Arafat's funeral—that Louise, Abdul, and Amos, a Christian, a Muslim, and a Jew, join hands in planting a peace-bringing honeysuckle bush—just another case of wishful thinking? Have hatred and vengeance won out in the end? Were all the ideas I've tried my hardest to inculcate in students over the years—reason over fists, freedom over the dull habits of authority—no more than childish fantasies? How could religious zealots win out over reason? *What went wrong?*

This was yet another riddle for me, but figuring it out was a bit like following Tom Thumb's pebbles out of the dark forest. You must be careful lest you end up following the wrong leads—by blaming Islam, for instance. The truth really isn't what it seems to be, for despite Hamas, Islam may well be part of the solution to healing our terribly violated land. The fanatics like to hold up the Koran, they just don't like to read what it says about the Jews and Jerusalem. Israelis would similarly be wise to read what their own prophets have to say about oppression.

One day, to clear my mind, I took a stroll with Naser, the head of Al-Quds University security, over to the part of campus he had helped save from Sharon's bulldozers. After the Israeli army agreed to move the wall over to the edge of campus, Naser turned the rocky plot of land, once slated to form the concrete border severing Jerusalem from the West Bank, into a flowering garden with a fountain in the middle. Here the local people of the village, cut off from Jerusalem by the wall, can sit and stare off at the Mount of Olives. In their imaginations they can stroll through the city of the ancestors.

I sat in the garden and was at once lost in thought. My mind went back over the last twenty years. Back in my days at the union no one could have imagined Sheikh Yassin's obscure charity in Gaza, given a kick-start by Sharon, someday controlling the fate of our people. Now, in my post-election funk, the appalling mental image came to mind of the new Ministry of Education's schoolbooks infesting young minds with the fable that the Jews are Crusaders and must be chased away by a modern-day Saladin. A whole host of Islamic characters flitted past my mind's eye: I saw how Hamas would put a sword in Mohammed's hand. Omar would no doubt have one, too.

Sitting in the garden listening to the bubbling sound of the fountain, my mind raced. The Hamas victory, for many final proof of an epochal clash of civilizations between Islam and the West, wasn't what it seemed to be. In fact, the more I thought about it the more I realized that the best witness against their perversion of Islam was the very tradition they claimed to defend, and used to justify their rejection of Israel. Our religious militants have imbibed a lot more revolutionary European nihilism than they are aware of. However much they dress up the ideology in a traditional garb, it remains a product of a very modern European obsession with purity. The cosmopolitan decency and tolerance of Islam, and the ability of Muslims to come to terms peacefully with erstwhile foes, will win out in the end, I concluded, because it is based on ancient traditions and texts. It is more deeply rooted than the slogans of contemporary extremists.

Whenever I think of how Islam has been twisted by fundamentalists my mind tends to drift back to Mother and Father, and the tales I heard as a child. The Jerusalem I was raised to love was not a geographic dot on a map, and was certainly not a purely Muslim city; despite No Man's Land, it was the terrestrial gateway to the divine world, where Jewish, Christian, and Muslim prophets—men of vision and a sense of humanity— met, if only in the imagination. This is worth mentioning, because the political divisions scarring the Holy Land begin in the *religious* imagination, and it is there they must be combated and overcome.

The tale that always comes back to me, and which over time has grown only more poignant, is Mohammed's Night Journey. It is a tale that seeped deeply into my mind as a child, and over the years has gone into the formation of my identity as a Muslim Jerusalemite.

Most Muslims will tell you that Jerusalem is sacred because Mohammed ascended from the Holy Rock during this nocturnal flight—a journey that brought Mohammed to God's presence, where he received instructions on how Muslims should pray and worship. Returning from God's presence, the tradition relates, Mohammed led all the prophets in prayer. But a question that is not asked is: Why was Mohammed's journey made through Jerusalem? Why was that Rock chosen as the place from which Mohammed ascended to God's presence? Didn't that affirm Islam's recognition of the Rock's prior Jewish (and Christian) holiness?

Travel books printed in Syria a hundred years ago had no problem calling the Noble Sanctuary the Jewish Temple Mount, just as the Islam that I was raised with left me no doubt that Jesus, the son of Mary, was a prophet of God.

As a child, and now in adulthood, the tale of the Night Journey has always been inextricably joined with the story of Caliph Omar, Islam's second caliph. In the story I was taught, already in his journey from the north, Omar prepared himself to enter the Divine City. He didn't arrive as a Roman emperor riding golden chariots and surrounded by soldiers, or as pharaoh carried on the shoulders of slaves. He and his manservant took turns riding a camel, as if Omar wanted to teach us that before God even the loftiest political office doesn't entitle one man to lord over another.

When he arrived in the Golden City, he slipped his sword back in its sheath. Jerusalem wasn't like Baghdad or Cairo: it mustn't be conquered with sheer force or desecrated by blood and plunder. Omar received the keys of the city and of the Church of the Holy Sepulcher from Bishop Sephronius. He then entered the city peacefully on foot. The caliph continued to the Holy Sepulcher. Next, a Jew helped Omar locate the place of the Rock over which the temple once stood. We are also told that, having determined its location, he cleaned the Rock with his own robe, as if to say that it was an honor for any man to serve this holy site, but by no means to dare pose as its master.

. . .

The Hamas legislators now running my country no doubt would bristle at the thought of the "enemy" being at the source of our identity as Muslims. But the religious fundamentalist can eradicate the Jews from Jerusalem only by first doing violence to Islam. At the deepest metaphysical levels, Jews and Arabs are "allies," and any attempt to separate them is a product of the modern European myth of a "pure" nation, purged of outsiders, as with Sharon's wall.

One of the best representatives of the Muslim spirit I can think of in these dark days of fanaticism is, oddly enough, Lucy, called Louise in my fairy tale, one of the three characters who was symbolically given the role to bring peace to a war-torn land. Lucy was one of the few people among the Palestinian peace camp able to resist the pall of gloom that fell after the Hamas triumph.

After the elections a reporter from *Ha'aretz* asked to interview her, doubtlessly expecting lamentation. Sitting with the journalist at the American Colony Hotel, across the street from Mother's house, Lucy mentioned her philosopher parents, and her decision to move to Jerusalem. "I came here because I fell in love with Sari." Mostly she talked about the organization she had founded, MEND (Middle East Nonviolence and Democracy); her "Smarter Without Violence" campaign; and her work with the Al-Qud University's *Sesame Street*, which is now back on the air beaming out the message of mutual respect and tolerance. She also mentioned two films she helped produce to illustrate her work in education and media: *Death of a Dream* tells the story of Fatma Moussa, who has a miscarriage while waiting in line at an army checkpoint. *A Woman's Determination* is the story of a woman eager to study law, despite her family's objections.

I say that Lucy embodies Islam infinitely better than the religious fanatics because, in her interview, she expressed a hope and openness to the future, and a belief in the miracles we as humans can perform using logic and will, which to my thinking comes straight out of the religion of the Prophet. "The future is still open," she declared. The Palestinian people didn't vote for Hamas because they wanted a religious dictatorship or endless war with Israel. They voted in Hamas because they were sick of Fatah. "The Palestinian public is fed up with violence. More than anything else it aspires to live a normal life."

To explain what she meant Lucy gave the example of one of her MEND activists in Tulkarem, who got a phone call from Hamas members interested in working together. "You see," she told the journalist, "it isn't all black." Even Hamas can come around to a belief in dialogue and peace.

"Neither is it all white," her Israeli interviewer replied.

"Do you know anything that is all white?" Lucy countered with her beguiling smile.

Lucy's wise words may be a good way to wrap up a chronicle of a life lived in a broken and violated land. Dualities of good and evil, black and white, right and wrong, "us" and "them," our "rights" and their "usurpation" have cut the Holy Land into ribbons. The only hope comes when we listen to the wisdom of tradition, and acknowledge that Jerusalem cannot be conquered or kept through violence. It is a city of three faiths and it is open to the world. Even after the erection of Sharon's wall and the ensuing Hamas victory, the way my fairy tale ends still seems right to me: three characters, each from a sister religion, join hands to plant a honeysuckle bush. Meanwhile, Mr. Seems stands off in the distance as a reminder that things are never what they seem to be. In Jerusalem's tangled, ancient alleys, wonder and surprise are always lurking around the corner ready to remind you that this is not an ordinary place you can map out with a surveyor's rod. It is sacred.

Notes

Acknowledgments

Notes

Chapter Two: The Pan-Arab Nation

1. David Hirst, *The Gun and the Olive Branch* (New York: Nation Books, 2003), p. 135.

Chapter Three: Promises, Promises

1. Hirst, *The Gun and the Olive Branch*, p. 209.
2. Ibid., p. 163.
3. Ibid., p. 177.
4. Vincent Sheehan, personal history, quoted in Hirst, *The Gun and the Olive Branch*, p. 189.
5. Ibid., p. 161.
6. Shabtai Teveth, *Ben Gurion and the Palestinians* (New York: Doubleday Books, 1981), p. 189. See also Benny Morris, *The Birth of the Palestinian Refugee Problem* (Cambridge: Cambridge University Press, 1989), p. 25.
7. Peel-Bericht (Berlin: Schoeken, 1938), p. 114.

Chapter Four: The Herod's Gate Committee

1. Walter Laqueur, *A History of Zionism* (New York: Schocken Books, 1976), p. 266.
2. In a speech at the House of Lords on April 23, 1947, Sir Herbert Samuel, the former governor of Palestine, said, "I do not support partition, because knowing the country as I do, it seems to be geographically impossible. It would create as many problems as it would solve."

3. John Bagot Glubb, *A Soldier with the Arabs* (New York: Harper, 1957), p. 294.
4. Izzat Tannous, *The Palestinians* (New York: IGT Company, 1988), p. 570.

Chapter Five: The Pepper Tree

1. Hirst, *The Gun and the Olive Branch*, p. 143.
2. Adonis, Mihyar songs, selected and translated by Kamala Bu-Deeb. See http://www.jehat.com/jehaat/en/poets/.
3. Bertrand Russell, *Problems of Philosophy* (Oxford University Press, 2001, reprinted 1972), p. 90.

Chapter Six: A Grapevine

1. *Le Monde*, February 29, 1968. Cited in Hirst, p. 414.
2. Hirst, *The Gun and the Olive Branch*, p. 398.
3. Ibid., p. 400.

Chapter Seven: Smashing Idols

1. Hirst, *The Gun and the Olive Branch*, p. 414.

Chapter Nine: Monticello

1. Seymour Hersh, "The Gray Zone," *The New Yorker*, May 24, 2004.
2. Quoted in Hirst, *The Gun and the Olive Branch*, p. 481.
3. Leo Strauss, *Persecution and the Art of Writing* (New York: Free Press, 1952), p. 17.

Chapter Ten: The Lemon Tree Café

1. Father published the article in *Yediot Ahronot* on September 7, 1979.
2. Quoted in Nizar Sakhnini, "Village Leagues," www.al-bushra.org/palestine/nizar.htm, accessed January 2005.
3. Quoted in Hirst, *The Gun and the Olive Branch*, p. 493.

Chapter Eleven: The Salon

1. Her comment appeared in *The Sunday Times* on June 15, 1969.
2. See Sakhnini, "Village Leagues."

Chapter Twelve: Military Order 854

1. Hannah Arendt, *The Human Condition* (Chicago: University of Chicago Press, 1998), p. 186.
2. Michael C. Griffin, "A Human Rights Odyssey: In Search of Academic Freedom," April–May 1981, *The Link*, vol. 14, issue 2, p. 4.
3. Alexander Cockburn, "Return of the Terrorist: The Crimes of Ariel Sharon," *Counterpunch*, February 7, 2001.

Chapter Thirteen: Masquerade

1. Quoted in Hirst, *The Gun and the Olive Branch*, p. 533.
2. David Ignatius, "Arafat, Upheaval," *The Washington Post*, October 29, 2004.

Chapter Fourteen: Murder on the Via Dolorosa

1. Sakhnini, "Village Leagues."
2. *The Jerusalem Post*, December 24, 1986.
3. Daniel Kurtzer, later American ambassador to Israel, put it this way: "Israel perceived it to be better to have people turning toward religion rather than toward a nationalistic cause." Quoted in Ha³aretz, Dec. 21, 2001.
4. The consul was Morris Draper.
5. Avinoam Bar-Yosef, "He'll Yet Be Their Mandela," *Ha³aretz*, December 7, 2004.

Chapter Sixteen: Annex Us!

1. David Shipler, *Arab and Jew: Wounded Spirits in the Promised Land* (London: Penguin Books, 2002), p. 216.
2. Central Bureau of Statistics, Statistical Abstract of Israel, 1992, 1994, 1996, 1997, 1998, 1999, 2000; Yesha Council Online; Peace Now; *Ha³aretz*, August 11, 1993; *Ha³aretz*, September 16, 2001.
3. 1984 Amnesty International report.
4. Hanan Ashrawi, *This Side of Peace* (New York: Simon and Schuster, 1995), p. 41.
5. Shipler, *Arab and Jew*, p. 464.
6. Lamia Lahoud, "Their Man in Jerusalem: Meet Sari Nusseibeh, Arafat's New Man in Jerusalem," *Newsweek*, July 7, 2002.

Chapter Eighteen: The Exorcism

1. Aryeh Shalev, *The Intifada: Causes and Effects* (Jerusalem: Jerusalem Post Press, 1991), p. 36.
2. *The Jerusalem Post*, February 3, 1989, cited in Hirst, *The Gun and the Olive Branch*, p. 19.
3. Ashrawi, *This Side of Peace*, p. 42.

Chapter Twenty: Interrogation

1. This was from an 1989 interview with *Ha³aretz* correspondent Gideon Levy.
2. *Ma³ariv*, June 26, 1992.
3. A summary of the charges appeared in *The New York Times* on May 5, 1989 and May 21, 1989.

Chapter Twenty-one: Ramle Prison

1. Quoted in Yoram Ettinger, "Dr. Sari Nusseibeh: Be Wary of Deadly Coral Snakes Posing as Harmless Skipjack Snakes," *Yediot Ahronot*, August 20, 2002.

2. John Wallach, *The New Palestinians: The Emerging Generation of Leaders* (Rocklin, CA: Prima Publications, 1992), p. 97.

Chapter Twenty-two: Madrid

1. Quoted in Dennis Ross, *The Missing Peace* (New York: Farrar, Straus and Giroux, 2004), p. 79.
2. Quoted in Mohamed Heikal, *Secret Channels: The Inside Story of Arab-Israeli Peace Negotiations* (London: HarperCollins, 1996), p. 413.

Chapter Twenty-four: Oslo

1. Heikal, *Secret Channels*, p. 496.

Chapter Twenty-five: The Disappearance

1. These settlements included places such as Har Adar, Givat Zeʾev, New Givon, Kiryat Sefer, Tel Zion, and the settlements in the Hebron area.
2. Sharon said this during a speech delivered on November 15, 1998, at a meeting of the right-wing Israeli Tsomet Party.

Chapter Twenty-six: Porcupines and Roosters

1. Michael Rubner, "The Oslo Peace Process through Three Lenses," *Middle East Policy Council Journal* 6, no. 2 (October 1998).
2. David Hirst, "Yasser Arafat," *The Guardian*, November 11, 2004.
3. Ali Abunimah, "The Men Who Would Sell Palestine," April 27, 2003, www.counter currents.org.
4. Sari Nusseibeh, "Islam's Jerusalem," *Jerusalem Religious Aspects* (June 2000): 75.

Chapter Twenty-seven: Holy of Holies

1. Aryeh Dayan, "Barak Began Referring to the Holy of Holies," *Haʾaretz*, December 9, 2002.

Chapter Twenty-eight: The Possessed

1. Neil MacDonald, "Three Days to the Brink," *The Magazine*, October 12, 2000.
2. Quoted in James M. Wall, "In the Pressure Cooker—Middle East Tensions and the Peace Process," *The Christian Century*, November 8, 2000.
3. Marwan was quoted in Arieh O'Sullivan, "Taba Talks Halted after 2 Israelis Murdered. Hamas Claims Responsibility," *The Jerusalem Post*, January 24, 2001.
4. In a January 16, 2002, Op-Ed, "Want Security? End the Occupation," in *The Washington Post*, Marwan asserted that while he and his Fatah colleagues "strongly op-

pose attacks and the targeting of civilians inside Israel, our future neighbor, I reserve the right to protect myself, to resist the Israeli occupation of my country and to fight for my freedom."

5. Amnon Kapeliouk, "Constructing Catastrophe," *Le Monde Diplomatique*, January 2002.
6. Cameron W. Barr, "Israel Strikes at Peacemakers," *The Christian Science Monitor*, May 22, 2001.

Chapter Twenty-nine: Allies

1. Vered Levy-Barzilai, "Noblesse Oblige," *Ha'aretz*, December 28, 2001.

Chapter Thirty: Checkmate

1. Levy-Barzilai, "Noblesse Oblige."
2. Ibid.
3. Ibid.
4. Israel News: A collection of the week's news from Israel. January 4, 2002.
5. Gideon Saar, "Sari Nusseibeh: The Trojan Horse," *Yediot Ahronot*, January 1, 2002.
6. Interview with Alain Cypel, *Le Monde Diplomatique*, December 22, 2001.
7. Quoted in John Pilger, "Tony Blair's Peacemaking Is Not What It Seems," *The New Statesman*, January 14, 2002.

Chapter Thirty-one: The Iron Fist

1. Graham Usher, "Palestine Militias Rising," *The Nation*, April 11, 2002.
2. Rabah Mohanna of the PFLP to the *Chicago Tribune*. Quoted in James M. Wall, "Bombing a Peace Plan," *The Christian Century*, August 14, 2002.
3. Baruch Kimmerling, "From Barak to the Road Map," *New Left Review* 23 (September–October 2003).
4. Marwan Barghouti, "Want Security? End the Occupation," *The Washington Post*, January 16, 2002.
5. Stanley Reed and Neal Sandler, "Powell's Visit Won't Shut the Doors of Hell," *Business Week*, April 22, 2002.
6. The article was by Yoram Ettinger in *Yediot Ahronot*, August 20, 2002.
7. Suzanne Goldenberg, "Israeli Raid Targets PLO Moderate," *The Guardian*, July 10, 2002.
8. H.D.S. Greenway, "Sharon's War on Moderate Palestinians," *The Boston Globe*, July 19, 2002.
9. Anthony Lewis, "Silencing a Palestinian Moderate," *The New York Times*, July 13, 2002.

Chapter Thirty-two: "The Tigers"

1. Spencer Ackerman, "Bracing for Impact: Fight or Flight in an Israel with 'Intifada Fatigue,'" *New York Press*, January 16, 2002.

2. Aviv Lavie, "The Peoples' Choice," *Haʾaretz*, July 11, 2003.
3. Christopher Thompson, *The New Statesman*, December 15, 2003.

Chapter Thirty-three: The Perfect Crime

1. Israeli public opinion poll, November 24, 2004, conducted by Hagal Hachadash. See http://www.geneva-accord.org/general.aspx?folderID=45&lang=en.
2. Ami Ayalon, "The Wrong Way Out," *The Jerusalem Post*, August 2, 2004.

Acknowledgments

I am grateful to everyone who helped us with this book. I want especially to single out our agent and dear friend Dorothy Harman, who, in a conversation with my wife, Lucy, first suggested I write my memoirs. Without her energy this book would never have been written. Jonathan Galassi, the president and publisher of FSG, believed in the project before a word was written. Paul Elie, our superb editor, helped craft it; and Cara Spitalewitz and Kevin Doughten, Paul's assistants, worked tirelessly to make it what it is. I would also like to thank the people at the Radcliffe Institute's Fellowship Program, who provided the physical and intellectual space for this book to germinate. In Jerusalem I am grateful to Adel Ruished. Adel took Anthony under his wing and drove him around the West Bank to meet many of my colleagues.